Me and Marlon

A MEMOIR

ALICE MARCHAK

BookMasters®, Inc.

BookMasters®, Inc., Ashland, OH 44805

ISBN: 978-0-615-22235-6

Disclaimer:
This book contains information and adult language that expresses the emotional upheaval in a life and not meant to titillate, or to offend the sensitivity of the reader.

Printed in the United States of America.

This book is dedicated to all the young ladies
who worked for Marlon Brando throughout the years
and have their own story to tell.

ACKNOWLEDGEMENTS

For encouragement when I contemplated and hesitated to write explaining my complicated relationship with Marlon Brando, I must thank friends Marie and Phillip Rhodes, David Watson, Harvey Kresky, Bernard Judge, JoAn Corrales, Don Whitbeck, Joel Pipes; and Marty Asinoff for his support.

I'm especially grateful to my friend and fellow author Robert Dorff, who through many months graciously interrupted his own work to give me encouragement and then put on hold work on his fictionalized book *22 Days Hath November* about the assassination of President Kennedy to read and critique my work.

To my great nephew, Christopher Thompson, I owe my sanity as he came to the aid of this computer illiterate when I became frustrated with the intricacies of my iMac. And further owe him a thank you for the hours spend editing my first draft.

A special thanks to Marisha, Meghan and Camielle who filled my heart with joy and broke up the solitude with laughter when they cajoled their mother into a weekend sleepover.

I would be remiss if I didn't acknowledge the encouragement and tolerance of family; Micki, Peggy, Boots, Marty, Mims, Todd, and John, Kathy, Michael, Bruce, Morgan, David, James and Thomas—also dear friends Florine, Cheryl, Mary Lou, Laurie, Scarlet, Ed, Rudy, Barry, Dave, George, and Don, who still embrace me as friend in spite of the fact that I have neglected them for the past year.

Above all my heartfelt gratitude to the professionals: Don Hunt; Anja Clarke, story editor, for her thoroughness and resolve, but also for her tolerance and understanding of my request to allow me my voice. And I'll be forever grateful to Claudine Mansour, book cover designer, who with utmost patience produced a cover that met everyone's approval—but mostly for referring me to Anja Clarke, who was more than editor, for without her guidance and expertise, I'd still have these words on my computer.

A.M.

Newport Beach, 2007

In writing this narrative about my personal involvement in Marlon Brando's life and career, it is not my intention to do other than to tell it like it was during certain times in Marlon's life—a life I saved in many ways, more than once, in spite of his destructive nature.

After Marlon's death certain people, including myself, sued his estate for money, property, personal items, etc., owed by, loaned to, appropriated by, or left with Marlon. These lawsuits were met with very derogatory articles which spanned the globe. I was portrayed by representatives of the estate as a "money grabber" and a "gold digger."

I received calls and letters from friends and relatives nationwide saying that they had read the articles on the Internet or in newspapers. It has been never-ending, and friends and relatives still call about reading items on the Internet and still send clippings referring to me and Marlon's estate. And the accusations still stand as true statements, since they have not been repudiated by me.

It is an undisputed fact that Marlon owed me money, which he had always acknowledged. During conversations with me and others, it was evident that it was always Marlon's intention to pay back the money he owed me. He also gave me a bungalow on Bora Bora—this, along with one he gave to Jay Kanter, his friend and agent at that time, was also known to everyone.

Unfortunately, he was unable to pay this debt during his lifetime because of a lack of cash flow as well as legal monetary problems in his business and with his extended family.

Therefore, upon his death, this circumstance required me to sue Marlon's estate, which had obtained cash after the dissolution of his properties. I'm certain, knowing Marlon as I did, that under these circumstances, he would have wanted me to do so.

Throughout my life, if accused of something, I would examine my conscience and if I did not find myself culpable of the accusation, I would dismiss it from my mind and go on. This time it is too encompassing for me to dismiss these untrue charges without a challenge, especially since I have also been depicted, in essence, as being a doddering old fool.

There were different ways I could respond: I could write a book, which was never my intention, even though I had been approached by several authors to co-author a book on Marlon; or, since I had access to the press through reporters who had called for interviews, I could refute the statements, and the articles would be written through their interpretation of what I had said in the space allotted them.

However, I want my own words to be heard, not filtered through anyone else. Therefore, I have decided not to respond to the charges in any of these ways. Instead, I am writing this "open letter" to my friends, my relatives, and Internet browsers who have read the untrue depictions and are interested in knowing about my personal relationship with Marlon, as employer and as a friend, and why he gave me property which I sued to retrieve from *his* estate after his death.

*****

This is not a biography of Marlon Brando. It is merely an answer to some of the myths that are being perpetuated by people who did not know Marlon Brando. Why am I so certain about that? Because Marlon did not allow anyone to know him. Even I only scratched the surface. Trying to understand Marlon was an exercise in futility. I "knew" him most of his life and yet he could surprise me. When he called late in life and told me another child was on the way and I queried, "Marlon, have you ever heard of condoms?" I, only then, discovered that he felt pregnancy was a girl's responsibility. Not his.

Marlon said of himself he was a private person and he guarded his private life. This statement is far from true. Marlon was more secretive than he was private. Marlon would consider something private and he'd tell me not to tell anyone, then I'd discover he had told several other people and said the same thing. His was a strange sense of privacy. But, there were secrets.

People say they were personal friends and yet they are unaware of anything I'm writing about. How can they pass themselves off as personal friends of 40 years, yet I never knew or saw them with Marlon, nor did he speak about them to me?

Were there people Marlon met and I didn't? Of course. Did he tell me about people he was acquainted with and I hadn't met? Yes.

I made a list of people in the hundreds that passed through Marlon's life and yet, now people representing themselves as intimates of Marlon are not on that list. People who met Marlon five or six times are suddenly authorities on Marlon. I hate to tell you what his reaction to this would be. I smile, but Marlon had no sense of humor when it came to people professing to know him.

Drawing a portrait of Marlon Brando is almost impossible, for he had many faces. And since he was, by his own admission, an accomplished liar, con man, seducer, crazy, and let's not forget actor, among other things, it complicates and shades the picture drawn. Was he wonderful? Yes. Was he funny? Yes. Was he charitable? Yes. Some people knew these faces. But didn't he show some people other faces?

When I began working for Marlon, he expressed the opinion that everyone in his life was crazy. Because if they weren't crazy, they wouldn't have anything to do with him. He thought they all should see a psychiatrist and voiced this, along with "stupid," often. Maybe he was right. I don't know.

I suggested that before I joined the ranks of crazy, maybe I should leave. He glared at me and said, "I'll pay for your psychiatrist."

Lest it's thought that Marlon and I only suffered confrontations, this would be untrue. Certainly we had different opinions. Occasionally we went toe to toe, most times because I protested his treatment of others or the children. I always championed them against unfair treatment, as most were too intimidated and afraid of Marlon to do so. Any wrong that was brought to my attention was addressed by me with Marlon. But always in private.

Despite the life style, daily events, lack of money, women, and crisis after crisis in Marlon's mid-life that tested us both, our friendship withstood all and lasted throughout his lifetime. Our relationship matured over time. We weathered many storms. Sometimes we came out of it with our relationship stronger, and sometimes I would wonder aloud how much longer I could take it. My life would be going along calmly and smoothly, and suddenly I was caught up in Marlon's perfect storm.

That I helped him get through these ten terrible years is unquestioned. And they were terrible. That sex was foremost in his life is also unquestioned. Note that I do not say love. Sex more than any other thing ruled his life.

And ruined it.

* * * * *

There have been many articles and books written about Marlon Brando during his lifetime; many, too, after his death. Some, not all, have opened the door a crack into who this man was. Most have written about his acting ability, a gift of the Gods honed by him. Some have quoted people who met him once, or twice, or even more. All have been representative of Marlon—who *he* wanted to be perceived as at that moment in time. He was an *actor*. On screen and off.

A few knew him as Marlon Brando, co-worker; few knew him as Marlon Brando, business associate; few knew him as Marlon Brando, employer; few knew him as Marlon Brando, friend; many, many knew him as Marlon Brando, lover; and many more knew him as Marlon Brando, movie star. But few, very few, really knew Marlon Brando. Not even the children who called him father.

Throughout Marlon's life and career, friendships and relationships were forged and split. In the end only a few persons had gained the trust and commitment that allowed them to know the true Marlon—not the off-screen actor.

As noted, by his own admission, he was: liar, con man, seducer, crazy; some of the words he tossed around to describe himself in print and conversation. What about the other words to describe him that he didn't toss around, that he kept close, hidden, or that one learned by being with him day in and day out, year after year, living in the same house or hotel suite? The unknown that would have gone with me to the grave but for lies that had been told and written about me and others who befriended Marlon when he was down for the count.

I was confronted with a big question that had to be addressed. Do I owe allegiance to Marlon Brando, a public figure who, by his actions and death, exposed us to the mercy of the press to define us by people who know us not, and who knew Marlon less? Marlon, who left us with so much unfinished business.

Of course, the answer had to be that I cannot allow people who do not know me, or my history with Marlon, to define me or, by extension, people Marlon and I have known a lifetime. And I owe nothing to the extended Brando family. They may owe me as will be attested by what is revealed about Marlon and how they were protected by me during the turbulent times of divorce, annulment, custody battles, and, yes, "crazy." The things revealed they are unaware of since they were not raised in his home, except for Christian from age 12 to 21, and as young children only came to visit a few hours each week—if Marlon was in residence.

Of course, as they grew older, there were vacations and outings. But others were tasked to care for, "entertain them," or they were left on their own. If asked, they would undoubtedly reveal that their father was locked in his room if in a rented house, or in bed ordering room service if in a hotel. His children were intimidated by him, as were most people. In fact, they would scatter like a bunch of cockroaches when a light was put on when they heard Marlon's bedroom door open and heard him coming down the hall. In truth, one of his children badly stuttered when he had to speak to his father.

I can't count the number of times they were away with Marlon that I received calls from the children and caretakers asking me to solve occurring problems, to make decisions because Marlon was unavailable to them. On holiday vacations, living in the same house or hotel, I would receive calls from them asking me to phone Marlon to relay messages, or relay what fist fights were happening in the house between girlfriends. And, when older, calls beseeching me to phone to tell Marlon they wanted to leave. And Marlon also calling, complaining he had to lock himself in his room for a week because he could no longer referee the fights between the women and disagreements between the children—and requesting me to extricate him from the situation.

This same scene was played out by his entourage on film locations when I didn't accompany Marlon. Only Marlon, too, was calling. Day or night, I was always available to any secretary or employee of Marlon's to solve any problem they were having and advise how to "handle" Marlon in given situations. Many, many times saving their jobs as Marlon was quick to tell me, "Fire them."

I would not be lying if I said there wasn't an employee who didn't owe me the longevity of their job or association with Marlon. And that includes lawyers, business managers, and, yes, some girlfriends and friends. I championed them all through the years, ignoring Marlon's emotional outbursts of "fire them" or "get rid of them," or "don't put their calls through." I never fired anyone, nor told anyone Marlon had asked me to do so.

It's not a pretty portrait that will be painted. But understand: Marlon Brando was the painter and Marlon Brando was the author of his life—the life I bore witness to. Marlon laughed at the book *Songs My Mother Taught Me*—the publishers giving him "all that money because I am *Marlon Brando*." He said he would "not autograph one book." This is not an indictment of the co-author of the book. This is Marlon Brando revealing a side of himself by his spoken word. Spoken not only to me, but to others as well.

He would say he was a private person, yet he bragged about his conquests. And upon telling him of requests for an interview, he often said, "You do it." He'd ask me to give interviews about him. "Oh, sure. I'm going to tell *blank* just left your bed and it's being changed to get ready for the next one. Is that what you want me to talk about, Marlon?"

I realized early on that the only way to work with Marlon was to recognize his moods, to anticipate his every move, and beat him to the punch, or, lacking that, batten the hatches and prepare for the storm. If you didn't know him, you were in for a rocky ride. One had to be vigilant as he was adept at pitting one against another with a plethora of lies. No one, but no one, was exempt.

There will be those who will still wonder why I'm writing about Marlon. I have struggled this past year with the same question. Even asking myself, *Would Marlon, this private man who lived his life on the front pages of newspapers and between covers of books and magazines, really want me to talk about him?* When I asked myself that question, the answer was simple: "Yes." Especially under the circumstances I found myself in.

Let's go back in time. Marlon and I knew this moment would surface if I outlived him. We discussed whether or not I should give interviews or write about him. We concluded that the decision would be mine. He said he'd be in a place where he didn't "give a f--k" what anyone said, "and "I know you, you wouldn't lie." I remember we laughed when I replied I'd be afraid to lie about him because he'd probably come back and haunt me since he *always* sought revenge. Throughout the years there were many times Marlon encouraged me to talk about him, which I was reluctant to do. Mainly because it is so easy to be misquoted or for words to be misconstrued. He gave me his blessings by saying, "Let it rip!"

Marlon and I had long concluded that I couldn't pretend I didn't know him and that I hadn't shared the greater part of his life with him. If he knew I was on the Web talking about him, he would again laugh and say, "Let it rip!" Also, he would be madder than hell at the way I was being portrayed when I sued his estate for money he owed me and for the property he gave me on Bora Bora. I've bailed Marlon out of too many financial difficulties to be labeled "gold digger" by people who know next to nothing about Marlon's personal and financial affairs throughout his life. And, obviously, nothing about me or our relationship.

But enough—let's get on and, as Marlon said, *"Let it rip."*

Part One

For some reason never ascertained till later, in 1958 Marlon decided he wanted me to become his personal secretary instead of production secretary for his film company, Pennebaker, located at Paramount Studios. I was approached by his father on Marlon's behalf and turned him down. Two of his previous secretaries had nervous breakdowns; I had no interest in being the third. Then Marlon asked his father to bring me to Borrego Springs, California, where they were filming *The Young Lions,* so he could talk to me. I didn't go. I sent word with his father there was nothing to talk about. Therefore, after finishing *The Young Lions,* instead of me, they hired a lovely girl, Rennie Laven, to work for Marlon as his personal secretary.

Marlon was *broke* and needed money, so he contracted to do *Sayonara* with Miiko Taka as his leading lady, and he left Hollywood for Japan where they were to film the picture. Word reached us he was giving the director, Josh Logan, problems. I didn't pay attention to what was happening with Marlon in Japan. I simply was not interested in him or what he was doing. Shortly after Marlon returned, Rennie became ill and retired as his secretary.

After Rennie had left Marlon's employ, Senior Brando asked me into his office and said Marlon had called. He wanted me to come to his house the next day because he needed to talk to me. We both knew what he wanted to talk about. Senior urged me to meet with him. Finally, I decided I'd better talk to him face to face about this rather than through his father.

We met. I had worked for Marlon's production company for about two years, so we were well-acquainted even though we had had no in-depth conversations—just the light-hearted flirtatious ones that he had with all girls, and hail and farewells. I knew he was aware I didn't want to work for him personally. Nor any actor. I didn't want a 24/7 job. He set out to convince me he was not "one of those movie stars with a big ego"—he was just "a farm boy from the Mid-West". Ha! Ha! That brought a hearty laugh from the both of us.

I did not "adore" him, therefore he had a different relationship with me from the other girls passing through his life. When he left the house, he was idolized—lionized. He was correct in his thinking that he was Marlon Brando, Movie Idol. Everyone wanted a piece of him. I didn't. I gave him friendship. I wanted nothing from him. Well, that's a big lie. For before I agreed to work with him, I wanted certain assurances. I wanted him to promise to treat me with respect, which I didn't think was too much to ask of him, as I felt all humans deserved the same treatment. I did not want to be spoken to or treated the way I saw and heard him treat others. I could ask this of him because I knew I was dealing with a man who thought of no one but himself—who thought that everything revolved around him. He was a very self-centered individual. That knowledge in itself didn't bother me when I was working for his production company and not directly for him, but now that he wanted me to become his personal secretary, it had to be addressed.

I said to him, "Marlon what I'm going to say may come as a shock to you—you may think because you're Marlon Brando, a movie actor, everything should revolve around you. I don't think that way. To me, you're just another human being, who has a special talent that I acknowledge and respect, but if you expect me to cater to you 24 hours a day just because you're gifted, you'll be very disappointed. It won't happen."

How I had the audacity to speak to him the way I did amazes me, but I have to admit, I did. I had nothing to lose. I didn't want the job.

Since I'm confessing, I have to confess I went further—I told him I thought he was "not couth."

Puzzled, he asked, "What's couth?"

Smiling to take the sting out of the words, I replied, "That's just my way of saying I think you're uncouth."

Again he questioned, "What do you mean by I'm uncouth?"

"Well," I said, "since you want to know what I mean by uncouth, I think you're vulgar when speaking. The F-word is used in front of women, you're rude at times, you're ill-mannered, you don't say "please," you order. Had enough or do you want me to go on?"

Laughing, he inquired, "There's more?"

"Yes. You should laugh at yourself more often."

He had a "crush" on me and had been propositioning me and trying for two years to get me to work for him. So instead of taking offence, he set out to convince me that, when I got to know him, I'd think differently of him. Putting self-centered movie star aside, we had a lengthy discussion and I agreed to, as he put it, "Take a chance on me." So in 1958 I became Brando's personal secretary.

A short time after I committed myself, Marlon and I met again for a heart-to-heart chat at his request. After this chat, I wished I had stuck to my guns and stayed in his production office, for Marlon opened the conversation by saying, "There are a few personal things you should know about me." Then he seriously said, "I'm crazy." I reminded myself that I had witnessed what would constitute juvenile and bizarre behavior, but "crazy"?

Aloud I said, "How do you know you're "crazy"?

He replied, "Oh, I'm crazy all right. Every psychiatrist I've gone to has told me that I am crazy."

"What about the psychiatrist you're going to now?" I asked.

"Dr. Aaronson. He thinks I'm crazy, too."

I can't presume to diagnose "crazy," but when someone in a serious conversation tells you he has been told he's "crazy" by numerous psychiatrists, you don't just raise your eyebrows, you run, because even though you can't diagnose "crazy," shouldn't you believe the psychiatrists?

Marlon continued by confiding, "You should also know, I'm a sex addict." If my eyebrows were raised to my hairline when Marlon told me he was "crazy," my mouth popped open and my chin dropped down to my chest when he said he was a "sex addict." I didn't comprehend sex addiction, but my immediate thought was he was alerting me to a sexual assault. Through the years I had known him, he would always ask, "When are we going to get it on?" My mind was telling me to get up and leave, but my backside was stuck to the chair and my feet were stuck to the floor.

First crazy, now sex addict. Who knew about sex addiction? I didn't. What next? *What have I committed myself to,* I was asking myself.

I knew Marlon had been romantically involved with several girls when he lived in New York City and was still flying cross-country to visit some of them. I also knew he had a romantic relationship with Movita Castenada and Celia Meredith. And he was engaged to Josiane-Mariani Berenger. At the same time, Marlon prevailed upon Robert Dorff, an associate producer at Pennebaker, to return shoes left behind at his home by a girlfriend. And drive Josiane around Hollywood, showing her the sights prior to breaking his engagement, while Marlon was working at 20th Century-Fox. He was also dating a few girls he had met on the set. I had heard one of the girls he courted had had a nervous breakdown. Marlon had also been introduced to Anna Kashfi by A.C. Lyles, who was a studio publicist, now a producer on *Deadwood*. So, I was well aware Marlon was playing the field—but *sex addict*? He was constantly referred to in magazines and the press as a "sex symbol" and a "stud" as well as a "great actor," but this was now Marlon, not a journalist, talking.

As I had asked him about "crazy," I now asked him how he knew he was a "sex addict." And he said, "When I awake in the morning, or at noon, or whenever, the first thing I think about is, *Who am I going to f--k today*, even though I turn and find a body and a hank of hair lying next to me. Most times I don't even know who it is lying there. Who I'm going to f--k is foremost on my mind."

And through the years I was to often hear of his sexual desires being foremost on his mind.

Since I had my office at Paramount Studios, I felt removed from his sex life, but the "crazy" bothered me. There are degrees of madness, and little did I know at the time, I would witness quite a few. And if I felt I was removed from his sex life because I had an office at the studio, oh, how the Gods must have laughed.

Marlon was dating Anna Kashfi, and during this time she was hospitalized, I was told, with tuberculosis. Marlon visited her at the City of Hope hospital in Duarte until she was cured and released. Meanwhile, he was romancing other women. Though Marlon thought Anna was exotic and beautiful, he, by his own admission, was not serious about her. He, after all, recently had his father help him break his engagement, and his father warned him he'd have to get out of any further entanglements by himself. So, after Anna quit the hospital, he stopped seeing her. I don't know if it was mutual, but he was dating everyone except Anna. Then, when he went to Japan to film *Sayonara*, he was contacting Anna. Go figure. Little did I know this was a pattern of Marlon's. He would drop someone and then pick them up, only to drop them again. He was like a child with a toy, playing with it a while, and then throwing it in a corner, only to pick it up later and repeat the process. I was also to witness variations on this theme throughout the years.

One day Marlon confided that Anna had phoned him. She was very upset because her father had died, and he spent the weekend consoling her. I don't know whether she had called him or he had called her, but he didn't mention seeing her again to me. By this time in our relationship, I had discovered that Marlon did not tell the truth if a lie sufficed; therefore, I never knew what to believe, and I dismissed this bit of information as of no special interest to me.

A couple of months later, Marlon phoned and asked me to come to his house at 12:30, he'd leave the door open, "Walk right in." I had just arrived when there was a knock at the door. I answered and Jay Kanter, Marlon's agent, walked in and said Marlon had asked him to come by at 12:30. I told him Marlon must be upstairs because I hadn't seen him. Jay called out to Marlon. Marlon shouted, "Come on up." I asked Jay to tell Marlon I was downstairs.

Soon Marlon came bounding down the stairs in his underwear and called to me as he went through the swinging door into the kitchen. Briefs were hardly attire to greet a newly hired secretary in, or anyone else for that matter. Ordinarily I would say, "Don't you have a robe?" but ignored it and followed him. We leaned against the kitchen counter near the refrigerator, and though he did offer me a piece, Marlon devoured an entire pecan ring, washing it down with a quart of milk. In between stuffing his mouth and swilling the milk, he said, "I want you to keep secret what I'm going to tell you." He paused, took a swig of milk. "I'm getting married."

I repeated, "Married?" Thinking he was kidding, I scoffed, "Who'd have you?"

"Anna Kashfi."

"I thought you told me you weren't seeing her anymore."

"She's pregnant. So I'm going to marry her."

"When?"

"Today. At my Aunt Bette's in Eagle Rock."

If this nonchalant marriage announcement had surprised me, you can imagine how surprised I was when he just as nonchalantly continued by saying, "There's a girl upstairs getting dressed. Stay out of sight until you hear the door close. She doesn't want you to see her. Then come on up."

With that he left the kitchen and I stayed there. My mind was trying to assort what I was seeing and hearing. Jay's here. Marlon just got out of bed. There's a girl upstairs. He's getting married this afternoon. Keep it a secret. What was going on here? Why did he have to confide in me? I could read about it in the paper. Soon I heard the front door close and then I, too, went up the stairs to his bedroom.

It was like entering a cave. Marlon had the drapes closed and a scarf over the bedside lamp. Jay was standing at the foot of the rumpled bed. Marlon was showering. I asked Jay if Marlon had said anything to him about getting married. I honestly thought this was another one of Marlon's lame jokes. Jay laughed and said, "That's what he told me."

Marlon rushed out of the bathroom in a white dress shirt addressing me and Jay, "Help me get dressed." He handed each of us a cuff link and held out his arms. When we had finished, he grabbed a tie and hurriedly tied it, then pulled on a pair of pants. He couldn't find his shoes in the darkened room and began to be concerned because it was now past one o'clock. The wedding was scheduled for 1:30 in Eagle Rock, 30 minutes away, and he was still in Hollywood looking for his shoes. Finally, Jay and I had him pulled together and he ran down the stairs with us in his wake. He opened the door and hurried out.

There were two teenage girls sitting at the curb waiting for him. When they saw him, they started jumping up and down, squealing, "Marlon! Marlon!" As he got into his car and sped away, I still thought he had to be putting me and Jay to some kind of test. I don't know what Jay was thinking—but we both kept his secret.

Well, he did get married. This was one time he wasn't lying or playing a joke. When the press discovered Marlon was married to Anna Kashfi, they had a field day. Among other things, they immediately questioned whether she was Irish or Indian, whether her name was Kashfi or O'Callaghan. And so did Marlon. The marriage and planned full-week honeymoon lasted overnight. Marlon spent the rest of his "honeymoon" with Walter Seltzer and George Glass, producers at Pennebaker, who were handling the press. I don't know where Anna spent hers.

After Marlon married, he moved out of the house he had been living in on Laurelview Drive in Hollywood and moved into a house in the Beverly Hills flats near MCA that Jay Kanter rented for him. Anna had moved into the vacated house on Laurelview. And both sides hired lawyers. Marlon also hired a detective to discover if the press reports were true while he hid out from everyone. I was glad I had an office at the studio and stayed far away from him as he really was "crazy" at the circus his marriage had become.

When the child, Christian, was born on May 11th, 1958, Marlon and Anna reconciled and Marlon leased a house on Mulholland Drive for them. Later, Anna would contend Marlon was seldom home during the night and she was frightened living in the remote house in the hills. In other words, she was married and he hadn't given up his bachelorhood. What she didn't know was that he still maintained the secret abode in the flats of Beverly Hills and kept the sheets hot. And they still battled. Eventually, Anna moved out of the house after the child's governess drowned in the pool. And Marlon moved in. Later, he would purchase the house from Robert Baltzer and reside there until his death.

Then Christian, whom Anna called Devi, was exposed to the limelight by endless visitation rights and custody fights fought in the press. This was the beginning of years of battling between Marlon and Anna in the courts and newspapers.

When Christian was a baby, Marlon went to Anna's house for visitation on Wednesdays and every second weekend—holidays were shared. This was in constant fluctuation. If Anna and Marlon were "fighting," there was no visitation and their lawyers and courts had to sort out their differences. And the press had a field day with the "battling Brandos."

To be honest, I must admit that Marlon was out to make Anna pay and pay and pay for what he contended, "She lied to me." Of course, this coming from one of the admitted biggest liars in the world is laughable. I never discussed with him the lie that was so unforgivable. I had not been working for him long and I didn't want to get in the middle of this "battle of the exes" using a child to hurt one another. I heard both of them angrily hurling hurtful words at each other. Marlon certainly knew all the buttons to push.

Years later, I foolishly intervened. He had expected me to commiserate with him, instead I accused Marlon of provoking Anna. Marlon went wild. Everything I heard him call Anna, he now called me. She was lucky; she was safe at home on the telephone when he had lashed out at her, but I was in the same room with this wild man who was spouting obscenities, calling me among other things a traitorous human being. He took out his anger on everything he could pick up and hurl. I retreated fast because I knew I'd be flying through the air next if he got his hands on me.

Once again, Marlon was *broke*. He was divorcing Anna Kashfi. Enormous lawyer bills ensued. He couldn't start the Western film he was committed to for his own company as there was no script. Consequently, Marlon contracted to do *The Fugitive Kind* with Joanne Woodward and Anna Magnani, which was to be filmed at the New York Studios with a Poughkeepsie location.

By this time I had had enough of Marlon Brando, Movie Star, Womanizer, Angry Young Man. I asked Marlon's father to seek someone else to work for Marlon. His father appealed to me to see him through the picture and his divorce. He assured me that once Marlon had all this behind him, the financial pressures and the divorce, Marlon would be a different man. I felt he knew his son better than I, therefore I agreed to go to New York City with Marlon. More importantly, it was an all-expenses-paid trip and I could visit with family.

Marlon had been romancing Rita Moreno, who was now living in New York City. He had also met and fallen in love with France Nuyen when she was filming *South Pacific* and who was now on Broadway in the hit play *The World of Suzie Wong*. So he was looking forward to New York City. Marlon was also anxious to escape the problems of finding a writer, a director, and a producer his production company was experiencing in an attempt to get the Western onto the sound stages. Marlon could not make decisions, and since he was producing the film and acting in it, everyone deferred to him when a problem arose and a decision had to be made.

What we all didn't know, along with his financial and personal life in shambles, the pressure to do a picture by Paramount executives was haunting him and driving him up the wall.

My concern at this time was that, along with leaving his marital troubles behind, he was also leaving his psychiatrist, Dr. Aaronson, behind. But his father assured me I need not worry because Marlon arranged to consult Dr. Aaronson by phone if he needed him. Regardless, as I confided in his father, Marlon was in a bad state, and being the actor that he was, he had his distress well hidden from those around him. Though he was very open with me. Why he allowed me to witness his anguish, I didn't understand.

Marlon and I flew to New York City where we met up with his makeup man, Phillip Rhodes, and his wife, Marie, who was an actress and Marlon's stand-in. They were old friends from the New York City days before Marlon became a Broadway and Hollywood star.

The mantle of despair and anger at everything and everybody that had been boiling beneath the surface in Hollywood seemed to have been shed as soon as Marlon settled into the "New York state of mind." He was contacting old friends; Janice Mars, Stella Adler, Maureen Stapleton.

But *The Fugitive Kind* location became a nightmare for me. I couldn't wait to return to Hollywood and the studio. I couldn't wait to see the last of Brando.

It started out badly the first week after our arrival. Marlon's involvement with Rita Moreno, he indicated, had ended. She, I believe, had dumped him. All I knew was, he was troubled about Rita. At the same time, he professed to be deeply in love with France Nuyen. After seeing them together, all indications were he was in love.

I did not want to become involved in his love affairs. Therefore, I managed to side-step any questions about what I thought of either one as I didn't know Rita or France except for an introduction and social greetings; hellos and goodbyes. So I'm not certain what this romantic entanglement entailed. I only know our relationship unexpectedly erupted like a sleeping volcano.

One day Rita left a note for Marlon at his townhouse. I had been there at the time so I informed him about it upon returning to the set. When we arrived home from the studio that evening he ran upstairs, found the envelope Rita had left, and discovered it had been opened, then resealed. I heard Marlon yell my name, then he came vaulting downstairs where I was preparing to leave. He was in a towering rage.

"How dare you open my personal mail!" he bellowed coming toward me.

I didn't know what he was yelling about and was stunned by the verbal attack and his fury. I merely denied opening any mail.

My denial sent him into a frenzy. "Don't you lie to me! You f--king c--t!" he shouted.

"I'm not lying. And don't call me a c--t," I said in a firm, low tone. My insistence of innocence made him wilder still.

He screamed, *"Liar!"* Then he spun away from me and furiously punched the banister. Such was his fury that the entire six-foot balustrade, which must have been unstable, shattered with a loud crack that further frightened me and made me jump out of the way as pieces of wood and posts flew in all directions and tumbled around me and Marlon. I had never had such uncontrolled anger directed at me, nor had I ever been in the presence of anyone that furious.

He turned toward me after venting his anger on the banister, still enraged, and stormed, "Get out of my sight before I punch you, too!" All this only took seconds. But after what he had done to the balustrade, I took the threat seriously. I ran and opened the door to the street. And with the little courage I could muster, I turned and yelled at him, my voice rising to his level, "I don't lie!" Then I slammed the door for emphasis as I left.

I hurried down the street away from the madness as fast as my shaking legs could carry me. I hightailed it to the Dominick Hotel, where I was staying, and immediately called the airlines to check the scheduled flights to California.

The scene I had witnessed, and been part of, whirled through my head like a movie montage. It had been so fast, so furious, so scary, I knew I couldn't work for Marlon.

My phone rang, and thinking it was my sister, Micki, whom I was expecting that evening, I answered. But, to my dismay, it was Marlon. A very contrite Marlon. In a soft voice, barely above a whisper, he said he was sorry he had lost his temper. After I had left, he had telephoned Rita and she had told him she had reopened the envelope to add something, and then she had resealed it. I thought Marlon was acting. I didn't believe he was sorry at all. I told him he terrified me. That I was unnerved by his behavior and that I expected to be believed. That if I had opened the letter, I would have acknowledged it. But, I added, I would never open a personal note. I also informed him I was leaving for California the next day. He again said how sorry he was and explained how he felt about intrusion into his private life and, particularly, how strongly he felt about people reading his personal mail. I understood, but after what had happened, I still thought it best if I left. He asked me to take a few days to think it over. So we ended the conversation on that note.

Next came the flowers, a bushel of them, with an apology from Marlon.

Marlon's father had talked me into working for Marlon. I enjoyed production work, having previously worked for John Farrow, director and Mia's father, and Irving Asher, producer at Paramount Studio. But actors were something else. I knew many socially and had dated a few, but I had no desire to work for one. Marlon's father had asked me to work for Marlon when Celia Meredith, his secretary, left to live in New York City. And also when her replacement, Rennie Laven, resigned because of illness. I turned down both offers. Nothing to do with Marlon personally, because I really didn't know him. I just loved production work; I liked writers, was enjoying Pennebaker, and I had a full, busy personal life, as well as going to college in the evenings and taking flying lessons after working hours. I didn't wish to interrupt this. But Marlon's father had talked me into giving Marlon a try, saying, "We'll be filming the Western at the studio, so you wouldn't be working out of Marlon's house as his other secretaries had. You would have a studio office."

I now reasoned that since Marlon's father had gotten me into this mess, he could get me out. So I phoned him in California, related, without exaggeration, what had occurred, and told him to find another secretary for his son as I was afraid of Marlon and didn't feel I could trust him enough to continue working for him.

Brando Senior tried to talk me into staying through the film, reminding me that Marlon was undergoing a great deal of stress and pressure because of his divorce, and that he needed someone he knew around him at this time, rather than a stranger. Of course, Marlon's father didn't know anything about his son losing sleep over two women here in New York.

And so, as Marlon had asked, I told Senior I'd think about it.

I hated to put more stress into Marlon's life and hated leaving him without a secretary in the midst of a picture, but he hadn't endeared himself to me by calling me a liar, among other foul things, and threatening to punch me out. Brando Senior spoke to Marlon as he said he would. Still I was conflicted. While I was pulling myself together, a soft-spoken Marlon called each day to find out how I was feeling. I had a few more telephone consultations with Marlon's father, and he persuaded me to continue working for Marlon until we returned to California at the end of filming *The Fugitive Kind*. After three days, I went back to work at the studio. But during a chat before I returned I was scared brave, for I warned Marlon to think twice about hitting me because he'd only hit me once, and I'd make sure he'd regret it the rest of his life. I laugh now when I think about me taking on Brando. I returned, but my defenses were up. And they stayed up. I kept my turmoil hidden. In that sense, I was as great an actor as Marlon. He acted as though nothing untoward had happened, and I went along with the charade.

We didn't have any major confrontations about his personal mail again, even when, years later, I inadvertently slit open a "personal" envelope and marked it *Opened but unread –Alice.*

And he never called me a liar again. Nor did he ever threaten to punch me out again, even in jest. Though he did warn me to get out of his sight in an angry outburst years later when I told him to grow up, to stop blaming others, that he was the one who was making a mess of his life. That time, he jumped up from the couch and vaulted over the coffee table toward where I was sitting on the opposite couch, yelling to get out of his sight. I ran out of his reach and in seconds, the living room was in shambles and I could hear glass shattering behind me. Since I had provoked him by my remarks, I cleaned up the mess in the living room and left him locked in his bedroom where I hoped he was thinking about cleaning up the mess of his life.

These were the only times he threatened bodily harm. I didn't believe Marlon would ever hit me.

Another matter was his language. In our agreement, he promised not to use the F-word in my presence, especially if there were other people present. I tried to impress upon him that I didn't want to be treated as if I were "one of the boys." It was difficult for him for some time, as everything was "F--k this" and "F--k that," and "F--k him" or "F--k her." I remember teasing, telling him I thought he had a very limited vocabulary—the only word he knew to express himself was f--k. That didn't go over too well, but he got the message and made the effort, and if he slipped, he always asked to be pardoned.

Marlon's agent had rented a three-story brownstone for Marlon on 65th street off Park Avenue, and I stayed at the Dominick Hotel within walking distance. It became my routine to walk to

Marlon's brownstone each morning, gather everything he needed on the set, and we'd leave together for the studio. I'd remain on the set with him and at the end of the day drive back to the house, give him his script pages for the next day's shooting, let him know the time of his call, make certain he had some money for the evening, and if he didn't need his driver, I dismissed him after giving him the time of Marlon's pickup call in the morning. Then I'd leave for my hotel after telling Marlon whether I was going to be in or out that evening. For some reason Marlon needed to know where he could reach me, even though we had an agreement that he respect the fact I had a life of my own. When I left his house, I was through for the day and he was on his own. I didn't want him living his life and mine. I made every attempt to keep our relationship a business one and stayed out of his personal affairs with women, though he continued trying to draw me in by telling me with whom he was sleeping. Of course, he didn't say sleeping.

I did work scared the rest of the location filming in New York, because he again lost complete control, smashed his fist through a mirror, shattering it, and thrashed his hotel room one night while shooting in Poughkeepsie. Nothing to do with me, thank God. Of course, as I did at the townhouse in the city, I dealt with the manager about damages and urged him to restore the room before Marlon returned from the set in the evening. Marlon didn't tell me what caused him to lose control again.

And I didn't dare ask.

I knew I had Brando Senior in my corner. Someone I could talk to should a problem occur. When something did, most of the time he'd hear me out, sigh and say, "This too shall pass." It was a favorite quote of his, and he used it often with me during this early period.

I don't think Marlon ever knew how influential his father was in keeping the two of us together. Senior was concerned about his son. And he also had this strong feeling that once Marlon and I got to know one another, we'd be able to work together. One of his big concerns was that, in the past, Marlon had had women working for him who were in love with him, and he felt strongly that Marlon should have a secretary who was not romantically involved with him, or intimidated by his celebrity. Well, I certainly fit those two categories. And so, in the beginning his father forever encouraged me to "stick it out" when things got rough. And, before I realized what was happening, the responsibility he felt for his son slowly transferred from him to me. I can't remember a moment in my life when I sought responsibility, but it certainly sought me, especially where Marlon was concerned.

I always tried to maintain an impersonal, business-like demeanor in public with Marlon. And I stepped out of camera range of the paparazzi when we dined or attended social events together. That's why there are only one or two photos of us together, except for set photos. But when Marlon and I were alone, I relaxed this pose and an informality embraced our relationship, which never went beyond a shared friendship, though he tried unsuccessfully to make it otherwise. Once he seriously offered me a million dollars if I'd have an affair with him. I laughed it off asking him if he was trying to get me to establish a price, as he was of the opinion that money could buy anything; it was just a matter of the amount. Of course, as the years went by, through the course of events that bound us, a deepening of the relationship developed without any thought of intimacy.

I stayed on with Marlon after filming was completed on *The Fugitive Kind,* and we returned to Hollywood.

Marlon and Anna's divorce was final in April of 1959, but there were still unresolved matters that kept them at each other's throat. Consequently, Marlon was upset for a few days after each child visitation at Anna's house. Anna was also upset. Therefore, she denied Marlon visitation and it was back to the lawyers and courts. Since there were visitations weekly and every other weekend, both parties were constantly at war and lawyers were kept busy trying to bring about a truce. If it was trying for both of them, imagine what effect it had on the people around them. I was not immune from attack by Anna, verbal and physical, thus my desire to escape the situation and Marlon.

*****

Marlon returned from New York City to his production company, Pennebaker, and the Western film. And Marlon, after interviewing director after director, decided he would not only star in, but also direct, the Western, now entitled *One-Eyed Jacks.*

I didn't see very much of him; he was not an office man. But that would change when Marlon decided he'd start shooting the film on location in Monterey and Big Sur in northern California. The film company stayed in a hotel at Monterey, but Marlon decided he would stay at Big Sur, so the production company took over the Tickle Pink Motel. The second floor housed Pina Pellicer, the female lead, in the end unit at the top of the outdoor stairway; Marcella Bruce, secretary to the writer and Marlon, was next, then my room. Next to me was Guy Trosper, writer, and finally Marlon's unit. Marlon had to pass all our rooms to arrive at his—and he'd knock on our doors as he passed.

The Tickle Pink Motel shared a common driveway with the Highland Inn. Some nights we'd all dine together at the inn, but most nights Marlon and Guy would work on the script and they'd order room service from the inn's dining room. If Marcella wasn't needed, she and I would drive into Monterey and join the cowboys who were working on the film for dinner. They were a fun group of cowboys whose names may be forgotten, though not the great tales they spun and the cowboy poems that touched the heart.

Marlon was extremely friendly toward me. I thought he was reaching out, wanting me to forget the New York City location. He was turning on the charm full force and was so very solicitous about me that Marcella observed it and warned, "Marlon's on the make." She'd hear him at my door after we came home at night. He'd saunter in, examine a book to see what I was reading, then gaze around, say, "Goodnight," and leave. It didn't take long for us to decide this was a bed check, Brando-style. Marcella and I found him entertaining. We laughed and didn't take him seriously.

But the laugh was on me. Almost every time Marlon observed me talking to a male on the set, he'd nonchalantly walk over and join us, or if he was at a distance, he'd call to me. Then by the time I'd walk over to him, he'd forget what he wanted me for. Marcella and I spent our time trying to anticipate his next move in the game he was playing. He certainly kept us from being bored sitting around on the set. Marie Rhodes often joined us in the fun when she wasn't standing in for Marlon.

When Pina Pellicer arrived from Mexico, Marlon wined and dined her. Then one night while making his midnight stop at my room, he confided that after dinner, he had escorted Pina to her room and made a move on her. She had rebuffed him by stating, "Marlon, I'm a lesbian." I burst out laughing, and so did he. He said it was a first for him. So much for seducing his leading lady.

We all ultimately learned she was fervently in love with a girl in Mexico who she constantly phoned, and who eventually joined her. They had many loud arguments, and soon her lover returned to Mexico leaving a distraught leading lady. Her tear-swollen eyes prevented her from facing the cameras for a few days, so Marlon shot around her. She was shattered, but Marlon lent a broad shoulder and urged us to try to cheer her up. We tried, but couldn't do much to lift her spirits. Our efforts were unwelcome—she made us feel she wanted to be alone with her unhappiness.

It was sad to hear she ended her life about a year after she returned to Mexico.

One day, a notice was left in our rooms by the motel and the inn alerting us to a "Peeping Tom." Marcella and I discussed moving into town to the hotel. Marlon thought we were being too dramatic. Maybe we were, hence we abandoned the idea. The next night Marcella saw the "Peeping Tom" tilting the louvered window in her bathroom as she stepped out of the shower. I heard her scream and phoned. We both hurried to the gallery walkway. Naturally, he escaped, having been scared off by the screams.

We talked to Marlon about it. He finally showed some concern and said he'd contact the hotel security about assigning a man at our motel until the "Peeping Tom" was apprehended.

A few days later, Marcella screamed again. This time I was in my bathroom, too, which was near the door. I ran out and caught a glimpse of the "Peeping Tom." Having dressed, Marcella and I hurried to the inn and told the manager about the two episodes since we hadn't reported the first one. Mainly, I needed to find out when our security came on duty.

After we left the inn, Marcella returned to her room and I proceeded to Marlon's room. This was to be my first confrontation with Marlon since New York City, and I didn't relish telling him I had recognized him, that he had lied when he assured us he'd arrange for a security man. I knocked, and he called out, "Door's open." He was surprised to see me; I'm sure he thought it was Guy, the writer, at the door since I would telephone if I had a message for him. I didn't give him a chance. As soon as I opened the door, I greeted him with, "Hello, Peeping Tom." He was sprawled on the bed dressed in a black turtleneck sweater and black trousers—obviously worn to blend into the night. Did I get an Academy Award performance from Marlon. His outraged denials fell on deaf ears.

Ultimately, he accepted that I had recognized him. And having admitted he was the culprit, he began to laugh as if I had told him the funniest joke. He was "having such a swell time scaring you." To him it was a game. But what a perverted game. And what about the people at the inn? It wasn't just me and Marcella.

"Marlon," I admonished. "What if a guest at the inn had recognized you? Did you ever think of that?"

Then he tried to convince me it was just a prank. What a childish one. Marlon was 35 years old! This wasn't a prank. I tried to reason, saying he had to remember he was a public figure, and certain social behavior was expected of him, whether he liked it or not. He could play a prank on me or Marcella, but he could not frighten the guests at the inn. I tried as best I could to make him understand this would not be considered funny to anyone if he were caught at the inn.

I was not qualified to deal with situations like this, with a man as complex as Marlon Brando. I just did the best I could. Marlon knew all the psychiatric jargon and mumbo jumbo, and if you attempted to make him understand his was not normal behavior, he, if you let him, would make you think *you* were the one who was "crazy." He could argue you into the ground.

"It was a crazy thing to do," he finally agreed, and then excused himself by continuing, "But I warned you I was crazy."

With that pronouncement the reasoning ended. But I was beginning to wonder, *How crazy is crazy Marlon?*

What I didn't know was that Marlon thought he could charm his way out of any situation. He believed he had the power to sweet-talk anyone to forgive him anything. He'd laugh and make everything a big joke. When he felt he wasn't quite succeeding, he fell back on "I'm crazy," and with that confession, everyone would overlook his transgressions.

I told Marcella that Marlon admitted he was the Peeping Tom and asked her to keep it between us.

It didn't end with Marlon being caught. He had too much fun tormenting us and continued to tilt the louvers and make his presence known every time he passed our rooms and heard water running in the bathroom.

It was at this time Marlon began using me to tell the production staff what he desired. I became a go-between. Marlon was, by his own admission, out of his depth as a director. He could have been spared much if he had taken advantage of the bright, experienced people who had been assembled to help him. The set designer on the picture was the brilliant Mac Johnson. He had worked with Zanuck for years at Twentieth Century-Fox before he moved to Paramount. Marlon couldn't have had anyone more willing or competent to help him if he had only reached out.

I first met Mac when I worked for director John Farrow. Mac was the set designer on two films for Farrow. Since I was now the conduit to Marlon, Mac felt comfortable asking me to tell Marlon he needed to show him the set he was scheduled to shoot the next morning. As per the script, it was a Mexican fishing village. Mac located it in a cove in Big Sur. With a set as large as this, it required days to build. Mac, as was his wont, had the set dresser dress the set, and casting bring in extras, thereby enabling the director to visualize where to place his actors to play out the scene.

Marlon arrived after he lost the light late in the day and could no longer shoot. With his cinematographer, Charles Lang, and assistant directors, Marlon was escorted around the cove fishing village by Mac. Mac, as usual, did a magnificent job with all the adobe buildings, Mexican artifacts and jars, Mexican male extras with serapes and sombreros, and Mexican women with bright colored skirts and shawls milling around. As you walked onto the set, you were immediately transported to an early Mexican fishing village.

After Marlon had the tour with Mac, he walked around the cove by himself, stopping here and there. Then he returned to where Mac and I were standing. Addressing Mac he proclaimed, "I've changed my mind. I really would like a Chinese fishing village." And with that pronouncement he abruptly left. Mac turned to me, before he could say anything, I, mimicking Marlon, also, proclaimed, "Mac, he wants a Chinese fishing village." Mac didn't say a word. He was speechless. The sun was beginning to set by this time, but no one tarried to watch the glorious changes in the sky and water. Mac and I, too, turned from the wondrous sight and trailed in the wake of

Marlon as he departed the cove with the Mexican fishing village.

The following morning, Marlon arrived and stepped into a Chinese fishing village. He was amazed and sought out Mac to acknowledge how pleased he was with the cove, as this was what he had imagined as he walked around the previous evening.

Marlon was amazed all right. He thought it would take days to rebuild the set, and he would have that time off. He had arrived on the set late and expected to leave immediately. But Mac had worked his magic. He had completely transformed the Mexican village. He told me Marlon was unaware all he did was strip the set of the Mexican jars, artifacts, and Mexican extras. There was not a serape or sombrero in sight. Then he populated the cove with Chinese fishermen with straw hats, plus Chinese women and children, all appropriately clad. The set dresser provided wooden fish traps, fishing poles, and nets galore.

Marlon was also unaware that when Mac was assigned to a picture, he, being an artist, painted a watercolor storyboard of all the sets. It was so complete that a director could see what the entire film looked like. It would have been a great help to Marlon if he knew this was in existence.

By the time we returned to Paramount studio, whenever anyone needed Marlon to check a set, check wardrobe, okay an extra, etc., they didn't approach him, they came to me. I would relay the request, get answers, or set appointments. Marlon was very pleasant to everyone, but he was not making decisions. He was also tired. If someone was lucky enough to approach him and get his attention, he put them off. Other times he was simply unavailable. Marlon was procrastinating, and I continued pestering him, actually sweet-talking him was what I was doing, until he okayed everything.

Marlon had a full-size bed put into his dressing room at the studio, and he would stay there nights, so he could sleep in late. Ironically, Marlon's dressing room was John Farrow's former office suite, which included my office when I worked for him.

The cinematographer, Charles Lang, had a bead on Marlon by this time. Each evening he'd prevail upon Marlon to give him the setup for the following day. That way, he would set the lighting, and Marlon could immediately start shooting when he arrived late on the set. Everyone was trying to help Marlon.

Marlon was aware of what Charlie was doing and set out to thwart him. One morning I went to Marlon's dressing room to awaken him and he refused to get up. He said he hadn't slept. He asked me to go to the set and have the lighting changed. Then he proceeded to tell me the shot he was going to make. I made a deal with him; I'd do as he asked if he'd promise to get up when they told me they were ready for him. He promised and I returned to the set.

Charlie's face was set in stone as he watched me approaching. I reached him and relayed Marlon's instructions.

"He told me last night he was shooting this angle and the lighting is all set," Charlie moaned.

All I could say was, "Charlie, I'm sorry, this is what he wants this morning. Let me know when you're ready and I'll get him."

Another day he asked me to tell Charlie, "Marlon, the director, was going to shoot Marlon, the actor, over his left shoulder."

Charlie again had to change the lighting.

Then one day Marlon arrived on the set and when Charlie saw him, he sought me out and asked, "Alice, what's going on?

Marlon only has one side of his face made up." I looked in Marlon's direction. Charlie was right.

"Will you please tell him," Charlie requested.

Bewildered, I crossed the stage to Marlon and asked what was going on. Smiling, he whispered, "Tell Charlie, I'm being photographed from the left side so I don't need the right side made up."

When I, in turn, whispered this to Charlie, he just shook his head.

Marlon knew what he was doing. By tormenting Charlie at every opportunity, he was attempting to get an angry reaction from the mild-mannered Charlie. Charlie was too wise to respond.

The filming went on and on, and Marlon was becoming more tired of it and wanted it over. But he did nothing to expedite things. At his behest I continued to deliver last-minute changes.

After dinner every night for a week, Marlon filmed a drunk-rape scene. During the scene, Marlon, the actor, decided he would drink whiskey instead of faking it with colored water or tea. Since Marlon couldn't handle liquor, he soon became intoxicated and thereby was unable to act or direct. The shots they did film were unusable. Each night filming came to a halt because Marlon was falling-down drunk. The next night they'd repeat the drinking and raping. Mostly, it was Marlon falling out of bed, staggering around thoroughly enjoying himself, having loads of fun along with members of the crew. I don't know how much they were drinking. All I know was, I had to get Marlon on the set sober each day. What nobody knew was that most nights before I left the studio, Marlon was so sick I had to hold his head to keep him from drowning in the toilet as he knelt and hugged while he threw up into the toilet bowl.

Of course, the front office became aware of what was going on, especially since there were no dailies from *One-Eyed Jacks*. Along with sleeping late and sending me to the stage with the changes in setup, I was also being pressured by the production office to urge him to speed up. Marlon and I were given the word "Get it done."

Production knew that I was keeping Marlon focused on finishing the picture. I did my best to cajole him into "getting it done." But by this time everyone seemed to think it was my responsibility to get the picture finished. Production was pressuring me, not Marlon.

Through the ensuing years, this became the norm.

During this period, I was ignoring Marlon's sex life, but not everyone on the set was. His "friends" were always in attendance and whispering in his ear, and they kept working. Marlon was not only "fooling around" with the extras, but also a particular married bit player, whom he carried on salary throughout the film. This presented another nightmare for me, as one night Marlon invited her to his home for the evening. Being a married woman, I know she must have given her husband a reason for the evening out other than spending it with Marlon at his house. What she didn't know, Marlon had phoned her husband before she arrived at his house and told him he was "f—king" his wife and had been all the months during the filming. Her husband refused to believe him. Marlon then invited him to the house, told him to walk right in as the door would be unlocked. His wife was in bed, nude with a nude Marlon, when her husband arrived. Needless to say, that was the end of the marriage.

As with the Peeping Tom episode, I questioned if he didn't stop to think that her husband may have had a gun and shot them both. The cruelty of it astounded me. But Marlon treated it as a joke to entertain his friends—another of his "pranks" that he related with glee.

I couldn't wait for the picture to end. If it wasn't for the pressure on me and on him by the front office to finish the picture, and his financial situation, I know I would have split. The only thing I knew to do was to urge him to keep the appointments to see his psychiatrist.

One of the things that slowed down the filming, both on location and at the studio, was rewrites. Guy Trosper, the writer, was on the set each day. He and Marlon would have story conferences and rewrites every day while the cast and crew stood around.

Marlon had endeared himself to the cast and crew. Every Friday night there were food and drinks after shooting finished for the day. Marlon also closed down the picture on location at Monterey and sent everyone home for the Christmas and New Year holidays. The cast and crew loved him. Paramount's front office was another matter.

Filming on *One-Eyed Jacks* finally came to an end. But since Marlon was the director, it was only the beginning. Now he had to edit the picture. He had shot so many takes that choosing one was getting to him. Marlon could not make decisions, and now he had to make important decisions every night as that was when he was editing.

I asked him one time about this aversion to making a decision. "Marlon, are you afraid of making a mistake?" I queried.

He glared at me for a long moment, then very coldly replied, "No. But you just made a mistake."

I knew better than to broach the subject ever again. But with that remark I was put on Marlon's revenge list. I was beginning to learn you had to handle Marlon with kid gloves.

Like the filming, the editing went on and on. Then one day it, too, finally ended. The studio had stepped in.

Marlon was out.

During the filming at the studio, the obsession with me that began on location in Monterey became more pronounced. Marlon wanted me on the set at all times. If he couldn't see me, he'd ask, "Where's Alice?" When I'd appear and ask what he wanted, he'd usually say something like, "Later, I'm busy." But later never came.

Of course, he was acting and directing, and it became necessary for me to tell someone where I was at all times. Then, he proceeded embracing me when we were alone—more of a clinging to me as if he were drowning and needed something solid to hang on to.

Marlon liked music and had a pianist and accordion player on the stage. They would play music between setups. If I was near, Marlon would reach for me and we'd dance. He was a peachy dancer, having studied with Dunham in New York. Later, when I worked at his house, if we met in the hall as music played, he and I would dance and up and down the wide hallway.

I had a birthday during the making of the film. I had never told Marlon when my birthday was. When he asked me how old I was when we were first introduced, I told him I was old enough to know enough not to tell him. But he went into my purse and checked my driver's license. So he threw a big surprise party for me in the studio commissary. His gift to me was white and black lace bra, panties, and petticoats. An appropriate gift? Enough said.

We were shooting late on the back lot one night and after the "wrap," everyone dispersed. I checked Marlon's portable dressing room after he departed and had just stepped outside and closed the door when I became aware of someone coming out of the shadow and an arm snake out to grab me. I spun away and ran. I have always been a fast sprinter, so I got away. But I knew I couldn't last too long at the pace I was running and being pursued. I was familiar with the studio lot so I ran toward Stage 5 and stars dressing rooms hoping I'd see a security guard or someone walking by. No such luck. But as I ran, and fear no longer controlled my senses, I suddenly recalled the scent of the person chasing me. I recognized the perfume as belonging to Marlon. By the time I reached the Stage 5 quad, I had a stitch in my side and I was panting. I stopped running and bent over holding my side. The idiot who was chasing me ran up huffing and puffing and breathlessly said, "Jeez, you can run!"

I was too angry to acknowledge him. I hurried to my car parked in front of Marlon's dressing room and sped off homeward. I had just opened the door to my second floor apartment when ol' Mar came bounding up the stairs. I didn't enter, but he did, and I watched as he went from room to room, then came out, said, "You're very neat," and departed. He didn't know how lucky he was that I didn't put my foot to his butt and help him down the stairs.

When Marlon began following me home, I could no longer ignore what was going on, and I had to talk to him about where our relationship was not going to go. He promised to change his ways in regard to me. Marlon did keep his word about one thing, he stopped following me home—until Tahiti—but that was later.

But then Marlon started to call me in the middle of the night. When I'd pick up the phone, he'd start singing a song. Sing it through to the end and hang up. Other times at three or four, he would call and say he had told someone I had said something awful about them just to see their reaction, and also to find out what they thought of me. So if they were mad at me, that was the reason. I'd go back to sleep wondering if there was a full moon. I had heard that that's when crazy people do crazy things.

Marlon was also monitoring my telephone calls. I didn't have many as I gave my office number to only a few people. Most didn't know I was Marlon's secretary as I had always said when asked that I worked for Pennebaker and George Englund, and when I became Marlon's personal secretary, I never mentioned the change.

One day I received a call from a friend and accepted an invitation to see Dizzie Gillespie that night. He was appearing in a club on Vine Street in Hollywood. The place was packed. We were eight, elbow to elbow, at our crowded table. The air was smoky; it looked like fog. Someone at the next table, which was so close it seemed it was an extension of ours, said Marlon Brando was in the audience. The buzz began at our table and extended to surrounding tables.

I ignored it, but only a while, for it wasn't too long before I looked up and there was Brando. Standing next to our table just staring at me, smiling. An angelic smile. Everyone at our table had their mouths open, gaping at me. Finally, through the smoke, the apparition spoke, "Aren't you going to introduce me to your friends?" I was the only one at the table that wasn't thrilled to see Brando for that's when I knew for certain that he was listening to my calls.

When next I saw Marlon, I confronted him with the knowledge. He lightly tossed if off with, "It's my phone, I'll listen anytime it rings. If you want a private conversation, get your own phone." Needless to say, very few I socialized with had my work number.

If I hadn't given my word to his father that I'd help him, I would have thrown in the towel long ago. But now his father was producing films for Pennebaker, and he and Marlon were not communicating. And Marlon didn't want me to talk to him, either. Marlon thought that if he was mad at his father, I should be, too.

And I knew if I did consult his father, he'd only again say, "This, too, shall pass."

*****

After Marlon finished filming *One-Eyed Jacks,* he decided he wanted me to work out of his house as he would no longer be going to the studio. I, reluctantly, moved my office from Paramount, where I had worked for 17 years, into the maid's quarters at Marlon's home, which I transformed into an office.

I had been in Marlon's new home only one time before he asked me to move the office. I had met his Aunt June once and grew to know her from telephone conversations. She wanted to see me again and wanted to see baby Christian. Marlon also wanted me to see the baby. So one visitation day, he invited both of us to the house. Anna, by court agreement, was not present when Marlon had child visitation.

As I parked my convertible in the parking area at the front of the house, I heard a baby crying—it was really a painful wailing. I wondered what was happening. I entered the house and saw Aunt June walking down the hall cradling the screaming child. She knew I was expected and greeted me. Then said, "I think this is a colicky baby."

Marlon appeared at that time and said, "Let me hold him," and took the crying baby out of Aunt June's arms. The baby continued to wail with intermittent sharp screeches. Marlon couldn't comfort the child, so he laid him on the floor in the living room on a blanket. That didn't help. Marlon picked him up. We all felt helpless. Marlon then gave Aunt June the baby and disappeared into the bedroom.

Aunt June and I didn't have much to say to each other as we were concentrating on the wailing baby. Soon I left. As I departed, Aunt June was again walking up and down the hall with the screaming baby.

I arrived at Marlon's house at 9:00 a.m. to begin work. Marlon's automobile was parked outside, which indicated he was home. The back door was unlocked so I entered. There was no one about in the kitchen. It was a galley kitchen with no place to sit. I looked into the maid's room, which was to be the office, and it was bare. I ventured into the living room. It was very sparsely furnished. I noted there were no chairs or dining table in the dining room I had passed through. I looked down the hall, whose outside floor-to-ceiling glass wall revealed the pond in the atrium and saw that Marlon's bedroom suite door was closed. I could only assume he was still asleep.

I sat on one of two love seats in the living room and waited for Marlon to make an appearance. He knew I was starting today. Maybe he forgot. I looked around. Anna obviously had taken her furnishings when she moved. Other than the sofas there were two Chinese chests and two candlestick lamps with cream silk shades. Nothing personal indicated that Marlon lived there or, for that matter, that anyone lived there. It had no warmth. The only thing it had going for it was a spectacular sweeping view of the San Fernando Valley out of the wall-to-wall, floor-to-ceiling windows. I sat gazing at the view, waiting for Marlon to appear.

There wasn't a book or magazine I could read, so I went outdoors, walked around the grounds, returned inside, sat and waited some more. Finally, I felt hunger pangs and realized it was noon. I was about to leave when I heard the sound of a door opening and saw Marlon come galloping down the hall in a rush.

As I surmised, Marlon said he forgot I was coming in today. He was full of apologies. We sat in the living room after exchanging pleasantries and I asked what he was going to do about furnishing the office. He stared at me and hesitantly said, "Look around and find something you can use."

Was he that unaware? I went through four rooms—there were only four pieces of furniture and we were sitting on two. "Marlon, you look around. There's no office furniture. There's not even a chair."

"Well, get what you need."

"How much money do you want to spend on the office?"

"I don't know. Whatever. Ask my father for the money." And he rose and walked away.

I returned to the studio, informed Marlon's father of the condition of the house, and that Marlon sent me for some money to furnish the office. He wasn't too happy with the move. He didn't like Marlon distancing himself from

Pennebaker—he was unaware Marlon had lost interest in movie making. Marlon wasn't worrying about his finances, but his father was, and here I was, presenting him with another monetary problem with the office move.

I don't recall the exact budget I was allowed for the office furnishings, but I know it wasn't enough as I had a table, painted and covered with a glass top, instead of a desk. A typing swivel chair and a three-drawer file cabinet was the extent of the purchases. I had no lamp. There were no overhead lights, but I felt that as it was August, I wouldn't need a lamp until later in the year. I would be leaving at six p.m. and it was still quite light. There was no telephone in the maid's room. I checked the bathroom; there were no toilet tissue or towels. I'd have to bring some from home or buy some.

Since there was no money left after my purchases, I bought toiletries and brought my extra large Webster dictionary from home. From the Pennebaker office, I expropriated a typewriter, office supplies, paper, clips, pencils, etc., and a typewriter stand, which was the property of Paramount studio.

I knew Marlon was a night person. This meant I didn't see him until after lunch, which would be after 1:30 p.m., but more often it would be about three or four p.m. I usually had lunch in one of the restaurants or the deli on Ventura Boulevard in the San Fernando Valley. When I had lunch with friends, it was either at the Paramount studio commissary or a restaurant in Beverly Hills. My office hours were from nine a.m. to six p.m., Monday through Friday. One hour for lunch, but since it took about half an hour to and fro the restaurant in the valley, lunch lasted one and a half hours.

After a few weeks, Marlon asked me to lunch at the house instead of going out. He wanted me there if he awoke early. That was fine, but there was no food in the house except a box of corn flakes, a carton of milk that certainly Marlon had chug-a-lugged out of, and a can of instant coffee. And some tea bags and lemons I brought from home as I didn't drink coffee.

This meant I had to brown-bag it, or I had to grocery shop. I could not cook, so I bought a loaf of bread, several cans of tuna, a box of saltine crackers, peanut butter, strawberry preserves, cheese slices, iceberg lettuce, mayonnaise, eggs, and salad dressing. This I thought would keep me for a while. Wrong. Marlon said he'd provide my lunch, but it developed I was providing the household with food. It wasn't long before Marlon and I needed to have another chat.

During this exchange I learned Marlon had a weekly allowance of, are you ready for this? 50 dollars! This was Marlon Brando, Movie Star. One of the biggest and highest paid stars in the world at this particular time.

As with the office furnishings, again it was ask his father for money for food. While I had his ear, I further made Marlon aware it was more than money for food that was needed. I was buying toilet paper, towels, soap, etc. I also informed him he needed a cleaning woman as the toilets and showers as well as the rest of the house should be cleaned. I didn't know who, if anyone, was cleaning Marlon's suite. I imagine his girlfriends may have helped him change the beds as there were pillow cases filled with linens to be dropped off at the laundry. Which, I reminded him, I had been paying for when I picked it up. He, much to his credit, remarked I shouldn't be paying for his laundry, I should get the money from his father. I told him I was not going to his father for money, he'd have to do it. And, incidentally, I continued, there were FINAL notices for his gas, electric, and telephone. Then I capped it off with telling him that Schwab's Drugstore wasn't going to allow him to charge until his PAST DUE bill was paid.

Marlon went through the roof when he heard about the cut off notices. Shades of New York. In an absolute rage he stood over me and commanded, "Get my father on the phone and have him send 3,000 dollars to me immediately!" Remembering what I went through getting money for the office furnishings, I told him I didn't want to ask his father for money, he should. He refused to talk to his father. We needed funds. I phoned.

When I requested the money, his father inquired what the money was for. I replied it was for the household and enumerated the household needs. He responded he didn't have the money and he'd like to speak to Marlon about his spending. I told his father I'd tell Marlon he wished to talk to him. Marlon was shaking his head "no." So I told Senior I'd have Marlon get back to him and we hung up.

I gave Marlon his father's message. He became angrier, shouting, "It's my money, get him on the phone and tell him to bring the 3,000 dollars to me immediately." Again, Marlon's father wanted to speak to Marlon, but Marlon had stated, in no uncertain terms, he did not wish to speak to his father.

I was giving Marlon Senior the sanitized request from Marlon. It didn't help me because when he later arrived with the money Marlon had demanded, Marlon summoned me to his room. The angry son, who had been screaming hateful epithets and threatening to one day do bodily harm to his father a short time ago, was this serene, loving son, who curtly said his father had told him I had been rude to him on the phone, demanding he bring the money immediately, and further I wouldn't let him talk to him. And in the future, if his father wanted to talk to him, I should tell him and get him to the phone.

I was struck dumb. I stared at both Brandos condemning me and walked out of the room. I was going to continue walking right out of the house, but decided to stick around and give

Marlon Brando, Movie Star, a piece of my mind before I left. I'd show him angry! Then I'd go to the studio and confront his father.

Marlon Senior and I always had a very friendly relationship; I liked him. He was the one who had been encouraging me to stay on with Marlon. After this episode, I felt betrayed by both of them. Especially Marlon, who had been standing near ordering me what to say. He knew I wasn't passing on the threats and obscenities spouting out of his mouth, and I certainly wasn't rude.

As soon as Senior left, I was ready to attack. I strode into Marlon's bedroom where he was lying on his bed. Before I could open my mouth, he smirked and said, "Did *we* pull one over on *him*! He thinks I was mad at you! He thinks I want to talk to him! *Don't ever put him through! When he calls, I'm not available!*" I stared and listened in amazement. As he ranted, he peppered his speech with the F-word, among other curses, and became louder and angrier. He went on and on about how much he hated his father, how his father had made bad investments for him, especially in cows, and that's why he, Marlon, was broke. Why he didn't have any money. The more he talked, the angrier he became. I tried to interrupt a few times, but by this time he was on another plane. He had transformed before my eyes.

I finally got through to him and said I didn't know he was acting out for his father, and further, I was certain his father didn't know it either. Again he transformed, for this delighted Marlon, and, in this exalted and angry state he was in, just as in Big Sur, I knew he wouldn't understand what he had done to the relationship between his father and me. But, on the other hand, maybe he did.

Marlon had been transforming in front of my eyes. In time I would recognize this transformation, but never did I understand it. One thing I did know, it was more than acting. Was this transformation what the psychiatrists meant when they said he was crazy? Had they seen it?

Marlon and his father had such different views in regard to money, therefore there were many financial disagreements. Earlier, Marlon's father had addressed this in a letter to Marlon. But lack of money was always an issue. Finally, by mutual consent, Marlon transferred the management of his financial affairs to Guy Gadbois of Gadbois Management in Beverly Hills.

At 35 years of age Marlon, making millions, no longer had to ask his father for spending money.

After I had the office furniture, such as it was, arranged and a phone and intercom installed, I had no secretarial services, as generally perceived—typing and shorthand—to perform. And filing was unheard of.

Marlon had had secretaries before me who had worked for years for him. So when I began to work for him and set up the office at the studio, I asked him for his files. He looked at me blankly. There were no files, not one file folder. Next time I saw him, he handed me two brown grocery bags overflowing with unopened mail. He said, "Get rid of this!" I checked the mail and, as instructed by his father, I sent all the fan mail to Claire Priest Fan Mail Service. The rest was cut-off notices and past due bills, which I took down the hall to his father, who was his business manager then. I, too, didn't need any files until I started them on *The Fugitive Kind*. I also retained and filed all legal papers. In the future, he referred to the office files as "Alice's files." Marlon's file was the waste basket.

In the beginning, he told me to throw everything away. He didn't want anything saved. Especially anything that had to do with his movie career. When he was finished with a picture, he was finished. No reminders. By this time, he had been working in the film industry for about fifteen years or so and had no personal files. Not one. His father may have had Marlon's business files and personal files, but I never saw them. At this time in his life, Marlon really did not need files; he was not a businessman, nor was he one to write letters. His form of communication was the telephone. He only needed an office in his home to stash a secretary to screen anyone trying to reach him.

Marlon had an answering service which I had transferred from his hideaway. In regard to answering the phone, Marlon outlined very specific instructions. The answering service answered the phone. I was to check periodically during the day for messages. When I wrote messages on a tablet, I was to disguise my handwriting by scribbling the message and turn my tablet at different angles for each message because he feared someone could read the messages from across the desk. My Palmer Method handwriting went by the wayside and I scribble to this day.

I was not to give him oral messages if anyone was around. I was not to mention any girl's name in front of another girl, and, if a girl called on the office phone, when I answered I was not to address the caller by name. I was *never* to tell anyone he was in; I was to say he was out or unavailable, and I would have him return the call. His current girlfriend would have his private number and I was not to answer his private line. There were no exceptions; he was *never, ever* to be disturbed by a telephone call.

I recall saying to him at the time, "Marlon, if there is a fire, do I disturb you or do I just call the fire department?" I stared at him blankly, awaiting his reply, and he stared back. I thought he would laugh. He evidently decided I was serious. And it was one decision he made. He said I could disturb him and walked away.

So much for my sense of humor.

I solved the telephone calls by typing every call that came in; name, telephone number, message, and handed it to him when I saw him. If he was out and I was leaving for the day, I put it on his pillow in his room. I gave him no verbal messages. These instructions lasted for some time. Then Marlon decided I should answer the phone when I was there and the answering service should when I left. I was to take care of all business calls; he would only take personal calls. Now, I had to determine if his business manager was personal, if his lawyer was personal, if his agent, who was also a friend, was personal. When I'd buzz, he'd ask what they wanted, then he'd tell me what to say. After a time, if I knew his disposition in regard to a matter, I handled it, otherwise, I'd get back or he would. Except for the girls. Some of them called numerous times and it was days before he returned their calls, then, in front of me, he'd lie and say, "Alice didn't tell me you called." And the girls believed him. Some of them would inform me that Marlon told them I was not giving him their messages or telling him they had called. I couldn't believe they didn't realize if that was the case, I wouldn't be there five minutes—I'd be out the door.

During this early period and for several years, Marlon was having visitation and custody issues with Anna Kashfi. She would call, at times daily, but Marlon's instructions were he did not wish to take her call because it would result in a war of words and ruin his day. Therefore, I took her verbal abuse. She called Marlon everything but a human being and included me in the diatribe. The night telephone operators received the same messages for Marlon. He instructed, "You don't have to take the abuse. Hang up." But it wasn't our fight. I didn't want to provoke Anna as he did and add fuel to the fire by hanging up. He had great emotional stress, as did she, and they became physically abusive at times. Even I was subject to physical attack, as well as the house with a table thrown through a floor to ceiling sliding glass window one day while Marlon was at work. There was never a dull moment during this time, nor for years.

I hated being in the middle of the mess Marlon had made, and was making, of his life. The fights with Anna were acerbated by the advent of different mothers and their children almost every year or two. This also brought on more lawyers, more court appearances, and more emotional and financial stress for Marlon.

There were times when I dreaded the phones to ring. For by this time, there was the answering machine, my line, which was the business line, Marlon's personal line, and Marlon's private line. Marlon's lifeline was the telephone.

Other than the telephone instructions, there were other directives. I was not to discuss movies, movie stars, or anything pertaining to the movie industry with him. He didn't want to be Marlon Brando, Movie Star, in his own home. He left Marlon Brando, Movie Star, at the studio when he left for home after the day's filming. He completely divorced himself from motion pictures and movie people once he finished working on a film. Except for the ladies he was romancing who worked in films.

And I was to stop calling him Mr. Brando. "Sweetheart, call me Marlon." When we were alone, Marlon called me sweetheart, or babe, or Ali. I had called him Marlon until I started to work in his house. Then I referred to him as Mr. Brando. He asked me about it and I replied that I didn't want anyone to think I was a girlfriend. He let me know he was "Bud" to his sisters and family and some boyhood friends and I could call him "Bud"—but as a rule, since he was older, his family now called him Marlon. He didn't want me to call him Mr. Brando. So I compromised, called him Marlon in private, but Mr. Brando when we were in public or when public figures were at the house. It took him some time to accept this, groaning each time I called him Mr. Brando, but eventually he became used to it and accepted it. Later on I called him Mar. And when I wanted to get a rise out of him, or get his attention, I called him, Marlon Brando, Movie Star. But only in private.

I had been mad at him and stopped calling him Mar for a long period—but when I stayed with him for a few months before he went to London and then to Spain to do *Columbus,* I began to call him Mar again. He noticed and brought it to my attention. He faxed one day and his P.S. read: "It comes strangely to mind that you're calling me "Mar" these days. It's almost like you calling me "Bud." Ah, well, will wonders never cease, Soon."

Now that Marlon had a financial management firm, he was given a checkbook. I considered this personal; I never looked at the checkbook, nor asked Marlon how much money was in this account. But, oh, what a big mistake that checkbook was. Marlon Brando checks were bouncing all over town.

I received a call from the business office asking what was going on with the checkbook. I inquired if anyone had explained the checkbook to Marlon. They were aghast to learn Marlon had never had a checkbook and probably didn't know it required record keeping. I didn't tell them Marlon had a problem adding, subtracting, and dividing. Later he was in his element with his handheld calculator. It was left to me to explain his checkbook limits and required record keeping. It didn't penetrate because he was constantly overdrawn. Ultimately, I was requested to confiscate the checkbook, and Marlon was back on an allowance.

In the meantime, with the aid of Marlon's Aunt Bette, who was an interior decorator, I was slowly adding the basic necessities for gracious living. We purchased much needed linens, and since there were no dishes or silver, I requested two sets; everyday silver, china, and glassware, and more pricey china, stemware, and silver for entertaining. Bette found a tortoise shell leather dining table at auction, which was perfect for the small dining area, and which would have blown Marlon's mind if he had known the cost. But we decided that if he did ask, she'd say, "Alice bought it, ask her," and I'd say, "Bette bought it, ask her."

Truly, though, Marlon never questioned my household expenditures. Once when I told him he had to go to work, I later overheard him lying, complaining to a girl, "I have to go to work, Alice spent all my money." He just laughed when I told him I overheard him and to "stop lying about my spending your money."

I never told Bette the state of Marlon's finances, so when I'd said to Bette, "It's a budget-buster, we'll get that later," she said, "With the money he's making, he can afford it." Little did she know, she was probably debt-free and had more money than Marlon. I know I did.

Slowly, the house was transforming and was becoming a home. But there was one big problem. Marlon did not want any household help. He didn't want his privacy invaded. Yet, he expected his household to have the same amenities as a first-class hotel.

Marlon was in the habit of divesting himself of his outer garments as soon as he entered his bedroom. Then, he'd walk around them if they landed on the floor. And so would I. I did not hesitate to, very politely, tell him, "I'm not your valet," when one day, when he was expecting a new girl, he asked me to pick up his clothes from the floor. I knew if I picked them up once, I'd be picking them up forever. I decided to buy him a wooden valet, which he began to use.

By this time, I was no longer schlepping his laundry and cleaning on my way to and from work. I had arranged for pickup and delivery. And, I made a deal with Marlon. He would leave the house one day a week and I would have someone come in to clean. My part of the deal with him: I would not let the cleaners know it was his house, I had to say it was mine, and I had to be in his suite while it was being cleaned to make certain no one went through his drawers or medicine cabinet. He was quite specific. I agreed to everything, assuring him of his privacy. I needed him out, one day a week.

Cleaning day arrived and our deal was blown. Marlon was in his suite. But I determined to have the crew clean the rest of the house. Everything went well until the industrial-size carpet sweeper was plugged in. I answered the intercom that was insistently buzzing in my office and heard Marlon bellow, "What the f--k's going on out there! Stop that f--king noise!" I asked if he was alone. He was. I said I'd bring him a cup of coffee and hung up. I'd make nice with him. I wanted him out. His suite needed to be cleaned. He was in an amiable mood and readily agreed to get up and, more importantly, go out. I suggested he sneak out his bathroom door, go around the house to the parking area, and make a clean getaway in his car. No one would see him. He didn't acknowledge my suggestion, but I knew he heard it and left him alone to shower and dress.

When next I saw him, he and giggling girls were sitting in the living room and I heard a low seductive voice dripping with honey saying, "Call me Marlon." So much for cleaning and for being certain it was my house, not his.

The following week, I requested the agency send elderly people. And since this house was replete with floor-to-ceiling windows and sliding glass doors, as most outer walls were glass, I asked for male window washers. Marlon henceforth tolerated the cleaning crew, and if he was disappointed his "giggling fans" weren't among them, he didn't let me know.

The money problems didn't end with the transfer of business managers. Marlon received a meager allowance which did not cover household expenses. I was spending my money and using my American Express charge card—then I'd ask to be reimbursed. This arrangement was playing havoc with my budget. Also, I drove a clean Cadillac convertible, and Marlon a beat-up, dirty, old car. He was near-sighted, couldn't tolerate contact lenses and didn't wear glasses, except for reading. So the sides of his car and fenders were dented and scraped where he had side-swiped whatever was in his way. Marlon developed the habit of running into my office, saying, "Ali, give me your car keys. And, oh, have you got a 'coupla bucks,' I'm taking so-and-so for a drive along the coast and we'll be stopping for a bite to eat." I'd open my purse, take out my keys and wallet. Before I could extract some money, he'd grab the wallet out of my hands, flip out some bills, and stuff them in his pocket. Then he was off on the run with me after him yelling, "Make sure you're back by the time I'm ready to leave at six."

Now, I had to remember to check the gas gauge because he'd usually bring the car back empty, or near empty, and I'd have to coast down the hill on fumes to a gas station. That was another thing. Before Marlon began driving my car, I only gassed up once a month. Now, I was constantly checking to make certain I had enough gas. I never was reimbursed for money he took out of my wallet or for the gas. Therefore, Marlon and I had another money chat in which I told him I couldn't afford to work for him, and why. He immediately called his business manager with the result that he and I were issued gas cards. Also, Guy Gadbois was unaware that there had been no household allowance. That was remedied. I was to receive a petty cash allowance. Now, when Marlon needed "a coupla bucks," it wasn't coming out of my wallet, and I was no longer paying for food for the house.

I wasn't the only one Marlon had been tapping for "a few bucks" here or there; he'd invite people to lunch or dinner, then ask them to pay the check as he had no money with him—then he'd forget and never reimburse them. That is, until I came along. He did it to me and I would reimburse myself from petty cash. When I discovered he did it to others, I waited until he was in a very good mood, then I brought up the subject. Teasing him, saying he was no better than a panhandler, I reminded him he earned thousands more than his friends; he should reimburse them when he asked them to lunch or dinner and had no money with him. If they asked him out, then, I said, "they should pay." And when he'd borrow a few bucks for cigarettes, etc., people should be reimbursed. He accepted this rationale from me with good grace and from that day forward, his friends would tell me Marlon asked them to call me, and I'd take care of what he owed them. Phillip Rhodes was happy about this as he had been giving Marlon cigarette and lunch money for years.

If I knew Marlon had a dinner date, I'd check his wallet to be certain he had a credit card and sufficient cash for valet parking, etc. The *et cetera* was someone he might run into who hadn't worked in a long time or had a sad tale that touched Marlon. Marlon allowed me access to his wallet, but did not tolerate anyone else the same liberty. I evidently had been tested and had passed. By this time he was aware that I didn't lie and I didn't steal.

There was another money problem that reared its ugly head. Marlon's business managers called, explained what they considered a problem, and asked that I talk to Marlon. Marlon refused to discuss finances with his business managers. As he did with his father, he just wanted them to send him money when he wanted it. If there was a monetary problem, since they couldn't talk to him, they all talked to me and I talked to Marlon. This time it was his charging habits. They appreciated he charged everything and had bills sent to them, but they became aware Marlon was having 35 to 50 dollar dinners with 150 to 250 dollar restaurant tabs. They felt that with his limited funds, he could not afford such generous gratuities. When I relayed the message, angered, he shouted, "F--k them!" He didn't appreciate the fact that they were attempting to keep him on a budget. I received the same "F---k them!" when they asked me to curb his generosity to everyone with their hand out and a sob story.

To understand Marlon's frustration with money, or lack of it, I must address his financial problems when I first started to work for him.

<u>Marlon Brando's finances:</u>

Business:

Pennebaker incorporated 3/30/55 with capital of	$5,000
September 1955 Pennebaker made a deal with Paramount for one picture, *To Tame A Land,* purchased for (funds borrowed from MCA)	$25,000

Script development, $47,500, was spent without results.

Shortly after George Englund was hired, he discussed a story based on the United Nations. Paramount agreed to finance. Stewart Stern was hired as writer and a photographer hired to record the location trip. This deal fell through.

Pennebaker was short of cash and Marlon loaned $5,000. Then another $3,000.

Co-production with William Goetz was made for *Sayonara.* Against the deal, Pennebaker drew $150,000 earmarked to pay Marlon's salary.

At that time Pennebaker's overhead was $3,500 to $4,000 each month.

Pennebaker had spent: $196,000. (Since Marlon owned Pennebaker, this was his debt.)

Personal:

Anna Kashfi divorce settlement in 1959:
$65,000 house in Beverly Hills
$5,000 per month living expenses
$1,000 per month child support
An automobile
$100,000 in trust for Christian—Christian to receive this at 21 years of age.*
Continuing lawyers' fees for visitation rights and child custody.
Investigators, security guards.

*Note: Marlon went to court and had the trust changed to 30 years of age. When Christian was 30, Christian signed over the money to Marlon to buy a house for him. But as he did with me and Jay Kanter and Bora Bora property he had given us at that time, Marlon kept the house in his name. Upon his death, Christian's house was still in Marlon's name and became part of his estate.

Any money investments Marlon had made before this time (1960s) had been lost. He was seriously in debt. He didn't like it one bit. It had him talking to himself and it was part of the reason for his rage. He really was a very angry man with a volatile temper. He definitely was a candidate for anger management. I don't know if rage therapy existed at this time. If it did, I wonder why his psychiatrists hadn't recommended it. Maybe they did.

I have since discovered that researchers at Harvard Medical have done a study on rage—Intermittent Explosive Disorder. I can't diagnose Marlon, but I can attest to the fact that he had intermittent explosive rage. And I wish I had known more about it when I first started to work for Marlon because his rage was *explosive.*

Marlon's business management sent Marlon financial statements and I would discover them in his waste basket. I approached him about this. He confessed it was all Greek to him. He could not read a financial statement. Consequently, I was not only administering his household, I was now explaining his financial statement to him. After a few months of this, when he saw me bringing him the financial statement, he'd say, "I don't want to look at that—you take care of it." I'd check it and then give him a rundown.

All the business managers Marlon had through the years were subject to Marlon's distaste for a financial statement; he even threatened bodily harm if a financial statement was handed him by any one of them. Though statements were sent and angrily discarded in the waste basket, they were retrieved by a secretary or housekeeper at my request and filed.

* * * * *

Marlon remarked that when I began working for him at the house, I had two expressions: My eyes were popping out of my head, or my mouth was popping open. Is it any wonder?

Marlon was a sex machine, if the number of different girls that passed through his portals was any indication of his sexuality. I met few. Many I never saw as Marlon would usher them out the front door while another was entering through the back door. If I was in the kitchen as a girl passed, we ignored each other by mutual design. I made the observation he really was living dangerously. This remark only brought a laugh from Marlon. There were occasions when a taxi arrived with a girl and I'd pay for the cab knowing a girl just departed and they probably passed on the winding driveway. Other times friends arrived with a girl for Marlon. Or Marlon would run by my office and say he was going to so-and-so's house. Subsequently, I learned from Marlon they had a girl who wanted to meet him.

One day, Marlon and I were discussing friendships and he remarked he had many female friends, but few male friends. Then he enumerated those—Wally Cox and Bob Hoskins from his youth, and Phillip Rhodes and Jay Kanter. I was surprised because this list contained childhood friends from Libertyville, and Phillip and Jay from his early days in New York City. That meant he hadn't made any male friends since he was about 20 years old. Though I did know he had many acquaintances. I ran a few names by him who I knew he had known for years and I said, "I thought they all were your friends." They were his callers, and some I always saw on the set when he worked. He gave me a shocking answer: "They're not my friends! They're my pimps!" These "friends" would have been as shocked as I if they had heard this, for they all referred to themselves as "a friend of Marlon's."

I discovered that day that anyone who got him a girl was in his mind a pimp, and at times referred to them contemptuously as a pimp in private conversations I had with him. He also revealed he thought most people who were acquaintances used him and that was one reason he didn't have many close friends. He felt exploited by most and he didn't like it.

In this open-hearted conversation he revealed a great deal about himself, how his distrust made him a loner, how the discovery of being exploited left him disillusioned. How qualities he thought he perceived in others, but did not exist in reality, left him with doubts about himself. And, some relationships with both men and women acquaintances left him bitter and remorseful. He mentioned names and volunteered he kept mental lists of people who had hurt him in some way. He remembered every hurt moment, every criticism, however slight, and each and every one would be addressed one day in a manner he deemed appropriate. He believed revenge was sweet and I can attest he enjoyed "getting back" at people, which he did, no matter how long it took.

Marlon and I had such different outlooks in regard to people. I thought everyone was intrinsically good, and Marlon looked at people with distrust and was determined they must be tested. Few passed. I remarked I thought there were certain people he enjoyed, and he should make the effort to get off his bed and spend time with them. I named names. He laughed at the those I named, whom I thought he enjoyed being with, and reminded me, "You forget I'm an actor."

Yes, I would forget. Forget the times I heard the laughter coming from the living room, his louder than anyone else's, and how guests weren't off the premises before he was instructing me, if they called, he was not available. Ever. He had better to do than waste his time with them. This spoken in the most colorful language with great emotion. How could I ever forget he was an actor?

I knew Wally to be a true friend. He was the only person I know, other than Marty Asinoff, who could come to Marlon's house without first calling and who could walk in day or night and stay. Marlon thought of Wally as a brother and Marty was family, his sister Jocelyn's son.

I was staying at Marlon's home; he was in Tahiti. I received a call that Wally had died and was asked to notify Marlon. I knew Marlon had left Tahiti en route home via Hawaii, where he told me he was going to visit a friend of long standing. I didn't know how to contact her as she was in Marlon's telephone book, which he had with him, not mine, and thought she may be at the airport as Marlon's plane was due to land.

I didn't want Marlon to hear about Wally by a press or radio report. I also didn't want him to hear it from a stranger. I phoned the airport manager in Hawaii, told him Marlon was on the plane arriving from Tahiti and prevailed upon him to whisk Marlon off the plane and keep him incommunicado until I could break the news of Wally's death to him. I also asked him to please help Marlon if he became too distraught. I didn't know how Marlon would react to my news. He was very kind and asked if there was anything further he could do. Since he was so accommodating, I prevailed upon him to arrange a flight to Los Angeles and advise me when Marlon was aboard.

After I broke the news to Marlon, who was stunned, the airport manager took over. He later called me with Marlon's time of arrival in Los Angeles, where he was again met by airport personnel and whisked away.

I'll never forget Marlon's anguish, the wailing, and cursing. He was so angry at Wally for dying that for months, every time he thought of it, I'd hear him yell and curse Wally for leaving him. I couldn't mention Wally's name. The anger lasted for years. And it was years before I could bring up Wally's name. Years before we could reminisce about the warmth and laughter he brought into the house and into our lives.

I stayed out of Marlon's personal life, but like everything else, the more time we spent together and we got to know each other, the more he trusted me, the more he confided in me, and the more he solicited my help in getting him out of bad situations. It was mostly advice on my part since I thoroughly disapproved of some of his crazy shenanigans and didn't hesitate to let him know I didn't want any involvement.

Most of his problems with women came from his lying to them. There's no way to sugar-coat this; he outright lied to them. And his penchant for having one girl coming in the front door while one was going out the back door afforded plenty of opportunities to hone his acting skill when he was caught. I refused to help him when he did. I made no bones about it; I'd remind him I was his secretary and I wasn't going to lie for him, or be an accomplice in any of his nefarious schemes. At times he laughed about it, at times he became annoyed because I refused to lie for him. And then, he'd tell lies about me to get even.

Marlon never had one girlfriend, but five, or not less than three, at one time on the string. He referred to them as his stable. Of course, they all thought they were the only one he was romancing. Why would they think that? Because he told them so. I would feel sorry for some of them when they told me how enamored Marlon was, as I knew about all the others. God, he was good at deception. A few months before he died, he phoned to talk about one of the girls he had on the string for years and said in complete astonishment, "Can you believe she really thought I loved her!"

"Yes, I can believe it, because you had her drop everything at a moment's notice and travel halfway around the world to rendezvous with you in New York, London, Paris, or Beverly Hills," I said.

"She's crazy. I never loved her!"

During the years, Marlon and I had enacted the same scene countless times, but I was surprised when he called me at this late date in our lives to marvel at her belief that he had loved her with great passion and wanted to know if I remembered whether he had ever told me he was in love with her.

If she said he loved her with great passion, I have no doubt it was because he had told her so—acting all the time. Through the years he'd remind me he was a liar and an actor. But, the girls he seduced had no such reminders from him. So they believed his lies.

The reason he was checking with me about her was because during one of our "heart-to-hearts," Marlon surprised me by saying he wanted me to keep a personal diary on him. I, naturally, knew what he did during the day while I was there, but he wanted me to record what he did every night and with whom. I refused. What if the diary was lost or stolen? The idea of a personal diary went out the window fast. But, he wanted me to know everything, because "I can never remember who I saw or what I did yesterday."

Then Marlon became obsessed with being blackmailed and took measures to protect himself. Thus, he began to tell me all and it continued throughout his lifetime. Even after I took up permanent residence in Newport Beach, he would call and confide his escapades and latest seductions. At times he'd call about someone who had done him wrong and he'd ask for my advice, though I don't know why he did; he seldom listened to anyone when he was hell-bent on getting revenge on the one who had wronged him. Through the years, Marlon used me as a sounding board or devil's advocate. But playing devil's advocate with Marlon could get you into a great deal of trouble. I always warned secretaries who were asked to play that role to beware of falling into his traps as later he would attribute some of the stands he had asked you to take as your own beliefs.

Because he was a night person, during this early time Marlon and I would seldom spend much time together, even though I was at his house every day, except weekends. We spoke mostly on the intercom from his bedroom to my office. Most of our encounters were in the kitchen at the refrigerator—Marlon stuffing himself. With his mouth stuffed, he couldn't speak, so I'd just stare at him in wonder. After a moment of silence, Marlon would invariably say, "What were you thinking just then?" *Where are you putting all that food,* is what I couldn't tell him.

But one afternoon, after a girl who had stayed the night left, and another two had just arrived as we were meeting at the refrigerator, him wolfing food, he talked about the girls. After a lull in the conversation, he asked me what I was thinking, and I said, "You know I'm a church-going Catholic and was raised to believe in Heaven and Hell and purgatory. I was thinking, "Marlon's going straight to Hell, I'd better start praying for him." He almost choked on his food. Fortunately for me it was because he started to chuckle. I had to guard my tongue because one never knew what would set him off.

I didn't know how to reconcile this gluttony with what he explained to me soon after I moved the office to his house. I was taking his clean laundry to his room. He was alone. I knocked and called to him. He was in the bathroom and said, "Come on in." I went into the dressing room and told him I had his laundry. He was standing at the sink. He tipped back his head, opened his mouth, tossed something in, picked up a glass of water, and washed it down. I asked if he had a headache, I thought it was aspirin.

"No," he said, "it's an amphetamine. I take it to keep my weight down."

"I thought you smoked cigarettes to keep your weight down."

"Only before I'm making a picture."

He noticed I saw the other prescriptions he had. He reached and held one up and identified it as Nembutal. Then he said the others were, Seconal and Miltown. Without my asking, he explained he took uppers and downers. And sleeping pills because he couldn't sleep at night.

I had previously remarked to him that he never walked. He was always in a hurry, always running. He had just laughed and continued on his way. At times he was also euphoric. Other times, he was very quiet and subdued. I didn't know anything about the drugs he was taking, but maybe the upper pill was the answer to why he was forever on the run. Maybe the drugs were the reason why he was so moody.

One noon Marlon was getting dressed to go out. He buzzed and asked me to help pull him together. He was in his dressing room and when I knocked, he asked me to come in and select a shirt and pants to wear. He had just showered, a large bath sheet wrapped his lower body. He was pouring "1711" in his cupped hand and slapping it on his face and torso.

There was a long, chest high, built-in set of drawers separating the toilet, shower area, and sink from the closet and dressing area. I noticed underwear at the end of the counter. But on second look, it appeared to be large ladies silk undies. I remarked his girlfriend who left them behind must have been an amazon. Marlon astonished me by saying they weren't any girl's, they were his, and offered the explanation that he liked the feel of silk underwear. I was dumbstruck. What other surprises did he have in store for me? I thought he was pulling my leg, but no, he was going to pull on the undies. I blurted, "Marlon, you're not going out in those, are you?" He replied he was. Then I took my life in my hands and told him if he wore those out, I would be out the door behind him. I reasoned with him, he was such a reckless driver, if he had an accident and was taken to the hospital, I'd die of embarrassment when it became known he had on woman's silk panties. He told me I was silly, he was not going to have an accident. I pleaded, "Marlon, if you won't think of yourself, please think of me." He studied my face for a moment that seemed like years, then without saying another word, slid the panties down to me. They ended in the waste basket and that was the end of that.

This was one time I didn't ask Marlon's father to hire someone else to work for his son, as on reflection, I believed Marlon had staged everything. But to what purpose? To see my reaction? He was always testing. But silk panties! The entire episode was weird. A girl probably left the panties behind. I never saw any woman's clothes in his dressing room in the years I knew him, except for those belonging to his girlfriends, or guests, which were sized much too small for Marlon.

I lived at the Balboa Bay Club in Newport Beach for a few years and stayed at Marlon's house if I had a date or was attending a party in town, instead of driving back to the Beach late at night. So I kept a change of clothes and pj's and robe in my closet. Later, I became Christian's guardian and lived in Marlon's house during the week and kept more clothes in my closet. Nothing was ever missing. Maybe it was because he couldn't fit into anything or didn't like my style or I didn't wear "bloomers," but I don't think so. I'd know if he was into cross-dressing because we lived under the same roof for so many years. I always kept most of my clothes in the trunk of my car, as one of Marlon's girlfriends checked my closet and thought my clothes were those of another girlfriend of Marlon's.

I did hear a story told by a friend of his that, as a young actor around town in New York City, there was a group of friends gathered in a ballerina's apartment, and Marlon disappeared to go to the bathroom. When he returned, he was garishly made up and had on the girl's silk peignoir in which he camped around amidst much laughter. But, who hasn't, at one time or another, seen someone do the very same or similar routine at a party. I know I have.

I remember as a child, I saw my Aunt Helen put on a bowler hat and man's black overcoat that lay across the bed, take a walking stick, go downstairs and imitated Charlie Chaplin, while my parents' dinner guests howled with laughter at her antics. Mickey Walker, the prizefighter, was one of the guests. I always remembered it because he brought my brothers big red, puffy, boxing gloves and I was the recipient of a bloody nose in one of the fights we staged, and that ended my boxing career.

Marlon seldom, if ever, thought about the consequences of his actions. He acted on impulse. I didn't judge him. I just tried to slow him down, make him think, stop him from going full bore ahead.

But this was one time I knew, without a doubt, that the "panty" scene was staged. When I mentioned the size of the panties, he just ran with it. Reflecting upon it, I was certain he was pulling my leg.

Through the years I would see him pull similar stunts with others, and when he gave interviews he would make provocative statements "off the record," "wink, wink," testing to see if it would wind up in print. Invariably it did and would end up in conjecture and/or headlines. He was adept at manipulating interviewers and would confide what he had made up and "planted" that would catch everyone's attention and make him the talk of the town.

I was learning more about Marlon every day. But as each day went by, I realized he didn't need a secretary as much as he needed a wife. I decided to become a matchmaker. I tried to subtly nudge him into marrying France Nuyen, whom he was still dating. He, of course, was soured on marriage. The continuing war with Anna Kashfi didn't help my matchmaking. And I failed. Marlon's final response to my nudging was a sorrowful, "She's too good for me, I'd only hurt her."

Many years later, after I knew both Marlon and France better, I had to agree with him. I didn't know it at the time, but any marriage would have been a disaster. As any romantic relationship Marlon had was.

One afternoon, Marlon dropped by my office and said, "Alice, I want you to go to Mexico with me tomorrow." I asked him why we were going to Mexico. He solemnly replied he was going to marry Movita and he wanted me there. Then he added, "She just had a baby and she said it was mine." With that pronouncement, he turned and walked away, leaving me staring at his retreating back as he walked out of the room. This came completely out of the blue as he had never mentioned Movita to me before.

I arrived at work the next day prepared to go to Mexico. Instead, Marlon came into the office and announced he was going to Mexico alone because Movita didn't want anyone else there. I didn't tell Marlon then, nor later, that I was acquainted with Movita. I had met her before I knew Marlon.

Upon his return, he was back to his bachelor ways as he was when he was married to Anna Kashfi. Wedding vows didn't change his way of life.

Marlon and Movita did not co-habit.

Soon, Marlon was confiding that he didn't think the child was his. He was troubled. He began quizzing his friends Marie and Phillip Rhodes about whether they thought the child was his. He was doing the same to me. Doubts continued for months—years.

Finally a few years later, Marlon consulted his lawyers with his fears and they suggested he hire a private investigator. Marlon confided he discovered that Movita was still married to Jack Doyle, the prizefighter, and that the child had been adopted in Mexico. Marlon went to court and asked the marriage be annulled.

Marlon wanted to tell the child he was adopted. I said he was too young. But Marlon was mad at Movita and wanted to use the child to get at her. I suggested Marlon consult his psychiatrist about disclosing to his son he was adopted by Movita. He was advised to wait until he was 12 or 13 before he told him, which he did.

Marlon always treated the child as his son, realizing he was not implicit in the deception and should not be punished for it. Although, when he came to the house for visitation, Marlon would warn everyone not to say anything in front of the child that could be taken back to Movita and used in their skirmishes. He believed Movita questioned the child when he returned from his visitation. Marlon would be out of sorts after a visitation and explain his mood by revealing that Movita had phoned and that they had had an argument about something that occurred while the child was visiting.

His relationship with Movita before and after the dissolution of their marriage was anything but friendly, to put it mildly. Marlon again was "an enraged man," venting his anger on the furniture and windows.

Movita had adopted another child, a girl. She had come to the house with her brother and had called Marlon "Daddy". Marlon was so furious he immediately called and requested Movita not to send her to his home for visitation as he didn't want her to think he was her father. Movita complied.

The months of investigation and lawyers fees, plus a settlement and child support, which Marlon assumed, took a toll on him emotionally and financially, for Marlon was mentally unable to work during this period of investigation into the adoption and, as he always said, "fraudulent Mexican marriage." He always said he received an annulment, but others referred to it as divorce.

Now Marlon had two families to support; Anna Kashfi Brando, and Movita Castenada Brando.

And no wife.

*****

I knew Marlon was constantly stressed out about finances. What I wasn't aware of was how bad it had become until one day he said, "Alice, I called the business office for some money. I was told they couldn't send any–I am *flat broke*. They told me I didn't have enough to pay your salary this week. I'll have to let you go until I can get some money. Then I'll want you back."

He looked pained, dejected. Was he acting? How broke could he be? My salary was only 75 dollars per week!

"Marlon if this is your way of saying you want to let me go, it's okay," I said. "I'm okay with that. You don't have to feel so bad. It's okay."

What I didn't tell him, I had been looking around to see if there was anything available in the industry as I didn't think I could go back to Pennebaker. I had learned from a friend who knew him that Gregory Peck was looking for someone, and she had said that she'd arrange an appointment for an interview. Had Marlon heard about this? I wondered. I hadn't talked on the office phone about leaving. I wanted to secure another job first.

Marlon assured me he didn't want to let me go. But he didn't know what to do, he had no money to pay me. There was a couple of crumpled one-dollar bills and some change on his bedside table. He gestured toward it and very soberly stated, "That's it."

He reiterated he didn't know what to do. No job. No money. Debts. He repeated that he didn't want me to leave, but he couldn't pay me. He didn't know when he'd work again.

I had seen Marlon in many moods, but I had never seen him so low, so defeated. My heart went out to him. I told Marlon I had 10,000 dollars in stock I'd sell. He could have it and repay me when he made his next film. I said I'd go off salary; I had an American Express card and we'd charge everything until he began working. He told me he didn't want me to sell my stock. I was grateful for that, as he'd saved me embarrassment because the market was low, and I probably didn't have 10,000 dollars to give him.

I asked if there wasn't a friend who could loan him enough money to tide him over until he worked. His answer saddened me as it did him. He revealed he had told two people he thought were friends he was broke, had no funds, and "They never even offered to buy me dinner." After all the meals he had bought them. Here was Marlon Brando, one of the world's greatest actors, and he was unemployed, and he was *broke*. Surely, there was a producer with a script screaming for Brando.

He was so completely helpless. With all the people he had helped financially, there was no one he could turn to, no friends. I told him he'd just have to forget about what had happened, get past it, pull himself together, stop feeling sorry for himself, and I'd help him through this financial crisis. I reminded him we'd gotten through others and we could do it again. In the meantime, while I was giving him the pep talk, I reminded myself that he had never been down to zero before. And I was soon to join him.

I went off salary for about eight weeks. I maxed out my American Express card, didn't pay my rent, and used that money, plus the money I had in my checking account, to pay my charge card at the end of the month. In this way I was able to keep Marlon and me afloat. I wasn't too worried because I knew if I got to the point of desperation, I had a fallback—I had family, and, of course, my stock. And I tapped both.

Marlon never forgot that I didn't jump ship and helped him financially. And from this time on, Marlon and I became a "we". He vowed that *we* would never be in this condition again. That whatever was his, was mine. That no matter where he or I was in the world, if I was in need, he would drop everything and be there for me. And he was. Not financially, because I never had monetary needs, but emotionally, when I felt my world was falling apart.

What I didn't know at the time was that he also made another vow; that the two people he told he was flat broke and who never offered to help him or "buy him dinner" would one day be repaid in kind. And he kept this vow.

Shortly afterward, Marlon and I were briefed by his business manager, Norton Brown, in regard to his financial affairs. And Marlon told Norton, along with his assistant, George Pakkala, who had accompanied him, that if I ever called for money for myself, he was to give it to me. Norton asked, "What if she asks me for one hundred thousand dollars?"

"Norton," Marlon replied, "I don't think you heard what I said." Then he went on, "It's the same as if I called." Later, when he gave me power of attorney, the head of the bank said, "Do you know you're giving her the power over your entire estate? You're trusting her with millions of dollars." Marlon replied, "If I trust her with my life, why wouldn't I trust her with my money?"

I never told anyone Marlon was broke, that I was not on salary, and that I was keeping Marlon afloat. And neither did he. The business office only knew I was off salary. Later, when Marlon started the film *Mutiny on the Bounty,* I was reimbursed.

Marlon phoned me with news. Producer Sam Spiegel had contacted Marlon. He had a script he wanted Marlon to consider—*Lawrence of Arabia.* Marlon and I discussed it. He wasn't thrilled with the idea of working in the heat of the Sahara desert. And he absolutely hated the thought of riding a camel. I tried to convince him he wouldn't have to spend much time on the back of a camel—I was certain he'd have a stunt double. But, then again, he had no choice. "We" were *broke.* This was the answer to prayers.

Marlon's agent, Jay Kanter, also contacted him about *Lawrence,* and Marlon also informed him about his aversion to the film. But he didn't tell Sam Spiegel, so I took that as a good sign. Maybe he'd realize he had no option. I didn't press. I'd let him think about it for a few days, then I'd wait for the right moment, and remind him again about the bleak financial picture. He had to go to work.

A few days later, my sister, Boots, and I were dining at the home of a writer friend, Bordon Chase, and his wife, Patty. He mentioned he was writing a screenplay for a remake of *Mutiny on the Bounty*. He was aware that I worked for Marlon, who incidentally lived about a mile east of Bordon, and we spoke about Movita, who had recently been in the press with Marlon, being in the original *Mutiny on the Bounty*. Bordon expressed his desire for Marlon to star in the remake.

Next day I told Marlon about the dinner with Bordon and the remake of *Mutiny on the Bounty*. Soon afterwards, Marlon ran out the door one afternoon calling, "I'm going over to see Bordon Chase."

Was Marlon interested in the *Bounty*? I wondered.

Upon his return, he was elated and said he was going to Tahiti with Bordon. I didn't know till then Marlon had the same romantic fantasies about Tahiti many men have. There was only one plane a week to Tahiti at that time, so they were to leave immediately. But it wasn't *Bounty*, it was the girls that had Marlon excited. I scrounged up some money for the trip to Tahiti. As it developed, MGM was interested in Marlon and picked up the tab for the trip. Our luck was changing.

Recently Jay Kanter revealed to me that Aaron Rosenberg, who was also an MCA client and the producer of *Mutiny on the Bounty*, had wanted Marlon for the picture. But I don't recall Jay speaking to Marlon or me about it at the time *Lawrence of Arabia* was being considered. Neither Jay nor I can recall who spoke to Marlon, other than me, to send him off on the run to talk to Bordon Chase.

In the meantime, Sam Spiegel was calling not only me, but also Jay Kanter, in regard to *Lawrence of Arabia*. Marlon had kept Sam dangling while he explored Tahiti.

Marlon returned ecstatic about Tahiti, the Tahitian people, and especially about Leone, a Tahitian girl he had met and wooed. Was he in love again?

Jay and I were informed by Marlon he had decided he'd rather the South Seas than the Sahara desert, and a ship instead of a camel. He was committing to *Mutiny on the Bounty*.

Marlon informed Sam Spiegel he would not do *Lawrence of Arabia*.

Marlon had no problem, as he had on other films, with the prospect of going on location to Tahiti to work. Where he would usually set up every obstacle he could think of to postpone the start of a picture, he now couldn't wait to return to Tahiti. Of course, Leone and the dozens of adoring girls he rhapsodized about, was the lure, and he absolutely fell in love with the islands of Tahiti and Moorea. When, later, he beheld the Tetiaroa Atoll, that was it. He had to have it.

Marlon met Tarita Teriipia during the filming of *Mutiny on the Bounty*. Another girl had been set as the lead, but she discovered she was pregnant and quit the picture. Tarita's then boyfriend, John, I believe was his name, brought her to the interview for her replacement. Tarita was the best Tahitian dancer to try out, as I heard it, so the part was hers.

The first time I saw Tarita was in Marlon's sleeping fare on the estate he was renting in Punaauia. The fare was a one-room Tahitian bungalow. In this case, a bedroom. Marlon had a leisurely breakfast with me in the main house, where I had my room, then told me he was leaving to visit Carlos Palacios, the Chilean consul, whom he had met on his previous visit. After he departed, the housekeeper asked if I would go to Marlon's fare and gather any clothes to be laundered. Marlon had informed her days earlier that she was not to go into his fare unless he told her she could, so she always asked me to check the fare for his personal laundry.

When I opened the door to the bedroom, I couldn't believe what I saw. In the darkened room I made out a nude Tahitian girl spread-eagled tied to the bed. I looked at her face and from photos I had seen of Tarita, I realized who it was. I immediately reached to untie her. She screamed at me, "No! No! Marlon kill! Marlon kill me! No! No! No!" She was so frightened, I stopped. I told her I would return and left.

I didn't know if she understood me because Marlon told me when we were talking about her getting the part in the movie that she didn't speak or understand much English.

I ran to my car and raced a few miles down the road to Carlos's house. Marlon was lounging in a rattan chair, thoroughly relaxed, having a cool drink in the shade of a tree with Carlos, who was sitting opposite him, his colorful parrot perched on his shoulder. We exchanged greetings, then I addressed Marlon saying I must speak to him privately and walked a short distance away. Marlon replied I could speak in front of Carlos. I apologized to Carlos and told them it was a private matter. Marlon, acting exasperated, reluctantly joined me.

I related my encounter with Tarita and said he must come home and release her. Turning to join Carlos, with a wave of his hand dismissing me, he said he'd be along shortly. It wasn't good enough, "Marlon, this is the tropics. It's hot and getting hotter." And I said he must leave immediately; I was worried about dehydration.

Fortunately, he decided to leave with me. We said our goodbyes to Carlos and, as we walked to our cars, I questioned

Marlon. What had possessed him to do such a thing? He grimly proclaimed she had to be punished for lying to him.

I thought *Not again,* and there was no Dr. Aaronson to send him to.

Once before in the States, I arrived at work and Marlon's car was not in the parking area. But it didn't mean he wasn't home, as sometimes girls would drive off in his car and return later. If his car was not there, I'd check to see if he was home.

The door was open to his bedroom, so I walked down the hall. I reached his door, looked in. No Marlon. But facing me at the foot of the king-sized bed, tied to one of the dining room chairs, was a girl. She looked as shocked to see me as I was her. We stared at each other for a moment. Then I walked to the chair and proceeded to untie her.

"Where's Marlon?" I asked.

"I don't know," she replied.

I discovered he had been gone a very long time. Upon his return a few hours later, I disclosed I had untied the girl and sent her home in a cab.

Why, Marlon, why? She had to be punished, she had lied to him. And now there was Tarita. She had lied to him. So he said.

Welcome to Tahiti, Alice.

If the girls were running in one door and out the other in Beverly Hills, Tahiti, in contrast, was a big parade. Tarita was one of many, but he thought he should be the only one in her life, so there were not many smiles or laughter that I recall in their relationship.

One evening, Tarita, Agnes, Carlos Palacio's Tahitian wife, and I drove into Papeete for a night on the town.

At Quinn's Bar, the three of us separated. Tarita said she was going outside to the bathroom; she never returned. Agnes met some "cousins." All Tahitians seemed to be related; you were always introduced to "cousins." She was off dancing the tamure with them. I met up with a few of the *Bounty* British. When I was ready to leave, I couldn't find either girl, so I departed knowing they'd bum a ride home with a "cousin."

The next day at lunch, Marlon appeared. In a controlled voice, he proceeded to quiz me about the evening. Whom we saw, whom we talked to, what time we came home. Did we come home together. I stopped him by saying if he wanted to know how Agnes spent the evening, ask her. If he wanted to know how Tarita spent the evening, ask her. He mockingly spat out, "I know you, you won't lie. That's why you won't tell me about last night—who Tarita and Agnes were meeting."

Then he became vicious and hurtful, his voice rising, reminding me he always told me everything he knew about my boyfriends, and I was not as loyal to him as he was to me, etc., etc., etc. By the time he was through with his recitation, I didn't know whom or what he was talking about. He was on a roll.

When I finally could interrupt him, I said he could interrogate me all day about my evening if he wanted to, but he could not interrogate me about anyone else ever. By this time we were both steaming. He abruptly rose from his chair, toppling it over. Shouting that I exasperated him, he fled.

A short time later, he was outside my room softly, sweetly pleading to take a drive with him. I really didn't like to drive with Marlon. He was a terrible driver. But I thought he felt remorse for the harsh things he said at lunch and wanted to make up. So I succumbed to his entreaties and reluctantly went along for "a drive around the island" of Tahiti with him.

When we approached Carlos Palacios driveway, he slowed down and turned in saying, "Let's say hello to Carlos."

Did he snooker me. He didn't want to go for a drive. He didn't want to see Carlos. He wanted to see Agnes and have a confrontation. Fortune was favoring him, for upon greeting us, Carlos dropped the news that Tarita was in the house with Agnes. That's all Marlon needed to hear. He was into the house in a flash. I sat under the tree with Carlos. Immediately, Marlon's angry loud voice could be heard, then Tarita cried out. Again and again. I asked Carlos to please intervene. He just shrugged and laughed and continued feeding seeds to his parrot.

Since the cries were continuing and becoming louder, I jumped up and ran into the house. Marlon was slapping and pushing Tarita around, yelling about her lying. Agnes just stood bug-eyed watching him. I pushed between them, persuaded him to stop, and hustled him outside. Needless to say, our "drive around the island" ended at Carlos's driveway.

Later when Agnes and I discussed the incident, she said Tarita thought I told Marlon she had disappeared with someone the evening before. I didn't see Tarita for quite some time afterward, and when I did, decided not to bring up what must have been an embarrassment to her.

Marlon was doing a great deal of entertaining with the Tahitian housekeeper and maid—and their friends and cousins. The kitchen was always overflowing with Tahitian girls clad in bikinis or colorful pareos. The housekeeper had a guitar and it seemed they all played, for the music and dancing never stopped as the guitar was passed from hand to hand.

Most nights there was a party at the house in Punaauia. Marlon liked beer, so did the Tahitians. I was purchasing case after case of Hinano, the Tahitian beer, each day, plus cases of wine and champagne, which was preferred by the French who stopped by. Everyone was welcome. Especially if they were female.

I decided to move out—to the Lotus Village, which was nearer town. Marlon didn't like it, but he had no say in the matter. I was becoming too involved in Marlon's private life and I had none of my own. That didn't stop him from the same routine of checking on me that he had on the Monterey location. Returning from a night on the town, he'd stop by my windowless, screened A-frame bungalow calling, "Alice, Alice."

When Marlon decided to do *Mutiny*, I put him on a diet. He stuck to it. Also, there was his amphetamines, cigarettes, and swimming each day, which made for a very slim Brando when he arrived in Tahiti for filming. He and his stunt double, Paul Baxley, were the same size and could swap wardrobe for the first time on a film. But not for long. For as the filming went on and on, with all the beer, wine and French dining, the pounds were beginning to show. Paul called it to my attention and I was avoiding Marlon's wardrobe man, David Watson, as he was too.

I couldn't enforce a diet, especially since I no longer lived in the same house nor dined with him every day. There was no way I could monitor what he ate. I tried to do what I could by buying more fish and fowl for the house, but what else he ate I didn't know as everyone at the house was lying, at his request, about what he ate. It was, "Don't tell Alice." And I certainly wasn't going to follow him around at night to the French restaurants. He was on his own after sundown. I only hoped he was enjoying every bite that landed on his waist.

I had discovered there were drugs—marijuana and cocaine. One of Marlon's "friends" offered me cocaine, which I declined. He assumed that since I was close to and living with Marlon, I was using drugs. I never saw Marlon use cocaine, nor did I ever see evidence of it around the house, Tahiti or Beverly Hills. I recall he once told me he was afraid of it.

Marlon was ill several times during the making of the film. Once he was ill with what he dismissed as a heat rash in the genital area. His wardrobe consisted of elasticized skin-tight breeches, which made him sweat, and since he had gained weight, his legs rubbed together when he walked. This, according to Marlon, gave him the red raw rash.

I was nearby as he was relating his condition to some of the guys, and I heard him telling them he had a social disease. Was he spinning a tale? When we were alone, I informed him I overheard him and asked why he had lied to me about the rash. He said he didn't lie to me. I asked why in the world he'd want anyone to think he had a social disease. He just laughed and replied, "That's what they're thinking anyway."

Well, if they weren't, they certainly were now. Didn't they get it directly from Marlon? I reminded him gossip traveled fast, especially in Tahiti via coconut radio.

It didn't take long, because I heard about it later in the day. I didn't understand why he had to make up stories, especially when the truth sometimes was bad enough.

I related Marlon's penchant for lying to a psychologist I met at a party, without revealing it was Marlon I was talking about, and was informed I was describing a pathological liar.

The problems mounted: script problems, director problems, rainy weather, illness among the many actors, so the film, like *One-Eyed Jacks*, went on and on. Marlon was beginning to tire of *Mutiny*, but not of Tahiti. Finally, filming was completed in Tahiti and the company returned to MGM Studios in the States to finish the film.

As *Mutiny* wound down, so did Marlon's involvement with Tarita. After he left Tahiti, his romance with Tarita and other Tahitian girls was at an end—for upon his return, he was back to his old ways; a different girl or two each night and each day.

Tarita came to California to finish the picture, but she was not invited to stay at the house. Marlon never mentioned her nor any other Tahitian girl he romanced on the film, though he did give a party for all the *Bounty* Tahitians and their friends who came to Hollywood to finish the picture. It was a blanket invitation, so all attended. That was the only time I saw any of his Tahitian girlfriends around. He was busy with all the girls he had left behind when he went to Tahiti as well as all the new girls he was being provided by his "friends" upon his return.

The film finally ended.

Marlon once again was happy he didn't have to work and he reverted to his habit of staying up until dawn and sleeping past noon. I had finally convinced him we needed a housekeeper on the premises, so housekeeping was no longer a problem. Marlon didn't have grave financial pressures. He was also seeing his psychiatrist regularly. Marlon seemed quite content. There was no evidence of "the angry young man." He wasn't "mad" at anyone. He wasn't plotting revenge. The phones were ringing—Marlon was back in town. The girls were coming and going. Singly and in pairs.

Then an article appeared in Saturday Evening Post magazine that spoiled the serenity we were enjoying. Marlon hit a high C in his tirade. And it was back to spending money on lawyers. For Marlon was accused in print of running up the cost of *Mutiny on the Bounty*. He sued and received a modest out-of-court settlement. But it forever rankled Marlon that the motion picture industry always believed he was the villain portrayed by the article.

Notwithstanding the problems of filming *Mutiny on the Bounty* in Tahiti that were now laid at his doorstep, Marlon still retained his love for Tahiti and the Tahitians. He was very interested in pursuing his dream of owning Tetiaroa and returned periodically to Tahiti in his quest. Each time coming home more enchanted with the South Pacific and the atoll.

*****

Marlon was in Tahiti once more when I received a call from MGM. *Mutiny on the Bounty* was to be released. The premiere, scheduled for Japan with the Emperor and Empress in attendance was unusual—and they expressed a desire to meet Marlon Brando. MGM would like me to persuade Marlon to attend and requested an immediate reply because they needed to arrange the audience with the Emperor and Empress. Marlon said, "No."

I prevailed upon him to think about it and call me in a day or two. He didn't phone. MGM-Japan was anxiously awaiting his decision. Finally a call.

"I'll bet you 10,000 dollars I can beat you to Japan." He never forgot I had 10,000 dollars in stock and forever bet me that amount.

"When do you want to leave?" I queried.

"Right now. I'm leaving for Fiji tonight. See you in Japan." And he disconnected.

I immediately notified MGM, notified my family, and hurried home. I had to pack not only my gown, cocktail and day clothes, but tuxedo and clothes for Marlon. I had to get myself together fast if I were to beat Marlon to Japan.

I called the airlines. I didn't think to ask MGM to arrange for my flight. There were no direct flights to Japan. I booked a flight to Hawaii, then caught a flight to Tokyo. In the meantime, I cabled MGM-Japan my carrier and time of arrival, for they said they'd meet me.

I flew in on the last plane to the Tokyo airport that evening at 1:00 a.m. No one to meet me. Neither I nor MGM-Japan remembered about the International Date Line I would cross, thereby changing my date of arrival. I arrived on Sunday and the MGM-Japan offices were closed.

I sat in the terminal with my two suitcases. All the passengers had long gone. The cleaners were mopping around me. All the airline employees had left. The cleaners finished and left. They evicted me and locked up. I stood outside with two bags and a few airport workers.

I had never been to Japan. I didn't know the names of any hotels. No one spoke English and I didn't know any Japanese except "sayonara," and that meant goodbye. A bus pulled up, all the workers embarked and so did I, with my two suitcases. I hoped it was going into Tokyo.

I only had American money. I extended a bill to the driver. It was refused with a torrent of Japanese. I didn't understand what he was saying. I sat down on a front seat, still extending the money. He refused to accept it. We were at an impasse.

One of the passengers called out something to him in Japanese. They had a rapid exchange and the driver reluctantly started the bus and we left. We drove for miles in the dark night. Finally, I spied lights in the distance. I thought it must be Ginza. Some of the passengers got off before we reached the lights. I didn't know where we were. I decided I'd get off at a building that looked like a hotel. We drove down darkened streets and suddenly I stood up and said, "Stop! Stop!" The driver understood "stop" and I got off dragging the two suitcases.

The huge building in front of me looked like a hotel, so I approached. The door was locked. I was aware hotels locked up at night in Europe, so I banged. Soon a sleepy man emerged and opened the door into a darkened lobby. He saw the suitcases and said, "No room." I asked him to check our reservations. He reluctantly consented. That got me in the door. I asked if he had a reservation for Marlon Brando. No. Alice Marchak. No. MGM. No. I asked if he had a room. No. I asked if I could sit in the lobby until morning. No.

He asked me to leave as he wanted to sleep. I said I didn't think that a hotel as large as this was 100% full. I insisted there must be one room available. I was being polite as I didn't want to be perceived as an ugly American. I was exhausted by this time. I was jet-lagged and needed sleep. He express his desire to go back to sleep and wanted to be rid of me. I imagine I insulted him when I said I didn't believe the hotel was full, for he retrieved a key and took me to a room the size of my clothes closet at home. It contained a narrow cot and a teeny sink. He dropped my two suitcases on the cot and disappeared. I had to walk on the cot to get to the sink to brush my teeth. I slept in my clothes curled around the two suitcases on the tiny cot.

I was awakened by a loud rapping on the door. I opened it to a bowing Japanese man repeating, "Sorry, so sorry, so sorry," as he reached in and took the suitcases. I grabbed my purse, followed the suitcases and wound up in the presidential suite. It developed that this was the hotel where, miracle of miracles, MGM had booked us. Marlon had the presidential suite and my room was next door. They were protecting Marlon's privacy, therefore we were registered under a fictitious name which they neglected to tell me. Of course, I could have had any room in the hotel—they were "so sorry." Actually, the manager was mortified. He couldn't raise his head to look me in the eye. The MGM representative was as apologetic. As for me, I just wanted them gone so I could shower and sleep. To this day, I can't believe my experience, which brought me to the right hotel.

In the meantime, Marlon had located me through MGM-Singapore. He was in Singapore, grounded by storms, and couldn't get out. He arrived a day later. I beat him to Japan. And I had won 10,000 dollars. My elation at winning didn't last long for Marlon contended he was detained in Singapore by an "act of God." I couldn't convince him that the storms, which he contended were an "act of God," favored me. We went round and round. I gave up. He was not going to let me win.

However, before we left Japan, Marlon was approached by the manager, who asked Marlon if he intended to buy any pearls. He would arrange for a man who was part of a pearl consortium to attend him in his suite. I was surprised when Marlon made an appointment to purchase some pearls as I don't believe it had entered his mind. He had been to Japan several times and he, to my knowledge, had never purchased any.

The pearls were beautiful and I was surprised when Marlon asked me to select a necklace. I picked out a string the color of heavy cream. Then had a diamond clasp put on, which Marlon paid for, when I arrived home. The pearls, I gathered, were in lieu of the 10,000 dollar bet I won in the race to Japan which Marlon refused to concede. Oh, how he hated to lose to me. Or any woman.

Upon arrival, MGM had given me the schedule of events they wanted Marlon to attend: a press conference, a TV appearance, and a few cocktail parties. It wasn't too bad. I thought he'd attend all. And, of course, the premiere and audience with the Emperor and Empress.

An MGM publicity man divulged Tarita had arrived for the premiere, bringing with her two friends, Leo Langamazino and his wife. Leo phoned and said he'd like to meet with Marlon and asked me to arrange the meeting. Upon being queried, he informed me it was on a personal matter. When I told Marlon, he was perplexed. He couldn't imagine what personal matter Leo needed to discuss with him that he couldn't tell me.

I set up a meeting. After his meeting with Leo, Marlon asked me to his suite.

"You'll never guess what he wanted." He paused. "Tarita's pregnant and said I'm the father."

No, I'd never guess. He went on, saying he had told Leo he'd pay for an abortion and had asked Leo to arrange it for her. The phone rang and I answered. It was Leo. He again wanted to see Marlon. Marlon asked that I stay, but I didn't want any involvement so I retired to another room in the suite. When Leo left, I returned to the sitting room and Marlon related that Leo had said Tarita wanted money to have an abortion.

Marlon had said he'd pay for the abortion. He didn't want to believe she didn't understand what he told Leo. He asked me if I would go to Tarita and tell her that Marlon wanted her to have an abortion and he would pay for it. I advised Marlon to speak to her. He refused. I told him I did not want to negotiate. But after a short discussion I agreed to tell her Marlon asked me to find out for him whether she was pregnant, and if she wanted an abortion. And if she did, Marlon would pay for it.

But Leo and his wife were in the room with Tarita, I did not see her alone. After I spoke to her in English, they spoke to her in French. She listened and all she said was, "No." I reported back to Marlon I didn't know what transpired in French, therefore, I didn't know what the "no" meant as it didn't seem to answer my questions.

Marlon again met with Leo to determine how much money Tarita wanted for the abortion. Again I joined Marlon after he had met with Leo. The sum for an abortion, Marlon told me, was 750,000 dollars. I was speechless. Marlon had refused and laughed at the amount. I understood why Marlon laughed. He would have loved to have 750,000 dollars at that time.

Marlon commented the cost of abortions had risen from 750 dollars. This, I learned, was in reference to a girlfriend he was romancing, when younger in New York City, who asked for that amount for an abortion, which Marlon gave her. But he gave and gave and gave. For every three months or so she said she was pregnant.

Marlon then ordered that when we attended any of the cocktail parties or go anywhere Tarita was present, I was to stick to him like glue. I was charged to make certain there were no photographs of him and Tarita. He ignored her completely. Her pregnancy, abortion, or money was never mentioned again during our stay.

Discussion had ended.

I was not present at any meetings between Marlon and Leo, though I was in his suite. But after each meeting, Marlon then discussed what had transpired with me. Therefore, I can only attest there were several meetings in regard to an abortion, and money was involved. And, from Marlon, the amount of money Tarita allegedly wanted.

Tarita gave birth to Teihotu in May of 1963. Four months later, Marlon went to Tahiti to see the baby. He fell in love with Teihotu, as I did when I met him. He was an adorable child. Marlon and Tarita were bonded by the child.

Years later, Tarita informed Marlon she desired another child as she didn't want Teihotu to be an only child. Marlon made arrangements with Dr. Red Krohn of Beverly Hills for Tarita to become pregnant by in-vitro fertilization. A daughter, Cheyenne, was born. Tarita later had children by men other than Marlon and he also paid for their upkeep.

Marlon was still married to Movita at the time Tarita became pregnant. Marlon never married Tarita. He always maintained marriage didn't mean that much to Tahitians. That and the sexual freedom appealed to him about the Tahitian girls.

Now Marlon had three families to support.

And living with none.

* * * * *

On a trip to Tahiti with Marlon sometime after *Mutiny on the Bounty*, Marlon asked me to accompany him to visit Captain Omar Darr a sea-going man. What he didn't tell me was he wanted my opinion about his home and property, which was located in Punaauia about 10 miles from Papeete. Marlon had made the captain's acquaintance, and while visiting with him earlier learned he was planning to sell. Marlon bought his house.

After its purchase Marlon and I stayed there when we visited Tahiti, though it was very sparsely furnished. It had three bedrooms. At one end facing the lagoon overlooking the island of Moorea was one large bedroom suite, divided by a great room with a huge fieldstone fireplace, and two smaller bedrooms and bath. Floor-to-ceiling windows provided stunning postcard views. The large kitchen and maids quarters, which backed the fireplace, opened to an atrium and a huge garden with tropical fruit trees, flowering foliage, and towering palms.

In 1966, during the early planning for the village on Marlon's atoll, Tetiaroa, Marlon's architect, Bernard Judge, also stayed at the Darr house, as it was then known. That is, until Bernard discovered the ghost that inhabited his room. Marlon, his sister, Jocelyn, and I were visiting Tahiti en route to Tetiaroa. Bernard, who had been staying at the house informed us at a standing-around breakfast in the kitchen that he was moving out because the ghost was too active during the night and he couldn't sleep. I wasn't afraid of ghosts as I was raised in a house that was inhabited by a friendly ghost. Marlon and Jocelyn said that they didn't believe in ghosts. We three stayed on in the house. Bernard moved out.

We always laughed about this because Bernard joined us on our trip to Tetiaroa, a first for me and Jocelyn, where both he and I espied the young girl ghost of Tetiaroa. This was when I learned that Tetiaroa also had a well-known ghost.

When Marlon purchased the Darr property there was one structure on the grounds–the house on the shore of the lagoon overlooking the island of Moorea. Years later, Tarita wanted a house. Instead of buying one for her, Marlon had a bungalow built for her to live in with her children on the roadside of the property. And later still, he built another for Cheyenne.

After Tarita moved in and discovered the house wasn't hers, she periodically petitioned Marlon for the house. Therefore, on one of our trips to Tahiti, Marlon took Tarita to Papeete and as he told me, "put her name on the house to make her happy and get her off my back."

Thinking the house was hers, Tarita, unsuccessfully, tried to obtain a loan on the house. Marlon kept the house in his name and had just added hers, therefore he was contacted, but refused to sign for the loan Tarita tried to make. In discussing it with me, he expressed the thought that her live-in boyfriend probably wanted the money. Also, he worried, he didn't know how Tarita could repay the loan. He felt he'd have to repay it, and after building the house for her, he didn't feel he should give her a sum of money on top of it. Besides, he didn't have the money.

I don't know if Tarita was ever aware that Marlon was always informed by the Tetiaroa business office about all of her expenditures, charges, and requests for money from the Tetiaroa accounts. When Marlon questioned the amounts, he was also informed who was living at the house with her. Marlon paid all Tarita's expenses and the large consumption of wine at this time was noted and was worrisome to Marlon. Since there was alcoholism in his family and he knew nothing about hers, he became concerned and questioned it.

His business managers also, at this time, brought to his attention that he was short on funds and that a great deal of money was being sent to Tahiti. This concerned him as money for Tetiaroa was his first priority.

Marlon informed me he did not include the land when he put Tarita's name on the house. Marlon divulged he did not want any of Tarita's boyfriends, or if she married anyone, to have any claim on his property. He was not concerned about Tarita as he felt, "She could always take care of herself." She was in her early twenties.

Marlon forever said that he made great investments in the South Pacific without the advice of his business managers. And he was right. Marlon once called, and in a whisper as if he were afraid to speak the amount aloud, told me, "Tetiaroa is now valued at 80 million dollars." When I queried the jump in value since we last spoke about its worth, which was 50 million dollars, he responded. "We didn't take into consideration what my name was worth after *The Godfather*." This was brought to his attention when the current potential buyer said that they realized the high price of the island included the value of his name, especially since he was the Godfather. And at the time of his death, his Tahiti, Punaauia property—complete with ghost—was worth in excess of a couple of million dollars.

*****

Marlon was enchanted with the islands of Bora Bora, Tahiti, and Moorea. When, later, he beheld Tetiaroa Atoll, that was it. He rhapsodized over it and was determined to acquire it. Marlon learned Tetiaroa was owned by Mrs. Duran, who was ill and no longer lived on the atoll. He pressed an acquaintance to arrange an introduction and meeting with her. After a time, he was able to—when she had a "good" day.

Marlon and I visited in her bungalow on the Tahiti waterfront. She was delighted to meet us and made us welcome. Though blind, she was so comfortable with her condition that after a few minutes in her presence, you were unaware of it. I remember her as being very gracious. Marlon, of course, charmed her. Her companion retired from the room and only returned to bring us a cool drink.

Marlon told her about seeing Tetiaroa and how its beauty had affected him. He expressed his great desire in purchasing it. And Mrs. Duran promised Marlon that if she decided to sell Tetiaroa, he would be at the top of the list. Although, she did inform us, she was bequeathing Tetiaroa to her daughter—Marlon would have to deal with her.

She and Marlon discussed her dream for Tetiaroa and he concurred that ultimately it should revert to the Tahitian people, that it should remain in its primitive state and environmentally protected. The more they conversed, it became obvious that if the atoll was ever sold before her death, it would be to him.

I believe she spoke to her daughter about Marlon's visit and Marlon's interest in purchasing Tetiaroa, for when Mrs. Duran died a few years later and Marlon contacted her daughter, she was receptive to his offer for the atoll. When Marlon's dream of owning Tetiaroa was fulfilled, he was one very happy man.

Marlon did not buy Tetiaroa to sell. It was always his intention to live there between pictures and retire there, but the vagaries of life had altered those dreams.

A few years after he purchased the atoll, he realized that building an airstrip and several fares (bungalows) would be too expensive when you considered they must be maintained or the jungle would take over. So he reluctantly decided to build a small hotel consisting of a dozen bungalows plus kitchen, dining room, bar, and reception/office. Day tours were also added to subsidize his dream.

Shortly after a storm destroyed a few bungalows, Marlon built some A-frames and two larger bungalows. He told me one of the bungalows was for me—to choose the one I wanted.

On my next trip to Tetiaroa, I chose a bungalow—I picked the one farthest from Marlon's. His was at one end of the row of bungalows on the lagoon near the airstrip and mine was at the other end, near the dining room and bar. When I was not on Tetiaroa, my bungalow was rented or Teihotu lived there when on the island. Tarita took the other bungalow for herself. Later, when Tarita brought more of her children to the island, she asked Marlon if she could have a larger place built on the island because she needed more room for the growing children and, of course, her relatives who visited and stayed with her and her boyfriend. Marlon arranged for a contractor to contact her and build to satisfy her needs.

Marlon and I went to Tetiaroa for the summer. Tarita's house had been completed. As per their arrangement, Tarita closed her house and moved with her boyfriend to Tahiti while Marlon was in residence on the island.

Marlon asked me to accompany him on a stroll along the beach. He wanted to view Tarita's new house. All bungalows on the island were low, thatched-roof, Tahitian-style houses surrounded by coconut trees and tropical foliage. We were anxiously looking forward to seeing her bungalow as both Marlon and I were planning our new bungalows on the opposite side of the island. We sauntered by the bar, past the turtle enclosure, which Marlon idly inspected, and continued ambling down the beach.

Suddenly both of us stopped dead in our tracks assaulted by what we beheld. Marlon, who had been in a happy frame of mind brought on by being on his island, and who was rhapsodizing about the charms of the atoll, stopped speaking in mid-sentence, turned grim and deadly quiet.

There before us stood a new house a couple of stories high, which rightly belonged in a small town on the corner of Main Street, U.S.A. It was anything but the tropical Tahitian house we had both envisioned. If the house didn't startle us, the six-foot-high chain link fence glittering in the sun surrounding it certainly did. Palm trees had been cut down or removed from around the house. It stood alone. It was not the Tahitian thatched-roof bungalow we had been anticipating.

Without uttering a word, Marlon abruptly turned on his heel and I followed him as he hurried back along the way we had happily traversed minutes ago. Neither of us spoke. I didn't dare say anything. I could see clenched jaw and feel the anger emanating from him. I stopped at the bar. Marlon continued on to his bungalow. I watched to see what would happen if anyone crossed his path. No one did.

Marlon didn't join us at dinnertime. I left him alone. I didn't go near his bungalow until he sent for me. We never discussed the house that summer. From his reaction, I knew better.

We were again summering on Tetiaroa. Tarita, as agreed, had left the island with her boyfriend. Marlon and I took our evening stroll to view the sunset. Instead of walking on the beach to the opposite side of the island as we had always done, we strolled down the airport runway as Marlon continued to avoid the sight of Tarita's house.

That evening, after dinner, I was readying to leave in the morning to spend a month on Bora Bora. I was packing the paperbacks I hadn't read in my suitcase when I heard a great commotion. I went outside on the terrace and saw towering flames and billowing smoke above the palms. I called to a Tahitian man running by, "What is it?" Tarita's house—it was on fire.

I didn't know if Marlon was aware of the fire, so I dashed to his bungalow. He was lying on the bed as I rushed in, alarmed and winded. Words rapidly tumbled out all at once. "Marlon, there's a fire! Tarita's house is burning! The island may go up in flames!"

Marlon didn't move a muscle nor blink an eye—just laid there and looked at me. Didn't he understand?

"Marlon...Tarita's house is on fire!"

He calmly whispered, "What else is new?"

I stared a moment, left and swiftly ran toward the blaze.

I searched out the island manager to ask him if everyone was okay and also inquired if there was any chance the rental bungalows were in danger. There was no chance of that he assured me because there were no palm trees near and the other bungalows were far enough away. Fortunately, there was no wind that night. There was no fire equipment on the island, so everyone just stood and gazed awed as the towering inferno engulfed and destroyed Tarita's house.

Later that evening in thinking about Marlon's reaction earlier, I realized the manager must have sent someone to notify Marlon about the fire. He had to have known, before I arrived to tell him, to be so unmoved while there was so much excitement all around him. I guess he didn't join the rest of us because he couldn't bear to watch his thousands of dollars spent to build and furnish the house going up in flames.

I didn't leave the next day for Bora Bora as planned. No one saw Marlon. He stayed incommunicado in his bungalow. I conferred with the manager and arranged to notify the Tahitian government officials about the fire, and also Tarita, for all that was left of the house was ashes surrounded by a scorched six-foot-high chain link fence.

I also notified Marlon to be prepared to talk to the fire inspectors who would be flying in at noon.

Marlon summoned the manager and instructed him to arrange for a special luncheon along with the best wines for the guests. Marlon very graciously greeted the inspectors upon arrival and escorted them to the dining room for a festive lunch where they dined not only with Marlon Brando, the owner of the beautiful atoll Tetiaroa, but also, Marlon Brando, Hollywood Movie Star. Lunch over, Marlon instructed the manager to escort the officials to the fire site, then bring them back to the airstrip where Marlon would see them off.

After their departure, Marlon returned to the security of his bed and was again contemplating the ceiling when I stopped by to bid him a happy remainder of the summer before I flew off for a much needed vacation on Bora Bora.

Marlon and I never discussed the holocaust. The house was never rebuilt.

Marlon and I were once again on Tetiaroa. He was very anxious to find an architect to build his island home. We had traversed the island numerous times, at different times of day, noting the winds, the sun, the views. He finally located exactly where he would build and had a road bulldozed through to the site. Now, he was determined on this trip to find an architect and get started on his house.

There began a series of interviews with local architects. He flew each to the island. They discussed at length with Marlon in minute detail what he wanted. They'd return to Tahiti to draw up plans. When finished, I'd arrange for their return.

They'd present Marlon with plans incorporating his ideas—a few even presented a model. But in the time it took them to draw up plans, Marlon had changed his mind and rejected what he had told them he desired. There were some very confused architects in Tahiti that summer listening to Marlon telling them, "That's not what I wanted, that's not what I told you." Then, after referring to their notes, they tried to convince Marlon that what they presented was exactly what they had discussed.

It was a very trying time. I, again, was anxious to leave for Bora Bora. Marlon said he needed me. He was determined to find an architect. And start his house.

Because I needed a vacation without Brando, I began to interview secretaries. It was difficult as they would have to leave their home in Tahiti and stay on Tetiaroa while Marlon was there. I finally found one who was agreeable to work the summer and ran her by Marlon for approval. I stayed around for a week to help her get used to Marlon's ways and routines.

I was ready to leave when she disclosed she couldn't work for Marlon. She was quitting. Marlon was too much for her. I had made plans to meet friends on Bora Bora; I wanted to leave. I convinced her to stay by telling her Marlon would only be on Tetiaroa for two more weeks and would be leaving for home. Then she would be working in the office in Tahiti. She'd only have to deal with Brando long distance. She very reluctantly agreed to stay.

I chartered a plane and left the island for Tahiti before she changed her mind. I also promised Marlon I'd continue to try to find an architect for him. Fortune shone on me. I had just arrived in Tahiti and the first face I saw was that of Bernard Judge, the architect who had built the original hotel on Tetiaroa. He was about to leave for home, but when I told him Marlon was looking for an architect to plan his island house, he became very interested. There was only one problem—Marlon was mad at Bernard and wasn't speaking to him.

I had found Marlon a secretary, now I had to convince Marlon to forget he was mad at Bernard. I called the Tahiti office and asked them to send Marlon the message that I was bringing him an architect—Bernard Judge. If I didn't hear from him that evening, Bernard and I would be there by noon.

The next morning, with Bernard in tow, I chartered another plane, radioed the Tetiaroa office to notify Marlon I was returning and descended upon Tetiaroa. I took Bernard to

Marlon's bungalow, where he was warmly greeted. Marlon had his architect.

I said goodbye to Marlon again and hopped into the waiting plane to take me back to Tahiti where next morning I flew out to Bora Bora.

Marlon's house wasn't started that summer. It took some time before work finally did begin on his house and then he began to nag me about having plans drawn for my house. I hadn't decided where I wanted to build, but promised I'd decide after I had another look at a site near his house that Marlon had approved for me. What caused my indecision was that the approved site was on the lagoon side with the rising sun, and I didn't know if I would rather live on the opposite side of the island with the setting sun. Marlon wanted me near him. Therefore, I was conflicted and kept postponing drawing up plans, because each site's location required different plans. Unlike Marlon, I knew what I wanted and he liked my ideas, so once I picked a site, it wouldn't take long to get my bungalow built.

Marlon was already on Tetiaroa when I arrived. I was looking forward to seeing the progress on his house. As the plane circled the island to land, we flew by Marlon's house site. I was amazed to see masses of concrete. It wasn't just a foundation I observed, but also massive walls. It looked like a fort. Could this be Marlon's house? What was he thinking?

Marlon met the plane and had my bags taken to my bungalow, while we strolled to the dining room. After lunch Marlon said, "Let's take a walk, I want you to see my house. It's really coming along fast now that I'm here."

I hadn't seen his plans. I didn't know what that concrete mass represented. It certainly didn't look like any house I saw in the tropics. We walked on a rutty road cut through the tropical forest of coconut palms until we came to a clearing where there were Tahitian workers, a massive bulldozer, a skip loader, mixers, shovels, wheelbarrow, etc.

Marlon shouted greetings to the workers as he led me up a flight of concrete steps explaining as we went along, "This is the entrance and to your right is the dining room." And pointing far beyond the concrete floor we were standing on, which was partially enclosed by a concrete wall, to a space being cleared, he said, "That will be the kitchen bungalow."

"Marlon," I said, "don't you think it's too far from the dining room? "

"It's not that far."

"When it's windy, or raining, are people going to carry food all that distance? Are you going to walk down the entrance stairs to get to the refrigerator for a cool drink or some food in the middle of the night? I think you need access on the far side of the dining room. The kitchen should be closer—with a covered walkway."

"Make a note of that," he said.

To the left of the dining room was an eight foot concrete wall. As we rounded the wall into a very large room, I noted it looked like a bunker separating the space.

"This is the living room." Marlon waved his arm encompassing the entire area. There was no roof so the room seemed enormous.

"Where are your sleeping quarters?" I inquired.

"Oh, you're going to love this. I'm going to have a loft bedroom built, under the roof on the far end. I'm not going to have stairs. I'm going to have a ladder. When I get up there, I'm going to have a pulley, and I'm going to pull up the ladder after me. No one can come up or down unless I put the ladder down for them. I'll have complete privacy."

I listened to him in wonder, then questioned. "Marlon, that's all good and well, but how in the world are you going to climb up and down the ladder? You're well over two hundred pounds. You're all belly. What kind of ladder are we talking about? It's going to be one big ladder. I can't see you climbing up after some wine at dinner or down the ladder in the middle of the night to go to the bathroom."

He stood there digesting this as I continued, "You'd need a mattress on the living room floor that you'd have to inflate every time you wanted to go up to the loft, so when you fell you wouldn't break your neck. Face it, Mar, you don't have a bedroom. And by the way, where is your bathroom?"

He didn't speak after I knocked down his plans for his sleeping quarters. So when I asked about the bathroom, he just turned and silently pointed to the "bunker" with a door opening into his living room. I didn't think Marlon liked what he was hearing. But it had to be said. I continued to burst his bubble.

"That's the bathroom? Marlon, the door is in the wrong place. Everyone who's going to use the bathroom will have to come into the living room. You'll have no privacy."

"But," I consoled, "it's not too much of a problem though, the door can easily be changed to the entrance wall."

He just gazed at the open doorway. I continued, "Where do you plan to put the closets?"

Marlon had had enough. He rushed toward the concrete stairway shouting, "Where are those plans. This isn't what I wanted!"

I knew Bernard wasn't the architect, Marlon had found his own builder. And it obviously was what he wanted. He had been on the island a few weeks supervising the building. He was yelling for the contractor, the foreman, as he flew down the concrete steps with me at his heels.

I thought, *Oh, God, what did I do? He wanted my input. Now, they're going to be blamed for his mistakes.*

Who listened to that fanciful loft idea of his? The ladder and pulley? Why the thick concrete walls? To withstand a typhoon, perhaps.

A huge Tahitian man got down from the bulldozer and approached Marlon. Marlon wanted to see the plans, he accused him of not following the plans he approved. The man was trying to tell him they were, but Marlon wouldn't listen. He was screaming, "Stop the building, stop everything." Then he clambered up onto the seat of the bull and revved up—still screaming every obscenity known to man.

The Tahitian worker looked frightened, bewildered, and asked, "What's the matter with him?"

I was yelling, "Marlon, calm down."

I was ignored. He got the bull rolling and smashed into the concrete wall, backed up and smashed again and again.

The Tahitian workers all ran off. I stayed and hollered, "That's fifty thousand dollars!"

I knew he had a couple hundred thousand in the house. So every time he knocked down another wall, I'd yell, "There goes another fifty thousand!"

Finally, he stopped. And sat there.

I waited below. He didn't move.

"Are you going to sit up there all day?" I yelled, "If you are, I'm going back."

He didn't answer.

So ended another day of "fun in the sun" in paradise with Marlon.

I didn't have to worry about plans for my house any longer on that trip. I wouldn't build until Marlon built.

The last time I went to Tetiaroa, the plane circled Onetahi Island to land. I looked down. The huge concrete foundation that remained standing after Marlon's assault with the bull was still unclaimed by the jungle. The ruins of Marlon's dream house still stood—and are still standing, last I heard. And my site still awaited my dream house.

During his lifetime Marlon had been approached by hotel chains, etc., to lease his hotel or lease the island of Onetahi to build a hotel complex. Marlon listened to all the offers through the years as it gave him some idea of what was happening in the hotel business. And he also used the information garnered without having to pay for studies regarding tourism in the South Pacific and elsewhere as some of these offers came from international chains.

Marlon would call and we'd discuss the proposals. But, after each and every offer, he would say in amazement, "Why do they think I would give them control of Tetiaroa? I would never do that!"

Through the years, it became a game to him. He began to enjoy the meetings, toying with the hotel representatives with their multi-million dollar offers, picking their brains, leading them on, and then total rejection. But, he gloated, he had all the latest figures without paying a dime. And he marveled that anyone thought he'd sell Tetiaroa, the atoll that was the answer to his dreams and that he loved above all other places on earth.

The secretary I hired, Cynthia Garbutt, who quit and I persuaded to stay, worked for Marlon in the Tahiti-Tetiaroa office until his death—about thirty years. Bernard remained a life-long associate and "mad and glad" friend—drawing up many plans and making many models which were at times scattered around Marlon's room and home office. Marlon had given permission to Bernard Judge to build a bungalow on the island. After Marlon died, Bernard sued his estate to honor his contractual right to do so. Ironically, in speaking to Bernard at the time of the lawsuit, I discovered he had chosen for himself the same site I had picked out for my bungalow and that Marlon had given me to build on.

*****

Even though Marlon found Tahitian girls appealing, he didn't lose interest in all other girls. Sometime in 1963, Marlon confided his yearning to speak Chinese. He particularly expressed the desire to speak Mandarin Chinese and asked me to phone the local colleges to determine if there were any Chinese students, of the fairer sex, who spoke Mandarin Chinese and who could tutor him in the language. I was to arrange for ten to 15 students to be interviewed.

I located Chinese female students and made arrangements for the interviews. There would be one each day for tea at 4:30 p.m. for two weeks. When the students arrived, I escorted them to Marlon's sitting room in his bedroom suite, where he preferred to conduct the interview, rather than the living room.

On the third day, when departing after the interview with Marlon, one of the Chinese students asked if she could speak to me privately. Of course, I obliged. She wondered if I was aware of the questions Marlon was asking. I responded I had no idea of the precise questions he would ask as I was not present during any of the interviews. She then said she was offended by the questions as they were of a very personal and sexual nature.

I was stunned and inwardly became furious with Marlon for putting me in this embarrassing position. She further stated she didn't believe Marlon was looking for a Mandarin tutor. She was quite candid regarding her interview and the probing sexual questions. I apologized and said I was sorry she was put in a discomforting position and thanked her for bringing it to my attention. She said she spoke to me because of our pleasant telephone conversation when she was being interviewed by me, and further stated that from my demeanor, she didn't feel I was a party to this situation. I thought, *I hope she didn't look upon me as a procurer.*

After she departed, I immediately cornered Marlon. This was one time he could not get away with such irrational behavior as he had involved me. He indignantly tried to say the student was imagining things, etc., etc., etc. I wasn't buying it. Finally, he admitted he was not looking for a Chinese tutor. He wanted someone "in-house" so he wouldn't have to think about who to call and then wait an hour for them to arrive when he desired sex. He wanted instant gratification.

Then he quickly changed the subject and laughed at how easily he had fooled me about wanting to learn Chinese Mandarin. While he was congratulating himself and enjoying the moment, I warned him I'd never forget he was Marlon Brando, Movie Star, Sex Addict again.

I cancelled all the remaining "teas."

Years later, he did hire a secretary that he called an "in-house" to me in private, but he procured her himself. Once a sex addict, always a sex addict? I wondered about it. But no longer do I, for the mystery of sex addiction was addressed when I discovered in the September 2006 issue of Redbook Magazine. Douglas Weiss, Ph.D., who runs Heart to Heart counseling center for sex addicts in Colorado Springs, answers the question: "What is sex addiction?" Dr. Weiss outlines "what you need to know to recognize the problem." Signs of addiction include: "short temper, secrecy, lying, viewing pornography, voyeurism, having affairs, seeing prostitutes, or visiting strip clubs."

Marlon met all the criteria. *Every sign of sex addiction.*

But now I wondered who had told Marlon that he was a sex addict. His psychiatrist? And why wasn't he helped? Or did he want to be helped? Another mystery.

Not long after the "teas," one morning when checking the answering service for calls that came in during the night, I noticed one of the messages was from a man who wanted to talk to Marlon on a personal matter and noted he had phoned several times. I had given the messages to Marlon, evidently he was not interested. But I decided to check with him about the persistent calls. After he awoke that afternoon, I broached the subject as he was sipping his coffee. He said he didn't know the person. Since Marlon's telephone number was unlisted, I thought he may have given someone the number. To tickle his memory, I mentioned that the area code was San Francisco. It didn't ring any bells.

Then the gentleman called and left a message for me by name. I informed Marlon of the call. Curiosity got the better of us. "Give him a jingle. Find out who he is and what he wants."

I called. The gentleman explained Marlon didn't know him but he had to talk to Marlon on a very personal matter. I asked how he had obtained Marlon's number. He refused to tell me. "I'm Marlon's personal secretary. He asked me to talk to you and find out what you wanted to discuss with him."

He was undecided whether to tell me, but since he was given my name and told to call me, he gave me a message for Marlon.

"Tell him Tarita had an abortion and I paid for it as she didn't have the money." Tarita had given him Marlon's telephone number, told him to tell Marlon and ask him for the money.

As in Japan where Leo Langamazino negotiated for Tarita, this gentleman was doing the same. Throughout her relationship with Marlon, and especially in the early stages, Tarita didn't ask Marlon directly for money. She had emissaries ask him. The household help, her friends, secretaries, business managers, and I were all used in this manner. So his asking for the money at her behest was no surprise.

When I passed on the message to Marlon, he exploded. "I haven't had anything to do with Tarita! If she was pregnant, it wasn't by me!"

Marlon became very irritated. "He's a con man, he's just after money."

He thought this might be a "shakedown" by someone who had met Tarita in Tahiti.

I passed on a message; Marlon was not going to reimburse him for Tarita's abortion. During this conversation I learned that Tarita had told him to ask me to obtain the money from Marlon. And I also learned that Tarita had been in the Bay Area for some time with a Tahitian dance troupe, headlining at one of the clubs, which Marlon didn't know, and that she was romantically involved with someone.

Marlon was right, he wasn't involved. But he was wrong about the gentleman being a con man. I gave the information gleaned to Marlon.

He seethed and said, "I'm not paying for Tarita's abortion! Let her boyfriend pay for it!"

I thought it ended there, but later in the day Marlon asked me to "run Tarita down and find out what's going on."

I located Tarita, gave him the number, and suggested he call her. He was unwilling. He didn't want to get mixed up in her affairs. "She's working, let her pay the man. I'm not paying for another man's abortion."

He was adamant. He didn't feel obligated to pay Tarita's debts. Marlon became concerned about the baby, Tehotu. "Was he with Tarita?" I didn't know.

"Find out."

I put a call to Tarita. Marlon wanted me to talk to her. He was loathe to. I handed him the phone, saying, "I'm out of it, it's all yours," and left his room.

Marlon was giving Tarita money for child care—he remarked at the time that since he didn't have any money, "She can work and take care of herself." She was about twenty, give or take a few years. But when Tetiaroa and the Tahitian government issues were involved years later, Tarita and Tehotu became his, as he said, "ace in the hole."

After this incident, dealing with another abortion, Marlon's days were filled with anger at women getting pregnant and expecting him to marry them or take care of the problem.

Soon afterward, one night Marlon was throwing a fund-raising party. I was expecting a telephone call, so I went to my office to await it. When my phone rang I answered, but it wasn't my call. It was another call from San Francisco—this time from Marie Cui, a girlfriend of Marlon's; she must talk to him. I returned to the living room, sidled up to Marlon and whispered there was a call for him on my office line.

Shortly, a maid approached and said Marlon wanted to see me in my room. When I entered, he gestured and said, "Sit." After I was seated, he solemnly announced that Marie was pregnant and that she had said it was his child. This was the very last thing I expected to hear. No wonder he wanted me to be seated when he broke the news. I laughed out loud. It was infectious. He joined me. Once started we couldn't stop laughing. Amid the laughter, I asked what he was going to do. He replied, "We're going to get drunk."

I let the answering service take my call and we went back to the party where Marlon proceeded to keep his word. I joined him in only one drink because I knew after the jolt he had just received, I'd have to see he made it to his bed when he fell over.

The following afternoon, Marlon and I were sitting in the living room "having a cupa," discussing the previous evening. Marlon suddenly said he'd been trying to remember when he last saw Marie. I, too, started to think back. I recalled the last time I saw her.

Marie had come into my office in the morning and had asked me for a Kotex. She said she didn't bring many because she hadn't expected to stay the night. I also remembered she had left soiled napkins next to the toilet in the guest bathroom. The housekeeper complained to me about it. That was a couple of months previous. I told Marlon about this. He said he couldn't remember having intercourse with her. That was the last time he saw her. He doubted the baby was his.

Marie came to see Marlon with Gene, a friend, when she returned from San Francisco. I stayed away from the meeting, but Marlon filled me in when they departed. Marie wanted 100,000 dollars to have an abortion. Marlon made the observation that the price was coming down.

Marlon persisted he didn't think he was the father. All these girls getting pregnant, thinking he was going to marry and take care of them, was really getting to him. He said he was not going to marry again. I informed him that I didn't want anything to do with his life decisions. He'd have to determine what to do on his own.

A few days after the meeting, Gene called and asked me to prevail upon Marlon to give Marie the 100,000 dollars. I reminded him Marlon didn't think he was responsible for her pregnancy. Gene was convinced by Marie he was. He didn't want Marlon to have any bad press if Marie decided not to have an abortion and said Marlon should think about having another baby by yet another woman. He was deeply concerned about Marlon and this problem. I passed his concern on to Marlon, but he was unmoved. He was not giving her 100,000 dollars. Period.

For months he'd ask, "Are you sure she asked you for a Kotex the last time she was here?" I reminded him that didn't mean a thing, as women were known to conceive regardless. That made him uncertain, but he was racking his brain trying to remember what had happened the last time he saw her. Time and again he'd say, "What did I tell you, do you remember what I told you?" He and I didn't discuss anything about the night she stayed over, that I recalled. I know I didn't tell him about the housekeeper's complaint at the time; maybe if I had, he'd have some reference as I had. He, nevertheless, had very serious doubts about the baby being his. And discussed them freely with me.

In July of 1963, Marlon became ill and spent a week in St. John's Hospital with acute pyelonephritis.

I was told by a doctor that pyelonephritis is a very serious kidney ailment which could travel to other organs and cause death. While Marlon was in the hospital, it was discovered he had four kidneys.

On July 19th,1963, headlines proclaimed that Marie Cui filed a paternity suit against Marlon. Marlon was so angry, he could chew nails and spit out battleships. When Marlon was discharged from the hospital, he immediately had a meeting with his attorneys in regard to the lawsuit. Now lawyers became involved.

I had suggested that since Marlon didn't think the child was his, he wait until the child was born, then have a blood test. When Marlon consulted his lawyers, they agreed. I can vividly recall the day Marlon was going for the blood test; you'd think he was on his way to the gallows. The last thing he said to me as he went out the door was, "We'd better be sure."

"Don't 'we' me," I laughed. "I had nothing to do with it." He was not laughing.

The blood test came back negative—Marlon was not the father. I thought he'd be ecstatic hearing the results. Instead, he was so mad at Marie for putting him through months of hell, he was raving. But somehow he controlled himself and didn't thrash a room or break a window. He, instead, vowed revenge. And years later, he took it. More than once. He never forgot or forgave Marie for the paternity suit as through the years he would bring it up and we'd relive it, then he'd again vow revenge.

Next, Marlon confided that another girlfriend was pregnant by him. She had the child, who did not assume the Brando name. She was independently wealthy, therefore Marlon was not saddled with support.

About a month or so later Marlon buzzed my intercom and summoned, "Come on in. I have something to tell you."

When I arrived in his room, he surprised me by saying, "I just heard Movita has a baby girl."

"Yours?" I asked, laughing at him.

"*No way!*" He shouted. "This time I'm *certain* it's not mine!"

It wasn't. Marlon revealed the child was adopted in Mexico.

It wasn't long before Marlon was again confiding—an Asian college student he was romancing, along with all the others, was pregnant. Since marriage was not on the table, she opted for an abortion as her family wanted her to have a degree before returning home. "She could not shame her family by having a child out of wedlock," according to Marlon. I don't know what this cost him in dollars, but I did know what it cost him emotionally.

All these females having children was affecting Marlon's relationship with women. He felt they thought that if they became pregnant, he'd marry them or take care of them. He let it be known that he was not ever getting married.

It was when he had to work on a film because he needed money that resentment against all the women having children usually came to the fore. He'd say to me, "They think when I die, I'm going to leave them all millions. They think because they got pregnant and had a child, I'm going to take care of them. They didn't love me. They wouldn't get pregnant if I wasn't a movie star. They're not getting a dime." He'd angrily rave on.

And on.

He meant what he said. He remembered the children, but he did not remember any of the women who had children in his will.

* * * * *

During this same period, in the early sixties, when Marlon was being besieged by calls from girlfriends telling him they were pregnant, I received a call asking me to give Marlon a message. Brando Senior had fathered a child. Marlon's relationship with his father took another hit. Marlon greeted the news by losing it.

Incidentally, Anna Kashfi wrote in her book that I was having an affair with Marlon's father and that I had coerced him into giving me the job with Marlon. Nothing could be further from the truth. Marlon's father was old enough to be my father. Perhaps it was because one night we were all at the same party and Anna needed a ride home. She asked Brando Senior for a lift. He asked me to go with him. His reasoning was that he didn't want Marlon, who was filming in Japan, to hear that he was interested in Anna. Since I accompanied Senior, she may have assumed we were dating.

Later, Anna and Brando Senior were dwelling in the same apartment complex in Hollywood, and she wrote that a girl she saw him with there was me. But Marlon's father was dating two others that I was aware of, and one of them had his child.

Contrary to what Anna thought and wrote, he and I were just friends.

* * * * *

These five years were a test of our friendship, as Marlon careened from one paternity crisis to another. And all the lawyers, investigators, women, and families, plus his generosity, were keeping Marlon broke.

Never a day went by without calls from one or another of the families—angry messages for Marlon, problems needing to be solved, and always requests for money from the families, friends in need, and his latest causes and pet project, or petitions to fund projects. There were occasions when Marlon couldn't cope, or simply wouldn't cope. At times he, in a state of exasperation bordering on desperation, would drop everything in my lap, saying, "You take care this." And leave town.

His emotional life was like a roller coaster and it, too, took its toll on him and his bankroll. He made many visits to his psychiatrist.

It was at this time Marlon first asked me to go to his psychiatrist for him. He claimed I knew more about him than he did himself, and he wanted me to discuss him with his psychiatrist. I refused. I felt he needed to attend his own therapy sessions and help himself. He dumped all his other problems on me to solve. I felt I didn't know enough about his idiosyncrasies, rage, sex addiction, craziness, dual personalities (acting?), fantasies, and paranoia to shoulder them, too. I passed.

Except for his psychiatrist who said he was crazy, and Marlon, who readily agreed with him, anyone who came in contact with Marlon during this period would have told you Marlon was kooky, juvenile, but sane. And I would agree. For, when I challenged his sanity or his craziness, he forever reminded me that he was an actor. Therefore, he left it to me to discover who Marlon Brando the Farm Boy, as he referred to himself to me, was.

Who was Marlon Brando the Actor? Who was Marlon Brando the Star? Which one did people meet? Which one would greet me each day I arrived at work? Which one was sane, and which one was crazy?

Or—who was this other person that he hid from everyone, but of whom he gave glimpses to me?

This person who broke windows, broke furniture at the slightest provocation. Who couldn't get out of bed? Who put hair or string or lint from his navel, as he told me, in closed drawers and doors, then checked to see it they were moved, if anyone was invading his privacy? Who was this person who lied, but said he hated liars, and accused everyone else with lying? And vowed they must be punished for lying. Who was this person who didn't trust anyone? Who was this person who constantly sought revenge? Who was this person who thought nothing of setting up scenarios? Who was this person who was constantly plotting? Who was this person who said he couldn't sleep alone in bed? Who was this person who relished the fact that he lied to his psychiatrist? Who conjured up elaborate dreams to tell him? Who was this person who abused and demeaned women verbally and physically?

Who was this person who thought the CIA was watching him, bugging his phones? One day after lunch, I saw a car drive up and park in the farthest corner of the parking area in front of Marlon's home. Marlon ran out of the house. A man got out of the car. They greeted each other with a handshake. I recognized the man as U.S. Senator Church. He returned to the car. The motor was turned on. The radio began blaring. Senator Church then returned to where Marlon was still standing. He and Marlon spoke for a short period of time. Then, shaking hands again, he departed.

Later, with the radio blaring, Marlon informed me not to let anyone know that he had called Senator Church and had asked him to meet. And had told Church about the CIA following him around, how they were tapping his phones, etc. Marlon was so paranoid at this time, he insisted the CIA had come into the house when he wasn't there and planted "bugs." He had all the rooms and his phones swept. No eavesdropping equipment, "bugs," was ever found. He'd ask me to whisper and monitor our speech with music blaring. Senator Church never appeared or was heard from again.

This phase passed, but resurfaced from time to time. He gave me the names of two men. Told me that they were CIA and that I was to remember their names for him. I don't know who the men were. CIA?

He was spinning out of control.

Who was Marlon Brando?

I didn't have the answers. I urged him to take control of his life. His psychiatrist had told him he was crazy, to take a Miltown. He tried, but there were too many crises in his life, too much rage, pain, too much of everything, and to add to this, he was hiding this from everyone. Acting. He cried out to me, and I was there, but he had to help himself. I begged him to exercise some control over his emotions.

At times, even I realized reality was too difficult for him to face. But there was always Miltown, and later Valium, lurking in the shadows. To an outsider, his was a busy life—girls, children, atoll, causes, marches, movie making—but there was a great deal of pretending everything was normal. Acting, lying, and, yes, protecting.

What had I gotten myself into?

I always ran away when Marlon went berserk as he had in New York City. I would hear him cursing, yelling. I heard the sounds emanating from him. I didn't hear the words. I heard the noise. The crashing. Everything breaking. When this happened, I became a survivor. I scrammed.

Till one day.

Without forethought I hung around, watching fascinated. Furniture went crashing, books were violently swept from the shelves, everything at hand went flying. His room was in shambles in seconds, minutes.

And I listened. To the snarling shouts containing threats and curses. Obscenities. The all-consuming rage that accompanied the wild outburst and wreckage.

This was more than the ravings of a disordered mind. This was a man exorcising the demons that tormented him. It was heart-wrenching to behold. But when sanity once more took control, I was glad I stayed, for I discovered the source of some of his torment. I began to understand how completely his past controlled him, and the actor kept the hurt, hate, rage submerged. Until someone or something triggered it.

Who was Marlon Brando? I could only venture a guess, and I declined to do so.

Afterward, when he had purged himself of his demons and his anger had exhausted him and he sat empty among the ruins, I made myself known.

We talked.

By this time in his life, Marlon had made: *The Men, A Streetcar Named Desire, Viva Zapata, Julius Caesar, The Wild One, On the Waterfront, Desiree, Guys and Dolls, Teahouse of the August Moon, Sayonara, The Young Lions, The Fugitive Kind, One-Eyed Jacks, Mutiny on the Bounty,* and *The Ugly American.*

Marlon was the highest paid actor in the world. He was the first actor to receive one million dollars per picture for *The Fugitive Kind.*

After all these films, and on this date, he didn't have a dime. He was seriously in debt. Here was one of the biggest movie stars in the world—unemployed and broke when I came into his life and home on a day-to-day basis and put food on his table and money in his pocket—and now here again, sadly, *broke.*

He was aware he was emotionally troubled. He sought psychological help. Also, he was confiding in me, or confessing if you will, things and feelings that were so personal and so private that I could never repeat. Why? Because he was such a masterful liar and con man that I didn't know if what he revealed about himself was true or if it was a big lie. And I would wonder why he was so open with me. I knew he trusted me as I had been tested, but was he still testing me? I didn't know, and rather than spend my time trying to analyze why, I just buried it. I didn't want to be controlled or consumed by Brando, The Master Manipulator. I knew if I allowed him to exploit the compassion I felt and expressed, we'd both be lost.

Marlon and I would have a most intimate conversation for an hour or so, for by this time we were best of friends. Then later, on the set or in public, he'd behold a very formal person, addressing him as Mr. Brando or Marlon. In time he became used to my formality. He got the message. In public he became Marlon Brando, Employer.

In this manner, I would distance myself from his personal life while maintaining an employer—employee demeanor. It was difficult at times, but it worked for me. Yet, I was available to him when he needed a shoulder, or needed to vent, or needed financial assistance, or a friend. In other words, from the beginning I defined our relationship—not Marlon.

And now here he was among the emotional and material ruins. His lack of funds was putting him into another place—it was blowing his mind; he was past understanding. All the money he had earned from all the films he had made through the years was gone. Where?

He had to go to work. By now, too many people were depending on him for their livelihood. His life style was becoming more expensive. Life was encroaching upon his personal freedom. Government, taxes, lawyers, and women had become his enemies. He was working for "them." What could I say? He had made his bed—he didn't want to sleep in it.

And so he escaped, hiding out from himself, acting for the world—that everything was wonderful in his private life—until reality would rear up and slap him in the face. For by now Marlon was in a profession he hated. He hated, as he told me, making faces in front of a camera, pretending to be someone else, digging deep into his emotional self. *Last Tango in Paris* comes to mind when he swore he'd never allow himself to be torn apart again.

The profession he had chosen—had revolutionized—imprisoned him and was destroying him. His lack of money, and the enormous amount of money he could make, kept him in front of the camera. He felt his lack of education prevented him from escaping. There was nothing he was capable of doing that would give him the funds to live the "free-wheeling life style" he desired and had become accustomed to living. His fame gave him the power—and the money he earned from each film gave him personal freedom and, moreover, freedom from responsibility.

Or so he thought—for he contended, and kept repeating in his tirade that people he trusted with his money had lost it all. He couldn't understand the fact that he surrounded himself with people who were intimidated by him, were afraid to tell him he was giving away money he didn't have or couldn't afford. It didn't matter. He didn't want to hear he made one million dollars and he was in the highest tax bracket and didn't have one million dollars to spend.

When I tried to impress him with this fact, he didn't understand what I was talking about. All he allowed himself to understand was he was making one million per picture. And he brushed me off, or tried to, because I persisted in reminding him most went to the government in taxes and families he was supporting.

Occasionally, his financial predicament would get through to him and he'd work. And still his overhead was escalating with all the mothers and children and their monetary demands, and he was constantly in debt. They thought that because he had made all these films, he was a multi-millionaire. Everyone else did, too. They thought he was kidding when he said he didn't have any money. He was Marlon Brando, one of the biggest stars in the world, earning millions. No one knew he only worked when he was up to his eyeballs in debt—when there was no other choice. They didn't know all the money he had made was lost.

So, Marlon was *broke* again. And again he raged against the world. People didn't see him. They saw a movie star. He raged against women. The women only had his children because he was Marlon Brando, Movie Star. They didn't love him. They didn't know him. They just wanted his money. They didn't care he was broke and had to go to work at a job he hated. They just wanted more money.

He escaped from the reality into a Miltown haze and took to his bed.

He voiced his resentments: people depending on him for money, people depending upon him for work. He said they were only friends with him because he was a movie star—

someone who could get them work on a film. And if he wasn't working, they'd attach themselves to another movie star. He resented those who, when they needed money, came around with a project and wanted him to fund it. They only came around when they needed money. They didn't come around "when I need money."

I tried to console him and explained that it was the nature of the movie business, if you were a star, when you worked, your friends who were actors, but not stars, worked. Unfortunately, he rejected this premise. They were not his friends, they didn't care about him.

All the films he had made, all that money lost, or given away, all the women whom he felt were using him, added to his feelings about his early home life and his parents, was taking its toll. His only release was the destruction of what was before him. And after his purging, the planning, and plotting for "getting even." Revenge.

Throughout all this, there was one glaring thing missing. Marlon did not take responsibility for anything that had happened in his life that he was raging about. Everybody did *him* wrong. He completely ignored the lives he had influenced for better or worse, or the lives and relationships he had destroyed. He was consumed by rage. And so utterly bitter. And yes, sad, too, as was I.

Whereas I had the capacity to perceive the results of an action—Marlon didn't seem to have the ability to perceive the results of his actions. If you touch a hot stove, you'll burn your hand. Cause and effect was foreign to his nature. He never showed any remorse for actions that injured or humiliated others, if it was something he had initiated for revenge. He exercised superiority over his victims.

After we had talked, I realized there was little I could do, except be there for him and try to talk him out of the vengeance he threatened upon those he perceived did him wrong, injured him in some way. Those he raged about during his uncontrollable destruction of his room.

Sex and *revenge* ruled his life. If he wasn't thinking about one, it was the other—or both. No one was immune to the Brando charisma. And no one was immune in his quest for revenge.

For instance, even his sister, Jocelyn, was the recipient of his revenge. He knew he caused her pain, but such was his nature that he ignored it until it was too late. Her "sin": She gave an interview to set the record straight, invalidating and contradicting Marlon's words—his lies against their parents. He felt betrayed.

I could do nothing to reconcile the two. He didn't ask me to take sides. He knew I wouldn't, and he had no intention of listening to a voice of reason. And through the long years of their estrangement, when I spoke to Jocelyn, I made a point of relating our conversation, which Marlon listened to in stony silence, then introduced a new subject completely unrelated to what I had imparted. He could ignore it, but I knew he heard every word I said. And I also knew that if he wasn't interested in her well-being, he wouldn't hesitate to cut me off as soon as I said, "I talked to Jossie last night."

And though they reconciled during the last year of his life, when Marlon, her brother, died and we discussed his passing, Jocelyn, anger edging her voice, lamented, "Ten years. I can't forgive him for the loss of years."

It was the sad lament of a broken heart.

Now along with the anger vented over personal hurts, most of his rage was directed at those he blamed for his lack of money. Because he allowed other people to handle his money, refused to talk to them except to ask for funds, and wouldn't look at financial statements, he had no idea how much he was throwing around. Until it was too late and he had to work.

I'd been working and taking care of myself since my teens. I had a healthy respect for money earned. I tried to impress upon him to exercise some control over his spending. I encouraged him to put the past behind him and live in the present. I encouraged him to take an interest in and have more say in his financial affairs, his investments.

Much to my dismay, he took my advice on investments. Marlon decided we meet with his business managers—and Marlon talked rings around them. They left confused and a day or two later, they called me to determine whether Marlon had agreed or disagreed with their investment suggestions, or whether they should act on any of his way out fanciful ideas.

It was a disaster, but he enjoyed the mental gymnastics and from then on, he would periodically meet with his business managers and engage them in all manner of ways to make a fortune—and to feed the world. World hunger was a huge problem that Marlon was constantly addressing, hence his years of working and traveling around the world as ambassador for UNICEF.

When he purchased Tetiaroa, he thought himself an expert on real estate. He would have meeting after meeting on developing and exploiting the island. Thirty years later, I would still receive calls from him about his plans for his beloved Tetiaroa. And he'd remind everyone what a great investment his house purchased from Omar Darr in Punaauia, Tahiti, was.

Marlon acted on an emotional basis when it came to investments. For instance, he visited Hawaii, had a wonderful time, loved the island. He expressed the desire to live there. Before he returned, he had purchased ocean-front property, sight unseen. The fact that there was no right of way to reach the property didn't concern him. He'd have privacy. He'd reach it by boat. Of course, he didn't have a boat. I don't believe he ever set foot on the property. I never went to "check it out" for him as he asked. He couldn't sell it and I understand it eventually was given to charity.

Same scenario. Only this time the property was in Mojave. He fell in love with the desert. Bought property where he could be private. He sent an emissary to view the property, which was 168 acres on the side of a steep mountain. To get to it was a very hazardous journey in a range rover. The road only went partway up the mountain. You could hike or take a burro the rest of the way to Marlon's property, that is, if you could get past the man with a shotgun who was guarding his own property from trespassers. It was determined that the only way to reach or view it was by helicopter. I know Marlon never saw this property.

Years later, he entertained a brilliant idea; he'd contact an Indian tribe and open an Indian casino on his property.

Marlon, his girlfriend Jill, Jocelyn, and I went to New Mexico with him as he wished to purchase desert property in or around Santa Fe. He promised us it would be "loads of fun." First we went to Taos. Leave it to Marlon to hear of desert property with water on it.

We had breakfast, then set out with the real estate woman to see the property. We drove a few miles into the desert when Marlon began complaining about the way she was driving. There was not another car on the road but us. Marlon seemed to think she was driving too fast—she disagreed. He said he had been watching the speedometer. They were arguing in the front seat; Jill, Jocelyn, and I were in the back seat not paying too much attention. Suddenly, Marlon screamed, "Stop the car. Stop the car." The car stopped in the middle of the road. Marlon said he wanted one of us to drive. We all refused. He jumped out of the car and ran around to the driver's side. She refused to move, because she had driven with Marlon the day before and she didn't want to trust her temperamental car to Marlon. He now threatened to drag her out by her hair. Still loudly objecting, she moved to the passenger side. Marlon got in and we rolled on.

There was silence in the back seat as Marlon now asked how long it would take to get to the property. She couldn't give him a definite time or number of miles and the argument was on once more.

After driving a few miles Marlon stopped the car. He got out, opened the trunk, and came back. He opened two boxes that he had brought with him. We whispered in the back seat, "What's he up to now?"

It didn't take long to find out. He had two walkie-talkies. He opened the back door of the car.

"Alice," he said, "I want to test my walkie-talkies."

I quickly said, "I don't know anything about walkie-talkies."

Jocelyn and Jill chimed in, "Neither do I."

Undeterred, Marlon asked me to get out of the car and he'd show me what to do. Then, he would drive a mile down the road and he'd talk to me on his walkie-talkie.

"I'm not going to stand here on the road in the middle of nowhere while you drive away."

"Are you telling me you're not going to do it?"

"I'm not getting out of this car and let you drive off leaving me stranded on a desert road."

Exasperated with me, he turned to Jocelyn and Jill and asked one of them to do it.

"Don't either of you do it," I advised. "He'll drive off and take his sweet time returning for you."

"Stop telling them what to do."

"Don't do it," I repeated.

Now the real estate woman got into the act. "We don't need walkie-talkies. Get in, let's get along."

Marlon yelled at her, "Don't you tell me what to do. You keep out of this!"

"I have a suggestion," I said. "Marlon, you stay here and we'll drive a mile down the road and you can test them." Jocelyn and Jill agreed. The real estate woman kept yelling. "We don't need walkie-talkies."

Marlon slammed the back door, threw the walkie-talkies on the front seat, slid in and tore off down the road. He was driving too fast for the real estate woman, now she was admonishing, "Slow down."

Marlon was still yelling, "Don't tell me what to do."

By this time, the real estate woman was so unhinged by Marlon's verbal attack, she became confused because she hadn't been watching the mileage and didn't know whether or not we had passed a turnoff. Marlon was giving her a very bad time.

We spent the morning looking for the property. Marlon became more annoyed every time we went down the wrong dirt road. Then we had a flat tire. In the middle of nowhere. Marlon now berated her for taking us out in the desert with bad tires. She contended we must have picked up something. And the war of words was on.

We didn't know how to fix a flat. We sat in the air-conditioned car. Finally he put us out in the sweltering heat. We handed him tools while he figured out how to change the tire. By this time, we were all sweating, thirsty and hungry. And very vocal about it. He threatened to leave us behind if we even mentioned that we needed to go to the bathroom. There was nothing in any direction as far as the eye could see. Marlon refused to abandon the search, he wouldn't turn around. He was getting more annoyed with us by the minute.

Luckily, we finally went down the right dirt road off the highway. He was right—there was water. And you had to have hip boots if you wanted to wade through the swamp to get to a higher piece of flat land where Marlon contended he would build his house. He was gazing around fantasizing about building a bridge over the swampland to get to the house. The real estate agent was extolling the beauty of the vista and the sunrises and sunsets he'd have. It took Jossie and me to talked him out of the madness of signing on the dotted line.

After that first day, Marlon wasn't talking to us.

He had called a friend and we all went in the rental station wagon with Marlon driving and Jill navigating to where we'd pick her up. Marlon was giving Jill a bad time because he claimed she wasn't giving him enough time to change lanes on the freeway. So by the time we reached our destination, they weren't talking.

When we picked up his friend, she was drunk. Marlon was furious, for now he was not only stuck with us, he had an intoxicated friend to contend with. She jumped in the back seat with me and Jocelyn and proceeded to take a bottle out of her huge bag, uncorked it, and took a swig. Marlon saw her in the rear-view mirror.

"There's no drinking in this car." he yelled.

"Marlon, there's always drinking in a car, you remember…"

He didn't let her finish. "You're drunk. There's no drinking while I'm driving."

And the fight was on. She gave as good as she got. He threatened to throw her out of the car. Jill tried to calm him as he was all over the road.

Jocelyn whispered to me, "Isn't this fun."

If everything could go wrong on a trip, this was it. Jossie and I had had it. We booked the first flight out we could get. But we were in Taos and our flight was out of Santa Fe.

We decided not to drive to Santa Fe, but to take the commuter flight. By this time, Marlon and Jill had had enough of Taos and decided to go to Santa Fe with us as we were going to the theater before we left. They packed and, as usual, Marlon was late, so when we arrived at the small airport, the commuter plane had departed.

Marlon went to charter a plane. We hung around until the plane was ready. We met the pilot and walked out to the plane. When I saw the puddle jumper, I said to Marlon, "I'm not getting into this plane." It was a four-seater single engine that looked like it was held together with bailing wire.

Marlon and I argued, at the same time he was ushering Jill and Jocelyn onto the wing and into the door. The pilot joined in, telling me it had just been serviced. It was safe to fly. I said I thought it wouldn't get off the ground with the four suitcases and the rest of the weight of the passengers. Marlon took umbrage and turned on me.

"You mean me, don't you?"

"Well, yes, Marlon. You're two people."

He got madder than hell, grabbed me, hoisted me onto the wing, and pushed me into the door of the plane, and followed behind me. That ended that argument.

It was a short flight and we made it.

The trip was a disaster. Jill wasn't too happy with us for abandoning her.

Jossie and I vowed we'd never go on a trip with Marlon again. And Marlon, he vowed he would never take us anywhere again. Jill, she was in love with him—so she was stuck with him.

There were other real estate deals and, of course, there was the infamous boat he purchased, sight unseen, that had sunk and been raised—and had sunk again the last we heard. Throughout the years, Marlon kept his business manager busy with any number of experimental investments—turtles, shrimp, hydroponics, growing coral, etc., along with his real estate forays.

I must confess to making outlandish investments myself. I bought a racehorse with Bob Dorff. I don't remember whether he won any races or not, though Bob said he did. The only thing I remember is the horse ate better than I did. I was constantly paying feed bills. I had also invested in a tavern. Then I owned Daffodils and Dandelions, a floral business. Real estate in Apple Valley and Newport Beach, both in California. And, always in the stock market. Of course, later I put a 2,000 dollar down payment on a bungalow on Bora Bora in the South Pacific, which Marlon eventually purchased for me.

*****

As I write to explain why Marlon gave me property—why I sued his estate for money he owed me and intended to pay when funds were available—I realize I have underwritten. I feel I must try to explain that, while Marlon had bouts of paranoia, as at the time of the secret meeting in his parking lot, he, when with others, was "acting" normal. And on a day-to-day basis exhibited normal behavior despite occurrences of destruction.

It's difficult for me to explain this for he seemed to be able to change character at will and hide behind a façade of a "happy-go-lucky" persona. But, he was living life on the edge. Hanging on by his fingertips. He knew he was troubled, but couldn't control his compulsions or addictions. There were times he completely lost it. He did confide in others, besides me, about the CIA "bugging his house and phones."

And he also confided he was unloved as a child and considered it a root cause of his emotional problems. I recall a conversation I had with Phillip Rhodes, who also was a confidant of Marlon's. We discussed Marlon's alleged childhood traumas and I brought up the fact that I felt strongly about his verbal abuse of Christian, putting him out of the house so Christian was hard pressed to put down roots and therefore lacked a true sense of "home," of "belonging." And the other children having to call to find out if they could "visit"—they could not just "drop in." They all referred to it as "my father's house," never as "home." And Christian, who was living there, was constantly reminded by his father that, "It's my house, not yours." Phillip laughed and said, "Isn't it strange that Marlon has become his father."

During the period I'm writing about—the sixties and then the year before he died in 2004—Marlon, and his interests, had evolved through the years. He was very, very active in, UNICEF, civil rights, politics, Indian affairs, aquaculture, solar energy, promoting and building on Tetiaroa (hotel, school, his home), court appearances, and, of course, acting in movies when he needed funds.

But these were not everyday happenings. He took care of many of his affairs from his bed by telephone. He also delegated—threw money at aquaculture, solar energy, Tetiaroa, etc., and let the builders, scientists, and others. carry the ball.

There was a sense of great activity, even if he wasn't the one who was physically active.

He did a great deal of traveling on behalf of his interests—and since he had "sex on the brain," he either traveled with a companion or had a "friend" meet him with a girl, or contacted a girlfriend in cities all around the world, telling them when he was arriving so they would be available, or he picked up the first girl he laid eyes on. He invariably returned from trips with new telephone numbers. There were meetings, parties, trips—people coming and going in his life.

But through it all he was alone. And I, I was the constant in his life.

Since he was a night person and there were girls during the day and half the night, he'd start telephoning people around two or four in the morning. The first time I ever heard of "phone sex" was when Marlon one day dropped it on me by saying, "You'll never guess who I'm having phone sex with." I didn't ask him to explain it, still couldn't tell you what it entails. I didn't try to guess who—he told me. I wasn't happy to hear she was married. Why? He delighted in breaking up relationships—and marriages.

I'm showing one face of Marlon Brando here—the hidden Brando. That Brando didn't surface every day—nor did the angry, moody, brooding Brando; the tortured soul. There was the Marlon Brando that was charismatic, compassionate, generous, childlike and childish, prankster, whimsical, fun loving, affable, charming. Marlon showed many faces to the world—the one you saw depended on the day.

There was the one who whistled. In 1992, when I stayed with Marlon a few months before he went to Spain to film *Columbus*, he called me from London one night to chat. During the conversation I said, "Mar, I didn't hear you whistling while you were here. I missed it. You don't whistle anymore."

His immediate response was, "I do. In fact I'm whistling better than ever now!" And we laughed at the defensive attitude he displayed in regard to him whistling. Though I hadn't heard him.

Throughout the years, everyone would stay out of sight, hiding from Marlon, when he was in one of his "dark moods." When I said good morning to him and he'd ignore the greeting by turning to me with a "how dare you address me" look, I'd invariably respond by saying I'd be leaving.

"Are you going to be grouchy all day? If you are, I'll plan to be out of the house. I'll call Florine and go to the Bistro for lunch, then go shopping." That ploy always worked. His attitude toward me would change. He didn't want me to leave.

One day, after everyone had been hiding from him the day before, when I saw him, I asked how long he was going to be "mad at everyone."

His immediate response was, "I'm only mad at you."

Surprised, I asked, "Why are you mad at me?"

"Because you were right. Why are you always right?"

This amused me and I laughed because he was serious. "Marlon, I'm not always right."

"Yes, you are!" he insisted.

"No, Marlon, it's just that you're always wrong."

That was the cue for him to enumerate the times he was right, and he forgot he was out of sorts with me. And I didn't even ask him what I was right about that had annoyed him so. Then, I thought, he probably was still brooding about what happened earlier in the week.

I had been away from the house and on returning, I came upon Wally Cox sitting on the kitchen floor, surrounded by tools at his feet and an empty, three-foot-long toolbox. Marlon was sprawled on the floor beside him with his head and shoulders partially filling the opening under the kitchen sink.

"What's the matter? Pipe broken?" I queried.

Wally replied, "The garbage disposal is broken, we're going to take it out and fix it."

Marlon stuck his head out and with a beguiling smile on his face and a large wrench in his hand, he said, "You didn't know I was a plumber."

I addressed Wally, "Did you turn off the electricity?"

"He was on the floor when I arrived. He didn't have tools so I got mine." Turning to Marlon, Wally said, "Did you turn off the electricity?"

I didn't give him time to answer, I said, "You're lucky you weren't electrocuted fooling around under there."

The smile had left Marlon's face.

I continued, "Marlon, before you pull out the disposal, press the red button."

Simultaneously, Marlon said, "What red button?" and Wally said, "Marlon, didn't you press the red button?"

"What red button?" He asked exasperated. Marlon couldn't look under the disposal, he was too big to maneuver.

"Feel under the disposal," I said, "you'll find a button. Press it."

Marlon did. I flicked the electric switch. Nothing happened. Marlon gave me his "you think you're so smart" look. I then pulled out the drawer under the counter next to the sink and took out a little silver thingamajig, and said, "Marlon, move over." I got down on the floor, leaned in and inserted it, worked it from side to side a few times, and then it unfroze and went around.

Wally was leaning against the drawers on the opposite side of the narrow galley kitchen, laughing at this interplay between me and Marlon, Marlon was annoyed with my telling him what to do, then taking over from him. Wally's laughter was getting to Marlon. I stood up and flicked on the electric switch again. A whirring sound filled the kitchen.

Wally quipped, "Marlon the Plumber!" and fell over laughing.

Marlon gave me a scathing look and loudly ordered me out of the kitchen, which only made Wally laugh more. As I retreated, I heard Marlon say to Wally, "She does that to me all the time—she drives me crazy!" I heard the dining room door slam and knew Marlon had left. I rejoined Wally, and laughing we both picked up the tools scattered around the floor. When finished, Wally locked up his toolbox, picked it up, and solemnly announced, "I think I'll go home."

* * * * *

During this early period, Marlon's special interest was women. Frankly it was an all-consuming interest. To get him out of the bedroom into the light, I encouraged him to take up a sport. He was not interested in tennis, golf, etc. He refused to attend any spectator sports, like baseball or football. He said he'd be mobbed. Even when I told him Bob Dorff and I sat in front of Robert Taylor, who was a big MGM star at the time, at a football game one Sunday and no one paid any attention to him—football fans were more interested in the game—it didn't move him out of bed.

I tried to interest him in the horse races. I told him Florine and I had sat at a table next to Cary Grant, whom we both knew, and no one had bothered him. At these spectator sports, no one was especially interested in movie stars. He evidenced no interest. I couldn't talk him out of the bedroom.

That Marlon was a high school dropout bothered him. I urged him to read, even if it took him forever to finish a book. I urged him to take some courses at college, telling him I'd go with him. I mentioned that Jean Peters was attending college at UCLA. His answer to that was, "I'm not Jean Peters."

It wasn't until much later that we learned of dyslexia. Marlon was dyslexic. That explained his learning problems at the schools he attended and contributed to his behavioral problems causing him to be kicked out. And then he eventually dropped out.

Marlon had books that he brought from New York City, some which he had purchased in secondhand book stores. Some were old and well read. But I knew Marlon hadn't read some of them. He'd have two or three books besides his bed—poetry and Shakespeare—which he memorized.

The only suggestion he acted on was reading. He'd purchase a book and begin to read it. When it became too tedious, he would ask me to locate the author. He only read non-fiction, and subjects that appealed to him: solar energy, Indians, the environment, etc. Most books purchased were written by college professors. I'd run them down, tell them he had read their book, and how much he had enjoyed it. I'd arrange a time convenient to talk.

He memorized script pages rapidly, and so with books. He would take passages from the author's book and quote it. Naturally, the author would think that Marlon Brando had read his entire book and, along with a few pointed questions, Marlon had a two- or three-hour lecture on the subject of the book. Marlon had a tap on his phone in his bedroom and he would tape conversations. After he talked to the author, he would listen to the taped conversations or, if you will, lectures. Marlon was like a sponge; he'd absorb everything, then become an instant authority on the subject. And he didn't have to read the book. Through the years, he developed this into an art. Though a few times it backfired as he would expound on something with a person who was more knowledgeable about the subject in question and then leave him speechless. But then he'd go away, having picked that man's brain dry.

If you went into his room, there was usually one or two, sometimes three, books cracked open with observations written in the margins. Marlon did have a thirst for knowledge and I encouraged him, sometimes to my sorrow, because he would introduce a subject into a conversation I had absolutely no interest in pursuing, like five-ton trucks or saw mills. He could bore you to death if you'd let him. I'd escape by interrupting to go to the bathroom. I'd leave and never return. After several times using this excuse, he got wise and waited for the right moment to take his revenge.

I was in a meeting with him and a few gentlemen in the living room. After the meeting was underway and I knew Marlon didn't need me as he seemed comfortable and was in control, I stood and was easing out of the room. Marlon abruptly stopped what he was saying, and calling attention to me, he apologized for my departure. "You'll have to excuse Alice, she has a kidney problem and has to go pee." The dirty look I gave him didn't stop him from continuing to relate how many times a day I excused myself to "pee."

When Marlon was making a picture, in the morning when I brought him coffee, he'd ask me to read the scene to be filmed that day, then he would go over his lines orally three or four times while I read all other lines. By then he would have them all memorized. When he had to read a script, he would ask that all calls be held, lock himself in his room and ask not to be disturbed. Sometimes, it would take him days to finish reading a script.

He memorized poetry, Shakespeare's soliloquies, songs, famous sayings, and they'd trip off his tongue, yet he would ask me to read letters to him. After we discovered he had dyslexia, it became apparent why he always asked me to read all his legal papers, which he would toss aside and never look at. Through the years, his reading improved, but he still had secretaries reading correspondence, legal papers, to him. He used his bad and failing eyesight to hide behind.

Marlon constantly used the F-word and I remarked that I thought he had a very limited vocabulary. I didn't realize I had hit the nail on the head. I had noticed paperback books with the titles "Word Power," "Learning Made Easy," and other self-help paperbacks. But when I discovered Marlon couldn't spell, I became aware of the reason why there was not a file folder. Marlon replied to all correspondence I read to him by a telephone call. As he didn't accept any formal invitations, I would pick them out of the wastebasket and RSVP.

When I urged Marlon to read, I told him I always read with a dictionary by my side, a habit I had developed as a child when I was reading literature beyond my years. I put a magnifying glass, which I purchased for him, and a dictionary where he had access to it, but when he read, he still buzzed and asked me to look up words for him. Unlike me, I don't believe he ever made friends with a dictionary. There were times Marlon would read off words that he had written on his hand while talking to someone on the telephone and ask me to look them up for him.

He had a thirst for knowledge. He knew a little about everything—and could expound on any subject as if he were an expert, he was such a superb actor. Years later I was surprised to learn I wasn't the only one who had consciously helped Marlon with his vocabulary.

George Englund was a producer for Marlon's Pennebaker production company. When I started to work for Pennebaker, I took note that he and Marlon complemented each other. This observation was before I knew either, and it didn't change. If I had known George better, I wouldn't now have raised an eyebrow in surprise when I learned George had covertly been helping Marlon expand his vocabulary.

I wasn't acquainted with George until I started to work for Marlon's production company at Paramount. Though I did know of him in connection with The Circle Theatre. Jack Kelly, an actor whom I was dating, took me to a few plays at the theater, and introduced me to the actors, directors, etc. I also knew a writer named Englund, who was his stepfather. So, George was no stranger to me.

I didn't know how, when, or where Marlon and George met. I did note, however, they had a warm, easy way with each other, like people who had known each other for a long time. I was wrong on that account because their relationship then had been of short duration. Nevertheless, a closeness developed through the years, and though they wouldn't see or talk to each other for long spells, when they did get together, they had the sort of affable rapport that their conversation seemed to be a continuation of the last time they spoke.

Marlon was very wary of anyone who was better educated than he. I didn't know anything about George's education, but since his stepfather was Englund, the writer, he was exposed to "words." This exposure must have stuck because George had an enviable vocabulary. I don't know if George envied Marlon's acting ability, but Marlon certainly envied George his way with words.

Through the years, I always knew when Marlon had either spoken to George on the telephone, or when George and he had had a night out, or when George had come by the house. Marlon would have a list of words I looked up in my huge Webster for him. Then in the next few days, I'd hear the same words sprinkled here and there in Marlon's conversation. Of course, after his association with Pennebaker ended, George was unaware that every time they met through the years, he was still tutoring Marlon. I was benefiting, too, as I was adding to my vocabulary when I had to look up words for Marlon that was not in my lexicon.

I'm reminded at this moment that Marlon often invited George to lunch and would, as usual, forget to tell me until a few minutes before he arrived. I'd not only want to tear my hair out by the roots, but also Marlon's, for not letting me know so I could order something for lunch.

You'd have to know the household to understand my reaction. First, you have to realize that I didn't know how to cook. Blame my mother; though she was a vegetarian and a gourmet cook, she never allowed us near a stove. Oh, I could slap together a sandwich, open a can of soup, or cut up some lettuce and pour store bought dressing over it, put a steak on the broiler, but to this day I can't prepare a meal where everything gets done at the same time and where something isn't missing from the menu—like not putting the garlic bread in the oven, or putting it in the oven and only remembering it when everyone starts to yell, "Something's burning!"

Blanche was a housekeeper, not a cook. And she and I were in the same boat when it came to preparing a meal. If anyone wanted something to eat, it took the two of us to put that something together. Second, Marlon was almost always on a diet of sorts. Therefore, the food selection was limited. But, I always had canned tuna on the shelf, lettuce and tomatoes in the refrigerator, hard boiled eggs, and some sort of crackers. So when George came to lunch, I'd prepare tuna salad while Blanche rustled up something to drink.

Marlon didn't drink so there was never any wine or spirits in the house unless there was a party, a special luncheon, or houseguests were expected. I can't pretend to be a wine connoisseur or have a "nose," but I did have the good sense to keep in touch with Robert Balzer, who did, and he always came through when I needed him. Robert had sold Marlon his house. He wrote for wine magazines, so at my behest he recommended a wine shop in Beverly Hills where I made friends and they helped me with wine selections. I decided we ought to have one bottle of red and one bottle of white in the house for emergencies. So I had a bottle of Pouilly-Fuissé and Valpolicella on hand.

I have to confess here I can't remember in those many years ever serving George anything else but tuna salad when he came to the house for lunch. And only one time do I recall serving him wine. Marlon asked me to bring George a glass of wine with his lunch, and since I was serving fish, I thought I'd bring him the Pouilly-Fuissé. But someone had beaten me to it and there was only a bottle of red wine. So that's what I opened. When I had put down the tray, George picked up the wine, sipped, and turned to me, "This wine is good, what is it?" he said.

"Valpolicella," I replied and hightailed it out of the room before he looked and saw that I was serving the tuna salad.

I've often wondered, but never asked, if George realized that for twenty-five years he was only served tuna salad whenever he came to Brando's house for lunch. If he was aware, at least he was kind enough to refrain from saying, "Not tuna again!"

And, wasn't I lucky George liked tuna.

*****

Marlon almost always had rewritten some of his dialogue in his movies. When I asked him about it, he said, "Some lines read well, but do not speak well." Other times he altered scenes to cause conferences and delays if he didn't feel like acting that day or wanted to frustrate the director. Sometimes the changes were laughable—taking the story line into an altogether different direction. At times he would give a line a reading foreign to the characterization of the person he was playing, by that means frustrating the director, or throwing the actor playing with him. Then the director would be left with the task of attempting to guide him back into his character, thereby spending time talking him back to the intention of the written words.

When I was trying to encourage Marlon to read, to keep his mind off his women problems and financial problems, I also encouraged him to try his hand at writing, since he would spend so much time rewriting when he was filming. Also, I thought he had such a vivid imagination, maybe he could take an idea and run with it. He tried. But he found it difficult to stay on one subject. He branched off in a myriad directions.

He didn't do well with pen or pencil in hand. He found he did better with a tape recorder. So, he would get an idea and tape it during the night when he couldn't sleep, then he'd hire a secretary to transcribe, and between the two of us, we'd bridge and make sense out of his flights of fancy. The more he taped the less self-absorbed he became, though if you read his works, you can discover Brando in them. With the aid of assistants and secretaries who transcribed, researched, contributed, and edited his meandering thoughts, Marlon produced a few scripts in time—as well as several ideas or projects for Tetiaroa and Tahiti. For Marlon wanted his island to become self-sufficient and planned to make a documentary or promotional film about Tahiti and his atoll Tetiaroa to create more tourism.

After he met Anita Wylie who was Chinese and an aspiring actress, Marlon tried to find scripts which might have a role for her and asked me to do likewise. We were discussing it one day, and as happens with Marlon, you started talking about one subject and it was discarded for another.

So we progressed from work for Anita to Marlon making a film on his island Tetiaroa. We tossed around a few ideas, but nothing moved him. Then I suggested he do a remake of the Jose Ferrer and Rita Hayworth picture, *Miss Sadie Thompson*. I thought Marlon would be wonderful in the reverend role, if a strong director controlled him. I urged him to contact his agent and check it out. He seemed very interested in that idea for filming on Tetiaroa, then he switched completely and he was back again wanting to do something that had a Chinese role for Anita.

I suddenly recalled reading a very interesting account about pirates still operating in the China Seas. I told him about their exploits. Some were Chinese pirates. I tossed around a few story ideas, even a Chinese woman pirate operating in the China Seas, and Marlon took off with the idea. Somehow Marlon got the plunderers from the China Seas to his island in the South Pacific, hiding their loot on Tetiaroa. Since the idea now included Tetiaroa, it excited him. He could write a part for Anita and exploit his island at the same time. Although we had an afternoon of great fun tossing around story ideas for the South Seas, and I could visualize Anita as Dorothy Lamour under a tropic moon, Marlon could only see Anita as a swashbuckling pirate shouting orders to her crew of buccaneers. But, as everything pertaining to work was put on the back burner, so was the story about the high seas raiders.

Time would pass. Marlon revived my pirate idea. Marlon would kick the story around, taping his ideas, hiring a secretary, and having them transcribed. Then it would lose his interest, it couldn't compete with his libido. And it would be shelved only to be taken up again on a lonely, sleepless night, hiring another secretary, then dropping it for a romp with his latest. The pirates would be put into dry dock once more. But not long forgotten, for it would continue to be revived from time to time.

One day Anita's daughter, Patti, approached Marlon for a loan. Her husband was Donald Cammell, a screenwriter. Marlon talked over the loan and repayment with me. He was concerned that Anita would not like him making the loan and also that the loan could not be repaid. We decided that since Donald wasn't working, Marlon would hire Donald to work with him on the China Seas pirate story he had abandoned and had once again dusted off. Donald's salary would be applied to the repayment of the loan. And he could tell Anita Donald was working on the script without mentioning the loan. In discussing it, I said, "Since Donald is a screenwriter, he could put the material you have into script form."

"That's a good suggestion, I'll talk to him about it." Marlon responded.

In the meantime, he asked that I gather all the material on the South Seas story, as it was now called, that he could hand to Donald to read after he spoke to him. So the pirates were resuscitated. It was full steam ahead with enthusiasm after Donald had agreed to work with Marlon on the script. Since Marlon was still interested in filming on Tetiaroa to make brownie points with the Tahitian government by making a movie and promoting tourism, he had determined to incorporate Tetiaroa in the script. Therefore Marlon decided to send Donald and his wife, Patti, to Tetiaroa to absorb the flavor of the atoll Marlon wanted in the movie.

They all left for Tetiaroa mid-December of 1978. They worked on the script in the South Pacific through the middle of January. Thereafter, for the next few years, they worked off and on at Marlon's house as Marlon could not sustain interest in a project for any length of time. Also, he and Donald locked horns over the project a few times and it would grind to a halt. Marlon wouldn't speak to Donald for months. Just ask George Englund how many times he was in the same position. All the Tahiti-Tetiaroa projects he was involved in with Marlon that was constantly shelved and enthusiastically resurrected, but never came to fruition in 25 years—that must have been maddening to George. When I'd ask him about it, Marlon would reveal after a dropped Tetiaroa project, "George is mad at me." He and George, as well as others, had a "mad/glad" relationship.

Though Marlon and Donald had many heated arguments regarding compensation and how much Donald contributed to the story content during their collaboration, the story evolved from a script to a novel that was rejected when submitted to a publisher, to a script that again became a novel, *Fan-Tan*, published in 2005 after Marlon's death.

Fan-Tan had a strange and unique history. The story idea started with me in a brainstorming session with Marlon. Marlon ran with the idea and expanded it. Then it proceeded to stormy sessions between Marlon and Donald Cammell. Elizabeth Hush did research. And George Englund was back with Marlon looking for financing for the screenplay. Unsuccessfully. It languished. Finally Marlon's friend and assistant, Joan Petrone, had an input in his writings. After Marlon's death, I understand, another writer also had input in the published novel, which received devastatingly bad reviews after finally reaching publication.

When it started out as a script, I was to receive monetary compensation when the film was made for the pirate story idea that I suggested to Marlon. He planned to star in the film. Anita was to have a role. But like everything else this, too, was lost in the shuffle and I never received any compensation, for the film was never made.

*****

Marlon's controlled and uncontrolled anger, along with his professed craziness, his sex addiction, and his penchant for not making decisions and not taking responsibility were not the only things I had to contend with during this period in his life. When Marlon confided he was "crazy" and "a sex addict," he neglected to tell me about bulimia. I was not aware that when he was gorging himself with food, he was able to do so only because he would then go into the bathroom and disgorge it. I found out quite by accident during what could have been a very, very tragic accident.

In the early sixties Marlon employed a private investigator, James Briscoe. James taught him how to pick locks. With Marlon's agreement, I put locks on the cupboards and the refrigerator. But food was missing and we didn't know how he was doing it. Then, James, inadvertently, let the cat out of the bag by stating he had bought Marlon some lock picks. Although he had agreed to the locks, he had retaliated by picking them. I confronted him, then threw the locks away. He kept the picks.

It was at this time that Marlon went to a consulate party and met an exotic beauty from Lahore, Pakistan, who was a college student. She was the most intelligent and bookish girlfriend Marlon had during this period of his life. He became enamored and pursued her with great intensity. If she said she was at class, he'd drive to her apartment in Westwood to check. He'd wait until she arrived home to satisfy himself she wasn't lying to him and seeing someone else.

One afternoon Marlon did this and I received a desperate call from him. He asked me to come for him immediately at this girlfriend's apartment as he was ill and could not drive. I arrived and discovered Marlon bleeding profusely. "What happened?" went unanswered. He was pressing a bloody towel across his mouth and chin area. He guided me to the bathroom, which was blood splattered, and asked me to help him clean it. Bloody towels were on the floor. He tried to help, but I stopped him. And I did the best I could.

I looked at Marlon, he was pasty faced. I asked again, "What happened?" From his mumbled answer I gathered he had picked the lock and come in to wait and surprise her. He had then raided her refrigerator, gone to the bathroom, put his finger down his throat, and thrown up as he usually did. Except this time, he began hemorrhaging and he couldn't stop the bleeding.

By now, he was white and I didn't know, but assumed, he was still bleeding into the towel. Worried, I stopped cleaning up and said, "Let's leave." And I hastily ushered him out. I helped him to my car. He refused to get in the back seat; he wanted to sit up front with me. I drove away with Marlon sitting close, leaning on me muttering, "Take me home." Over his weak protestations, I drove to St. John's Hospital, ignoring his pleas to take him home.

I was convincing the desk that I'd be responsible for the bill and trying to answer their questions as I was desperately urging, "Please get him into emergency immediately." My arms were around Marlon, holding him up. He was almost passed out by this time. Someone finally took him from me, put him in a wheelchair, and pushed him away. I don't recall what name I gave other than my own.

En route to the hospital, Marlon had expressed his concern about the press. He didn't want the press to know about his condition and he had kept insisting, "Take me home." But he didn't have to worry. They didn't know who he was. For by the time I got him to emergency, his head was drooping to his chest and his face was immersed in the bloody towel.

A short time later, a doctor approached me. He asked about my relationship to Marlon. I told him. Then he calmly informed me Marlon was not expected to live because he had lost more than half his blood supply. I was shocked. His next words also chilled me as he asked me to notify his next of kin.

I phoned his father at the studio, gave him the news and asked him to call his sister, Jocelyn, as I did not have her telephone number with me, as well as Frannie, another sister in Chicago.

Marlon's father and Jocelyn arrived at the hospital separately and were allowed five minutes with Marlon. I was not allowed in to see him because I was not related. I stood vigil outside in the hall.

When Marlon's father came out of his room, I inquired if there was any change. He gravely replied, "No, they do not expect him to live." I asked his father if he could get permission from the doctor to allow me to see Marlon for a few minutes. He sought the doctor and informed me the doctor said, "Only five minutes." Then he departed.

Jocelyn came out into the hall. I entered Marlon's room. He was lying there. Not moving. I could hardly tell where the sheet that covered him ended and he began, he was so white. His eyes were closed and he was whispering. I stood where I was, not wanting to intrude, for I heard him petitioning God. Softly praying, pleading, "Help me, please God, help me." Then he sighed and was quiet. I silently walked to the bedside and gently took his hand in mine. He opened his eyes, saw me, tried to smile, and weakly said, "This is it, babe." I shook my head from side to side and quietly confessed I had heard his prayer and if I did, so did God. His eyes closed. We held hands. His hand in mine was limp. No further words were spoken.

Too soon, a nurse entered and asked me to leave. He opened his eyes and addressed the nurse, "Let her stay." He didn't want me to leave, but I knew he was very ill and she was only carrying out orders. I assured Marlon I wasn't leaving. I'd be outside his door in the hall and I'd see him later. Not knowing if I'd ever see him alive again, I caressed his hand, left the room, and continued my vigil.

Marlon survived. And he was forever grateful to me for not listening to him and taking him to the hospital instead of home, as he had insisted. And I forever reminded him that I knew he believed in the Almighty whenever I heard him telling someone he didn't believe in God.

Marlon was diagnosed as having Mallory-Weiss Syndrome. This, I understood, is a ring where your esophagus ends and your stomach begins. He had ruptured this ring while he was heaving, discharging the contents of his stomach.

After this, Marlon again vowed he would take care of me for the rest of my life. That I was to consider what was his was mine. And I was to ask him for anything I wanted or needed. This incident alone cemented our relationship.

I never took advantage of this generous offer. I was a very independent woman and I didn't want to be "kept" by Marlon. Besides, the thought of "payment" for, as he said, "saving my life," was repugnant to me. I just did what any friend, or human being, would do.

But Marlon never forgot it.

Another time I rushed Marlon to the hospital when he was hemorrhaging. Someone had told Marlon that eating lemons and Greek feta cheese would enable him to lose weight rapidly. So Marlon ate nothing but the juice of lemons and Feta cheese for days. Needless to say, it took its toll. He developed bleeding ulcers and ended up in the hospital. Again, petitioning God as I entered and stood by his bedside. When he opened his eyes and saw me, he said, "I hope he heard me."

For someone who didn't believe in Him, Marlon certainly made God work overtime, answering his prayers.

Marlon hadn't learned his lesson in regard to eating and purging. The next time the bleeding was caused by a laceration of the esophagus. Again, Alice to the rescue. This time it was one o'clock in the morning. I couldn't handle this alone. I needed help. I phoned Anita Wylie, who lived nearby. She drove us to UCLA Medical Center. The nearest hospital.

Again, Marlon was extremely grateful that I had rushed him to the hospital and taken care of him.

I attempted to keep Marlon on a sensible eating regimen. But when he woke up late afternoon, it was difficult as he then ate at night when I wasn't there. And he would go on a binge with girlfriends who were always admonished, "Don't tell Alice." Of course, I teased him I was only trying to keep him alive because, after all, I wanted to work for a big movie star. But, did he ever listen to me when it came to food? No.

One night Anita Wylie phoned me at home. She revealed Marlon called her at four the previous morning, told her he was starving, and asked her to pick him up and take him to the Pacific Dining Car in downtown Los Angeles. She did. Then she related what he ate. He had ordered a steak, eggs and hash browns breakfast, which came with toast. While they were waiting for it, he had cornflakes and milk and a stack of pancakes. I didn't ask her if he had gone to the bathroom between orders. By the amount of food, I knew Marlon was up to his old tricks.

Another habit Marlon couldn't control was his love of ice cream. He'd buy a cone of ice cream and eat it while they were scooping a quart carton which, he would inform them, was for the children. Then he'd leave, sit in the car with a spoon he had brought from home and eat it. If he forgot the spoon, he would go to Phillip Rhodes's house, which was nearby, and eat it there. And I was wondering why he wasn't losing weight on the diet I had him on.

After I moved my office to Newport Beach and wasn't there to remind him of his eating transgressions, he, sad to see, ballooned. He would phone and tell me about his dieting and how much he had lost. I was always encouraging, but it was painful to see him. He had been fighting obesity all his life. Now he had given up. I was no longer there to prop him up. And those around him didn't have our history. No one challenged him. Marlon had a cutting edge to his voice that intimidated secretaries and the women around him—they wanted to please him. No doubt thinking the way to a man's heart was through his stomach.

No one had the courage to do what I did during the filming of *One-Eyed Jacks*. I had a sign made and put it on the set where everyone, including Marlon, could see it: DON'T FEED THE DIRECTOR.

*****

There were other occasions I rushed Marlon to the emergency room. Several times when he had chest pains during the night and thought he was having a heart attack, I drove him to St. John's Hospital, then took him home and got him through the night.

One night Phillip and Marie Rhodes were at the house and he thought he was having a heart attack. We rushed him to the emergency room. But, like all other times, this, too, was an anxiety attack.

I knew that every time Marlon heard that someone he knew, or didn't know, had died of a heart attack, I'd be rushing Marlon to the emergency room with "pains in my chest." And he'd be diagnosed as having a stress attack. There was a period we became well-known at St. John's emergency ward after midnight.

I didn't call the paramedics when Marlon was ill or having imagined "heart attacks" because he'd beg me not to, and I didn't want to add to his stress. My taking him to the hospital gave him a sense of security. He was known to have said, "I trust Alice with my life." Also, he didn't want anyone in the movie industry to know because if he was diagnosed as having heart problems, he felt there would be insurance issues. He was convinced the paramedics would notify the press.

Marlon and I were in Tahiti before Marlon was to start *Bedtime Story*. He and Tarita had an agreement that when he was in Tahiti, she would not have her current live-in boyfriend on the premises. Marlon did not want to be confronted with a boyfriend when he visited his child, Tehotu. On this particular occasion, Marlon heard she was not keeping to their agreement. Evidently it bothered him, but he did nothing about it until the night before we were to depart for the States.

After dinner at which we had wine, Marlon drove off to say goodbye to some friends while I finished our packing. I was in bed when I heard Marlon's car roaring up the driveway. Instead of going to his fare, he came into the house, banged on my door calling me. I went into the living room. The first thing I noticed was he had been doing more than just saying goodbye. He was intoxicated.

Marlon had been told that Tarita's boyfriend was at the house with her and he had not yet left Tahiti. He urged me to get dressed and accompany him to catch her. I, of course, refused. He wanted a witness. I still refused, and in the condition he was in, couldn't talk him out of leaving. He ran out, jumped into the car, and sped down the driveway. I could hear his car in the stillness of the night as he roared along the highway. There was no way I could warn Tarita he was on the way as she had no telephone. I went back to bed.

About ten minutes later, I heard a car coming up the driveway. It didn't sound like Marlon's, so I hopped out of bed and went to the open doorway of the house to see who it was. A big Tahitian man was approaching. He asked if I was Alice. When I said, "Yes," he explained that Marlon had had an accident, was injured, and was calling for me.

He drove me about a half mile away, and in the gutter on the left side of the road, Marlon's car was totaled. Marlon was slumped nearby on the ground. A few Tahitians were standing near. He was bloodied from head to bare feet. I asked the man to get a doctor. Marlon was hissing, "No! No!" I asked Marlon if he felt he had back injuries. Neck injuries? He only pleaded to, "Take me home."

I asked the man who fetched me if he would take us back to the house. There was someone with a lantern and in the dim light, I couldn't see how seriously Marlon was injured. But by the look of him and the car, he was. Nevertheless, before I had him moved, I checked as best I could to be certain he didn't have neck or back injuries. I concluded he had rib injuries because of the evidence of pain in his chest as I was probing him. Besides, I saw the steering wheel had been broken. There were no seat belts in the car, so Marlon had been thrown through the windshield, which was completely shattered. His face was a bloody mess. His four upper front teeth were missing. His lips and face were already swollen. I could see that his knee was bleeding profusely through his torn blood-and-dirt-splattered white trousers.

With the help of a man and a young boy, I had Marlon moved to the house. I couldn't stop the bleeding, there were too many lacerations, and I didn't know if there was glass in the cuts on his face. He had a huge bloody gash that crossed his knee. I assumed Marlon had fractured ribs. He was in terrible pain, evidenced by every breath he took. It was after midnight. I had to get a doctor. I asked the kind man who helped me if he knew a doctor. He did, but said he'd be asleep. I convinced him to go fetch him. In the meantime, I boiled some water and gathered clean towels because Marlon needed to be cleaned of the dirt and blood, so the doctor could assess his injuries.

While we were waiting for the doctor, Marlon bid me to ask the doctor not to tell anyone he was injured because he didn't want the studio to know, since he was due to start working in a few weeks.

When the doctor arrived, he wanted Marlon moved to the hospital in town, but Marlon refused, insisting I was capable enough to care for him. He dressed Marlon's wounded leg. He couldn't know without x-rays if Marlon's ribs were only bruised or fractured. He thought Marlon had a concussion. Marlon's four missing front teeth were caps I didn't know he had.

I walked the doctor to his car and passed on Marlon's message. The doctor gave me instructions for the care of Marlon. He had given Marlon antibiotics and pain pills and assured me Marlon should be all right till morning. The doctor said he'd be by in the morning to check Marlon and to re-examine his face cuts for glass shards, which concerned me.

Because Marlon was due to report to the studio for wardrobe fittings, I cabled Jay Kanter that we had missed the plane. I hid Marlon for two weeks, taking care of all his needs. The doctor stopped by daily. Marlon's most serious injury was the large gash across his knee and rib injuries, which plagued him with each breath.

I found a dentist, gave him my name and, when able, I brought Marlon in for temporary caps. He recognized Marlon, but he didn't mention the accident. Since I prevailed upon the doctor to say Marlon had a fever, and since he had no serious injuries from the accident, we didn't worry about the dentist.

While I had been keeping Marlon comfortable with all his cuts and bruises, and playing nurse, I also had the rental car picked up and arranged payment for damages. Then there was the family and the man who had helped Marlon at the time of the accident and had come for me, to whom I needed to express appreciation with a monetary gift.

We were surprised so few people knew of Marlon's injuries, as it was very difficult to keep anything secret in Tahiti. Marlon didn't want anyone in the States to know about the accident and injuries. I told no one and neither did he. That statement's only half true.

Through the years, I can't tell you the many versions I heard of how Marlon received the big scar across his knee in the Vietnam War. The last person to commiserate with him about his war experiences and injuries was JoAn Corrales. I had warned her to beware of what Marlon told her as he preferred a lie rather than the truth. But she didn't yet know him well, disregarded or forgot my warning and fell for his tale. I had a big laugh when she told me she didn't know Marlon was wounded in the Vietnam War. And I had a bigger laugh when I thought that 30 years later, he would still be lying about how he had received his injury to gain sympathy and compassion from his listeners. For the record, Marlon was never in the Vietnam War.

And he never played professional football either, which was the other version he related. One day he began to give me the football story. That's how I discovered it. He didn't even have the grace to be embarrassed when I told him that Marlon Brando, Farm Boy, may have received it playing football, but Marlon Brando, Movie Star, received it while speeding intoxicated one midnight in Tahiti and ran off the road into a deep ditch.

The one time I didn't rush Marlon to the hospital was when he received a nasty forehead wound administered by a lady friend. She had heaved a heavy glass ashtray at him during a violent argument, which had nailed him in the forehead.

I had driven up from Newport Beach on a Sunday afternoon because I was going to a barbecue that evening and we met as I was turning into his driveway and he was driving out. Marlon shouted, "Follow me!" I could see blood running down the side of his face, dripping onto his white shirt.

I followed him, not to the emergency room, but down a dirt road off Mulholland Drive near his house. He leaped out of his car and came to mine. He related what happened while we both tried to stem the flow of blood. I was putting pressure on it, but was having no success. He refused to go to a hospital because they would want to know how he received the gash. For once, he couldn't think of a lie to explain it. When we saw the lady involved drive by on Mulholland Drive in her Rolls Royce, we drove back to the house and I dressed the wound there.

He hadn't exaggerated about his room being thrashed during the melee. I had to take care of that, too. He wouldn't tell me what caused the argument. But she did. My response: She hadn't hit him hard enough.

He carried the scar on his forehead for the rest of his life as a memory.

I received a call from Los Angeles Airport personnel in the middle of the night to pick up Marlon, who was arriving from Tahiti drunk or drugged. I don't know why, but I took a pillow and blanket from my bed, tossed them into the back seat of my car, and drove to the airport to pick him up. I had requested that the airport personnel keep him on the plane until all passengers had disembarked, then put him in a wheelchair and bring him to the curb where I would be waiting in a tan Cadillac Seville.

He looked sick when I greeted him and, while helping him into the back seat of the car, I discovered he was sweaty and burning with fever. He only had on a Tahitian shirt and he started to shiver. As I wrapped the blanket around him, he thanked me for coming for him and asked to be taken home.

I had no intention of driving him home. I took off like Mario Andretti down the freeway to St. John's Hospital. Marlon sat behind me leaning on the seat and hung on to my long hair, telling me how much I meant to him. At St. John's, it was discovered he had picked up a tropical bug and had a raging fever. He was not drunk, nor was he drugged. But when asked by a nurse if he had taken anything for his condition, he said no, but had taken a Valium. He was hospitalized this time.

There was another emergency call from Tahiti. Only Marlon called. He asked me to pick him up at the airport as he was very ill. This time I called his doctor who was on staff and drove him, while he was calling on God to help him, directly to St. John's Hospital, where he was diagnosed with a urinary infection and prostate problems.

Then, in London while in the midst of filming *A Countess from Hong Kong,* Marlon had a bellyache in the middle of the night. He crawled from his bedroom at the rear of the house we were leasing to my bedroom in the front. I'm a light sleeper. I heard something, but dismissed it as being in a strange house and I wasn't yet accustomed to the night noises. I dozed, then heard a faint voice calling my name. Marlon was on the floor alongside my bed. He had crawled from his bedroom to mine. He couldn't rise, he was in agony. He was a dead weight; I couldn't lift him.

I quickly dressed after I phoned Phillip and Marie, who rushed over. Then called a taxi, and somehow we were able to get him to the University College Hospital, where the doctors couldn't diagnose the problem. They wanted to do an exploratory. We all discussed it. We weren't qualified to make a decision. I knew Dr. Kositchek, an internist. I called him, filled him in with the little I knew, and prevailed upon him to take the polar flight from Los Angeles to London to see Marlon.

I don't know the details of how it was arranged between the doctors and hospital, but they allowed Dr. Kositchek to examine Marlon. He diagnosed a twisted bowel. Sometimes a bowel will unwind, therefore it was decided not to operate for 24 hours. I stayed at the hospital all night with Marlon, as did Phillip and Marie. Fortunately for Marlon, his bowel unwound without surgery.

Dr. Kositchek was not Marlon's doctor at this time. Marlon was mad at him, but I didn't care. I made the decision to call him. He stayed for a week with us at the house while Marlon was hospitalized.

It was his wedding anniversary and he wanted to buy a gift for his wife. He'd like to buy her new dinnerware. I took him to Harrods, and if you've never been there, believe me, it's the wrong place to take a man to buy dishes. They have hundreds of patterns. He had to see them all. We were there for hours; I was cross-eyed when we left.

When Marlon was released from the hospital, Dr. Kositchek returned to his practice in Beverly Hills. And though Marlon was grateful to him for coming to London, he remained mad at him.

And when I returned from London, there was a call from Dr. Kositchek telling me how delighted his wife was with the dinnerware we had chosen.

I received another call. It was from Marlon's business manager. He was inquiring about a statement received from Dr. Kositchek for 10,000 dollars. I was glad Marlon didn't know how to read a financial statement and didn't tell him about this "little item" at the time, since he was still mad at the good doctor.

Years later, Marlon was relating the incident in a conversation and mentioned Dr. Kositchek as saving him from an exploratory by diagnosing a twisted bowel and waiting 24 hours. I took this opportunity to mention the money for the polar flight and week's stay till he was out of danger. And also told him how I spent my nights while he was in the hospital—entertaining Dr. Kositchek at Annabelle's, also with his money.

*****

Marlon didn't work until he was broke and/or needed money. He made a picture with Anna Magnani and Joanne Woodward, *The Fugitive Kind,* to pay for his divorce settlement with Anna Kashfi. He made *Sayonara* to jump start his movie production company, Pennebaker, which was broke. He made a movie to enable him to buy his house from Robert Baltzer. He made another movie to purchase the Tetiaroa Atoll. He made *Mutiny on the Bounty* when he was again flat broke. He made *Désirée* for 20th Century Fox to settle a lawsuit with that company. He made *The Godfather* to get him out of the hole after not working before and after his annulment (divorce) from Movita Castenada. He made *Last Tango in Paris* because he had no cash after enormous lawyer bills, investigators, security guards, gaining custody of his son Christian. He made *The Night of the Following Day* because he was broke and also wanted to help Rita Moreno while helping himself. He made *The Missouri Breaks* because he was again broke. He made *Bedtime Story* to fulfill a Pennebaker commitment with Universal when he needed funds. He made *Superman* because of debts, and once again there was no cash flow. He made *Reflections in a Golden Eye* with Elizabeth Taylor in Rome because Montgomery Cliff was ill and opted out—and Marlon needed money.

There were constant money problems, and I could always count on Jay Kanter and Elliott Kastner, friends and producers, to come to the rescue. They never failed me or Marlon.

And, of course, Marlon always asked for an advance when he signed to do a movie. Usually, it was a million dollars. This would pay his current debts and keep him afloat until filming started and he would receive additional funds.

Where was the money going? Marlon certainly wasn't living in grand style. The figures were all there before him, but he put blinders on and refused to look, and ear plugs so he couldn't hear.

Marlon not only had his household, but also three families to support. Seldom a week went by without demands from one or another of the families—angry messages for Marlon concerning problems requiring immediate funds, and always requests for additional money for the children.

But this wasn't all; there were friends in need as well—rents to be paid, cars in need of tires or repair, medical needs, psychiatrists. And his latest causes and pet projects, and petitions to fund projects. And always lawyers.

His response to everything was not to get involved emotionally, but to throw money at requests or problems, forget it, and go on his merry way, never looking back. It was the swinging sixties and he was too engrossed in living a self-indulgent, free-wheeling life.

Shortly before he died, Marlon phoned and said Anita Wylie had asked him for repayment of 25,000 dollars she had loaned him. He didn't remember any loan, any 25,000 dollars or repayment. He wanted my recall.

Marlon, as usual, didn't have any cash flow and he was aching to develop his atoll Tetiaroa in the South Pacific. He had hired an architect and environmentalist, Bernard Judge, who was in Tahiti working on the project. In 1972, Marlon was being besieged by Bernard for funds—primarily to build an airstrip. Marlon didn't want to work, he wanted to go to Tahiti, get the project off the ground and build that airstrip. Consequently, he borrowed money from Anita.

When Anita arrived at the house with the cash and gave it to Marlon, he wanted her to have a receipt for the funds. She refused a receipt from him as she didn't want her family to know she was loaning him money. Marlon asked me if I would sign for the money. I signed a note as having received 25,000 dollars from Anita, which I gave to her. I didn't have anything in writing from Marlon stating the funds were for him and that he would repay the loan. Such was our trust in each other.

This will give you some indication of my involvement with Marlon's financial entanglements. Marlon gave me his power of attorney when he and I went to the Banque de Indochine in Tahiti to deposit the funds from Anita. Marlon died without repaying the 25,000-dollar loan from Anita Wylie, as was his intention. Anita can't get the money from his estate because the receipt is signed by me.

In 1978, before *The Formula,* Marlon was again in such dire straits that when his friend, Wally Cox, who evidently was in the same predicament, approached Marlon for a 3,000-dollar loan, he didn't have the money to give him. Marlon asked me if I'd loan Wally the 3,000 dollars, promising he'd give me the money if Wally was unable to repay the loan. I wrote a check to Wally, and Marlon didn't have to worry because Wally repaid me in due course.

I always pulled Marlon through any cash flow problems through the years, except for the one time Marlon came through on his own, which sounded wonderful, but which turned out to be a disaster for me.

After Marlon's children reached an age when they could have visitations at his home, Blanche, the housekeeper, requested a raise as she had more work with the visitations of the children. I knew Marlon was again in a cash flow crisis, but I discussed it with him. He understood the situation and called his business manager to determine if raises for both of us could be managed under the circumstances.

A few days after I had talked to him, he summoned us to his room. He couldn't give us a raise, but he and his business manager had worked something out that should please us. He continued that in lieu of raises, he would set up a Profit Sharing Plan for us. A percentage of each picture he made would be put in the plan. The plan would also include a pension for him. We agreed to the plan. At the time it sounded wonderful to us and we received no raise. We gave up wages in return for future benefits. I was aware that, at one time, there was 1.7 million dollars in the Profit Sharing Plan. What happened to the money? I received no monies from the plan after Marlon's demise.

I wonder about this, for ever since my house in Newport Beach was sold at the urging of others to help him financially again, he continued to bring up the fact that he "owed me a great deal of money."

*****

Although Marlon neglected to tell me about bulimia, he did tell me he was taking amphetamines to control his appetite, and also other prescription drugs. I don't know how much these drugs contributed to his erratic mood swings. I didn't think they caused his angry outbursts, but I could be wrong because I know next to nothing about these drugs or their effects. I was aware that Miltown was a tranquilizer, and he was never without it. I had only seen him take an amphetamine once. I didn't order Marlon's drugs, he did. I only knew because Schwab's Drugstore delivered to the house at least once a week. Marlon would alert me about a delivery arriving from Schwab's.

One afternoon upon awakening, Marlon buzzed and asked me to bring him a cup of coffee. When I brought it to him, he asked me to stay. This usually indicated that Marlon wanted to talk to me about his previous evening, or he had something on his mind, wanted to run it by me and get my opinion. Was I in for a surprise.

Marlon was reclining on his king-sized bed as usual and after a few minutes of small talk, he soberly remarked he needed a very big, big favor, and he'd owe me BIG.

He was so solemn, I was afraid to inquire what this entailed. I feared the worst, but nevertheless asked what the big, big favor was I could do for him. He hemmed and hawed, then he asked me to go to our doctor, Dr. Kositchek, and tell him my boyfriend was having a problem with impotence. I burst out laughing.

"Dr. Kositchek," I laughed, "would know who I was talking about, call him yourself." He couldn't do it.

"Okay, I'll do it, but you'll owe me BIG time." He prevailed because I really felt sorry for him—a "sex addict" with an impotence problem.

Of course Dr. Kositchek knew who I was talking about. Thereafter, whenever I went to see him, he would inquire, "How's your boyfriend?" Never Marlon. He informed me all the drugs Marlon was taking, and the marijuana Marlon was smoking with his girlfriends, were most likely the causes of his impotence. But he'd have to see him.

I returned with this information. When I passed it on, Marlon let me know in quite colorful language what he thought of Dr. Kositchek and his diagnosis.

After the harangue about Dr. Kositchek had run its course, Marlon centered on me. He thought I would be shocked to hear he was impotent and was surprised that I took it so lightly, was amused, and laughed. He was the one who went into shock, for I told him I was aware he was impotent and how I knew. A few weeks prior to his confession I attended a Sunday night party. Cheryl was a friend of mine, as was her husband, Jimmy, who had been in "show business." His friends were "show people," and after attending several of their parties, I became acquainted with a number of them. Some were comics, like Joey Ross, Jackie Gayle, Lenny Bruce.

I also met Lenny Bruce's mother, Sally Marr, at their parties. She taught the strippers appearing at The Pink Pussycat on Santa Monica Boulevard in Hollywood their routines. She invariably entered the apartment with bumps and grinds and livened up a party with a bawdy story or two. Mostly Hollywood gossip. On this occasion, you guessed it, Marlon Brando was the subject. As the story unfolded, I learned that Marlon had been at The Pink Pussycat on Saturday night. After the show, he invited two of the strippers, envied by the other girls, home with him. As the girls reported to Sally and the others, "Marlon Brando, reputed to be the sexiest guy in Hollywood, couldn't get it up!" Fortunately, Sally had other gossip, and I took that occasion to quietly slip out. But Jimmy never let me forget it.

I knew Marlon went to Largo on occasion, but that was the first time I knew he frequented The Pink Pussycat. I was surprised I hadn't seen him there as when the girls were trying out a new routine, Sally would ask us to drop in and critique it. Comedian Jackie Gayle did the same when he was trying out new material. And on a Saturday night out on the town we all usually stopped by for the last show. But, I never saw Marlon there.

Marlon and I didn't discuss impotence again. I don't know how Marlon dealt with it. I know he didn't stop taking drugs as Schwab's was still delivering on Fridays.

There were several drug related emergencies at his house. None related to Marlon.

Christian Marquand, a French actor friend, was married to Pierre Aumont's daughter, who, I was informed, was a heroin addict. She overdosed at the house one night while they were house guests. Marlon was away at the time. When Marlon heard about it, they were asked to leave. She died shortly afterward in Paris from an alleged drug overdose.

A few years later, an artist friend of Christian's, who had accompanied him from France to arrange a show in Beverly Hills, was a guest at the house. Again, Marlon was away at the time. He phoned that he was coming home in a few days and asked me to clear the house of guests, as he wanted to be alone. The night before Christian and the artist were to depart, they had a large farewell party. I decided not to attend. Next day I was told there had been drugs at the party. And I was also informed that the artist had walked through one of the large plate-glass windows in the living room. He was taken to the emergency room and hospitalized. After his release, he was in no condition to travel to France. He returned to the house. I moved the bed out of the guestroom and rented a hospital bed. He had cuts from head to toe. And like Kaufman's *The Man Who Came to Dinner,* he stayed on and on. I provided nursing care for a month until he was well enough to return to Paris. Marlon arrived home to a house full of people, as the patient and Christian had many visitors.

Shortly after he and Christian returned to France, we received word he was suing Marlon for the injuries he had sustained while a guest in his home. I turned everything over to Marlon's lawyer for resolution. Marlon was incensed at the news. If anyone had been near him at the time I revealed there was a lawsuit, they would have been thrown out the window.

Marlon had a few girlfriends who would bring marijuana when they visited in the evening. But not when the children were very young and stayed over.

When I first began to work daily for Marlon at his house, he had a "ready to take on the world" attitude. He whistled around the house, he sang, he played the bongos. We had funny, sometimes ridiculous, conversations. He was very affable, charming, outgoing. The amphetamines and uppers and downers he told me he was taking to keep his weight in check did not seem to put him to bed in a stupor for a week at a time. The time he spent in bed was with women.

Lack of money during this period flipped him out, and anger and demons would take possession of him.

When drugs became prevalent in our society and the sexual revolution exploded, with the burning of bras, the wife swapping, anything goes, that's when there was a dramatic change in Marlon. Whereas formerly he was the galloping stud, now he was a dour, black moods Brando. There were days when he was light and cheery, but as time went on, there were more dark days.

Did the variety of drugs involved cause these personality changes?

I didn't know he was "doing drugs" at the parties he was attending until he talked me into going to a party in Malibu with him one night. When we arrived and entered the house, I thought the people who lived there hadn't been able to pay their electric bill. There were flickering candles all over the place. Whatever electric lights that were on must have been on dimmers, or had low-wattage bulbs.

It was one of those parties attended by several Academy Award-winning Best Actor and Best Actress stars—it was star studded. Even though I personally knew about seven or eight stars, I recognized all. That is, all I could see in the dim room.

We were late in arriving, the party was in full swing. The air was redolent with the odor of marijuana, there were bodies sprawled out on the floor. No one had a glass in their hand, so I knew this wasn't a cocktail party, but "cigarettes" were being shared, passed from mouth to mouth. I don't know what else was being shared. It wasn't too long before Brando left my side and was lost in the crowd.

If a bomb had been dropped in Malibu that evening, the Hollywood motion picture industry would have been mortally wounded. So would the record business, as there were familiar faces in the music world lost in space.

Marlon drove to the party. I drove home.

I did not attend all the gatherings Marlon had, or parties, which were few. I'd laughingly tell him I had enough of him during the day, I had my own life to live. And I'd leave. If it was a large party and he was unattached, or had no special girlfriend, he'd ask me to be the hostess. But I was required to hostess all business-related cocktail and dinner parties at home and on location.

At one gathering, Carlo Fiore, a long-time friend, smoked marijuana in one of the guest bathrooms. Marlon exploded and ordered him to leave, yelling he did not want drugs or drug users in his house. That was the end of their friendship. Friends said Marlon made quite a scene as only he could.

This was another performance by Marlon—he was smoking marijuana in the house. Of course, the house was his and he could do whatever he wanted in it. It seemed extreme to me, ending the friendship. And I thought at the time that he created the scene in front of everyone to bolster his denial if word leaked about his excessive use of drugs and his dependency.

Or, could he excuse himself, but not tolerate anyone else?

Maybe it was like cigarettes. Marlon put a ban on cigarette smoking in the house, and then on the premises. He instructed me to have a NO SMOKING sign made. He even went so far as to lecture everyone he saw smoking about the health hazards and paid his friends and strangers 1,000 dollars if they stopped smoking for one month.

But Marlon was smoking. I never bought him cigarettes. He would go to the "Open 24 hours" market in the valley downhill on Coldwater Canyon and Ventura Boulevard at three or four in the morning and purchase them, along with a lemon meringue pie and ice cream. He didn't smoke in the house; he would smoke on the patio outside his bathroom. Of course, he excused this as part of his diet.

He never could discover how I knew he was smoking. He knew I didn't go through his private drawer, where he felt safe stashing the cigarettes, but never guessed I smelled smoke on his clothes—or his hair, if he hugged me in passing.

After I began to work for Marlon, he listed the drugs he was taking the day I saw him toss an amphetamine into his mouth. What other drugs he took I had no way of knowing. Who could anticipate what now would be dropped in my lap?

Late in the day, Dr. Kositchek, whose office was in Beverly Hills, phoned and asked me to come to his office at my convenience. He wished to speak to me. I was curious about the nature of his call and said I'd be right down. He instructed me not to enter through the reception; a nurse would admit me through his private entrance. I told Marlon I was leaving for a while.

Upon arrival, the nurse ushered me into his office and said the doctor would be in shortly. He was with a patient. A very serious Dr. Kositchek entered and apologized for the summons to his office. Then he continued. He had to refuse Marlon any more prescriptions for drugs as he, Kositchek, would get into trouble. He was not prepared to give up his practice for Marlon. He asked me to tell Marlon he was a "drug addict". This was the last thing I expected to hear. I sat there in stunned silence at the announcement. Then I expressed my disbelief. He proceeded to convince me. He impressed upon me not to take this lightly. Marlon had a very serious problem and needed help. He had other patients to attend to, and apologizing to me again, he left, as did I.

I didn't know how I could tell Marlon. Highly troubled, I returned to Marlon's house.

I had never known or heard of anyone being a drug addict from taking prescription drugs. I always thought addicts were hooked on street drugs. After my conversation with Dr. Kositchek, I became aware of how little I knew about drug addicts, drugs, or drug abuse. Or, importantly, Marlon's drug history, as his "faked ailments" usually required pain killers. I also was alerted by the doctor to some of the ploys addicts use to obtain drugs.

In a few minutes, my life and relationship to Marlon had changed drastically. I had to look at him with different eyes. I no sooner entered the house when Marlon buzzed and asked where I'd been. I had not told him before I left. I said, "I'll be right in."

Dumb me, still brain numb, I blurted out what Dr. Kositchek had wanted. He shot up off the bed, where he had been reclining, like a rocket. Marlon went ballistic. He stormed, calling Dr. Kositchek everything but a human being. He turned on me, accusing me of "being in cahoots" with Dr. Kositchek. I tried calming him, repeated I was only the messenger. I didn't know what was being delivered by Schwab's Drugstore. My soothing voice finally penetrated. He flopped on his bed. Stared at the ceiling. I realized he was as shocked as I had been upon hearing he was a drug addict. Likely more so.

After the outburst, Marlon and I stayed immobile, enveloped by the silence that descended on the room, only broken by nature's occasional night sounds or a car speeding along Mulholland Drive. We were both out of words. I broke the silence by softly inquiring if he wanted me to stay the night. He assured me he'd be all right. He needed to be alone. We said "Good night," and, troubled, I left him alone with his thoughts.

Marlon didn't talk to, or see, anyone except me for a few days. And he was not very happy with me. He was being forced to make a decision. I wasn't helping him by agreeing with the doctor that he needed help. He was in constant denial. He reasoned that since he was taking prescription drugs, and not street drugs, he was not a "drug addict."

He wanted me to tell him he wasn't a "drug addict," but, bad as I felt and sympathized with him, I couldn't. Dr. Kositchek had been quite concerned and convinced me Marlon had a very serious problem. Not to take it lightly.

Finally, Marlon capitulated, he would stop taking all the prescription drugs and pills he obtained from others, but, he told me, he would not stop taking Miltown. He said he couldn't face his problems without it. And he warned me I wouldn't be able to be around him.

Without letting Marlon know, I returned to Dr. Kositchek and asked for his advice. I had no one else to confide in. I didn't know how to handle this situation because Marlon was almost out of Miltown. Kositchek changed the Miltown to a new tranquilizer, Valium, 10 milligrams. This change forced me to tell Marlon I had consulted Dr. Kositchek. It didn't sit too well until I convinced him I needed to obtain enough pills to wean him off the drugs. And, of course, I also had to convince him Valium was better for him than Miltown to reduce anxiety.

It took considerable time to wean Marlon off the drugs, but I hung in there, and difficult as it was, so did he. Marlon, much to my surprise, was very co-operative. He was extremely frightened at the thought of being a drug addict. I was the monitor of the drugs, so he couldn't cheat. We had an agreement that he wouldn't see any girls who would share their pain-prescribed drugs.

I weaned him off everything but Valium, which he refused to give up. He really needed it. I tried to convince him it was a crutch and he could face the world without it, but after test days, I realized his brain would not accept that premise. So Valium was the one drug, from this period on, he continued to take for the rest of his life.

Neither Marlon nor I ever revealed why he was incommunicado, even though everyone blamed me for not getting Marlon to the phone, or having him return their calls. It was a trying time for me, keeping him occupied so he wouldn't think of drugs, and keeping everyone at bay.

He couldn't thank me enough. I was exhausted and couldn't take any time off because he had become more emotionally attached to me, calling at all hours when I wasn't there. Even accusing me of lying to him, saying I was meeting someone for lunch if I told him I was leaving the house at noon to run errands. He was afraid I'd abandon him, as he felt others had, even after I solemnly promised him I wouldn't.

My life was not my own.

I was the only one he depended upon at this time. I promised him I'd be there for him. But his deep-seated sense of abandonment from his youth was always there. I assured him that when I was leaving the house I would return and always told him where I was going, so he could reach me. I gave up a great deal of my privacy and personal life, so Marlon would feel secure and not revert to drugs. I knew he would call whenever I was away at this time, checking to find out if I was really where I said I was going, but I didn't mind as I committed myself to help him through what was a very difficult period for him. And me.

I had been troubled about Marlon's possessiveness and attachment to me since his near-death experience. I called Jocelyn and asked her if I could talk to her about her brother. I confessed I was having a problem with his obsession with me. I related what he was doing: stalking me, following me home, calling at all hours of the night, wanting to know where I was at all times, wanting to know where he could reach me if I went out. Leaving me love notes. Sending me flowers signed "Your secret admirer," or "Love and kisses," or names he made up. She laughed, amused, and said that what he was doing to me, he had done to his mother, then later transferred to her. She explained he had been obsessed with his mother, demanding all her attention. His parents had favored him, but it was never enough. Then when he left home, he transferred to her until she married and had her own family. He was angry about being what he termed "abandoned."

"And," she said, "now he's attached to you."

I questioned, "What do I do?"

She laughed again and replied, "Just hope he finds someone else. In the meantime, you'll handle it."

But could I? After what I had just been through with Marlon, I didn't think I could handle much more of anything. By now we were joined at the hip sharing a secret life. An amputation might save me, but what would it do to Marlon?

It wasn't too long before I discovered Marlon was using drugs again. With the aid of a writer, whom he had met in Tahiti, he found another doctor who gave him drug prescriptions. And he found other means to get drugs without prescriptions. He, being Marlon Brando, had loads of "friends" who were suppliers or would get him a new doctor. And as usual it was, "Don't tell Alice."

I was devastated. Soon, he was no longer hiding it from me. Marlon would stay in a stupor in his room for days on end. I never knew when I arrived in the morning whether I would find him dead or alive. And I spoke to him about this as this fear was getting me down.

One time when he had been spaced out, I caught him awake and very boldly told him he had been in bed for days, that he stunk, and stated I wanted him up and in the shower. Before he could digest all this and attack, I changed tactics and very gently said I was going to make him a cup of coffee, and softly, with a smile, threatened if he wasn't out of bed by the time I returned, I was going to put a match to the mattress. I escaped before he could argue me out of my intentions.

The smell that stunk up his room wasn't necessarily emanating from Marlon, though that may not be true. He had not used the bathroom, instead he had urinated in a pitcher and other vessels which I saw filled alongside his bed. That was the source of the overwhelming odor permeating the room. You know, the gas station bathroom odor.

He managed to get into the shower before I returned with the coffee, as I was in no hurry to bring it to him. I didn't empty the chamber pots. He did.

I didn't know what to do. I felt so helpless. I tried everything I could think of to help him "kick the habit." I didn't have anyone to confide in who could help as I was also protective. And besides, I had given him my word I'd always be there for him.

Marlon didn't want anyone, but no one, to know. Neither did I. Besides, I knew if I told anyone what I was going through, they wouldn't believe me. He was the consummate actor. I'd be no match for Brando when he denied it. Which he would. I was afraid that by the time he got through with me, he'd have everyone believing he was the one trying to help me. I was in a no-win situation. He especially didn't want anyone in the industry knowing; he was afraid that would give them another reason not to hire him.

Promises were meaningless. I was exhausted. So this time, in desperation, I fell back on a woman's greatest weapon.

Tears.

I cried. There were copious tears. And they were for Marlon. The tears almost did him in. He never expected it of me. I had always been the strong one. I didn't have to tell him they were tears of frustration and stress. And, yes, pity.

He knew.

I was a person who couldn't swim—trying to save a drowning man. What surprised me later on was that I had the fortitude and the strength to hold on, and he didn't take me under with him. I brought him into the shallows where I let him go, but stood by, and he had to save himself.

He shaped up. He only did it knowing I was there.

When one day I facetiously told Marlon I'd pray for him, little did I know he'd begin to creep into my prayers at Mass. By this time in our relationship, I was constantly battering the gates of heaven with prayers begging for help. I needed direction, both in my life and Marlon's. My prayers went unheeded—I wasn't getting any answers to my petitions.

My mother was very spiritual and was psychic, and so was I to a lesser extent, as I ignored my "knowing." Though I could read Marlon like a book. So when troubled, I'd run down to Newport Beach to the comforts of "home." And without mentioning what I was praying for, we'd discuss faith and my frustration with unanswered prayers.

My mother once responded to my frustration, "You're where you are at this moment in time to learn lessons of life—don't fight it." She listened with her heart and was aware that I was questioning and losing my faith.

I had never told my mother or my sisters what I was going through with Marlon. My sisters never knew Marlon was a drug addict until now. I gave Marlon my word I wouldn't tell anyone, and I kept it. He released me when he told me that if he died before me, I could write *all* about him. Especially "if the knives came out," as he believed they would. But at the time we spoke, he thought it would come from a different source.

People will question how Marlon performed and was involved in so many causes, projects, etc. The honest answer is, "I don't know." But he did. He controlled his drug intake, not me. And, as he reminded me from time to time, he was an actor.

I'm reminded that during that same period in time, the sixties, we had a president of the United States, John Kennedy, who was reputed to be taking "pain killers" during his time in office and received injections from Max Jacobson, referred to as "Dr. Feelgood." These shots were reputed to contain amphetamines, procaine, cortisone. What other drugs made up his "drug cocktail," I hadn't heard and don't know. Also, as I write this, there is now another Kennedy, who is also in Congress, admitting to drug addiction.

Unlike these men in government, Marlon was not running a country, nor legislating. He was acting. And very, very good at it. I can attest to the fact there was no one better on screen, and off.

Is that how he got away with it?

Some actors through the years have been known to be addicts and have kept it hidden. Others in recent years have gone public with their drug problems surprising everyone except their intimates, and sought help through rehabilitation. Was Marlon's sometime bizarre behavior caused by the mix of drugs he was taking? I'm not qualified to say. I can only report on the behavior patterns. I can also attest that when Marlon was off all drugs except Valium, which, as he said, "keeps me on an even keel," he was what one would consider acceptable in social behavior and rational thought. He was also more approachable. His deep-seated anger, though, was ever present, always waiting to surface and explode.

*****

I wasn't schooled in psychiatry. I just used common sense in dealing with Marlon and made certain he went to his psychiatrist, whom I discovered he lied to by his own admission. Dr. Aaronson, Marlon's psychiatrist, after many years, finally gave up on him. Marlon returned chastened from a therapy session and said Aaronson told him he was crazy and couldn't help him. In other words, he gave up. Marlon was too much for him.

It wasn't until Marlon had been drug free, except for Valium, for some time and was being treated by another psychiatrist that I reluctantly agreed to Marlon's beseeching to talk to his new psychiatrist about him. The only reason I agreed was I had always wondered if Dr. Aaronson would have been able to help Marlon if I had done as Marlon asked and talked to him. Now I felt I had another chance to help Marlon. I agreed to telephone sessions. I had only one request of Marlon. He had to refrain from listening in or taping the calls. He was so anxious for me to talk to his psychiatrist that he readily agreed.

I had about four 90-minute to two-hour telephone sessions with his psychiatrist. They were probing and, according to the doctor, very productive. Marlon was grateful for my cooperation with the doctor on his behalf. It wasn't long afterward that Marlon came home from a therapy session brimming with happiness. "I'm not crazy," he sang. The doctor's analysis: Marlon was eccentric, had fits of explosive anger, displayed juvenile behavior, did crazy, bizarre things, had flights of fancy. But he was not certifiably insane.

Marlon embraced this diagnosis. Eccentric? He could live with this type of crazy.

I recalled I looked up "eccentric" in the dictionary at the time. It stated: "Odd or whimsical behavior; divergence from the usual or customary, and suggests at least mild mental aberration." Marlon certainly was eccentric. Synonyms are: erratic, odd, queer, peculiar, strange, outlandish, curious. Marlon embodied all. The psychiatrist got that much right. All other sudden and abrupt character changes were attributed to the fact that he was an actor and could change roles at will. Was this the interpretation of what I and others referred to as dual personalities, Dr. Jekyll and Mr. Hyde?

Now Marlon thought he was normal. His verbal and physical abuse of women was not addressed nor was his sex addiction—and they continued. Now, I wondered how he was going to excuse his behavior, or if he would, since he was told he was not "crazy." And what about the lying? And his penchant for revenge?

I didn't call to determine if Marlon's interpretation of the psychiatrist's findings were true. Marlon was happy he was no longer crazy, and that was all that mattered to him.

Is this why Marlon went to another psychiatrist? To invalidate Dr. Aaronson's diagnosis? As I've said, his abusive behavior toward women continued and so did his eccentricities. And everything else. Nothing changed except Marlon now thought his aberrant behavior was that of a sane man. And since that was so, he stopped going to a psychiatrist.

But years of habit were too engrained. The "games" he played were too much "fun." It didn't take long for him to revert to character. And he once again was seen by others as "crazy."

Through the years, I refrained from calling Marlon crazy. Whenever he referred to himself as crazy, I retorted, "Yeah, crazy like a fox." And I said he did crazy things. My theory was that if I told him he wasn't crazy enough times when he used the word "crazy" to blame his behavior, he wouldn't think of himself in that manner and start taking responsibility for his actions. Now, I thought maybe that's what the psychiatrist was doing. Who knows?

One thing I did know, when Marlon was not taking drugs, he was a much different person. But after the doctor told him he wasn't crazy, he continued to exhibit eccentric and outlandish behavior, and long engrained aberrant patterns still came to the fore seemingly at will.

And "suggests at least mild mental aberration" haunted me.

*****

Marlon decided to do the film *Morituri,* to be directed by Bernhard Wicki, which was to be shot on a derelict freighter off Catalina Island in Southern California.

We had rented a house for the duration of filming on the island of Catalina, 26 miles off shore. It was located on the hillside overlooking the casino with a magnificent panoramic view of the town and yacht-filled harbor.

Marlon and I, with housekeeper and cook, weren't the only occupants for long. Soon we were joined by Wally Cox. Not long afterward, Christian Marquand and guest arrived. Then Marlon sent for another girlfriend from the East. She was a sight to behold on the waterfront when she arrived, for she wore a startling-colored silk sari, long white opera length gloves, and a large bag. Then there was the huge umbrella. She was hiding from the sun's rays while the sand and street was filled with mini-bikini-clad, bronze, all-American girls and boys basking in the same sun. She turned heads.

With her arrival, cultures were about to clash.

Filming was on a rusted, old ship that was anchored offshore, reached by motor boat. I get seasick, therefore I didn't go to work with Marlon. I would walk with him through town to the dock where a speedboat took him to the ship. And late afternoon, I would meet him. After a few weeks living at the house on the hill, I moved to a motel in the middle of town.

Christian had brought "mushrooms" from Mexico and I don't know what else, but the nights were wild. If the house was going to be raided, it would be without me. Marlon wasn't very happy with me over the move and tried to entice me back. No way.

If Marlon was unhappy with me for moving out of the house, it was multiplied the very next day. Before I had waved him off the dock in the morning, he asked me to send his girlfriend out to the ship after she awoke. I returned to the house and, when she was up and about, I gave her Marlon's message. She was thrilled because this was the first time Marlon had ever invited her to visit the set while he was filming. Yul Brynner was co-starring with Marlon. The thought of meeting him also thrilled her.

She retired to change her sari. While changing, she had piled her brown hair on top of her head in an elaborate do, was fully made up, had on a stunning silk sari not suited to a yacht in the harbor, let alone an oily, rusted, battered ship. Jewelry and those long, white opera-length gloves completed the picture. And all this teetered on a pair of heels. She walked into the salon looking as though she was attending a grand ball instead of going to a beat-up, dirty, old derelict. The housekeeper and cook raised their eyes to the ceiling at the sight and made a fast escape. I was stuck.

The employees had complained about her overbearing attitude and I had spoken to Marlon about it, but he was amused by her autocratic behavior. I ignored her; I wouldn't let her bother me, but she looked down on every employee, critical and demanding to the point of annoyance to them. Marlon did nothing about it when it was called to his attention.

I was always courteous to any and all of Marlon's guests, whatever their attitudes. I must say, most were very nice. I don't know what she could have done to set me off that day, but whatever it was, I lost it, which was unlike me, and she was in the line of fire.

We left the house. She opened her umbrella. As we started down the hill, I politely told her she had a choice to either walk in front of me or behind me, because I was not going to walk through town to the dock beside her. I told her if she wanted to know the reason why, she just had to look at her bejeweled, gloved self, then look around her. She elected to walk in front of me, as it was insulting for me, a servant, to ask her to walk behind me. She haughtily informed me she was going to tell Marlon how rude I was to her. I nonchalantly tossed off, "Be my guest." And followed her through town to the dock.

Needless to say, she told Marlon about my "rudeness," for, when I met the speedboat that evening, Marlon, with her at his side, angrily sailed into me about it. I had been expecting a reaction from him because he was unhappy about my leaving the house, but when he demanded I apologize to her, I spit back at him, "And is she going to apologize to me for referring to me as your servant?" This stopped him cold. She had only told him what I said. I didn't wait for a reply. I was off. Let him continue to condone her behavior. As for me, I had had my moment.

Actually, I didn't give a hoot that she referred to me as Marlon's servant. I just took statements like that, dismissed them, and chalked them up to ignorance. I was upset with him for allowing her to speak down to the housekeeper and cook who made complaints about her demanding, demeaning behavior that I had called to his attention, and which he had dismissed with a laugh. They did not find her behavior amusing. And neither did I.

I no longer went to the dock. Instead, I went to the beach every day and had a wonderful time for a week or so. It took Marlon that long to plan and seek his revenge. One noon, he sent a production assistant to search for me. Marlon wanted to see me—on the ship. I loaded myself with seasick pills and went out on the speedboat. I boarded the freighter and was informed that Marlon was in his cabin and did not wish to be disturbed. I looked for Marie Rhodes, his stand-in. She was surprised to see me because she knew I got seasick, and we spent the rest of the day together.

I never saw Marlon until we boarded the speedboat for shore as I didn't go where they were filming. He just smiled smugly, acting as though nothing had happened between us and I had not spent the afternoon onboard the ship. He looked so pleased with himself, I wished that I had not taken the seasick pills so that I could have puked all over him to wipe that smug grin off his face.

We never stayed on the outs very long.

Every Wednesday, Marlon would leave work early and go by helicopter to the mainland for his visitation with Christian, who was six years old. And almost every Friday night, he would helicopter home for the weekend. Needless to say, twice a week he was late returning for his on-set call. Soon the production staff, producer, and director were becoming frustrated.

When I approached Marlon, and beseeched him to be more co-operative, he gave me his standard reply, "F--k them." Marlon was, once again, at odds with his director. Even though I wasn't going to the set, I was the conduit to Marlon. And I was in the middle between Marlon and the director, Bernhard Wicki, through his wife. Each time his wife saw me, her mantra was:

"Marlon is driving my husband mad. Marlon is driving my husband mad." That was all Marlon needed to hear. He ignored my pleas to, "Stop the games. Let's finish the picture and go home."

One thing Marlon did that may have been frustrating Bernhard—having his girlfriend come onboard, retire with her to a stateroom, wouldn't come out to rehearse with Yul Brynner, saying he was busy. Marie, his stand-in, would take his place rehearsing with Yul Brynner. Then, when Bernhard was ready to shoot, Marlon would not appear until *he* was ready. One day I heard that after having them wait for him, he came out of his room smiling, zipping up his pants.

Later word came back to us that Bernhard was admitted to a sanitarium in Switzerland at the conclusion of the film. Did Marlon's actions help put him there? His wife had continued to tell me "Marlon is driving my husband mad" till the end of filming.

Whenever I think about our film location on Catalina Island, I'm reminded that my sisters Marty and Peggy were on Catalina one weekend, as was Marlon. I had been working for Marlon a few years, and when they saw him in passing, they decided to introduce themselves. Asked to be excused for intruding, they said they were my sisters. Marlon said that no one named Alice worked for him. My sister said, "She's your secretary, Alice Marchak."

He replied, "I never heard of her."

They again politely excused themselves and walked away wondering why he was lying.

They didn't mention this to me at the time. If they had, I would have encouraged them to deny knowing me, or that I was his secretary, when he called them trying to locate me. They ignored it; they were too nice. If he had done that to me, I would have made him eat his words and had some fun doing it.

*****

I decided not to go on location with Marlon while he was filming *The Appaloosa* on location in St. George, Utah. It wasn't too long before I received a call from the production manager—Marlon was out of control and it was urgent I come to St. George. I arrived on a Saturday night and checked into a motel room the production office had reserved for me, instead of going to stay with Marlon at the house that was leased for the film duration.

After I unpacked, my friend Paul picked me up and drove me to Marlon's house. A wild party greeted us that included, I discovered, most of the crew and their guests, which must have been half the town. The rooms were wall to wall with people. Some of the guests were openly smoking marijuana. Marlon was surprised to see me, but very happy I had decided to join him. He was too high for me to tell him of my mission. I didn't think I'd be missed, so we left.

The following morning I returned and confronted the housekeeper I had sent on the location to keep her ears open and an eye on Marlon and let me know if he was misbehaving. When I asked if there were any drugs on the premises, she hesitated. She didn't want to squeal—Marlon had told her not to tell me. But she did.

I took all the pills and marijuana I found in the house and flushed everything down the toilet. She was almost apoplectic as she watched me. I comforted her and instructed her to tell Marlon everything I had found and what I had done with it. That was my way of telling him he was working and was not there to play around and lay around. Then, while Marlon slept, I returned to the production office to confer with the producer about Marlon's behavior.

Later in the day, I told Marlon I hadn't come to visit him, nor to stay, but had been summoned by the production manager for a meeting to discuss his antics on and off the set. Marlon gave me his side by merely saying he was having trouble with the director, but not being specific. He refused to discuss any problems he was having. His only interest was in having me stay, which I did until he straightened out.

Shortly after I arrived back in Beverly Hills, I was called about his daring escapades—like getting out of his car at the top of the mountain at dusk and telling the driver he'd meet him at the bottom, he was going to climb down. As Marie Rhodes related, he had persuaded Phillip, her husband, to join him, which he did over her objections and the driver's apprehension. They had slipped and slid down the side of the barren mountainside, almost over a steep precipice. They couldn't make it down and had to climb back. Marie was furious at Phillip, but more so at Marlon for putting them in such danger. The production manager was greatly disturbed, and rightly so, because if Marlon were injured, it would cause the film to shut down. I phoned, informed Marlon the production manager had called me again. We discussed his behavior and I received Marlon's promise he wouldn't do any more mountain climbing.

Soon, I received another call. Marlon had flown in a Chinese girlfriend from New York City over the weekend and had driven up the same mountain one afternoon. As he told it, a helicopter had circled low above them as she was performing oral sex while he laid on a large flat rock. Asked what he did when he saw the helicopter above him, he said he just smiled and waved.

When I phoned and asked him if he had made up the story for entertainment as he was wont to do, and to find out if anyone believed such an outrageous story, which they did, he laughed and admitted it was true. Was it? He lied so much. I didn't know what was truth or fiction. I couldn't question the other person involved in the story, because I would never cause her further embarrassment by revealing Marlon was peddling the story.

But the production office was not amused, even though it happened on a weekend and did not disrupt filming. They had to deal with the town elders.

And this, too, becomes Brando lore.

*****

I've been candid about Marlon being difficult for producers and/or directors to work with. Even those he professed to like. And I was always put into the middle by Marlon. And I always tried talking Marlon out of irrational behavior.

While we were filming *Reflections in a Golden Eye* in Rome, Marlon had an ongoing feud with Ray Stark, the producer. It was over funds that were slow coming from the backers. Marlon would send me to Ray with his demands. Ray would send me back to Marlon. Marlon wouldn't talk to Ray, and Ray wouldn't talk to Marlon. It escalated when Marlon requested I demand the last million dollars owed him. Ray repeatedly responded through me that he was awaiting money from Switzerland and that he would wire it to Marlon's lawyers in Beverly Hills as soon as it was received.

Marlon was harassing Ray because he discovered that Ray had confided that Marlon was driving him mad. Here we go again. That was all Marlon needed to hear. Every couple of hours I was obliged to inquire of Ray if the money had been sent to his bank. This continued for a few days. To add to the mix, the next day began the weekend and Ray was really feeling the pressure. I didn't understand what was holding up the money, but I think it was the value of the dollar; foreign currency and high monetary finance was beyond me. In the middle of the day, I gave Ray a heads up, remarking if the money hadn't arrived at day's end, he shouldn't expect Marlon to work the coming Monday. The money didn't arrive and Marlon didn't work that Monday—because of my heads up, he had no call, so the company didn't lose any time or money.

Monday I heard from Ray that the money was received in Rome and forwarded to Marlon's lawyers. Marlon returned to work Tuesday. But Marlon and Ray never spoke to each other during the filming of *Reflections in a Golden Eye*. Ray was very supportive and said if I had any problems to let him know.

There did become the problem of weight. I always made certain that Marlon lost 25 pounds before every film and usually lived on the premises with him when on location, so I could maintain some control over his diet. Also, I asked David Watson, his wardrobe man, to immediately advise me if his waist was expanding, as he could tell if Marlon was having a problem zipping up. Now I was being pressured about the "pasta pounds" Marlon was putting on. The situation at home and his grumbling about having to ride a horse, which he hated, the girlfriends he was juggling, and his thinking of ways to frustrate Ray made it almost impossible for me. I would order lunch for him, but I couldn't stop him from ordering a second one and have it delivered when I wasn't there. Also, he was having pasta dinners.

I could become a nag or throw in the towel. I threw in the towel after I told Marlon his weight gain was showing up on the screen and I had been asked to do something about it. He stormed at them through me, the messenger and, as usual, said, "F—k them!"

I wasn't very happy with Marlon when I received the stills, which Marlon never looked at—I did all the "kills." I took the fat ones and put them in front of his nose. He had to look at them. I asked if he'd like to have them published. He brushed them aside and shrugged, "I don't give a f--k." I killed all. But I hoped he got the message—"Skip the pasta."

A few days later, I was shown the front page of the newspaper, and there was one of the fat photos on the front page along with an unflattering story about Marlon's obesity. I searched out the publicity man and informed him I was going to Ray Stark about the photo I had "killed" and he had used. He surprised me by saying that since I had "killed" all the photos, he had approached Marlon on the set, told him what I had done, and asked him to okay the photos, which Marlon did.

The photographer was very pleased with himself. I was unhappy because you don't do what he did to people who have an obesity problem, as everyone knew Marlon did. But I was upset, too, with Marlon.

Now, I went into Marlon's dressing room, dropped the newspaper in his lap and said that from now, on he could okay all the stills. And, I continued, it was less work for me, which I appreciated. He stared at the paper for some time, then looked up at me and soberly said, "When you're right, you're right. And you know how I hate you to be right."

The set wasn't the only place Marlon and I were confronted by problems. Tarita arrived in Rome with Teihotu, unannounced, on a Sunday morning. Marlon and a girlfriend were in bed when I left the house after telling him I was going to the flea market with Phillip and Marie Rhodes. Tarita called from the airport; Marlon took the call. He was surprised to say the least. I returned by noon. She had just arrived from the airport in transportation arranged by Marlon. Marlon went immediately on the attack for my failure to have Tarita and Teihotu met and for not advising him of her arrival. I tried to tell Marlon she never notified me she was arriving. Tarita stood there mute while Marlon performed, dressing me down, and never said she didn't call me or send any message that she was en route to Rome.

Tarita had been in Paris with a boyfriend, unbeknownst to Marlon. I knew she was in Paris. I was notified that Tarita had the housekeeper at home make the arrangements for the flight from Los Angeles to Paris, and Tarita told her not to let either Marlon or me know she was in Paris. Or that she was meeting her boyfriend. I later learned that when her friend had said he couldn't spend more time with her, they had had a fight, so she had left Paris and taken the flight to Rome.

Needless to say, I was angry with Marlon for making me the fall guy, and I was disappointed in Tarita standing like a statue, not owning up to the fact that she had never notified anyone she was coming to Rome Sunday. This was a case of both Marlon and Tarita caught and covering up. I felt justified in being angry with both.

I didn't go to the studio with Marlon. I secluded myself in my room, planning to have it out with Marlon as soon as I had a chance to get him alone. He knew I'd want to address what transpired. He kept out of sight and made no attempt to see me.

A few days passed, then Marlon sent a message to me complaining there was no hot water for his shower when he arrived home from the studio. I sent a message back that if there was no hot water, then shower in cold water. That's what everyone else did.

In the meantime, Celia Meredith, former girlfriend and secretary, had flown in from New York City. Hired by Marlon to keep Tarita company. The only one I opened my bedroom door to was the child, Teihotu.

One day, Teihotu arrived at my door with a lighted cigarette in his mouth. Evidently, Tarita, who led Marlon to believe she didn't smoke, but smoked when he wasn't around, had put the cigarette down. He must have picked it up and came to visit me. He was about four years old at the time.

We sat on my bedside. I ignored the cigarette and talked to him. He would look up at me, puff the cigarette, and blow the smoke at me. Continuing to ignore it, I kept chattering. He finally screwed up his face, said, "Fue," and extended the cigarette. I took the cigarette, put it back into his mouth, and said, "Smoke." He shook his head from side to side, saying, "No. No good." I disagreed, "Yes, it's good. Smoke." I insisted he take several puffs, until I saw him start to tear up. He cried, "I hate you. You make me smoke cigarette." I pulled him close and trying not to laugh, I said, "I make you smoke cigarette because I love you." He didn't believe me. It took a few chocolate kisses before we made up and he smiled at me once more. He didn't come into my room with a cigarette again.

That night Marlon sent another message to me about the cold water. I was to "make sure there was hot water to shower when I come home." I sent a message to him to tell everyone not to shower.

The water tank in the two story apartment we were leasing on the Isle de Tiburina, I discovered, was very small. I knew I'd be receiving another message from Marlon, possibly my door flying off the hinges. I consulted the Italian cook and asked where I could buy a water tank immediately. I had good luck. She made a call. A relative could bring one and install it before Marlon arrived from the studio. But, since he had to get it and a helper to put it in that day, it would cost "a little more." I assured her money was no object. Marlon wanted hot water, he'd get hot water.

Now we had two water tanks. I put the bill on Marlon's pillow. Because I solved the hot water problem it didn't mean I wasn't mad at him. I still planned on having it out as soon as I could get him alone.

I didn't go to the set and he avoided me when he was home, until one night he sent word to my room that he wanted me at dinner that evening. He said he did not expect me to insult his guests, whom I was friends with also, by not appearing. At the dinner table, Marlon behaved as if nothing had happened between us, but then, didn't he always.

Marlon and I had been working on the Paris UNICEF Gala-TV Show for the United Nations for several months, so we flew to Paris on the day of the performance. Marlon thought that since I had shown up for dinner the night before, all was forgiven. I didn't want to make an issue of his behavior while on the trip, so we had an enjoyable time at the gala and partying in Paris. Afterward, Marlon flew to London for a day to visit a girl, and I returned to Rome.

I still remained away from the studio. Then one day Marlon sent his car and driver to bring me to the set. We settled our differences between takes since we couldn't talk at home in front of Tarita and Celia.

I remember it as one of the worst locations I had been on. Marlon ignored Tarita and Celia. He was meeting with women away from the house. Tarita and Celia spent their time together indoors as it was the rainy season. At times, Marlon didn't come home, and when he was home, there were house guests and cocktail and dinner parties.

Naturally, Tarita and Celia thought I spent more time with Marlon than they did, as he forever sent for me when I didn't go to the set with him. Or if he stayed out at night and wanted to talk to me, he'd send his car for me. He was not seeing or talking to them, and I was relaying messages from him. Their attitude toward me was not very friendly.

And though I spoke to Marlon about the atmosphere he was creating by ignoring them, he continued to do so, I accused, out of perversity.

These were two girls I had known for years. I had constantly helped Tarita obtain funds from Marlon for her needs as Marlon intimidated her and she was afraid to approach him for money. And Celia, who had worked for Marlon before Rennie Laven and I, was drawn into my social circle as she couldn't meet anyone because she was also a girlfriend and waited around for Marlon to call. Marlon was engrossed with others, and she just sat by the phone night after night at the Marmount waiting for a summons. I had felt sorry for her and had befriended her, invited her to parties and introduced her to a friend, who dated her for quite some time. And now there was frost in the air. It was not a happy household.

One night, I received an urgent call from Marlon to meet him—there was an attempted suicide by a girlfriend. Marlon had found her. He sent his car for me. Upon arrival, he whispered he thought it was a fake attempt. The odor of marijuana permeated the room. The girl was sucking a joint. Marlon seemed high. He wanted me to know first hand what was transpiring, that's why he had sent for me.

Marlon didn't come home and didn't go to work until he was certain she wouldn't try to take her life again. He refused to work until she left town. That was his story; I was stuck with it.

And, I was again in the middle, placating Ray Stark, the producer, and daily urging Marlon to please shape up and go to work. Ray was very kind to me, understanding who and what I was dealing with since he had recently gone a couple of rounds with Marlon.

Marlon finished *Reflections in a Golden Eye* and departed for London on December 23rd, 1966, then returned to Rome on January 18th through 21st, 1967, for retakes on the picture.

A few months after we had completed the film and returned from Rome, Marlon and Ray Stark were socializing and having meetings. Will wonders never cease? Marlon and Ray were certainly not interacting during the filming of *Reflections in a Golden Eye*. Marlon did everything he could think of to frustrate Ray. It worked, and he enjoyed every minute. I can attest to that as he stretched my patience to the limit. But now Marlon had an agenda: *UNICEF* and *Tetiaroa*—he was promoting both.

Shortly after all these dinners and meetings, I received a surprise call from Ray Stark. He said, "Alice, you can't work any longer for that mad man. I'll get you a job anywhere in the industry, just let me know." Before I could say a word, he hung up, leaving me wondering what had brought that on.

Remembrances of Rome? Or did something happen at those dinners and meetings? Nothing came of them that I heard about.

*****

Marlon and Christian Marquand, a French actor, were friends of long standing. Christian was charming. When he visited Beverly Hills, or when he worked in American films, he headquartered at Marlon's house. The housekeeper didn't like his condescending manner. She didn't complain to Marlon, but to me. One of her complaints would have irritated me too. He brought out his dirty laundry, dropped it on the kitchen counter, and ordered the housekeeper, "I'd like this as soon as possible." Then proceeded to detail how he wanted the shirts done, how to do his tennis shorts, how she should wash his silk shirts by hand, etc., etc, etc. Much to her credit, she said she wouldn't have minded his attitude so much if he had said please or had inquired if she had time to do it, of if she even did laundry. I told her she didn't have to do his laundry. I sent it out. I was incensed about what he had done, so when it came back, I said I was going to put his laundry on the bed in the guestroom with the bill on top. She didn't want me to do it. "Babe, you're not going to do that. There'll be trouble." I guess I was in a devilish mood that day. Things were quiet. Marlon hadn't been stirring up the pot. I put the bill on the top of Christian's laundry.

The next day, Marlon said he wanted to talk to me. We knew it was about the laundry bill. I went into his room. There he was sprawled on the bed. Marlon didn't utter a word. We were correct. He silently handed me what I knew to be the laundry bill. I wanted to laugh, but I kept a straight face and innocently asked, "What's this?"

Marlon wasn't buying the innocence. He was very succinct. "You know what it is. Pay it."

Swallowing laughter, I inquired, "Anything else?"

He somberly said, "No."

When I returned to the kitchen, we were hysterical with laughter as I related the scene. But Christian got the message. He left his laundry in the laundry room with his instructions. And I sent it out with Marlon's laundry.

With time Christian changed and there was no friction in our relationship through the years when he stayed at the house months at a time.

Though Christian was an actor, he yearned to be a director. He had the project *Candy* and asked Marlon to play a part so he could raise money on his name. Marlon decided to help Christian.

Marlon's schedule was so short, I decided to pass on Rome to take some R & R at Newport Beach. I didn't like what I was hearing from the location about the drug use being out of control. Maybe Marlon wasn't involved. I hoped.

*****

Marlon finished filming and was returning from *Candy* Rome location. He called to let me know he wanted a few days to himself to get over jet lag. He said he was tired. Tarita, Anita, and Tehotu, who had been visiting while he was away, left for Tahiti and I also departed for Newport Beach before he arrived.

I returned a week later, dropped my bag in the office, and went to see Marlon. The house was quiet; there was no one around. Marlon was dressed, lying back against a couple of pillows on the king-sized bed. I belly flopped on the other side of the bed and said, "I'm back."

He didn't reply, but was glancing toward the doorway. I turned my head in time to glimpse the startled look on the lovely face of a slim, young girl with long, light sandy hair, who quickly turned on her heel and disappeared. I looked questioning toward Marlon. Quietly he said, "That's Jill."

Jill was an actress whom Marlon met and fell in love with while making *Candy*. She later told me she hadn't heard me come in; she had been in the guest bathroom putting on her makeup. She said she had almost had a heart attack when she walked in the door and saw this "beautiful brunette" (her words, not mine) sprawled on her belly on the bed with Marlon. She had heard Marlon liked brunettes and she thought I was a girlfriend. She didn't know what to do, so she ran and hid in the guest bathroom—and sat there until Marlon came for her after I left his room.

We always laughed about it every time she told others of our first meeting. Jill was a great laugher. That was one of the things about her that appealed to Marlon. He loved a good laugh, someone to make him laugh, someone with a sense of humor. And, of course, someone who appreciated his brand of humor. Another appealing factor was that she, like Marlon, was from the Midwest. They had Midwest roots in common. Marlon thought of himself as "a boy from the farm, who struck it rich and was living on top of the world." One summer they took a trip and explored their roots—she took him where she was born, and he took her where he started out life.

Marlon also appreciated that though she was an actress, she was not ambitious. She went on calls, did some TV spots, but mostly made herself available whenever the whim to travel hit him. Another thing he appreciated—she only stayed three or four days. She was perceptive enough to realize Marlon became restless after a day or two and would go into silences, so she'd gather all her possessions and depart. She never left anything behind, as some girls did so they could return. She knew Marlon was having his flings, but didn't confront him.

Everyone in the household was very fond of Jill. We would check out Marlon's room to be certain there were no telltale signs of any other girl being at the house when he told me she was arriving.

The one thing I appreciated was that she wasn't in competition with me for Marlon's attention. She confided that Marlon told her about our close relationship. Saying how much I had done for him. How he had had a crush on me, but I had rebuffed him. He said I had an important place in his heart and life that no one could replace. He told me the same in a tender moment, but I was surprised hearing it from her. She was young, but understood and accepted that Marlon and I had bonded through many crises and would always be there for each other.

I was also surprised that Marlon confided that he could get exasperated with me, and other times he would bug me until I became annoyed with him. And, when this happened, that he or I would make ourselves scarce, but eventually make up, even though at times reluctantly.

In time, Jill became an ally of mine, and I of hers, and through me, she came to better know and understand Marlon. Their relationship had many ups and downs, as all of Marlon's relationships with girlfriends. Marlon became very possessive. He wanted to know where Jill was at all times. This was before cell phones, so if she was visiting a friend for the day, she'd let me know. There were a few times Marlon phoned and she didn't answer. He transferred his actions to her—he thought she didn't answer because someone was there. Another boyfriend. He rushed to her apartment, knocked and called her name. No answer. Convinced she was inside with someone else, he broke down the door. He did this twice early on in their relationship. He phoned, told me what he had done and asked me to meet him. Help him out of this mess. He wasn't kidding, it was a terrible mess. I suggested he stay and tell Jill what had happened when she came home, and I'd help by taking care of the landlady. I visited the landlady, gave her funds to cover the cost of repairing the door, along with something for her trouble and promise to keep the incident quiet.

Each time this happened, Jill called to confide that Marlon excused his violent behavior by saying he was "crazy." She was to learn that wasn't all he was, for he almost destroyed her.

From conversations I knew Jill had experimented with marijuana and other social drugs before she met Marlon. She was by no means an addict. On the contrary, she was always very alert, with a bubbly personality.

But after a few months with Marlon, I began to notice a change in Jill. When at the house, there were times her speech was slurred and she was spacey. Other times extremely subdued and introverted. I asked Marlon about it. He vehemently denied he was giving her anything. Then there came a time when there was no denying.

I was having boyfriend problems. Marlon knew about them because he was, according to Jill, monitoring all my calls. His panacea was always, "Ali, get packed, we're going to Paris, or London, or Tahiti for a few weeks; we'll have loads of fun. Forget him." This time he rushed me off to Paris. Marlon and I were in Paris only two days when he began to miss Jill. I laugh now, as I did then, when Marlon told me what transpired when he placed a call asking her to join us.

"I'll meet her plane," I volunteered. "When is she arriving?"

"Can you believe she can't come today because she has to shampoo her hair!"

"Yes, I can believe it. She's a woman. Hair is important."

"Why can't she wash her hair in Paris? Why does she have to wash it in California?"

"Because the water is different in California."

Punctuating every word—in utter disbelief—Marlon repeated, "The...water...is...different...in...California!"

"Yes, just like spaghetti doesn't taste the same in California as it does in Rome."

"What does spaghetti have to do with Jill washing her hair in Paris?"

"The water. Water in California is not the same as it is in Rome—so Italians say that makes spaghetti taste better in Rome. Maybe Jill thinks the water in California is better than water in Paris to shampoo her hair," I reasoned.

In a state of exasperation, Marlon tried shaking the cobwebs out, sighed and said, "I give up. I'll never understand women."

And he picked up his handy black telephone book and dialed a few digits. He was sweet-talking someone as I walked out of the room.

Jill arrived next day and that was the end of "loads of fun." She and Marlon were both drugged out for our entire stay. They never left their suite. We were at Hotel Raphael, our usual address when in Paris. The concierge sent for me and politely informed me we'd have to leave because the suite belonged to Darryl Zanuck and he was coming to town. I got the message as he didn't suggest moving us to another suite. I asked for 24 hours. I had to get them both in shape to leave.

Another time I received a call from a stranger—Jill was in her car and couldn't drive. She had given the man my number. I took a cab, thanked the man for staying with her until I arrived as I had asked, and drove her home. I couldn't stay with her, and in her condition I couldn't leave her alone. I phoned her mother to take care of her. When she arrived, Jill told her mother that she was suffering with a migraine and had taken a pill which made her sleepy. Her mother, who was a sweet woman, sympathized with her and took her home for a few days.

A few months later, Marlon phoned Jill. She answered with slurred speech. Marlon asked me to go to her apartment to see if she was all right. I suggested we both go. He refused to accompany me. I was concerned for Jill, but felt I shouldn't go alone. If she was as bad as Marlon said, I was afraid she may have to be hospitalized. So I phoned her mother and asked her to meet me at Jill's apartment.

Jill was in bad shape, and once more told us she had a migraine. I informed her mother Jill did not have migraine headaches, she desperately needed help. Her mother and Jill were in denial. Her mother believed her daughter, not me, and took her home again for a few days.

Jill would be great for a time, as was Marlon, then both were out of it again.

We were in Cambridge, England, where Marlon was working on a film, *The Nightcomers*. Jill had joined us. We had finished shooting, but Marlon still had a few days of post-production work in London. So Marlon, Jill, and I were staying at the Savoy Hotel. After about five days, I received a message; the manager of the Savoy wanted to see me. He apologized to me, but he wanted us to leave. He told me he didn't "want any drug-related incidents happening in the hotel involving such a prominent actor."

This took me by surprise.

It seemed Jill had been walking around the suite like a zombie or was completely out of it in bed. Housekeeping and room service personnel had observed her while cleaning the suite when Marlon was working and had passed the information on to the manager.

I hadn't seen Jill since the night we arrived and Francis Coppola had taken all of us to Mr. Chow for dinner. I was doing the town on my own with friends. Marlon had been busy looping for about four or five days and had kept a few luncheon dates. Our meetings were brief, and when we talked on the phone, I'd inquire about Jill and ask Marlon to give Jill my regards. By this time Marlon was finished looping, so I knew I'd find him in their suite, which was connected to my room. The door was unlocked, so I entered their salon. I discovered Marlon—completely out of it; nothing I said penetrated. Jill was in the same condition. I finally got them where we were able to leave with a little dignity.

I couldn't handle Marlon by this time. He had many new "friends." I turned Jill over to her mother again and convinced her that Jill was not suffering from migraines. It was much more serious. This time she believed me. She moved Jill in with her. Her mother wouldn't allow Marlon near. She refused his calls. Jill cleaned up her act.

Marlon, as I mentioned earlier, had picks that he received from a security guard and knew how to pick locks. He was now using them to break into his friends' homes when he knew they were out. One day, Wally Cox came storming into the house and he and Marlon had a shouting match. A raised voice was highly unusual for Wally. It seems that Marlon had been taking Wally's prescription drug– it was the drug Fiorinal.

After this, Marlon persuaded Jill to call her doctor and obtain some Fiorinal—for him. When I discovered this, I confronted her and insisted she must stop as she wasn't helping me, herself, or Marlon.

Marlon was again spinning out of control. And I was not only burdened with the responsibility of caring for his household, his business, and problems of his extended families, but also him. I couldn't reach him. He was drugged beyond understanding. Talking did no good. He felt that since he was taking prescription drugs, and not street drugs, he was not a "drug addict."

Now, we know different.

Another doctor phoned and asked me to come to his office. As with Dr. Kositchek, he couldn't fill any more prescriptions for Marlon. He flat out told me Marlon was a "drug addict." I was in a quandary as I went through hell with Marlon when I told him Dr. Kositchek said he was a "drug addict." I confided in the doctor. I confessed I didn't know what to do. He said he knew where Marlon could get help. He had arranged help for others—alcoholics and drug addicts. He could arrange for Marlon to go to a place run by Jesuits, where the church sent their alcoholics for rehabilitation. I said Marlon wouldn't go. He replied he would arrange for me to go with him. He assured me no one would know Marlon was there. I was agonizing aloud about telling Marlon. "I can't tell him. I just can't tell him." He felt sorry for me. He realized it would be difficult. He would do it by letter. He then had his secretary type a letter to Marlon, telling him he was a drug addict, that he needed help, and that he could make arrangements for him to "kick the habit." He gave the letter to me to hand deliver to Marlon.

Marlon was reclining on his bed when I entered his room and handed him the letter from the doctor. He read it without any change in his demeanor. Marlon looked up from the letter and gravely asked me if I knew what was in the letter. I acknowledged I did.

Then, there was a big explosion. He supposed I agreed with the doctor. There had been a big blowout when I had told him Dr. Kositchek had said he was a drug addict, but the second doctor's confirmation, and his offer to make arrangements for Marlon to go away to "kick the habit," was too much. There was angry denial after denial. He eventually wound down. After all the denials and anger, he firmly stated he would not go into rehabilitation. He didn't want anyone to know. Wasn't he aware that people would eventually begin to know? How did he expect to hide it much longer? He would not address the questions, nor admit anything.

We were at an impasse.

Finally, he told me he would stop taking pills as we had done it before without his going into rehab. Only, he said, he would go "cold turkey" this time. I didn't think that was a good idea. He was still fuming at the doctor and me and angrily bellowed not to tell him what to do. He was determined to do things his way, regardless what I thought. He was going "cold turkey." Period.

Marlon phoned Jill, confided in her, and prevailed upon her to accompany him to New Mexico. He and Jill left for Santa Fe.

He decided they would stay in a small motel where no one would recognize him while he went "cold turkey."

Marlon was not talking to me before he left. He was mad at me. I was the enemy.

I didn't hear from Jill or Marlon telling me that they had arrived at their destination, wherever that might be, nor where they were staying. After one day, Jill called me in a panic. She couldn't control Marlon. He was climbing the walls, had the runs, was vomiting, was cramping, bugs were crawling over him. You name it, it was happening to him. She didn't know what to do. Neither did Marlon.

Marlon wanted me.

Jill urged me to fly in. I realized he needed immediate attention. I calmed her. Asked if she had any pills. No. Marlon hadn't brought any along, either. He really thought he could go "cold turkey."

I advised Jill to seek the motel manager and ask him to refer a doctor, saying she had a migraine headache and that she took Fiorinal for the migraine. Fiorinal was one of the last drugs for which Marlon was getting prescriptions. This she did and, as I suggested, she gave it to Marlon, then drove him home where I took over. As before, I obtained some prescription pills, including Valium, and weaned him off again. Marlon still needed Valium. He refused to give it up. I never insisted because it was a tranquilizer. He couldn't face the world without it.

Was he grateful? *No!* I was still the enemy! After several weeks, yes. *Very* grateful.

This time, Marlon faced it and admitted he was an addict. After his admission and acceptance, he was afraid. He did not want to be a drug addict. Or any addict. Which was why he seldom drank—he did not want to become an alcoholic, either.

He elicited a promise from me that I would help him. I assured him I wouldn't abandon him. I'd be there for him. But, he had to help me, by helping himself. He desperately needed professional help, but his pride and fame prevented him from seeking it.

Caught in this secret life, I have to admit it was not the glamorous life everyone envisioned me living, working for one of the biggest movie stars in the world. When girls would say they envied my being with Marlon Brando all day, wishing they could be me, that's when self-pity came to the fore. All everyone saw was the designer clothes and high heels I wore to work. No one penetrated the wall to discover the reason. It was a barrier against Marlon he knew he had to respect. Also, I never knew when I'd be summoned to a doctor's office, or a lawyer's office, or a studio head's office. I never knew when I'd have to appear with Marlon at a meeting or in public on a moment's notice, or greet another celebrity or businessman at the door.

I usually wore light colors—beige or white, silk and linen, and pastel dresses in the summer—then when he'd ask me to help on a project in his workshop, I'd say to him, "I'm not going to soil these Ralph Lauren trousers" or "this white silk blouse." There was no way I was going to let him treat me the way I observed him treating the women around him. When he'd start a request with, "Sweetheart, will you...," my mind would go into overdrive and get ready for a negative retort.

He was a master when it came to his women, he controlled them, and he eventually did everything to debase them—destroy their dignity. He was Marlon Brando, Movie Star. With great charisma. He exerted sexual power. He charmed. He intimidated. He corrupted. He destroyed.

If you let him.

During the years, when Marlon was taking too much Valium, or whatever, I would call it to his attention, reminding him what it would be like going "cold turkey" again, or in rehabilitation. After a few days he would ask me to tell all the help not to come to work until notified. They would all remain on salary. Then, Marlon stayed in the house alone, with his dogs, for seven to ten days, until he weaned himself off Valium, except for one or two a day. Then he'd contact me. I'd return to the house and call everyone in.

No one but me and, of course, Marlon knew what was going on. I always told everyone Marlon desired to be alone for a while, and so did he. This was the pattern for years. Marlon did not return to dependency on prescription drugs, except for Valium, while I was around on a daily basis. Then I quit and was not there for about two years or so.

In about 1972, after Marlon and I were given guardianship of Christian and he was living at the house, I discovered Marlon was abusing Valium. I did not know how bad it was until one day I chastised Christian for smoking marijuana and he whined, "Why are you always on me about marijuana? Why don't you get after 'Bunky'?" Bunky was Christian's name for Marlon, which we used when talking about him. Other times, he was "Pop."

"Because he's not doing anything, or I would," I responded.

Christian then revealed that Marlon at night would come out of his room drugged, stand in the hall not knowing where he was, and then Christian would turn him around and lead him back to bed. "If you don't believe me," he continued, "ask my friend. He was here the other night and we both took him back to bed."

My heart sank. Christian wouldn't lie to me about Marlon's nighttime wanderings. Usually, it was to the refrigerator for food. I knew, or thought I knew, he didn't have any other prescription drug except Valium. His prescription was for 10 milligrams. I soon learned, after questioning Marlon, he was taking two pills each time, which was 20 milligrams. His rationale was that he was twice as big as when the Valium was first prescribed, he needed twice as many milligrams. Sometimes he didn't remember taking the pills and would take more.

When he was working on *Bedtime Story* with David Niven and Shirley Jones, he was clean of all prescription drugs except Valium. He took one pill in the morning before he left for the studio. I would arrive at the studio around noon, but not go to the set. We would meet in his dressing room for lunch and discussed his calls and what was happening with everyone. I noticed he would take a Valium before he returned to the set.

I believe I only visited the set twice during the filming. Each time he had called and wanted to see me. One time he asked me to get him a Valium from his dressing room. Then I sat talking with Marie Rhodes and he came by, requesting another. I reminded him it was only a half hour since he had taken the Valium. He confided he was having a problem with the scene and was uptight. I asked him if he would try to get through the scene without another pill. He thought a minute said, "Yeah," then added, "Stick around," as he walked away. He was really trying.

This was one picture I didn't have any trouble getting Marlon to work on time. He liked the sense of humor of both his co-stars Shirley Jones and David Niven; he came home from the set laughing.

*****

During lunch with Jill one day, I was bitching about a notice that my rent was being raised. I was living in an apartment on Doheny Drive in Beverly Hills at the time. This was the second rise in rent. The first time was shortly after I had moved into the apartment; they painted the apartments, then sold the building. The new owners had redone the lobby and were now raising our rent. My budget would have to be revised or I would have to move. I hated the thought of apartment hunting and moving.

Jill phoned me at home that evening. Marlon had asked her what we were talking and laughing about at lunch. She told him I had started out bitching about the rise in rent on my apartment and ended up bitching about everything else that was going wrong in my life. She and I had laughed about it. Jill said Marlon inquired how much rent she was paying, then asked how much I was paying. He was speechless about our rents even though she resided in the Valley where rents were lower than in Beverly Hills. Marlon hadn't lived in an apartment since he was twenty years old in New York City. He had no idea what rentals were.

She said he had lapsed into one of his moody silences, so she decided to leave. He had walked her out to her car, and before saying goodnight, he had said, "I'm going to buy Alice a house. I don't want her paying rent." She had said she thought that was "Swell, it would be a generous gift."

He had then said, "I owe her more than a house. A house is nothing."

She admonished me to "act surprised when he tells you."

The next day, when he awoke, he asked me to bring him a coffee. I brought it, and put the tray on the bed next to where he was reclining. He patted the bed and said, "Don't go." Then he asked me to call his business manager to find out about the house across from him on Mulholland Drive that was for sale. He said he wanted to buy it for me.

Jill didn't have to worry about my acting surprised. I went into shock. The last place I wanted to live was in Marlon's front yard. Fortunately, his business manager called with the news the house was for sale, but there was another parcel adjacent to it they wished to sell at the same time. His business manager advised Marlon he didn't have the money to purchase both properties. And he said that if they knew Marlon was interested, the price would escalate. I had been holding my breath until we heard, now I let out a sigh.

Next, it was call a real estate agent immediately; he didn't want me paying rent. The real estate agent took time to line up properties for me to look at, but Marlon was impatient. He nagged me every hour about the house, even commenting, "I don't think you want a house." He took matters into his hands, called the real estate agent and the Brando charm worked. She phoned and said she could show me a few places that afternoon.

Miko stopped by the house and Marlon sent him with me. Miko was great to have along; he was enthusiastic about finding me a house. I thought there was one possibility.

Marlon still was fixated on the property across the street, so while Miko and I were canvassing Beverly Hills, he called his business managers again and asked them to inquire if the lot was for sale, then we could build a house. When Miko and I returned, he related his new idea. I thought this was getting out of hand. I did not want to live across the drive from Brando.

That weekend I went to visit my folks in Newport Beach. While visiting my sister Marty, who lived on the Bluffs close by, I explained my dilemma and my need to live as far away from Marlon as I could get. She noted, "If that's what you feel, there's a house for sale on the Bluffs, three houses away across the street."

Someone was holding an open house, so we decided to look at it. We walked in and almost turned around. It certainly was nothing I could live in. The entrance, stairwell, and upstairs hallway were bright orange, bedrooms were dark brown. Downstairs living room, dining room, kitchen were rough redwood. The kitchen and downstairs hall were painted black. The patio deck was rotting. But there was a 360 degree magnificent view of the Back Bay, sailboats and all.

My sisters and I agreed it needed a lot of work. We also agreed it had good bones. I'd paint it. I wrote a 1,000-dollar check to hold it. Next morning, I phoned Marlon's business manager and asked them to look at the house and negotiate the purchase. The house was purchased and I did have it painted before I moved in. Marlon's Aunt Bette and her assistant, Bill Huston, helped me with some furnishings, which Marlon paid for.

One day when Bette was at the house checking on the powder room wallpaper, she and I visited over a cup of tea. We discussed Marlon and I remarked about Marlon's very difficult childhood. Bette challenged my comments. I recounted what Marlon had told me. Bette was aghast. She then proceeded with a history of Marlon's parents, sisters, and his childhood, unlike anything Marlon told me, eliciting my sympathy. This was the first time I learned Marlon had lied to me about his early life. Later, Jocelyn confirmed what Bette related. I had discovered Marlon was a liar since I started working for him, but I never imagined he'd snow me on his early life. To what purpose?

I didn't tell him I knew he lied about his childhood. I didn't give him the opportunity to laugh at me, for he always laughed at people believing anything he said. I was glad that Bette had stopped in to check the house, or I may never have known that I had been taken in by Marlon.

Years later, Marlon was without cash flow again. Because of huge lawyers' fees and the demands of a new family, property he owned was mortgaged, except for my house. He called and explained his situation and asked if I would agree to mortgage my house. I had never refused to help him out of any financial difficulties. I didn't now.

The house was in joint tenancy. I signed a loan for 300,000 dollars. Marlon received all the money. When the loan was due months later, Marlon was unable to pay the loan. Marlon didn't have any money. He was *broke*. Again. I received another call. I was asked to sell my house to pay the loan which I did. Subsequently, I learned it was not Marlon's idea to sell my house. I was informed that it was his business manager and his personal assistant at the time. After it was sold, it gave him great guilt and greater remorse—and he turned on both.

<u>Property:</u>

ADDRESS:	315 Avenida Cerritos, Newport Beach, California
JOINT TENANCY:	Alice Marchak and Marlon Brando

SOLD: July 24, 1998,
for the amount of 483,000 dollars.

In today's market, the property is worth in excess of 1.5 million dollars.

Marlon's stated intentions to me were that he would replace the property sold. When I told him I didn't want another house, he said he would give me the money he felt he owed me from the sale of the house he had given me. I might add that, as always, he was extremely grateful I had agreed to the sale of the house, which helped him out of a financial bind during a difficult time in his life. Marlon was also extremely grateful I had taken my tax exemption of 250,000 dollars, which I could do since I also owned the house and had been living in it, thereby helping him further.

From the time of the sale, almost every time we spoke, he referenced the money he owed me and his intentions to replace the house. In time he accepted the fact that I didn't want another house, but he insisted he would give me the money from the sale. He always felt guilty about the sale of my house. Whenever he spoke about it to others, he would say he owed me a great deal of money.

I did not receive any money from the sale of the house, nor any compensation for the work I did on the upgrades of the property, which greatly enhanced its value. Nor, at the time of the sale, did I receive my original 1,000 dollars to hold the property, nor a 10,000-dollar down payment.

After Marlon died, I sued his estate for the money, as he had stated in his will that "all outstanding debts should be paid first." My thinking was that this was a debt. And I knew Marlon wanted it paid.

*****

I had purchased a bungalow on the island of Bora Bora in the South Pacific. I put a 2,000-dollar down payment. I cautioned the acting agent she could not refer to Marlon Brando's secretary when promoting the complex as I never used his name for my benefit, and he never allowed his name to be used for any promotion. She wasn't selling many bungalows; they didn't have models built and she was becoming anxious about losing the complex to another real estate agent. She moaned, if only Marlon would purchase a bungalow....

Marlon and I were chatting one day and I mentioned I was buying a bungalow on Bora Bora. He wanted all the details. I used this opening and made an appointment for the agent to show him the floor plans, etc., and explain the investment prospects. The agent came out of the meeting ecstatic. Marlon had not only bought a bungalow for himself, he had purchased one for Jay Kanter and one for me. He then turned everything in regard to the Bora Bora complex over to me. I flew to Bora Bora frequently while the bungalows were being built.

Upon completion of the project, I selected the two models—one over the water for Marlon and the other model for Jay, which was on the hillside. Jack Nicholson also purchased a bungalow. My bungalow was situated between Marlon's and Jack's over the water in the lagoon.

I believe the over-water bungalows' purchase price was about 45,000 dollars and the hillside ones 40,000 dollars. Don't hold me to the exact amount because Marlon's business manager, Norton Brown, and a French lawyer, Claude Girard, handled the finances. I oversaw the building, the furnishing, including Jack's, the rental, housekeeping, and maintenance throughout the years. I opened an account in the bank on Bora Bora. Monies for the Bora Bora bungalows and rentals were put into this account. Dick Johnson, who had worked for Tetiaroa, was hired to go to Bora Bora periodically, check with the manager, and send a report as to rental and maintenance of the properties.

Marlon called me one day and said all rental monies would now be sent to Tahiti. And Maimiti, Tarita's daughter, would handle the funds. At the time my bungalow was rented by the year at 3,000 dollars per month. He stated that Maimiti would be sending me a check for that amount each month. I did not receive monthly checks, but assumed the rental money was being held in a Bora Bora account in Tahiti and used for maintaining the bungalows. I subsequently discovered the money received from my rental and the other rentals was spent in Tahiti. In 2004, I called, requesting 10,000 dollars from my Bora Bora rental money to pay for dental implants. I was informed there was no money and no Bora Bora account. Marlon was apprised of the situation—my request for money from my Bora Bora account by his business manager. Marlon said, "Give her the money." Linda, Marlon's accountant, questioned whether he understood the amount was 10,000 dollars and Marlon, as Linda relayed, repeated, "Give her the money. I owe her much more than that." Linda forwarded the money directly to my dentist in Newport Beach.

At this time, I was also informed that the bungalows had not been maintained and that my place and Marlon's needed new pandanus roofs. The Bora Bora account would no longer be handled by Maimiti, and the rental money would be used for the new roofs, repairs, and furnishings, as was originally intended. We were obliged to wait until more rental money had accrued in the Bora Bora account before the roofs could be repaired.

During the years, offers to sell were all rejected. Periodically, an offer to buy came from someone who had stayed at the bungalow. When Marlon discovered the increase in value, he phoned and advised me not to sell as he had heard there was a ban on building in the lagoon, and our property would go higher. He added, "If you need money, I'll give it to you."

The last offer for the three Bora Bora bungalows, Marlon's, Jay's and mine, was one million dollars. Marlon couldn't believe it. He phoned everyone to find out if the price was right. One person he spoke to was Mr. Biggerstaff, who had managed hotels, and his advice to Marlon was we shouldn't sell, everything would go higher.

Again, Marlon advised me against selling and reminded me my bungalow was giving me an income of 3,000 dollars per month. He was unaware I never received any checks from Maimiti or Tarita, who was in charge of the Bora Bora and Tetiaroa accounts at the time. When I sued Marlon's estate for money owed me from the sale of my Newport Beach property, I also sued for my Bora Bora property. I lost it.

Several years after the bungalows had been purchased by Marlon for me and Jay, I received a check for 2,000 dollars from Mr. LeJeune, a Tahitian lawyer. This represented my down payment. I discovered at this time that Marlon's business manager had made a down payment on three bungalows, not knowing I had already bought and put a down payment on my bungalow.

*****

Jill phoned me at home after she had left Marlon's one night. She was disturbed by Marlon's behavior and said I must talk to him. "You're the only one he listens to."

Marlon had been gaining weight. He wasn't taking amphetamines and he wasn't smoking. He couldn't stay on a diet. Oh, I'd try, but he had too many friends who'd bring him food during the night, no matter what time he'd call. Jill began to call him Fatso. It didn't stop him from satisfying his nocturnal yearnings for pie or ice cream.

The more obese he became, the more his clothes became a problem. The only thing he felt comfortable in were yukata, a Japanese robe. Marlon had always sprawled on his bed. I would urge him to sit on the couch in the living room, rather than just lying in bed day after day. He would occasionally sit in the living room, tucked in the corner of the couch near the phone. One person who tempted him out of bed was Wally. He'd drop by and they'd go for a hike. Or Florine Monteverdi, a friend of ours; he'd take a hike with her. But this wasn't often enough to make him lose weight. After a time, we all gave up. He was too old to bully and too tired of dieting. So, he just piled on the pounds and laid on his bed or sat in the corner of the couch.

But that wasn't what was disturbing Jill. As Marlon put on weight, he wanted comfort in the clothing he wore. He no longer wore briefs, he changed to boxers, which he cut up each side, so they wouldn't bind. And, the yukata became larger and larger. When he now sat down, he would spread his legs, the yukata would open, his underwear would be scrunched around, and he'd be exposed. When Jill called his attention to this, he snapped, "This is my house, I'll sit any way I want." Jill appealed to me to reason with him—which I did. She also had other worries which she asked me to address.

I put Jill on Marlon's revenge list when I called Marlon about the way he was sitting, because my opening gambit was, "I hear you're becoming a dirty, old man." Jill received a call from an angry Marlon. He sailed into her as he knew she told me about their confrontation and blamed her for calling him a dirty old man. Jill denied calling him a dirty, old man. She tossed it right back to me, and rightly so, because these were my words, not hers. She reported that Marlon had had a few hundred words about us. And he put us in deep freeze for a while.

Marlon had asked Jill to marry him. He suggested she pick out a ring. Instead, she opted for a ruby and emerald apple, that he had made for her, which she wore on a gold chain around her neck. Jill chose the apple for sentimental reasons. Marlon affectionately called her "the apple of my eye." The engagement was of short duration—the wedding bells would not be ringing.

They were en route to Tahiti via Hawaii with some friends and, as Jill recounted, they were on the balcony of the hotel. There were large waves crashing over the rocks below. Marlon was in a very surly mood; he was trying to antagonize everyone. He picked on her until he got a rise out of her. She uttered something that sent him round the bend. He went for her. He missed her, but not the ruby apple, which he tore from her neck and threw over the balcony into the sea and rocks below. As far as Jill was concerned, the engagement was broken at that moment. There was no way the jeweled apple could be retrieved from the rocks and the sea. The attack, and loss, naturally upset her. That's when, she confided, Marlon urged Valium on her. But she had cleaned up her act. She wasn't going to allow him to control her ever again. And certainly not with drugs, as he had in the past. She decided she had to save herself. She couldn't go to Tahiti with him. She returned to California.

Called me. I applauded her decision.

Jill left California. She didn't say goodbye to anyone. None of her friends would tell Marlon where she was if they knew. Her mother professed not to know where her daughter was. When I spoke to her, she said Jill was saddened by not being able to let me know where she was, but she was afraid that out of loyalty to Marlon, I might tell him.

It was a year before I heard of her whereabouts, but I never told Marlon. A friend of mine, who lived in Santa Fe, had seen her. I never tried to contact Jill directly, but periodically I would call her mother to inquire about her. I wanted her to know I cared.

Jill was away for a few years. Then one day I learned from Marlon she had returned to California. Marlon revealed that a friend had seen her and had invited her to dinner. Marlon dropped in. He didn't tell me the reception he received, but it must have been cool, because he didn't see her again or he would have told me.

She hadn't phoned me. I decided I'd give her space and time since it was evident after several weeks that she did not want to resume her relationship with Marlon. Then she called. We buried the past, but the future was in doubt. She was afraid of a relationship of any kind with Marlon. She had changed, but she realized he hadn't. And she didn't know if she was strong enough to withstand a Brando onslaught, or even wanted to prop him up as I had through the years. We'd stay in touch. After we terminated the call, I realized I failed to obtain her telephone number.

Marlon and I were leaving for Tahiti, Tetiaroa, for the summer. I promised myself I would call Jill upon my return. I wanted to see her again, have one of our enjoyable lunches.

Vacation over, Marlon and I were on the plane en route home and Jill came to mind. It was about an eight-hour flight and during it, she came to mind several times. After the last time she flitted across my mind, I reminded myself I must contact Jill through her mother as soon as I arrived home. The thought had no sooner crossed my mind when Marlon turned to me and just above a whisper confided, "I think I'll marry Jill. I'm going to call her when we get home."

It was late Friday night when I arrived home, tired from the trip and the airport. I felt Jill's mother would be asleep; I'd call in the morning. I had thought that when Jill came to mind so many times during the trip home, she may be thinking about me, or something may be troubling her that she wanted to discuss with me. But when Marlon surprised me with his announcement about marrying Jill, I surmised he had been thinking about her and I had been picking up his thoughts. Therefore I dismissed the strong compulsion I had to get in touch with Jill. Since Marlon slept past noon, he didn't call Jill either. Instead, we both received a call. About Jill.

Jill had been killed, mid-morning, in an automobile accident on the Ventura Freeway in the San Fernando Valley.

Marlon was inconsolable. As was I.

* * * * *

Marlon hadn't worked for a time, and producer Eugene Frenke, whose daughter was married to Marlon's father, was aware of Marlon's financial situation. He had a script he thought Marlon might be interested in, so he called and spoke to me about it. I asked him to send it to me and I'd put it into Marlon's hands, but "Don't get your hopes up," because Marlon was rejecting my suggestions that he begin thinking about going to work. Instead of sending it, Gene invited me to cocktails and I picked up the script.

Of course Marlon rejected it without a reading. He wasn't ready to work. I felt he owed Gene the courtesy of a call, so I'd remind him to call Gene as I wasn't going to call him.

A few weeks later I received another call from Gene. We spoke about Marlon's, as Gene put it, "laziness." He couldn't understand Marlon's reluctance to work when he was in demand and had such great responsibilities. From his conversation with Marlon, he received the impression Marlon was broke again, but didn't want to work until it was absolutely necessary. Gene had read Marlon correctly.

I received another call from Gene. He had returned from a trip to Japan, and with Marlon's conversation fresh in mind, when one of his associates there dropped the desire to have Marlon do a commercial for his product, he immediately volunteered to submit the offer to Marlon. Now, he wanted me to approach Marlon with an outrageous monetary offer to do a commercial, to be shot in one day that would only be shown in Japan, for a limited time.

Marlon was hurting for money. I thought he might be receptive to a few days' work. No time was the right time to approach Marlon about making another movie or go to work. Consequently, I waited until he was in a good mood before I made my pitch.

"Marlon, Gene called and said that while he was recently in Japan, he was approached to extend a very lucrative offer for you to do a TV commercial only to be shown in Japan." He looked at me with scorn and said, "What makes him and you think I would do a commercial?"

"You don't want to do a movie, you need money."

"I don't do television."

"I'm not asking you to act on television—I'm asking you to do a commercial."

"That's acting.... I'm not a TV actor."

"I know you're Marlon Brando, Movie Star. But Marlon Brando, Movie Star, doesn't want to do a movie. Marlon Brando, Movie Star, needs money."

"I'm not going on television."

"Marlon, I don't know where you've been all these years, but Marlon Brando, Movie Star, is also Marlon Brando, TV Star. You are on television."

He stared at me, disbelieving what had just come out of my mouth.

I continued, "Look at television every night and there is Marlon Brando, Movie Star, on the screen. Kids who never saw you in a movie theater are seeing you on television, some seeing you for the first time. You might be a movie star, but you are on television."

He glared, and vehemently repeated, "I'm not doing a commercial."

"Think about it."

"I don't need to."

Marlon didn't do that commercial, nor a few offers for commercials from Italy, only to be shown in that country, as well as many, many offers in the United States. For years he turned down millions in offers for television. He was Marlon Brando, Movie Star. Period.

*****

Journal Entry:

October 18th, 1968—I leave for Cartagena, Columbia, where *Quemada* is to be filmed.

Marlon is in Tahiti. Marlon returns and immediately leaves for Cartagena on the 25th.

Marlon used visitation to the children as an excuse not to work at every opportunity. If he had one day off, he'd run home from the location. All these departures from the location would cause consternation in the production department because they knew Marlon would return late. And frustration would begin to show in the director. This was part of the trouble between Marlon and Gillo Pontecorvo, the director of *Quemada.*

Below is a list of Marlon's efforts to frustrate Gillo by leaving the location in Cartagena, Columbia.

Nov. 30th—Marlon departs for *Beverly Hills.* Stays through Dec. 4th

December 5th—Marlon returns to *Cartagena* this evening

Dec. 19th—Marlon and Sam Gilman leave for Christmas vacation at home-*Beverly Hills.* Marlon becomes ill with the Hong Kong flu during holidays. Does not return until after the new year

Jan. 5th—Marlon causes bomb scare on plane—he is detained and misses his flight to *Cartagena*

Jan. 6th—Marlon and Sam Gilman return to *Cartagena* at 9:00 p.m. from *Beverly Hills*. Marlon goes directly to set for night filming

Jan. 29th through Feb. 3rd—Marlon departs for *Beverly Hills*

February 4th—Marlon returns at 6:00 a.m. to *Cartagena*
Feb. 15th—Marlon and Alice leave for home in a.m.—*Beverly Hills*
Feb 24th—Marlon and Alice depart for *Jamaica—Montego Bay – Kingston*
Feb. 25th and 26th—Missed flight to *Cartagena*—overnight stay—arranged for charter plane
March 8th—Marlon departs for home, *Beverly Hills.* Marlon home for weekend
March 10th—Marlon returns to *Cartagena*
Mar. 15th through Mar. 17th—*San Andreas Island*—Marlon visits for weekend
Mar. 22nd through 26th—*San Andreas Island*—Marlon visits again
March 27th—Marlon leaves *Cartagena* for home—children's Easter school vacation
April 7th—Marlon arrives *Cartagena* to resume filming
April 9th—*Barranquilla*—Marlon leaves for home after fight with Gillo—crew follows Marlon, persuades him not to leave
April 26th—*Cartagena* Marlon finishes filming in Columbia—leaves 8:55 a.m. for Miami en route home
April 29th—*Beverly Hills*—Marlon arrives home from *Quemada* location

Marlon refuses to return to Cartagena to finish picture. Location changed to Marrakech.

June18th—*New York City*—En route *Quemada* location in *Marrakech*
June 21st through July 12th—*Marrakesh—Quemada* filming. I refuse to go on location. Miiko Taka is hired by Marlon to go in my stead
June 23rd—The first day of shooting on *Marrakesh* location

July 10th—Finished shooting on *Quemada*
July 11th—Depart *Casablanca* en route to *Paris—London—Paris*
July 24th, 1969—Depart *Paris*—Returned home

*****

In Cartagena, Columbia, while we were filming *Quemada* (*Burn* in the United States) Marlon and Gillo Pontecorvo grew to hate each other. I don't know where this animosity began. It first came to my attention when they were filming on an island fort. It was hot, hot, hot. I was sitting in the shade of the fort wall watching Gillo filming a close-up of Marlon in a very confined space. Marlon, like everyone, was trying to bear up under the intense heat, but he was wilting with the addition of heat generated by the hot lights. And it was only mid-morning. Gillo showed no mercy. I watched as Gillo repeatedly did take, after take, after take. Phillip Rhodes, Marlon's makeup man, checked his makeup after each take to ascertain if it was streaking with sweat. The camera ran out of film and they stopped to reload. Mercifully, that gave Marlon respite from the hot lights. Marlon slowly walked over to where I was sitting. He had a strange, amused look on his face. I offered him some water and, in a whisper, I asked what the problem was. He softly replied it was a power play, but he'd outlast Gillo any day. If this was a just a power game, I advised him to forget it, it was too hot. I warned him he could pass out from the heat of the lights. Get it over with. He chuckled and repeated he'd outlast Gillo, heat or no heat. This was ridiculous.

I had always stayed out of an actor's eye line when on the set and they were filming. Now Marlon asked that I stand in his eye line. Since Gillo was doing a close-up, Marlon would rather look at me instead of Gillo while he was reacting. This went on for 52 or 56 takes, most of which he printed before Gillo gave up. Marlon later said he was giving him the same facial expression and same delivery each time. Marlon thought he won, especially when he visualized Gillo trying to pick out the "best" take.

As the filming continued, their relationship deteriorated to the point when Gillo began to carry a gun to the set. Word reached us he was heard threatening to kill Marlon. They were speaking to each other through me, or when I wasn't on the set, through Phillip or Marie or Sam.

Mario, the production manager, would leave messages for me to call him at his home when I returned in the evening. He sought me after he had received calls from Alberto Grimaldi, the producer in Italy, and urged me to use my influence with Marlon about easing the situation so they could finish the picture. Beseeching Marlon only brought Gillo more frustration. For the more I reported to Marlon that the production manager and Gillo were receiving calls from Alberto Grimaldi about delays and slowness of the production, the more Marlon did to frustrate Gillo. He was constantly leaving Cartagena.

One thing Marlon did that sent Gillo out of control was his refusal to work until all the extras were receiving the same meals he was. There were a couple of hundred Columbian extras working on that day. They received box lunches of local fare. Marlon insisted they should eat the same food as he and the Italian crew, who had their spaghetti each day. This stopped production cold. There were numerous meetings and two warring camps were set up—Brando's camp and Gillo Pontecorvo's camp. Naturally, a few more days of filming were lost while negotiations took place. The sad part was, the natives were the losers. The local fare was taken away and they were given the Italian food the cast and crew were eating. They refused to eat it; they didn't like it and wanted their own food. That created another problem. Marlon relished it. Gillo was losing it. I was making myself scarce. After this episode was settled, the warring camps remained in place. Tensions heightened.

Gillo sent word he wished to see me after work. As soon as I entered his office, he began ranting about Marlon and his actions, screaming he wasn't going to allow Marlon to drive him mad. At that moment, I felt Marlon had already succeeded.

Suddenly, a gun appeared in his hand. Evidently, the one he had been carrying on the set with the threat of killing Marlon. He advanced toward me, waving the gun up and down from my face to my upper chest, using it as punctuation while he was screaming at me in Italian and English—completely out of control. He repeatedly said he wanted me to tell Marlon he was going to kill him while he was terrifying me, pointing the gun at my face and chest. Scared as I was that the gun would go off, I kept backing toward the door, Gillo following, repeatedly threatening to kill Marlon. As I opened the door and backed out, I found my voice and became very brave. I raised my voice to match his and threatened, "If you kill Marlon, you better kill me at the same time because I'll kill you!"

And I ran down the promenade, running into Marie Rhodes and Sam Gilman, who were walking toward me. Gillo had followed me out the door and they saw that he still held the gun in his hand. I ran on, and Marie later told me Gillo had gone to the water's edge, got into a rowboat, rowed to the middle of the bay, and had fired the gun into the water. When she reported this to me, she remarked how lucky I was the gun hadn't gone off while he was menacing me with it by waving it in my face.

Gillo had threatened to kill Marlon. I had threatened Gillo. What was happening here? Where had that threat come from? What an idiot thing to do. I was becoming as crazy as the two of them. I debated telling Marlon of the threat. In the end I did. I knew my threat wasn't serious. But, I didn't know how serious Gillo was about the threat he gave me to deliver. Marlon had been aware that Gillo had been carrying a gun to the set and had been concerned.

Thereafter, Marlon insisted I go to the set with him. He reasoned that Gillo wouldn't kill him while I was around, because I had threatened to kill him. Did Marlon really think I would kill Gillo? This was getting nuttier and nuttier. But, because of my big mouth, I was forced to accompany Marlon to the location and swelter in the heat while they played make-believe under the unrelenting sun in the sugar cane fields.

There was one consolation: They were worse off than I, as I was sitting in the shade with a cool drink. Their consolation: They were being paid a heck of a lot more than I was.

This location was riddled with drugs. The drug dealers, some of whom were children about ten years old, openly approached you on the beach and asked what drugs you wanted—then named the availability of everything from marijuana to heroin.

One day, we were invited to a spaghetti dinner at Divo's apartment. Divo was a member of the Italian crew. During the cocktail hour, I was warned by the architect on the film not to eat the spaghetti—there were drugs in the spaghetti sauce. I passed on the information to Marlon, he disregarded it. His choice. Also at the table, joints were lit up and passed around. There must have been 12 people present, all Italians except me and Marlon. It wasn't too long before everyone was out of control; the place was bedlam. These Italians, when not on drugs, were quite exuberant and loud. The spaghetti sauce heightened their exuberance.

The apartment was on the fourth floor. Divo had the window wide open in the dining area. One of the "high" guests was leaning out the window, exclaiming about the million stars. Marlon joined him at the window, sat on the sill, and bent back looking skyward. I was sitting near the window. Marlon was laughing and exclaiming in wonderment about the millions of stars so near when suddenly, he leaned further backward, his legs went up in the air and were following the rest of his body hanging out the window. I grabbed and caught his legs, preventing him from falling. I cried out for someone to help me haul him in as I was unable to, since I wasn't getting any help from Marlon, who, not realizing the peril he was in, was still marveling at the heavens. The architect who warned me about the spaghetti sauce was near, trying to calm down a girl who was having a bad reaction to whatever drug was in the spaghetti. He saw my predicament and hastened to help me pull Marlon back into the room. Marlon was struggling and was unaware as to why we were wrapped around him on the floor beneath the window. The architect said he would take care of Marlon if I would look after the girl. By now, she had run screaming hysterically out of the apartment, and when I reached her, she was standing on the wide concrete rail, ready to jump off the gallery. I dragged her down, but my arms were tired from the struggle with Marlon and I was having trouble holding her as she was fighting me. The architect fortunately showed up, assured me Marlon was being cared for by one of his men, who was not drugged. Not to worry, he would take Marlon home.

He and I couldn't control the girl and she ran away from us shrieking. We chased and caught her before she could try to jump again. By now, she thought we were trying to do her harm, when all we were attempting to do was get her struggling body into the elevator. It was a small elevator and she pummeled us all the way to the lobby. He held her while I ran out to the street to hail a taxi.

In the taxi, she still wasn't aware we were helping her. Even though we were all friends, she thought she was being abducted. She continued to fight us while we tried to convince the taxi driver we were friends and meant her no harm. We brought her into our hotel; she still resisting all the way. As we didn't have the key to her room, we struggled to the architect's room where she stayed while he suffered through a sleepless night.

I didn't get any sleep either; I was too battered. I was also afraid of the nightmares and "what ifs" that might follow the Brando episode. I picked up a paperback and read the remainder of the night away.

As I relive the evening, I still feel certain that Marlon would have fallen to his death that night. He did not remember any of the evening's occurrences, even when confirmed by the architect. Therefore, as far as he was concerned, it never happened; he went blithely on, dismissing my admonitions to be careful.

There were many other situations not including drugs that occurred on the location. But I was not staying with Marlon. I opted to stay at Hotel Caribe, thereby having some respite from the madness. Nevertheless, the Cartagena location was one that I couldn't wait to leave.

Marlon flew home for a visitation with Christian. On his return, as he was boarding the plane at Los Angeles Airport, he asked the hostess if this was the plane to Havana. She reported the incident. Marlon was immediately removed from the plane and held in custody until his lawyer had him sprung. This was at the height of the plane hijacking scare. Marlon was the one who got the scare. He phoned me. I had to break the news to the production manager that Marlon was detained in the States.

Gillo was furious when he heard of the incident. Marlon didn't take the brunt of his fury. As usual, it was me. I was again asked to see Gillo in his office where he vented his wrath upon me, screaming that Marlon only said this to miss his flight, hold up the picture, and drive him mad, which he was not going to allow to happen.

I was beginning to wonder if I were to be the one who would end up mad, dealing with all this craziness.

Marlon and I flew home on February 15th. When we were returning, I called the production office, giving our time of arrival. I hadn't consulted Marlon. I ticketed us Los Angeles-Miami-Cartagena. Marlon insisted we go Miami-Jamaica-Cartagena. We argued. He wanted to frustrate Gillo. He won. I was not talking to him. We landed in Jamaica. He loaded our bags into a taxi and instructed the taxi driver to take us to the best hotel. We had no reservations, but he assured me they'd believe him when he'd say his secretary made them. The ploy worked. Especially when he mused that maybe we were in the wrong hotel. They were very apologetic about the misplaced reservations.

"We've never been to Jamaica together. Isn't it beautiful," Marlon rhapsodized. I couldn't see beautiful. I was seeing red. I had to call the production office again and tell them we were in Jamaica. I didn't speak or understand Italian, but I knew that what was almost bursting my eardrums were words not spoken to ladies. I also had to tell them we couldn't leave until the next day, and I'd call with the time of our arrival. More Italian yelling in my ear. Marlon was being mischievous. He was enjoying their reaction. I was the one being screamed at. He tried to convince me they were yelling at him—and he wasn't upset, so why should I be?

We were crossing the lobby after checking in. Coming toward us was the movie actress, Dorothy McGuire. She and Marlon were acquainted and greeted each other warmly. Marlon introduced me as "Alice" and then nonchalantly put his arm around my shoulder and drew me close. He told her we were on our way to Cartagena, but decided to stop by Jamaica a few days for a little R & R before resuming filming. His delivery of rest and relaxation made me want to kick him. After we walked on, I said, "Thanks for not saying 'This is my secretary.' She might forget Alice, but she'd remember meeting you in Jamaica with your secretary, and she'd really think I was your latest squeeze." He laughed and said, "She's thinking it anyway."

Well, he made sure of it. With all that I had to take in Cartagena, I wasn't very receptive to Marlon's mischief-making at my expense. But this was only the beginning. Marlon said he was going to take a nap. That freed me until dinner. I played tourist and went shopping. I returned in better humor.

That evening, Marlon and I dined at the hotel. Marlon requested a secluded table. He immediately began behaving as if we were on a romantic date. It started when the waiter came by to take our drink order. "Sweetheart, what would you like to drink? Sweetheart, would you like some champagne?" He was dripping sweetness. I decided I'd have a rum drink, and so did he.

Marlon drank as if he was downing a glass of water. He did not sip drinks. He ordered another round. I had only sipped one third of my drink. Before we received our first course, he was on his third drink and I had two lined up. The waiter was hovering and, before Marlon could order another round, I replaced his glass with one of my full ones. He was drinking his and mine. He then ordered a bottle of wine with our entrée. He proceeded to gulp that. I again sipped mine.

All through this he was sweethearting me to death. I decided to play along when the waiters would come by. If he was sweethearting me, I was out-darling him. Whenever Marlon and I had gone out socially and I saw him drinking, I would only have one alcoholic beverage because I'd have to take care of him by the end of the evening. This evening was no different. He was so engrossed in his seduction scenario, he didn't notice that I wasn't drinking drink for drink. I must confess something: I had a great capacity for liquor. When challenged, I could drink anyone under the table. Of course, I sometimes became inebriated. But not this night.

When we had walked through the tropical grounds to the restaurant, we had passed a wishing well surrounded by exotic flowers filling the night air with fragrance. Now, on return from the restaurant, as we neared the wishing well, a huge yellow moon hung above, bathing the path in moonlight. What a night for romance! And here I was, weaving along the path, linking a staggering, drunken sex symbol, movie star.

Life wasn't fair.

This man didn't know he was drunk. He thought he was a sexy, romantic movie star. "Sweetheart, let's stop by the wishing well." I propped him up next to the well. He began to extol the beauty of the night, the silence, the fragrance. He was on a roll. Then he said, "Sweetheart, in all this world what's one thing you'd wish for?" I answered I couldn't think of one thing at the moment and asked what he would wish for. Big mistake. He wished that I'd love him enough to let him make love to me.

In all the years we've known each other, he's only kissed me on the cheek. Now, as he was romancing, he was drunkenly swaying forward, off balance, so I neared to prevent him from falling. I knew I'd never be able to lift him if he went down. He took this as my succumbing to his romantic ramblings and reached out, clasping me in his arms, and clumsily proceeded to try finding my lips to kiss me. I was trying to keep us balanced. I pushed away, this was ridiculous. I started to giggle at the absurdity of it. And then he joined in the laughter.

Finally, he said, "What are we laughing at?"

I replied, "I don't know what you're laughing at, but I'm laughing at you. You've been romancing me all evening. A few rum drinks and a night under a Jamaican moon are not going to get me into your bed. You're a great act, Brando."

We started to laugh again and he proceeded to tell me how unromantic I was. He couldn't accept that his plan to seduce me in Jamaica was failing. He may have been intoxicated, but I could sense he felt rejected. I was soon to find out how right I was.

I linked him back to his suite, into the bedroom. I noted the bed was a very high four-poster with a two-step bed stool to reach it. Marlon would never make it alone. I told him to undress and I'd help him into the bed. I sat down, and instead of going to the bathroom to undress, he sat too. Then suggested we call his housekeeper.

"Marlon, it's late, we have to catch a plane in the morning. Let's call from Cartagena."

"No, I want to call her now." He picked up his telephone book and phoned her number. He asked how she was and then proceeded to tell her about the film, and finally, he got to the reason for the call. He said we were in Jamaica and were just in from dinner. Then, it came. "Do you know what Alice said to me at dinner? She said she thought I was f--king you."

I couldn't believe what I was hearing. We had never mentioned her at dinner. I had said no such thing. I didn't know what she was saying. Marlon said no more, he was listening. Our eyes were locked.

He said, "She's right here, you can tell her yourself." And he handed me the phone. I told her I had said no such thing. She didn't believe me. She'd rather believe Marlon, even though we had shared many laughs at the lies we heard Marlon tell to girls through the many years she had worked for Marlon as his housekeeper. I was terribly hurt—and couldn't even get mad at Marlon because he had to satisfy his deep-seated desire for revenge.

I say I wasn't mad at him, but inwardly I must have been, because, as I was listening, Marlon disrobed. After I hung up, as if nothing dreadful had happened, he asked if I would help him up the steps into bed. He lurched to the steps, and as he started up the first step, I nudged the stairs with my foot and he fell back towards me. I side-stepped and he sat down hard on his butt.

I said, "Good night, Marlon," and left him sitting on the floor, saying to my back, "Aren't you going to help me up?"

Nothing was ever said between us about the night the next morning. But years later, Marlon brought up the night, "If I wasn't drunk that night in Jamaica, would you and I…"

I didn't let him finish. "No way," I said.

The next day we were informed there was no space on any plane from Jamaica to Cartagena for a few days. I called the production office again. They were not amused. I was informed that Marlon was scheduled to be on the set that night and I was to get him there. Marlon and I conferred; we had to exert every effort to leave. We weren't getting any results by phone, so I suggested Marlon go to the airport and throw his weight around. He agreed to go. I admonished him, since he got us into this, not to come back without a flight.

He returned. All flights out were booked, so he had chartered a plane. I called the production office again and informed them we'd be leaving in an hour. We checked out and went to the airport.

To my amazement he had chartered, I believe it was either a Boeing 702 or 727 for the two of us. Well, I had told him not to return without a flight. On board I thought he'd sit in first class, so I took a seat in the tail end while he was flirting and charming the air hostesses and steward. Then, he sauntered down the aisle and plopped next to me. I teased, "Mar, with the hundred seats, do you have to sit right next to me?" His reply was typical Brando, "I'm paying for the plane, I'll sit anywhere I want." Then he gave me the farm-boy routine. He looked around and, shaking his head in wonderment, remarked, "A farm boy who struck it rich, can you believe it?" The steward with refreshments and the hostesses, who also joined us, ended our conversation. He made some new fans during the short flight to Cartagena.

Marlon returned to work welcomed by all except Gillo. Marlon continued to ignore him and also continued to leave the location at every opportunity. During March, he left Cartagena three times and in early April departed for Beverly Hills to spend Easter vacation with the children.

Gillo, in the meantime, was being pressured by the producer in Italy to finish the picture, so there were tense working conditions upon Marlon's return. And Marlon, knowing he was frustrating Gillo, added to the pressure. He had stopped production earlier for days over food for extras, now he disagreed with Gillo over an interpretation of a scene. He not only left the set in Cartagena, he left for home. There were no flights out of Cartagena, so he drove two hours or so to Barranquilla to catch a plane for the States.

The Italian film crew rounded up transportation and followed him. It was an airport scene to be remembered, for one of the highly emotional Italians had brought a crucifix with him. Amidst everyone surrounding Marlon, loudly begging him to return to the set, was this man on bent knee, with the crucifix extended, beseeching Marlon in the name of all that was Holy to "pleeese come back."

Marlon sprung for lunch and wine for everyone and allowed them to escort him back to Cartagena.

Another memorable moment came en route. The caravan stopped as Marlon had to relieve himself after all the drinking, and it was one time I longed for a camera. If I had had one, I would have a shot of Marlon urinating alongside a jungle road with a soldier in full garb, Uzi ready, standing guard shoulder to shoulder—and not a rebel in sight.

Marlon hated the heat and location filming in Columbia. And the necessary security. There was a guard at his house, a guard with a machine gun in the car, who drove with him to the location or when he went to dinner at night, guards walking around the perimeter of the set.

There were also barriers at each end of town. We were told not to go beyond the barriers without a guard. You went at your own risk. Columbia was not a safe place—especially for Americans.

I returned from location one day and discovered sand bags stacked on each side of the entrance of the hotel. In the center of each stack, a soldier was positioned with a machine gun pointing at the car as I exited. I walked into the lobby—more soldiers with machine guns positioned around the doorways.

I continued to the new section of the hotel, where my room was located, and started up the stairs. Three soldiers were on the top landing, pointing machine guns down at me commanding, "Halt." I said I was a guest in the hotel and my room was at the top of the stairs. They didn't understand me. I was detained at the point of the guns. One of the soldiers left and returned with another soldier who spoke passable English. I explained who I was. He demanded identification, which I turned over. He checked it, then said I would be allowed into my room.

I learned that a government official and his entourage had taken over the floor and that an important meeting was taking place, but since I was Marlon's assistant, and American, I was allowed to stay. Everyone else had been evicted. And for two days, I was greeted with three machine guns pointed at me as I started for the stairs, chanting loudly, "Alice, Alice, Alice."

This location terrorized me as I have always feared guns. I couldn't believe what I was going through—hand guns, machine guns, all pointed at me, and riding in a car with a gun-toting soldier. I couldn't wait to leave.

A short time later, we were notified that the production would shut down the following day and we were admonished not to go outdoors. We were to stay in our rooms and off the beach until notified.

A coup had been planned to take place the next day. All stores in the old town were closed and shuttered. Everything was in lock-down. I couldn't believe we were going to be in the midst of a coup. What next? A notice came to our rooms at the hotel to close our drapes and stay away from the plate glass windows. There was a strange silence as the hotel closed down.

The next morning I awoke to loud talking and laughter coming from the pool dining room, which was below and left of my balcony. I peeked through the slit in my closed drapes and was overwhelmed by the sight of the Stars and Stripes flying over a warship with American sailors aboard. And, as I pulled back my drapes further, I discovered the noise from the pool dining room was made by sailors from the ship, enjoying breakfast ashore.

There was no coup that day. America had shown her colors.

But Cartagena, Columbia was not a safe place at that time. I had been informed that the guards around Marlon were for his protection, because the Columbian government was protecting him from kidnappers. American men on the set, standing around with the Italian crew, were pointed out to me as being CIA. One, who I'm certain followed me from Cartagena to Bogota, helped me to leave the country when I was having trouble doing so at the Bogota airport.

Soon afterward, the film had to shut down. It was because of money problems and evaluation of the film they had shot. Marlon opted to go home instead of staying in Cartagena. Before he left, he wanted to throw a party for the cast and crew and asked me if I would try to have it at an old fort. I consulted the production office to determine if they would help obtain permission to have the party at the fort. I surmised that since they were spending a great deal of money, they'd have some clout. But they informed me they couldn't even get permission to film there.

Undaunted, I learned the names of all the city officials and made the round of their offices. And throwing Marlon Brando's name around like confetti, I invited all to be Marlon's guest at the party Marlon was having at the fort. On my rounds, I discovered there was a big bash at Hotel Caribe on the same night for beauty contestants, and the officials were committed to attend. I didn't let that deter me. I told them they were all invited to Marlon's party, too. Then I rushed to the Hotel Caribe and gave a blanket invitation to the Miss Columbia contestants who would then be vying for Miss Universe.

And a few hours later, I called the official who was in charge of the fort and told him Marlon didn't realize he required formal permission to throw a party at the fort, and could he use his influence to obtain permission for Marlon. I was sooo surprised when he said the fort was under his jurisdiction, and, of course, Mr. Brando could have his party at the fort. After thanking him profusely on Marlon's behalf, I was on my way to make arrangements for catering, flowers, a band, etc.

I went to the best restaurant and told the manager that Marlon was giving a party for the cast and crew, the government officials, and beauty contest contestants. Since no one would be eating at his restaurant, would he like to close and cater the affair? And, oh yes, could he please take care of flowers? He was wonderful. He took care of everything.

I knew everyone wanted a photo of Marlon because the cast and crew had been requesting one. I arranged for a photographer and instructed him to take everyone's photo.

That night, I requested the guests to stand near or next to Marlon at some time during the evening, and the photographer would take their picture. I also made certain all the officials would meet Marlon and have a photo taken with him. Needless to say, Marlon's enemy for months, the director, Gillo Pontecorvo, is shown in a photo with his wife and Marlon. Both are grinning like the very best of friends.

I had Marlon's bongos brought to the fort hoping he'd keep his promise to me that he'd entertain, because I couldn't hire a headliner and get them to Columbia in the short time I had to arrange the party. And Marlon obliged by playing solo, and also with the band, which thrilled them. Come to think of it, I guess I did get a headliner to entertain.

Brando.

Along with Marlon's security, who accompanied him wherever he went, the government officials with their guards; and the beauty contest officials and contestants with their guards, I also had to arrange for security for all the other guests, so there was a small army of soldiers on guard, cradling guns during the entire evening.

The next day, cast and crew and all officials said it was the best film party they had ever attended. Of course, all end of filming parties are remembered the next day as "the best." And all were photographed with Marlon. The government officials received their photographs, as did the beauty contestants who attended the party before going on to their bash at the Hotel Caribe.

Marlon confided that he was not returning to Cartagena and asked me to arrange for an animal, whose Spanish name I don't remember, but which looks like a raccoon, to be shipped to America. I made all the arrangements, paid for shots, cage, quarantine quarters, official papers, etc. I had to stay behind until the animal was out of quarantine and shipped.

Marlon had hired a secretary for the Cartagena location, who was living at the leased house with him, and she had responsibility for the house. She wished to leave when Marlon did and wanted me to close the house. I felt it was her responsibility, and since I had far too many other things to attend to before leaving Cartagena, I politely refused. She complained to Marlon. He called to say he couldn't understand why I was being mean to her, as she had led him to believe. I therefore proceeded to list all I had to do, starting with the animal who had a week more in quarantine before I could get him out. The quarantine had been extended, and I had to arrange payment for his food and board for another week. And, I reminded Marlon, I had to arrange boarding school for the young boy whose mother gave him to me when I had arrived.

Marlon was aware I had been caring for the child for several months. My architect friend was kind enough to allow him to share his room, as my room only had one bed and I didn't want him sleeping on the floor, as he wanted. His mother had also sent me a slightly older brother, but I obtained a job for him with the film company and he was on his own. The mother and father also moved to town from their island home and I had arranged for them to lunch each day with the extras on the film. Now I had to see to their welfare before I departed, since the film company was leaving.

Mosquito, as I called him, was a very bright, small child of ten. He had no schooling, but he was clever, as most children are who survive by their wits. I wanted to arrange for his education before I left. I met with the priest at a Catholic boarding school and he attempted to find a spot for Mosquito. In the meantime, I told Marlon, I had to get papers signed by his parents, so he could go to the school and board there. I had to hire an interpreter to accompany me to obtain their permission and arrange to pay them a weekly sum, because they would be losing the income Mosquito earned on the street while he attended school.

Added to this, I informed Marlon there was another issue I was dealing with that I hadn't wanted to bother him about. I had received a call one evening from a man telling me he had information that would be of concern to me and Marlon. He wanted 1,000 dollars for the information. I told him that I would not pay him 1,000 dollars and that I was not interested in any information he had. Further, I would not speak to Marlon about it. He phoned every evening lowering his asking price, insisting it was of great interest to us. After relating this, I asked Marlon if he was interested in finding out what the man was trying to sell.

He replied, "You handle it." Then said, "Ali, take care of the house. She doesn't know what she's doing and she keeps bothering me."

I asked him if this was his way of telling me she would be leaving when he did. The answer was yes. That left me no choice. I capitulated, "Have her take care of everything she can before you leave, and I'll take care of what remains."

After Marlon had departed, I went to the house. All his personal effects were still there. I had to pack his bongos and electronic equipment, personal items and clothes, etc. His "secretary" hadn't arranged for the house to be cleaned. She hadn't paid the housekeeper. She hadn't taken inventory. And, an angry housekeeper informed me, she had sent the owners baccarat crystal glassware as well as dinnerware to California.

Later on when I would arrive back home, I would discover that she had put the crystal and dinnerware in a cardboard box, without packing it individually, and everything was broken. I paid for the damaged goods, but the owner was devastated because the set of glassware and dinnerware were wedding presents and had great sentimental meaning to her because they were from her and her husband's family. I understood how she felt, and sympathized, but could only offer money and heartfelt apologies.

Marlon was right, his secretary didn't know what she was doing and I was glad the location was over, so I wouldn't have anything further to do with her. There had been more than one confrontation in Cartagena and I was happy to be home and rid of her unpleasantness.

In the meantime, the man was still phoning me at the hotel about the information. Finally, he realized I was not going to buy his information at any price. He then revealed he worked for the government quarantine department. The animal Marlon had bought, paying a large sum, did not exist. There was no animal. The shots, the cages, four weeks of quarantine, food, official papers, plus the added week, were for a non-existing animal. I asked what I would have been told when I arrived to pick up the animal the next day. He said I would have been told it had died during the night. I asked his name and told him to stop by the hotel desk in the morning and pick up an envelope I would leave for him—and thanked him for the information. Before we terminated the call, I realized from our conversation that, though I had never seen him, he knew who I was. He may have seen me when I brought money for the food, etc., to quarantine headquarters for the non-existing animal since that's where he worked. I may even have been giving him the money.

When Marlon arrived home, he notified the *Quemada* production office that he refused to return to Cartagena to finish the film. The film location was changed to Morocco. By now, I had had enough of being in the middle of the madness between Marlon and Gillo Pontecorvo. I refused to go to Marrakesh with Marlon, no matter what he promised.

I was well aware of the availability of drugs in Marrakech. Because my sister, Mary, was living in Spain and visited with friends who lived in Marrakech, I had learned about the drug situation from her. I didn't need a repeat of Cartagena and drugs.

Since I opted out, Marlon hired Miiko Taka, a friend, who was the female lead in *Sayonara,* to go to Morocco in my stead. Marlon let me know what a wonderful time they were having and what I was missing. Miiko also called and asked about my favorite color because Marlon wanted to buy me a caftan. She had good taste, she purchased a beautiful blue one encrusted with gold threads, which Marlon brought home at the end of the picture.

In the first part of 1976, Marlon actively tried to get an Indian film—*Wounded Knee*—produced. He had many meetings with Jay Kanter and Indian representatives Dennis Banks and Mark Banks. But surprise of surprises, Gillo Pontecorvo, who had threatened to kill Marlon, showed up at the house. Marlon had contacted him and asked him to direct the Indian film. Gillo arrived from Italy to meet with Marlon and then departed to return in April for further meetings, before going to the Pine Ridge Indian Reservation with Mark Banks.

After the hostility and hatred and murderous threats Marlon and Gillo exhibited during the filming of *Quemada,* and Marlon doing everything he could think of to frustrate Gillo, one would find it hard to believe they would team up to discuss doing another film—the Wounded Knee project. What was Gillo thinking? But such was Marlon's power of persuasion, he seduced Gillo into coming to Hollywood. And further, Marlon the Actor greeted Gillo like his very, very best friend.

As with Ray Stark after *Reflections in a Golden Eye,* Marlon didn't remember, or else put out of his mind, everything except his desires or needs of the moment, and he treated his former adversaries as if nothing had happened.

* * * * *

While Marlon was in Morocco, I was relaxing, lounging around Newport Beach, recovering from all the stressful events of the past several months in Cartagena. When Marlon returned to the States at the end of filming, I wasn't at his house. I left word for him that I was at the Beach. I knew the time he usually needed to get over jet lag, therefore, I returned to Mulholland Drive a week later.

I walked into my office—my nemesis from Cartagena was sitting at my desk, surrounded by a half dozen photos; her family, I assumed. She had taken over.

I dropped my purse and strode down the hall to Marlon's domain.

Marlon was dressed, lying on the bed. He was waiting for me; he knew me well enough to know we'd cross swords about her. I didn't lose any time. Without any greeting, quietly, I asked him if that girl in the office was his new "secretary."

Translated, his "in-house." He said yes, he had hired her and, "She'll be working here."

"Well, then I won't be," I flatly stated in a conversational tone of voice.

He bristled and said, in measured tones, "Don't try to tell me who I can hire."

Still softly, I said, "I'm not telling you who you can hire. I'm telling you I'm not going to work in the same house."

He wanted an argument. He had prepared for it. Instead, I started out of the room.

"Are you telling me who I can f--k?" he countered, his voice rising.

I didn't want him to have the last word, so I turned, looked him in the eye, and calmly said, "I'm not going to argue with a hard c--k."

And I walked out of the room. Silence followed me. I stunned him with my remark. That was the way he talked. Not me. I picked up my purse where I had left it, walked out of the house, got into my car, and drove to Newport Beach.

And I was not coming back.

I quit.

I knew Marlon's pattern with women. Two or three days—a week was rare—then he grew restless and asked them to leave because he "wanted to be alone." Translated, he desired another girl. I knew she wouldn't last long. He knew my pattern, too. I'd stay away a week, then he felt it safe to call. But this time, he didn't know I had had enough. I wasn't coming back. Cartagena and *Quemada* was too much. As was his behavior.

A few weeks passed. Then he phoned, "Hi, sweetheart!"

I cut him off, "Go f--k yourself!" and hung up.

I was still talking his language. Language he'd understand. He'd give me a few days to cool off, then call again. Every time he called, I told him what he could do and hung up. I couldn't speak to him. I had had it. I was burned out.

He then had several of his friends call on his behalf every few days. He importuned his friend, Stella Adler, who was a house guest at the time, to call. I still refused to speak to him.

Days later she again called saying, "Marlon's locked in his room. He hasn't been out of bed for a week. He's not talking to anyone." Her entreaties didn't move me.

The third time Stella called on his behalf, the message was, "Marlon is dying, you've got to come back."

Dying, indeed. The man had no shame.

I stayed with my mother in Newport Beach. I worked at my sister Boots's museum, Movieland of the Air, at the Orange County Airport. Later I had a floral business, Daffodils and Dandelions.

After all the hang-ups, Marlon refrained from calling me. Periodically, he called my sisters, Boots and Marty, and talked for hours. He also continued to send me a weekly check. Checks which I cashed, and which my mother made it known she disapproved my accepting since I said I had quit.

I didn't call to thank Marlon for the money as he thought I would. Manners be damned. I couldn't talk to him. I had had enough of Brando.

I went on with my life after Brando, involved in the community and my business, as well as spending more time with my family and friends. It was a life completely without stress. I enjoyed the freedom of making decisions for myself only, and no one else. I had left the madness and chaos behind. And shed the burden of responsibility for another. I had broken the ties that bound.

I had blithely moved on, unaware of what destiny had in store. Events in my future, beyond my control, were being formulated and being put in play. I was to find that the ties that bound had not been broken, but had just been stretched—to their limit.

For Marlon wasn't idle, he had time to lie on his bed and stare at the ceiling and plot. And plan. It took him quite some time, a few years, to figure out a plan to bring me back. And he set it in motion.

* * * * *

Out of the blue, Marlon called me. Before I could hang up, he quickly said, "It's Christian. Don't hang up, I have to talk to you about Christian." He proceeded to tell me he had gone to court to obtain custody. The judge had refused to give him or Anna custody of Christian, deeming both of them unfit. The judge asked him if there was anyone he could recommend to the court as guardian for Christian, and Marlon said, "Alice Marchak." The court investigated me.

I recalled my mother asking me if I was in any trouble with Brando and was hiding out with her. I had assured her I was in no trouble and was not hiding out. I had inquired why she asked. It seemed the neighbors had told her there had been an investigator from court asking about me. I had been puzzled, but had dismissed it.

Now, Marlon had solved the mystery. Then he floored me by revealing he had been notified that I, the court, and Marlon were given custody of Christian. I was aghast at what he had done without my permission. He asked me to come up to the house to discuss it.

It developed that indeed the judge had made me 12-year-old Christian's guardian until he was 21 years of age, along with the court and Marlon, who was to provide for us and give us living quarters at his home. Marlon confessed that he had told the judge I was living at his home from time to time, notwithstanding the fact that I hadn't stayed there in a couple of years.

I returned to Mulholland Drive, not as personal assistant, but as Christian's guardian, with the understanding that the child, Christian, came first. Marlon second.

Again, Marlon reiterated what was his was mine and I could have anything I wanted. He would have given me the moon if I had asked for it, but I didn't even want the stars, one at a time. By now I imagine Marlon felt he could promise me anything with impunity, as I had never asked him for any financial assistance. Nor anything else.

As for me, I merely called Brown and Kraft, his business managers, and told them I was back working for Marlon. I didn't receive any more money than I had been receiving two years or so ago, nor compensation for the added responsibility of Christian's guardianship. Nor did Marlon name any amount of money as salary—he just considered "what's mine is yours," and if I needed any money or wanted anything, I could call for it as he did. I never did.

I informed my family that I was now Christian's guardian. Everyone else just assumed I had returned as Marlon's personal assistant, and I never corrected their assumption. As time went on, everyone close knew I was Christian's guardian.

It was at this time Marlon asked me to legally change my name to Brando. His rationale: I would be living at his house with Christian per court order, and since I was now his guardian, we should all have the same name. Suffice to say I laughed him out of this absurd idea.

I made a big mistake when I told Marlon that Christian would come first and he'd come second. Marlon being second to anyone was a blow to his ego he'd never tolerate. I didn't think his possessiveness would extend to his child. Through the ensuing years, I learned otherwise. I walked a tightrope in so far as showing any affection for Christian or any of the other children. He would make Christian suffer, along with me, if I expressed what he thought was the slightest favoritism. Of course, the child was unaware of this. But when Marlon was out of town and Christian and I were alone, Christian was carefree. He lived in a different atmosphere.

*****

Marlon received many unsolicited scripts and novels through the mail. One day, a book arrived that I had heard about. It was *The Godfather* with a note from the author, Mario Puzo. I took it to Marlon. He asked what it was.

"It's *The Godfather,* a new novel about a mafia don," I said as I handed him the book.

He didn't even look at it; he tossed it back to me. "I'm not a mafia godfather, I'm not going to glorify the mafia," he muttered.

That weekend, I took the book home and read it. I brought it back to the house, but didn't take it to Marlon. I merely told Marlon that I had read it and that he should, too. Ordinarily, Marlon did not read novels. If he did any reading, it was non-fiction. So, naturally, he declined. He wasn't the least bit interested in *The Godfather*.

But I was interested. I knew Paramount had bought the book and was searching for someone to play the part of the head of the mafia—the Don. The part I wanted Marlon to play. Thereafter, each time I heard someone mentioned for the part of the Don, I brought it to Marlon's attention. He listened, but ignored it.

Till one day he said, "Maybe I should call and thank Puzo for thinking of me for the part—and for sending me the book." I got Puzo's number fast before Marlon changed his mind about calling him. But that call didn't change Marlon's mind.

Next, I nonchalantly dropped the news that Laurence Olivier was testing for the part.

"Laurence Olivier!" he sneered, unbelieving. "He *can't* play a Mafia Don."

I had finally caught his attention with Olivier and gotten a reaction. He was now interested in discussing *The Godfather*. I had really worked him over for a few weeks, but now I was no longer a pest; he was not glaring at me when I dropped *The Godfather* into our conversation.

Who first contacted Marlon from Paramount? Robert Evans or Francis Coppola? Had they contacted him before he surprised me by what happened next?

Marlon came into my office and asked if there was any black shoe polish in the house. I told him where it was. About a half hour later he buzzed me and asked if I'd come to his room. I walked in, and there was Marlon's version of a mafia don sitting in a chair. I burst out laughing. He had darkened his eyebrows and lined his eyes, and the black shoe polish glistened on his hair that was slicked back. He asked me what I thought. I laughed and said I expected him to jump up and tango me around the room. I didn't know if he was Rudolph Valentino or a gigolo. He laughed, too.

I returned to my office, and again he called and asked me to his room. This time, when I entered, he was George Raft, fedora, top coat, and all. When he took off the hat, his hair was still slicked back close to his head, but not quite the patent leather look.

"What do you think?"

"The slick hair has to go. The hat's not a bad addition. Keep the hat." He still looked like an old movie idol gigolo rather than a gangster. But he was thinking and evolving.

What next? Edward G. Robinson?

A few days passed. I was still giving him updates on who was being tested for the Don. I was naming every male on the "A" list of stars. I didn't feel bad about doing it because, like Scarlett O'Hara and Rhett Butler, when every publicist in town was getting the stars they represented considered for the parts in the press, I was now touting every star I could think of to Marlon, saying they were being considered for the part. I was one busy girl.

Then one day he said he wanted me to look at some photographs with him. We sat in the living room and he began to pass me photos of different men. I asked who they were. He said he had asked Francis to get him some photos of the Mafia. I knew who Francis was as I had been following all the news about *The Godfather* and updating Marlon. This was the first time he mentioned he had spoken to Francis Coppola, who was to direct. Surprise! Surprise! Marlon had been busy, too.

We perused the photos of mafia members that had been snapped on the street, in cars, in restaurants. After we had gone through the stack a few times, we concluded the Don should be an ordinary looking man you passed on the street—it could be himself. That's when the germ of the idea to start with himself, as he would look when he aged, began, and then Marlon morphed into the Don.

We heard Paramount's New York office had nixed Marlon. They remembered the trouble he had given them on *One-Eyed Jacks,* in which he acted and directed. His past was coming back to haunt him.

I don't know whether Marlon had called Francis or whether Francis had called Marlon, but on the evening of January 7th there was a meeting which included Al Ruddy, the producer.

Marlon disclosed that he was going to test for the Don. I wasn't surprised. For by now, he was trying different accents on me without telling me what he was doing. I was told to "keep it under your hat."

Early one morning, Francis Coppola arrived with two crew men. Phillip Rhodes, Marlon's makeup man, arrived. Marlon was still asleep. The night before he had asked me to wake him when they arrived. I brought Marlon coffee and managed to scrambled some eggs for the others. In the meantime, Marlon had showered and Phillip went to his room with a makeup kit. I left Francis, the cameraman, and soundman waiting for Marlon in the living room.

When next I walked into the living room, Marlon was sitting on the sofa and they were making a test for the Don. Marlon looked toward me and said, "will you get me a cigar?" I thought he should have asked for a "stogie." Either way, he was out of luck. This was a non-smoking house.

Marlon was only 47 years old. I noticed he looked older. Phillip had aged him and put Kleenex in Marlon's mouth along his jaw bone to give him jowls. There was not the slightest hint of black, shoe-polished, slicked-back hair.

Robert Evans, studio head, and Marlon met late afternoon on the 14th at Paramount studio after *The Godfather* test had been made.

It was only after the fact we became aware of what happened with the screen test. Robert Evans evidently liked it enough to bring it to the Paramount New York executives who had wanted nothing to do with Brando. At his behest, they looked at the test, and they, too, saw the Godfather. Marlon's lawyer, Norman Garey, took over from there. I happily stepped aside. I was only interested in Marlon getting the role Mario Puzo wrote for him. And we both wanted him to play.

Marlon liked Francis Coppola and I don't believe Marlon tried to frustrate him as he did other directors. No, it was Francis and the studio that were having problems. As Marlon related, the studio wanted to fire Francis. He told me why, but the only thing I remember of that particular time was Francis punching in a door, knocking it off the hinges.

The reason Marlon confided in me was that Marlon had threatened to leave if Francis was fired and had told Francis so. He feared I would think he would never again work at Paramount if they were both told to "take a walk." He also knew how much I had invested in getting him interested in playing the Godfather, and he wanted to assure me the studio wouldn't fire both of them. They didn't. And the rest is history.

The Godfather was being readied for a big premiere in New York City. Publicity was heralding the opening. Robert Evans, Paramount studio head, contacted me in Paris, where Marlon was filming *Last Tango in Paris*. He said Life magazine and Newsweek were featuring Marlon on their cover as The Godfather. And further, Time magazine would give him a cover if Marlon gave them an interview. Robert wanted the covers of "the Big Three" for *The Godfather*.

I remarked that I doubted Marlon would do it, as he hated Time magazine because they had written something about him that had offended and evidently hurt him deeply. He had never forgiven them and had refused all interviews in the past. But I told Bob I'd tell Marlon about his request and get back.

I relayed the message to Marlon. There was a resounding, "No." I phoned Bob, then asked if he'd give me a day or so to try again. I did and received the same answer. Bob then proposed to give Marlon a percentage if he would grant the interview. I thought that might be a talking point for me and told Bob I'd get back to him. I had to wait for the right moment because Marlon was having personal problems with *Last Tango in Paris*. I finally approached him and found him receptive. Marlon would grant the interview to Time. And as he was walking away, in an aside to me, he said, "You can have the percentage."

Bob went to work and made arrangements for the Time reporter to travel to Paris for the interview.

Bob and I spoke several times and set the time and date. It was to be early evening, as Marlon was filming *Last Tango in Paris* during the day.

The day of the interview, I was out shopping and passed a flower shop showcasing the most beautiful tulips. I was so enthralled I purchased three dozen different pinks, peach, mauve—glorious colors. Upon returning to the apartment, I arranged most in a large bowl and centered them on the coffee table in the salon where Marlon was to be interviewed that evening by the Time reporter.

Marlon was at his most gracious. The reporter was put at ease and spent a few minutes testing his tape recorder. Satisfied, he positioned it on the coffee table in front of Marlon. They sat on opposite sides of the table. I sat at one end.

The tulips were beautiful the way some draped over the bowl, and from time to time I gazed at them, marveling at the different hues while Marlon was being interviewed. The interview wound down, Marlon continued to talk to the reporter. After a short interval, the reporter reached across the tulips to retrieve the recorder which Marlon had picked up and now handed to him. Then Marlon escorted him to the door.

"That wasn't so bad, was it?" I observed after he left.

"Not at all, I enjoyed it," Marlon responded lightly and withdrew to his room.

The following day, I received a distressing call from Bob Evans. Something had happened; the tape was blank. My heart sank. Bob wanted to know if the Time reporter could return and redo the interview. Stunned, I said I'd call back.

I accosted Marlon. "What did you do? And when did you do it?"

I repeated Bob's call. He laughed loudly, he was overjoyed. He had been waiting all day to hear that he had had his revenge on Time magazine. He was very proud of himself for pulling it off. Marlon did it behind the beautiful huge bouquet of tulips. After the reporter had set up the cassette and I was playing hostess serving drinks, he had reached down and turned it off. He picked it up after the interview, flipped it on, and handed it to the Time reporter when he had reached over the tulips to retrieve it. I dreaded telling Bob Evans that Marlon would not redo the interview.

I was unhappy. I felt Marlon had used me and Bob Evans to get his revenge on Time. Marlon didn't care, he had exacted his revenge on Time after years of waiting. That's all that mattered to him. Not what he had done to me and Bob. He could care less about us.

He was happy.

Robert Evans was disappointed, but didn't lay the debacle at my feet. Instead, he big-heartedly sent me a round-trip ticket from Paris to New York City, tickets for the premiere of *The Godfather*, and paid for a week's stay at the Carlton Hotel. He also laid on a limousine to and from the theater and reception for me and my guests, Shana Alexander, Robert Loggia, and Kevin McCarthy. I was grateful for that as New York City had the biggest snow storm of the winter season, and transportation, other than limousines, to the theater was nowhere to be seen.

Marlon knew I was unhappy about being used, so he made no attempt to prevent me from leaving Paris for New York City and the premiere. If he wanted to know anything about the film from me when I returned, he'd have to ask or he could get it from the newspapers.

The only reference to the picture was one I made months later when I reminded him he owed me 50,000 dollars for a bet he lost to me on how much money *The Godfather* would make. He never paid the bet—but he remembered it as he brought it up one day and said, "Double or nothing." He was betting with me on a George Foreman prizefight. And I won. So now he owed me 100,000 dollars. He wanted to bet again; I called him a welsher and refused to bet with him. Through the years, he would bring up the money and ask me to bet "one more time." I'd tell him I only bet on sure things and when I found one, I'd bet.

Marlon died owing me that 100,000 dollars, too.

In 1992 when Marlon was going to write his autobiography, Marlon did not remember Richard Smith, a makeup man who journeyed to Cambridge, England, where Marlon was starting *The Nightcomers,* to take a cast of his face, so he could make pieces to age him for *The Godfather,* until I reminded him. He also forgot that Francis Coppola spent a week with us at Duxford Mill in story conferences and writing the screenplay of *The Godfather.* He also forgot that I had put him on a diet and he was in the best shape he had been in a long time. Then he had to be padded for his role. And, he didn't remember how happy he was he could eat again; for once he didn't have to worry about a diet while making a movie.

But when I reminded him, he did remember with great joy that he had mooned James Caan and Robert Duvall while driving through New York City streets after work. And, he remembered they had mooned back. He also remembered that he had admired and enjoyed working with, and being challenged by, both. He also remembered he liked Al Pacino and thought highly of his talent.

I spoke at great length to Mario Puzo several months before he died. During the conversation, he confirmed that he wrote *The Godfather* with Marlon in mind, and hoping Marlon would agree to play the Don he had sent the book to Marlon. In regard to Marlon portraying the Don on the screen, when Puzo brought Marlon's name up at Paramount, he said it was rejected. He had had problems at Paramount: "At one point," he remarked, "they threw me off the lot."

Mario was very amused when I related how I had worked Marlon over to get his attention and interest in playing the Godfather. He assured me Marlon had always been first choice with him to play the Don.

And though Mario was in the midst of writing a new book, he graciously extended an offer to help Marlon in any way when Marlon wrote his autobiography.

*****

A friend of mine from my Paramount studio days, Luigi Luraschi, phoned me from Rome, where he was now living and working. He called in regard to Bernardo Bertolucci, who was contemplating a movie and would like to meet with Marlon to discuss it with him, hoping to interest him in appearing in it. Luigi would produce. Because of my friendship with Luigi, Marlon agreed to meet with Bertolucci and Luigi, who would accompany him, since Bertolucci only spoke a smattering of English. Marlon was going to London and Paris in June of 1971, so I made arrangements for them to meet in Europe during that time.

While I was in the midst of arrangements for Marlon's business trip to London and Paris, I received a call from Marlon's business manager with the news that Marlon was being sued and all his funds were frozen. He was only allowed "living expenses" until the suit was settled. Marlon would have to forgo his trip to Europe.

Now I had to call Luigi Luraschi in Rome to cancel the meeting with him and Bertolucci, which I dreaded as I knew he'd be disappointed. But when I informed Marlon about his funds, it didn't deter him—Marlon was determined to make the trip as he had arranged to see French government officials in regard to Tetiaroa, his atoll.

"You figure something out. I'm going!" he declared when I told him.

And I did.

I thought of a way out of my dilemma—getting Marlon to Paris for his meeting with the French government. I called Luigi. Since he was a lawyer and would understand Marlon's predicament in regard to the lawsuit, I confided in him. And Luigi came through, all expenses would be picked up by the production company. The meeting was still on. Problem solved.

When Marlon returned from Paris after his meetings, he asked around about *The Conformist*, which Bertolucci had directed. The good reports made him open to *Last Tango*, so when Bertolucci showed up in Hollywood a few weeks later and called with a "draft" I again set a meeting with Marlon. The "draft," Bertolucci had was a several page outline, and it was written in Italian. Marlon couldn't read Italian, therefore Bertolucci again pitched his ideas for the movie. After this meeting, Marlon's interest waned. Bertolucci's trip was in vain.

At the end of July, Bertolucci was in Beverly Hills. Anita Wylie had met him and she contacted Marlon, urging him to meet with Bertolucci. Marlon resisted. Anita phoned me and asked that I press Marlon to meet with Bertolucci again. I did. He did. Marlon had four meetings with Bertolucci in regard to appearing in the untitled—not one script page—movie.

Marlon had finished *The Godfather* the first week in June and had no interest in working. He had been involved in a bitter custody battle for his son Christian and an annulment/divorce. This, along with lawsuits, taxes, lawyers' fees, security guards, investigators, several households with children, Tahiti property, and Tetiaroa were keeping him broke again. *Last Tango in Paris* was in the future. He needed a project ready to go whether he felt like working or not. He needed money.

Marlon decided to do *Child's Play*. In October we flew to New York City, where it was to be filmed. The director decided to have an entire cast reading and two weeks of rehearsal before filming. They met in a rehearsal hall. Marlon mumbled his way through the cast reading the first and second days. It was painful for me to watch as I knew he was dyslexic and was having a very bad time. After two days of trying to follow the reading of the script, Marlon announced to me he was not going to rehearsals—he could not face another day of fumbling through a reading. He informed the director he did not feel he was right for *Child's Play*. I called his lawyer, asked him to get Marlon out of his commitment, which he did. And Marlon and I returned to California.

Marlon finally decided to do *Last Tango in Paris*. And at the end of January, 1972, I left for Paris to meet with the production staff and also arrange for our housing, household help, etc., for the duration of the filming. My friend, Luigi Luraschi, was no longer the producer. Alberto Grimaldi, who had produced *Quemada*, was now the producer.

Marlon joined me the first week in February at Hotel Raphael.

* * * * *

We were again at Marlon's favorite hotel when visiting Paris, the Raphael. Before we left home, Shana Alexander, Life magazine correspondent, author, and friend of both of us, phoned, requesting an interview with Marlon. I explained we were leaving for Paris.

" I want to make a call. Let me get back to you," she said.

She had called Harry Craig, a writer friend who was working in Italy. He would fly in, and we'd all meet at the Raphael. I ran it by Marlon. He agreed to the interview.

The day they arrived, we all had cocktails in Marlon's suite, then planned to go on to dinner. Marlon had a scheduled script conference with Bernardo Bertolucci, so we prepared to leave. Marlon suddenly announced his desire to have me stay with him during the script conference. Marlon was disturbed; Bertolucci made him uneasy. He expressed sorrow for keeping me from spending time with Shana and Harry, but he'd feel more comfortable being with Bertolucci if I were present. He promised to make it short, then he'd dine with us. Marlon had had a couple of meetings with Bertolucci and had attended a concert with him and his wife prior to this. I had met Bertolucci three or four times previously. I thought he was very nice, but reserved. And since his English was limited, we had little conversation.

Bertolucci arrived with material, not a script, and it was still written in Italian. Consequently, he and Marlon had a prolonged story conference as Bertolucci outlined the expanded plot concept and Marlon's role once again. In this meeting, I could have been invisible. I don't remember having eye contact with him once after he entered and Marlon greeted him. He only had eyes for Marlon. I began to understand what was making Marlon so uneasy.

And I was like a jumping jack, answering my phone in the adjoining suite as Shana called reporting they were getting drunk waiting. I would order them another round and return to the story conference.

At the conclusion, Marlon felt too exhausted to go out and suggested we eat in. Shana and I didn't want room service. We left without him.

Marlon and Shana spent the next day together while she interviewed him for Life magazine.

Marlon was dispirited about *Last Tango* after the previous evening. He said he wanted to see a script and had flown to Paris with the expectation of getting one. Marlon began to wonder about his commitment to do the picture with Bertolucci. He was in flux.

Meanwhile, I was going full steam ahead. Setting up meetings, arranging wardrobe fittings—anything to firm a commitment in Marlon's mind. I was concerned about the financial picture if he opted out. His money situation was a problem. Marlon had to work. And I had to convince him to do *Last Tango in Paris* without a completed script, though Bertolucci had promised an English translation of the material.

First day of filming on *Last Tango* on February 7th finally arrived and I could stop worrying about whether I had convinced Marlon not to bolt *Last Tango* as he had *Child's Play*.

It wasn't too long before I received Marlon's script pages. When I read them, I immediately sought Marlon and asked if he realized what he was doing. It was pornography. I was scandalized. I hadn't realized what I had gotten him into. Marlon placated me, assuring me it wouldn't be shot as written. He wasn't going to do explicit nude sex scenes. I wasn't certain. I urged him to leave the movie before any more film was shot. I didn't know what Bertolucci and Marlon had discussed in their several story conferences as Marlon came out of each one dazed and rolling his eyes, and continued to ask for a script. Now I was receiving pages that I questioned, and Marlon was asking me "not to worry."

Marlon continued to go to the set.

At the end of February, Miko arrived to visit his father for his birthday. While Marlon was working, I tried to make his stay memorable. The first day I took him to lunch at the top of the Eiffel Tower and after we hit the ground, he looked up and asked me what the record was for trips made to the top of the tower in one day. The question stumped me. He decided at that moment that while in Paris, which would be just a few days, he would establish a record.

We had silly photos taken with our heads sticking out of the Eiffel Tower. Marlon had given permission for him to visit the set, as this was one of his birthday requests. So we spent some time with Marlon, then went shopping for souvenirs. It was a full day with his birthday celebration that evening.

The next day was fuller still. I sat on the balcony of the apartment while Miko went up and down the Eiffel Tower until he had spent all the money allowed for his quest. He did establish a record for one day, in our group at least. Though I believe I hold the record for a tourist having lunch at the restaurant at the top of the Eiffel Tower. That was where the boys wanted to eat lunch every day.

After Miko departed, I enjoyed a few days with Jill, who had joined Marlon. I was beginning to think that maybe Paris would be the "fun" Marlon promised.

But trouble came from afar.

Marlon had agreed for Christian to have a visitation with his mother, since Christian would be with us the entire time Marlon was working in Paris. Now that it came time for Anna to send Christian to us, Christian was missing. Anna said he was kidnapped.

Greatly disturbed, Marlon and Jill left Paris for Beverly Hills. Marlon had contacted his lawyers from Paris and immediately went into consultations upon arriving. Jay Armes, renowned Texas investigator, was hired to locate Christian. He trailed Christian to Mexico, where Christian was found sleeping in a hammock on a Baja beach, and returned him to Marlon. Now Marlon was obliged to go to court once again.

We had asked Dr. Troup, child psychiatrist, who had evaluated Christian at the time of the custody hearings, if she could find a tutor for Christian while we were in France filming. She recommended a tutor, Mrs. Marie Paul, who was located in Paris.

A girlfriend of Marlon's, who Christian had met at the house when he visited, was hired by Marlon as "governess," but changed to "companion" as Christian objected to a governess, saying he was too old to have one. All three returned to Paris after a few days visiting with Marlon's sister, Frannie, at the Mundelein family farm in Illinois.

Following two days rest and relaxation after his ordeal, and getting over jet lag, Marlon reluctantly returned to work.

In Paris, we leased a large apartment at Rue Buenos Aires near the Hilton Hotel. The Eiffel Tower was framed in the French doors of each room that opened on to small balconies. It was so near, it seemed as though you could reach out and touch it. The apartment was airy and lovely.

I hired a cook and housekeeper. She arrived and made breakfast for me and Christian, whom I awoke at seven. I sent him off to school each morning with Marlon's driver, who returned and took Marlon to the set.

I picked Christian up from school at noon and took him to lunch. He always chose to eat at the Eiffel Tower, so we'd walk around the corner from the apartment and lunch overlooking Paris. Evidently, Christian had heard about Miko's feat establishing a record going up and down the Eiffel Tower, so he set out to beat Miko's record, which enabled me to establish one too as I went with him.

Christian spent the afternoons with his companion to give me some free time. Marlon would have dinner with us, then I'd help Christian with his homework, and he went to bed by nine.

After dinner, Marlon would retire to his room and make phone calls most evenings. There were times he'd ask me to join him for a while. Mostly he honored my request for alone time evenings when I shared quarters with him. He and I went to dinners a few weekends, but I soon began to beg off because it developed that everyone was smoking marijuana, and some were on other drugs. It wasn't my scene. Marlon hosted only a few dinner parties, but mostly Marlon wanted to relax, talk to Jill or friends on the phone, sleep, or bitch to me about the demands of the movie and Bertolucci.

Since Marlon's return, he hibernated until he overcame the stress of the ordeal at home, but he was complaining and stressed about work. I thought it would pass, but when I'd wake him in the morning, he'd ask me to tell Bertolucci he was ill, and to let him sleep. I'd refuse, of course, and keep him talking until he realized he had no option but work. This went on for a day or two.

Then one morning, when I went into his room to arouse him, I found him wide awake. He moaned that he hadn't slept all night, he couldn't move, he had a bad back. He was unable to get out of bed. He implored me to summon a doctor as he couldn't stand the pain when he moved.

The doctor, procured by the production manager, gave him muscle relaxing pills. Marlon stayed in bed for a few days until all the pills were gone. When he wanted more pills, I realized he did not have a bad back. And told him so. When he attempted to convince me he did, I had a serious talk with him. I tried to impress upon him the consequences of getting hooked again. He kept insisting he had the bad back. I wasn't buying it. We went a few rounds, quietly arguing about whether I knew when he was acting or lying. He insisted he could fool me most of the time, then began to elaborate on the times he had. I went along, to get along. At least I had him up and dressing as he had a work call. And he forgot he wanted me to ask the doctor for a refill of the pain pills.

Marlon began complaining about Bertolucci from day one. I tried to visit the set in the afternoon if I had the opportunity. The street scenes were being shot one day I attended, and Marlon was at it again—testing the director.

He and Maria Schneider rehearsed the scene. Marlon was wearing a camel cashmere designer overcoat. Right before "Action" Marlon ripped the pocket of the coat and let it hang. The director, the wardrobe designer, the cameraman all stared. Marlon gave them the, "I dare anyone to say something to me" look and slowly walked to his place down the street for the beginning of the shot. Here we go again! Marlon had thrown down the gauntlet—Bertolucci wisely ignored it.

Where I had been disturbed by the script pages I had received at the start of the film and wanted to bolt, now Marlon was becoming disturbed at the direction Bertolucci was going. We were constantly discussing what to do. By this time finances was determining our decisions.

Marlon notified me Bertolucci wanted a sex scene. Marlon had ruled out any nude scenes. Now Marlon wanted me on the set with him. What could I do? Marlon said he needed me there as he had to take a stand. He required me as a witness if he walked and there was a lawsuit. I accompanied him to the set. Marlon won one. The sex scene was fully clothed. Overcoat, torn pocket and all.

Another day, another sex scene—the so-called butter scene. Marlon again complained to me. I suggested he talk to Bertolucci. Marlon said the scenes were improvised. No script. Bertolucci wanted more, more. Marlon, very upset, called me. He said he had sent his car to bring me to the set. As requested, I brought his Valium with me and stayed with him on the set all afternoon.

Each night I was staying up later, and later listening to Marlon's complaints about Bertolucci's demands, propping him up, urging him not to do anything to slow down the film. Except for the few days when he had faked the bad back, he was drug free, except for Valium, and only took one Valium, unless he was really stressed. This was beginning to be of great concern to me as he was under a good deal of stress. And I didn't want him to start popping Valium to get through the picture. I, of course, was only hearing Marlon's complaints. I don't know what he was putting Bertolucci through, and knowing Marlon's history in regard to directors, I didn't want to know.

On the other hand, this was Marlon's way of preventing my spending time with Christian. For years there was only me and Marlon in the house, and girls running in and out. But now with my circumstance changed, I had assumed responsibility for Christian while he was in my care. And with Christian living with us, the household took on a dramatic change.

Marlon wasn't importing women, nor was he having friends drop by with a girl that wanted to meet him. Marlon's privacy was being invaded by cooks, housekeepers, companions. Instead of taking calls from girls, I was talking to child psychologists, tutors, drivers, lawyers, scheduling, arranging visitations, plus managing a household. I was not always available to listen to Marlon or share his exploits as I had in the past.

And it wasn't because Christian took up all my time for he was, here in Paris, at school till noon. I always had breakfast with Christian and, when able, I saw him in the afternoon and also spent a few hours with him in the evening doing homework. Marlon took note of this, and now I was being reminded that he had hired a companion for Christian. I didn't have to pick him up after school and have lunch with him, then entertain him in the afternoon. I explained that this was Paris. I wanted him to experience more than the Eiffel Tower. Nevertheless, Marlon would call or send the car for me to bring me to the set where I sat around chatting with the girls.

One day when he needed me on the set with him, I returned to the apartment to check on things and heard Christian's companion, who was standing away from the wrought-iron grill surrounding the balcony, saying, "Christian, I think you better come back."

And I heard Christian yelling, "Help me, help me, I can't hang on!"

I ran to the balcony. I couldn't believe what I saw—Christian dangling from the third-floor balcony.

He couldn't swing back. He was beginning to panic. I had his companion hold me and asked Christian to "Hang on" while I leaned over the railing as far as was safe and tried to grab his pants at his waist as I had him swing to the side. The first attempt failed and, on the second attempt, I was able to get a good grip on him and eased him up where he could get purchase, and he was able to help as I pulled him over the balcony rail.

His companion thought he had been kidding when he said he couldn't get back and couldn't hang on. They were screaming at each other. Then they turned to me with a hysterical, "Don't tell Bunky, don't tell Marlon" from both. They didn't know I couldn't tell Marlon because Marlon had enough problems without this.

Near Easter time Marlon had again sent for me. I discovered the film was going to shut down for the holiday. And I also discovered there were drugs on the set. You could smell the marijuana. Maria Schneider, Marie Rhodes, and I were discussing what we were going to do over the holiday.

Maria said, "I'm going to take a trip."

I innocently inquired, "Where are you going?"

All the crew who heard us talking, as well as Maria, burst out laughing. Maria had told them she was going to take an LSD trip over the holiday.

After dinner one night, Marlon asked me to come to his room when I was through helping Christian with his school work. We had to talk. He was highly agitated. He said he was going home. He was leaving the picture. He couldn't take it. He was adamant about leaving.

I tried soothing him. I placated, "Let's not be hasty, let's talk about it." I couldn't imagine what had happened to bring him to this.

It was Bertolucci.

Bertolucci wanted another nude scene. We were back to that. Marlon explained that this time, he wanted a bathroom scene. Maria and Marlon nude. He stormed, "Bertolucci's determined to see my c--k!"

How did I deal with this state of mind? I was ready to pull out my hair, but when he was in this agitated state, I couldn't let him know my feelings. I had to submerge them. Bertolucci's adoration of Marlon had been in evidence since the beginning. It was a problem for Marlon. He was becoming more disturbed as we talked. I calmed and appeased him as best I could.

Then I enumerated reasons why he couldn't walk. One, and primary, he needed the money. He was *broke.* Still. And his household had changed. He had more familial monetary obligations. Two, they'd sue. He couldn't afford another lawsuit. Lawyer bills played a big part in his monetary problems. Three, he'd have a difficult time getting work; he had walked out of *Child's Play*; if he walked, he'd be outlawed. I had his attention. I continued talking. He was listening—the Valium he had taken before I came to his room probably kicked in where I could reason with him. I reminded him he had been an actor for years; he had been a director. He certainly knew about camera angles. He certainly knew all the tricks. Goodness knows, he'd perfected them through the years.

"Let's think it over. The bathroom area is small and cramped—you'll do the rehearsal with a robe or towel around you. You're smart enough to figure something out. Do some business so your penis won't be photographed. And, you'll negotiate to only do X number of takes."

He let me talk. He was taking everything in. But I didn't know if the seeds I was planting were taking root. His greatest fear was that not his entire body, only his lower frontal parts, would be photographed and not in the picture, but in someone's private collection.

I emphasized again and again throughout the night that he was savvy enough to know the camera. Since, as he said, most was being improvised, he had control. He would do the improvising. He had taken control of a scene from some of the biggest directors before. He could do it to Bertolucci. As far as I was concerned, Bertolucci had to take care of himself. I wasn't going to make him my problem, too. Marlon was starting to relax by this time. I kept jawing.

After hours of cajoling and strategizing, a decision was agreed upon. I'd accompany him to the set in the morning. He'd rehearse and figure out what Bertolucci wanted. Then, if he felt uncomfortable with the camera angles and couldn't control the number of takes, we'd walk, I would phone Italy, lay the cards on the table, and negotiate with Mr. Grimaldi, the producer.

Alberto Grimaldi had been the producer of *Quemada,* the Gillo Pontecorvo film Marlon had so many problems with in Cartagena, Columbia. He and I had numerous discussions at that time in regard to the problems that arose on that film. He was a reasonable man and understood actors and directors. And he also understood my position. I knew we could solve any problems Marlon entertained, as we had in the past.

After a few hours' sleep, I had breakfast at seven with Christian and sent him off to school. Talked over the dinner menu with the cook. Then, I arranged for Christian's companion to go with the driver and pick up Christian at noon, take him to the Eiffel Tower restaurant for lunch, bring him home, and help him with his homework. That done, it freed me to concentrate on Marlon and his nudity problem.

Marlon was fortified with Valium as we left for the vacant apartment where *Last Tango* was being filmed. After arriving, I took Marie, Marlon's stand-in, aside and questioned her about the scene. We both went to the bathroom, scrambling over cables, and around the camera, because I needed to see the set. Marie told me when she had rehearsed the scene, Maria Schneider was in the tub and she was standing beside the tub, washing her. I reported to Marlon, "Piece of cake." Marlon would not be ogled by the entire crew, and I felt he could outwit the camera.

The space was so tight, I was unable to observe what was happening in the bathroom when Marlon rehearsed. Instead I sat talking with Phillip Rhodes while they were rehearsing. Marie had been watching the run-through and then joined us. I asked her how it went. She laughed and said Maria was in the tub with her back to Marlon and he was washing her back. Then Bertolucci told Marlon he wanted him to wash her backside which he did, but Bertolucci wasn't satisfied. He wanted Marlon to take the sponge up and down through the crack and soap it thoroughly. Marie said Marlon had turned to her and whispered, "How silly this all is, it's embarrassing. I don't want to do it."

She agreed saying, "I think it's stupid," and advised, "just try to have your hand showing."

Marlon, she reported, kept his back to the camera.

I didn't know what they finally shot, but Marlon didn't seem upset.

The scene over, now I felt I needed to run home. I didn't want Christian to feel I was neglecting him because I was spending so much time with Marlon at home and more time with him on the set.

I opened the door to the apartment and was greeted with silence. I thought they might be at the Eiffel Tower. I went to the library balcony and looked out, didn't see them among the tourists at the base of the tower. That didn't concern me. They could be in the restaurant at the top.

I had just left the library when I heard voices coming from another room. They were home. I went to the door. They were in bed. Again, it was hysteric cries of, "Don't tell Bunky! Please don't tell Bunky!" And, "Please don't tell Marlon!" From both.

Christian was 12; she was in her thirties. Who seduced whom? My mind had shut down. They were both screaming, accusing each other about who got who in trouble and entreating me not to tell Marlon. They ended up fighting. I was tiring of the soap opera. I had to leave this scene and return to the set to make sure I didn't have another one with Marlon. They didn't want to upset Marlon and again beseeched me not to tell Marlon about their behavior. I departed after telling them I'd deal with the situation later, and in the meantime, I'd decide about telling Marlon. And they could stew over that for the rest of the afternoon.

After the previous night and the morning on the set with Marlon, now this. What else? Well, I soon found out when I returned to the set.

It was late afternoon. A cheerful, Valium-relaxed Marlon asked me to arrange for cheese, salami, bread, wine, etc., for the cast and crew when they finished work—in about an hour. I approached the production manager, and begged him to please spare someone to go with me to run to all the shops, which he did. And along with the help of Marlon's driver, we delivered.

I escaped before the party and went home. Christian and his companion were not in sight. They were in their rooms, doors closed. I closed my door, too. I was a no-show for dinner.

At nine Marlon, knocked and talked through my door. He wanted to see me about Christian. I went to his room. He greeted me with the fact that the companion had talked to him. He felt too much was happening on the set, he couldn't deal with any problems at home, so he decided she should leave. He asked me to give her money for an apartment, since she had elected to stay in Paris, and also give her a food allowance. He would have kept her on, but because of what he put me through last night and during the day, and since I hadn't shown for dinner, he was afraid I'd leave if there was another scene with her and Christian.

The next crisis came with the "death of his wife" scene. Again Bertolucci, according to Marlon, didn't have the scene written. He broadly outlined an idea; what he envisioned the scene to be. He wanted Marlon to take it from there, to improvise. Throughout filming, Marlon complained to me that too much was asked of him. Now he made many notes to himself. He was low, thoughtful. He withdrew into himself. He agonized over the scene. He dug deep. But the scene took so much out of him that after it was finished, he was an emotional wreck. Again, he wanted me on the set when they were shooting the scene. Christian was at school, so I was able to accompany him. Bertolucci wrung him dry.

At home afterwards, Marlon confided he would never allow a director do that to him again. He couldn't leave the scene on the set where it belonged. He took it home with him and was living with it. And because of it, was living on Valium.

Now that the companion was no longer with us, I spent all my days with Christian. I didn't go to the set again with Marlon. It was nearing the end of the film and I was just biding time until I could have a vacation. I was planning a trip to Rome.

Our lease was up on the apartment, so we moved to Bernie Cornfield's apartment on the Etoile. It was a spacious apartment and, again, we all had our own space.

Christian had seen me going in and out of Marlon's room evenings in the previous apartment, and now he came to my bedroom and asked in a shy, hesitant manner if I was intimate with his father. Marlon's door was always open when I was in with him and I didn't know what brought this on. Perhaps it was because Marlon would enter Christian's room and ask me to come to his room after finishing homework, or he heard Marlon knocking at my door. I told him our relationship was strictly business, which was a ridiculous thing to say on the face of it, as Marlon and I had a very close, warm relationship. We lived in the same house at times. And here we were now, where he saw me going into Marlon's room when no one else could do so. Also, Marlon felt free to hug me in passing and whisper, "Thanks," or things in my ear he didn't want others to hear. Intimate, but nothing romantic. Though it might seem so to a 12-year-old.

I thought I'd let Marlon handle this. I took Christian with me to Marlon's room, where he was lying on the bed, and asked Marlon to talk to his son about our relationship. I left them together. I didn't know what Marlon said, but Christian felt free to come to my room and sleep on my chaise evenings, even though my room had twin beds.

I had been keeping my door open instead of closing it as I usually did, and when I observed him in the middle of the night coming in dragging a blanket, I assumed he may have been disturbed by new sounds or was having a bad dream. This was the first time I felt that he was beginning to trust me completely and that we could be friends.

Christian was still going to school and I was picking him up at noon. Our lunch routine changed from the Eiffel Tower restaurant to the Champs-Elysées. I had taken Christian to a matinee of *The Cowboys* with John Wayne. Thereafter, Christian set a record for the times he saw that movie. And, I even bought him a pair of black cowboy boots. I only went with him two or three times. I liked John Wayne, but enough was enough. So, each day after lunch, I dropped him off at the movie and picked him up when it was over, until they changed the bill.

We also did the tourist thing. He didn't like the museums, but like *The Cowboys* movie, Notre Dame took his fancy and we visited several times as he loved the gargoyles and the tour. He even accompanied me to Notre Dame for Easter mass.

His former companion was still in Paris, and one day when I returned with Christian, she was at the Etoile apartment, welcomed by Marlon. She had been his friend of many years and it became quite obvious that, though interrupted, their friendship had been renewed and she was back—living at the apartment. Companion to Marlon instead of Christian.

Along with touring Paris, Christian and I spent time together perfecting our crepe-making and tossing technique. The cook would leave us a pitcher of crepe mixture in the refrigerator, and we became experts at having those crepes flying in the air and back into the pan without a miss. When home, our time was spent in the kitchen eating crepes till bedtime.

Then I found out that Christian wasn't coming to my room in the middle of the night when he thought I was asleep because of strange house noises. He was stationed at the window after midnight, watching the "ladies of the evening" below on the sidewalks.

I discovered this when I couldn't fall asleep one night, arose, and pulled a chair to the window to watch the Paris nightlife at the Etoile. To my amazement, I thought I saw Christian in my chesterfield-style long mink coat, walking back and forth past the "ladies" and their full-length mink-coated, fedora-clad "pimps." I almost had heart failure. We had one kidnapping scare at the beginning of *Last Tango,* I was terrified we might have another under my watch. I tracked him, or who I thought was Christian, with my eyes, then lost him. I searched, but couldn't see him. I hurriedly left the window and was on my way to check his room and run out when I heard the door to the apartment opening and softly closing.

I accosted Christian, dragged him into my room so we wouldn't disturb Marlon. He confessed he had been watching the activity from my window and then decided he'd go out. He had been going out every night. He thought nothing of it as he had been doing this when he was living at home, sneaking out at night to roam the streets. I remembered my friend Jimmy calling at one o'clock, telling me that "Brando's kid," who was seven at the time, was on the street outside a night club. But now he was my responsibility, I had to put a stop to the nighttime meanderings. I threatened to tell his father. With all that had gone on before, he begged me not to tell. I agreed not to, only after he promised that if he wanted to go out in the evening, he'd let me know and we'd go out together. Which we did. Every night. I wore the mink. Christian had taken my coat only because he had seen all these men at night in mink coats, and since my mink was available, he had worn mine.

Then one day Marlon arrived home jubilant. He was finished. He had done his last improvisation. He had mooned them all. This was Brando! I didn't believe him. Marie and Phillip acknowledged it was true—Bertolucci has asked him to do something outlandish. He did. Bertolucci had filmed it.

My friends Florine Monteverdi and Babs Shoemaker had arrived in Paris, but I spent little time with them as I was involved with Marlon. I wanted to leave for Rome, but hesitated to leave Christian with Marlon as Marlon took to his bed in a Valium-drugged state the day the movie finished.

I know the girls, especially Babs, who had never met Marlon, wondered why I didn't invite them to the apartment, but always met them at their hotel or at a restaurant. But Marlon was in no condition to meet anyone. I remember I lunched with them and upon returning, I went to his room to discuss plans for the evening. He was so drugged out, I could not talk to him. Since he had taken so much Valium to get through the filming of *Last Tango,* I was trying to make sure he was tapered off the drug so he could go back to Beverly Hills with Christian. After about two or three days, he finally came out of his stupor. But he was still in bed. Florine visited. Marlon asked her to accompany me to Rome and then on to the Greek Isles. He didn't want me going off alone.

I hung around Paris until Marlon and Christian departed, then closed the apartment. Florine and I traveled to Rome, Casablanca, Marrakesh, St. Tropez, Cannes, back to Paris, and home. We skipped the Greek Isles that Marlon insisted Florine take me to. Upon arrival, I went directly to my home in Newport Beach to recover from jet lag.

After a week, I drove up to Marlon's, dropped my bag in my office. Everyone at the house warned that Marlon was in a very bad mood—and he was mad at me because he didn't know where I was, and my family didn't know where I was when he called, trying to find me. They were happy to see me, but still wary of my reception, since Marlon was in such a foul mood.

I walked into Marlon's room with a cheery, "Hi! I heard you're mad at me for taking up your offer of a trip to the Greek Isles after *Last Tango*."

He scowled at me and growled, "What are you talking about?"

"My trip to the Greek Isles."

He didn't remember our conversation about my plans to visit Rome after Paris. He didn't remember Florine being at the apartment. He didn't remember telling Florine to take me to the

Greek Isles. Was I that wrong about his condition when I left? I didn't dare ask how they had managed to get home from Paris.

While he was digesting all I presented him with, I picked up his phone and dialed Florine. Laughing, I told her we were in trouble, Marlon didn't remember saying he'd treat us to the trip. She didn't know what I was talking about. "He insisted I take you to the Greek Isles," she said.

I put Marlon on to talk to her. After he hung up, he looked at me, shook his head and mused, "I don't remember a thing about a trip to the Greek Isles. I didn't know where you were."

I laughed, "Well, we certainly had a grand time spending your money because I maxed out my credit cards. And your business manager is getting my statements at the end of the month." He had to laugh, too.

I started out the room, turned around, and asked, "Did you hire a secretary?"

Bewildered, he asked, "What do you mean, hire a secretary?"

I responded, "I'm Christian's guardian. Remember?" And I left him to go back staring at the ceiling.

Asking Marlon to hire a secretary was my way of reminding Marlon I was going to be spending time caring for Christian and I'd have less time for him and his projects.

After *Last Tango* wrapped, Marlon planned to take Christian and spend the summer in Hawaii and the South Pacific—Tahiti and Tetiaroa. After my wanderings, I was going to return home and then join him in August on his atoll. Now that I was back, Marlon felt free to depart.

Marlon left via Hawaii, but my plans were thwarted by a call from Alberto Grimaldi, producer of *Last Tango in Paris*. He needed Marlon by the first of August to loop his lines. It seemed Grimaldi had to have *Last Tango* at the New York Film Festival at the end of September. He had to obtain a seal of approval; an art picture classification was needed. Time was of the essence. Grimaldi declared I must get Marlon to Rome for looping.

I was having difficulty reaching Marlon. When I did, he uttered, "Don't I have contractual agreements I would loop in September?"

I agreed he did and tried to explain the unforeseen circumstances that had arisen.

"I don't have to loop until September," he stated, "You handle it."

More trans-Atlantic and trans-Pacific calls ensued between me and Grimaldi, and me and Marlon. Finally, I persuaded Grimaldi and Marlon to meet halfway. The looping was done in Hollywood instead of Rome. Marlon flew in, looped, and immediately flew back to Tetiaroa.

I was now readying to depart for Tahiti, but there were more problems. Marlon had contractual rights in regard to promotion. Marlon was not available. They'd have to wait until he returned to town. United Artists, distributor, needed immediate approval from him on United States and international theater posters.

Again, when I called Marlon, it was, "You take care of it." I chose photos and made the approval on the posters, and also chose photos to be used on the record album and the paperback book. That ended the post-production problems and my involvement with the production of *Last Tango in Paris,* which all began with a call from my friend Luigi Luraschi.

Well, except that:

I received another long distance call. It was from a gentleman affiliated with the picture, who thanked me for my accessibility and for all I had done for them during the filming and post-production of *Last Tango*. He asked if there was anything they could do for me. Yes. I had one request. I asked if he would send me the poster I had selected for theater promotion of *Last Tango in Paris* in U.S. He would be more than happy to do it. The reason I desired the poster was that it was representative of Marlon—reclining, looking upward, plotting, dreaming, fantasizing.

Because I was leaving to meet Marlon in Tahiti and wouldn't be home to receive mail either at my home or at Marlon's, I asked if he would mail it to Norman Garey, Marlon's lawyer. Before I left town, I called Norman's secretary, alerted her the poster would be sent to me care of Norman and to please hold it until I returned from the South Pacific.

Upon returning from Bora Bora, I called Norman's office. I was informed the poster had been received—and given to Norman. I asked that it be sent to me. In a return call, I was informed that they were mistaken, nothing had been received for me. I phoned the office in New York, discovered it had been mailed to Norman immediately after we had spoken. They regretted, but they could not replace the poster. A limited number were made and none were available, but the nude poster of Marlon and Maria Schneider, which was used outside the United States, was attainable and they mailed that to me. I was disappointed as I wanted the U.S. poster I had chosen.

Subsequently I received an anonymous call—the poster addressed to me had been received at the law office and given to Norman. Since he denied having the poster, there was no way I could prove he was given it. I decided to forget it.

I thought that was the end of it, but weeks later I was crossing Wilshire Boulevard, and approaching in the opposite direction in the crosswalk was Norman Garey. We rapidly passed in the middle of the crosswalk with only a greeting. But I was utterly surprised, for Norman was carrying the framed U.S.

Marlon Brando poster for *Last Tango in Paris*. When I returned to Marlon's, I called Norman's office—but he was not available to take my call. I was going to tell Marlon what happened. But rather than upset him about it, I thought if Norman wanted the poster that badly, I'd leave him to Heaven.

* * * * *

Throughout the years, if Marlon made a monetary commitment, or borrowed money, or asked someone to pick up the check and I became aware of it, I honored his commitment and reimbursed the persons. While I worked for Marlon at the house, this was carried out. Of course, I always reported that I had done so. I wrote thank-you notes in his name, sent flowers or gifts in his name, then had to remind him when we'd meet the person why they were thanking him.

I recall one time I forgot to tell him I had sent flowers from him to one of the airline personnel, who had helped us on our many trips to Tahiti, when she was ill. The next time she saw him, she began thanking him so profusely, he stared at her as if she had gone berserk. I was trying to get his attention. Finally, I caught his eye and rapidly blinked a few times. Fortunately, he picked up on it. After she departed, Marlon said, "My God, Ali, what did you send her?"

In defense of Marlon, he was very, very generous, but to strangers. Not his immediate family or intimate friends. The modest jewelry he gave women was either out of guilt or seduction. He helped with medical needs, bringing people from Tahiti into his home for months while they were undergoing treatment. Gave of time and pocketbook to UNICEF and causes too numerous to mention. Gave the clothes off his back. But wouldn't give his son an allowance—until I insisted he had to learn how to handle money. It didn't last long. He cut him off. "If he wants pocket money, he should get a job."

* * * * *

Marlon did not celebrate holidays. I came from a family of ten, so we had birthday cakes almost every month. And along with birthdays we celebrated name days, and the months that didn't have a birthday, had a holiday. So one party ended and another was being planned. We celebrated every holiday. We weren't Irish, but were on St. Patrick's Day. We celebrated Christmas and New Year's, and then we celebrated Christmas and New Year's in January by the "old calendar" dates because, as my mother contended, we didn't know the true date. My mother had a list of every holiday during the year and we celebrated all, even whooping it up for political candidates on election day.

When we left home, we all carried on this "any excuse for a cake or party" tradition. I always thought other people celebrated certain occasions in their life, if not state and world celebrations, as we did.

Not so with Brando. When I started to work for Marlon in August, the big holidays (Halloween, Thanksgiving, Pearl Harbor, Christmas, New Year's) to my surprise were overlooked. Marlon professed to hate birthdays, holidays.

After the first of the year, I began to change all that. He was surprised to see a few red heart-shaped cookies, then green shamrock cookies, then bunny cookies turn up on the kitchen counter. And he was shocked when I brought him a birthday present and cupcake with a candle, and gave him a Father's Day card and gift. Then I talked him into holiday dinners. The first was a Thanksgiving dinner—I planned it with his sister Jocelyn and stayed to celebrate with him and his family instead of my own. Anything to start a tradition.

Marlon particularly professed to hate Christmas time.

He'd ignore it, as long as I let him.

I recall one Christmas time, Tarita and the children came from Tahiti, along with an aunt and her child. They were going to be at the house for a few weeks. I asked Marlon about presents for not only all of them, but also the other mothers and children. Daily I'd remind Marlon the number of days until Christmas. Daily I'd question if he had made his Christmas list. I'd ask if he wanted me to shop for gifts. He'd brush me off, saying he would do the shopping himself.

In the meantime, I festooned the trees around the house with white Christmas lights, I bought 50 poinsettias and put them on the patio outside the kitchen door, and I gave one to everyone who came to the house during Christmas week. Marlon also grabbed one and took it with him when he left the house to visit a "friend." The rooms were decorated with Christmas arrangements and looked very festive. I bought a giant Christmas tree, ornaments, and lights and it was standing in the living room, waiting for the tree trimming party planned for Christmas Eve. I bought Christmas cookies and candies, food, etc., for the party and Christmas day. The little children were beginning to get excited, because my gifts and others were showing up under the tree. All this activity was going on under Marlon's nose, but was being ignored. Marlon, as I said, professed to dislike Christmas.

In the meantime, I finished my personal shopping. I'd remind him I was through wrapping my gifts and planned to leave early on Christmas Eve for the Beach. I wanted to avoid the heavy freeway traffic and also wanted to have time to dress for our traditional Christmas Eve family dinner and party. Even when I offered to compile a list and accompany him shopping, there was no movement on his part.

Finally, it was the day before Christmas.

I was ready to leave for the Beach, and went into Marlon's room, where he was reclining on his bed, to report that all preparations for the holiday were taken care of, and to wish him a Merry Christmas. All he had to do was buy his presents.

It was after four and I wanted to be on the road before dark. I turned to leave.

"Just a minute," he said.

Then he picked up the phone and dialed. I heard him ask, "Could you send me 25,000 dollars. I want to buy some electronics." He was speaking to the business office. He listened, then put down the phone and rather dejected said, "I forgot they told me last week I was broke. They're closed and are having their Christmas party."

I waited for him to tear up the room. Show anger because he was broke and couldn't obtain any money from his business manager to buy Christmas gifts for the children. Instead it was a quiet, "What do *we* do now? Forget the adults, I need to have presents for the kids."

I could make a scene, but refrained. I asked why he hadn't informed me before that his business manager had advised him he was broke. He had forgotten to. It was too late to discuss it. It was Christmas Eve. I'd have to deal with "broke" when I returned after the holidays.

In the meantime, there was shopping to do. I had charge accounts at Saks, Neiman Marcus, Bullock's. I wasn't maxed out, but close to it because, after all, it was Christmas and I had charged my gifts for my large family and friends. I had bought Marlon a beige cashmere robe that cost 750 dollars, which, along with other gifts, took me to my limit at Bullock's. I offered to charge his presents, but, I reminded him, I wouldn't be able to buy expensive electronics because I didn't carry a large balance in my checking account, nor did I carry a large limit in my charge accounts. We compiled a short list of people he decided he'd give gifts to. I reminded Marlon a girlfriend had called to tell me her daughter wanted a Cartier wristwatch for Christmas. Now I inquired if he wanted to give her a Cartier watch. We discussed cost and his lack of money. She was in her early teens. He had recently come home with a new watch that had a black dial and a white dot on the face. He told me to buy her the same; he thought she might like one like his.

I had to hurry since the stores would be closing. I went to Saks first. I looked at gold chains with lockets, hearts, etc., for the girls, and then I saw the watch. They only had one; it was a girl's. I felt lucky. I reached my limit at Saks and had to write a check. Then went on until I had something for everyone on the list. There weren't very many choices as it was Christmas Eve, but I did the best I could, considering the circumstances. The stores were no longer gift wrapping, but I took boxes, tissue paper, and loads of ribbon. Someone at the house would have to wrap, I couldn't take the time. It was now dark. I would be caught in traffic and late for our family Christmas Eve dinner.

I raced back to the house and dumped everything on Marlon's bed. He had opened my gift while I was shopping and was coming out of his dressing room wearing the robe. He gave me a big hug and told me how much he loved it. He looked at the pile of packages on his bed and thanked me profusely for coming to his rescue financially again.

He then merrily said, "I want you to take a trip to Acapulco as your present."

I hugged him, kissed him on the cheek, and said, "Thanks. Merry Christmas," and left to phone my folks, tell them I was just leaving, and hit the road. I gave Marlon no inkling I was furious with him. I knew he resented my leaving to have Christmas with my family. I had declined to stay and spend Christmas with him. I knew if I were there, he would not have the responsibility of entertaining his guests. Alice would take care of everything. He'd have no decisions to make. It would be, "Go ask Alice." So he deliberately made me late for our Christmas celebration at home by not asking his business manager to find some money earlier, and by the phony call in my presence to the business office, which we both knew to be closed.

And my reaction to this stemmed from having not only me, but my family, punished because of his vindictive nature. Christmas Eve—and he had to take revenge because I elected to spend Christmas with my family instead of him.

Also, my Christmas present from him was a joke. I had taken a trip to Acapulco and upon my return, I regaled Marlon with the wonderful time we had had. Actually, Florine had married a jockey. Me, Bill Shoemaker and his wife Babs, who hosted the wedding at their Beverly Hills apartment, had joined them on their honeymoon to Acapulco.

Marlon remembered how much we enjoyed that trip and for six years, every Christmas, he gave me a trip to Acapulco, which I never took. Till one Christmas I told him that six trips were enough; I had no girlfriends I could join on their honeymoon to Acapulco.

The watch Marlon was so certain the teen would love because it was like his became a bone of contention. Her mother called me after Christmas and said her daughter was very disappointed she didn't receive the Cartier watch she had expected from Marlon. She told Marlon how disappointed she was and Marlon lied, saying "I sent Alice to get her a watch, I didn't know what she bought."

She wanted me to return the watch to Saks and buy a Cartier tank watch. I had to make excuses and at the same time cover for Marlon's lack of funds as best I could, so I very politely said I didn't have time to return gifts—she'd have to take it back. Further, I could not buy her a Cartier watch. And I threw it back to Marlon like a hot potato by saying that she'd have to ask Marlon to buy a Cartier watch. I didn't tell her Marlon was broke. I never asked Marlon if he sprung for the Cartier tank watch. So much for the teen liking a watch like his.

So much for hating Christmas. And so much for being "broke again" at Christmas time, and Alice to the rescue. And so much for revenge.

But I did start traditions—albeit most of them calamitous. And, oh yes, he bought me a "To My Sweetheart Valentine" card one Valentine's Day. That was one tradition I put an end to as soon as it began.

We did have our light moments.

*****

I had discovered early on that Marlon had social anxieties and wouldn't accept invitations unless it was one of his long-time acquaintances and in an informal setting without strangers. Later, after Marlon and I had known each other some time and he realized socializing didn't faze me, he'd ask me to accompany him. But whenever I went out with Marlon socially, before we left the house or hotel, no matter the country we were in, we seldom left without the promise from him that he'd watch his manners and behave himself, none of this playful business at the table if we were dining with people.

I can laugh at it now, but it wasn't funny then, because I never knew what would come out of his mouth; an insult, a sexual query, or a lie. He'd appropriate something that had happened to another person and dramatize it as he went along, thereby having everyone hanging on to his every word. As he embellished the story, he'd get lost, and since it wasn't his, it had no denouement. Therefore he would go off into fantasyland, and confused expressions would begin to appear on his listeners' faces as they tried to follow him into wonderland. After Marlon entertained with one of his lies passed off as a true story that had happened to him, invariably someone would walk away shaking their head.

I noticed when I first started to work for Marlon that he was very self conscious around well-educated professionals or writers. Jack Beck, a writer at The New Yorker magazine, comes to mind. Marlon would be a wreck before a meeting or luncheon.

Only after long acquaintance, and when older, did he become more self assured.

Throughout his life, before a meeting, he would stand in front of the wall mirror over his sink and rehearse what he was going to talk about. Visitors were unaware he would pick a subject and introduce it in a conversation. He was adept at taking center stage, expounding on his chosen subject. And I became adept at tuning him out, as I knew it was a game with him. He would revel in it later—how he had had everyone in the palm of his hand, hanging on to every word.

Another ploy—he'd use street language, thinking it would put people at ease, but it only made some of his guests uneasy. Especially in mixed company. When this happened, he'd make it worse by calling attention to the fact that they were uneasy and then begin an analysis of their reaction to the common language he had used.

Marlon would have a meeting with people and then not allow them to speak. He was a master at dominating the conversation, leaping from one topic to another before anyone could make a comment or get a word in. People would be subject to a lecture as he didn't converse. And, he didn't tolerate interruptions when he was speaking. He held the stage. Then, bored, he would pick up the phone, buzz a secretary, and have a one-sided conversation, saying, "What time was I suppose to be at the doctor's office? Call and tell them I'm going to be a little late. Okay, I'll get going." Then he'd terminate the meeting saying he had a doctor's appointment and was already late.

After one of those days, a gentleman who had been exposed to Marlon at his worst, left the house and I escorted him to his car keeping Marlon's St. Bernard and Mastiff dogs, who frightened everyone, at bay. He prepared to enter his car, stopped, then turned to me with a curious look and queried, "Is he for real?"

*****

In 1973, when Christian was about 13 years old, Marlon employed Marty, Jocelyn's son, at 250 dollars per week as companion to Christian. When Marty received his first check from the business office, he took it to the bank and couldn't cash it. Marlon didn't have enough funds to cover the 250-dollar check.

Marlon Brando was *broke*. Again. Marty called me and I took care of the matter.

It was at this time that Christian first ran away from home after a terrible, terrible experience with his father—and brought back.

It was a glorious California day. The sun was shining, the birds were chirping, and a peaceful calm had settled in the house after another father-son, angry, obscenity-filled shouting match.

I had made a cup of tea and brought it to my office. I stood sipping, letting the quiet seep into my bones with every sip as I gazed out the window following a jet silently cutting through the blue sky above the oleanders that lined the property. As I was turning from the view, a movement at the end of the driveway caught my attention. I focused and saw it was Christian who knelt down on the ground. My breath was taken away as I saw him raise his arm and put a gun to his left temple.

I quickly turned, set the teacup down, picked up the phone, buzzed Marlon, and asked him to hurry out—Christian had a gun to his head.

"If he has a gun, I'm not coming out."

Marlon disconnected.

I became stone cold. I ran out the back door. Kept my eyes on Christian as I slowly walked across the parking area toward him. In a voice without alarm, I called his name and said I needed to talk to him.

"Keep away," he called.

I ignored him. I kept walking and talking. Asking him not to frighten me. Reminding him how afraid I was of guns.

"Will you put the gun down so I can talk to you?"

"Don't come near—go in the house."

The gun hadn't moved. I was now right behind him. I heard him crying. The gun still hadn't moved from his temple. Quietly I asked, "Please put the gun down. After we talk, I'll go away."

I was holding my breath, afraid to breathe. Christian lowered his arm, but held the gun. I knelt next to him and once again asked him to put the gun away from us, repeating I was afraid of it.

He released the gun and pushed it away on the ground. I reached out and put my arms around him. I held him close as sobs racked his body—comforting him until his emotional distress ran its course. I persuaded him to come into the house with me. As he moved to rise, I bent over and picked up the gun before he could.

I settled him in the den where he curled into a fetal position on his pallet near the window. I sat and stroked him. Soon he was asleep.

I took the gun and went to Marlon's room to give to him for safekeeping. The door was closed and locked. I knocked and called to Marlon through the door. He opened it part way. I handed him the gun.

"I knew he wouldn't kill himself," he said as he was pulling the sliding door closed again. I turned and walked back to my office and sat there in a daze.

The next day Christian was not in the house and Marlon's door was still closed. This was the first time Christian left the house without telling me.

He had run away from home.

I subsequently learned the gun belonged to Marlon. I didn't know at the time that he owned a gun. He kept it under his bed within arm's reach.

It was much later that Marlon thanked me for taking the gun away from Christian.

Christian was 16 when Marlon tried to throw him out. He and Marlon had had a loud argument. I could hear it in my office at the other end of the house. Christian, very upset, came running through my office, letting me know in passing that Marlon had kicked him out. He had to leave immediately.

In the den, which was now where he slept as Marlon had given his bedroom furniture away, he was pulling clothes out of a drawer. I stopped him. I said he was not going anywhere. Christian retorted that Marlon had expressed in no uncertain terms it was "his house" and he had to "get the f--k out now!" I calmed Christian and convinced him to stay put. I was going to talk to his father.

Marlon knew I'd be coming and he was waiting for me. If this was going to be war, he was going to lose because I had all the ammunition. He started the battle of wills. Loudly and with authority, he proclaimed that Christian had to leave—it was his house and Christian was no longer welcome. Of course, this was peppered with foul language. My response was a serene yes, it was his house, but the court gave me guardianship, and the court agreement was that he had to supply a roof over our heads and food, etc., until Christian was 21 years old. "You can't put *us* out. *We* elect to live here." And besides, I reminded him, if he put Christian out, he'd only go to the Beach with me, and since I'd have sole responsibility, "I wouldn't have any time to spend here with you."

He glared at me all during my recitation. Then responded curtly, "Keep *him* out of my sight!"

I arose to leave and my parting remark and advice was, "Thanks. Take a Valium." I thought I had the last shot at him, but I didn't. For he brusquely said, "I've already taken two."

Marlon was so harsh that Christian would misbehave in defiance of his father. I couldn't be only an observer. I'd intervene and then I'd be in the doghouse along with Christian, as Marlon thought I sided with Christian and against him.

Christian left home a few times with my knowledge if his father was too tough and he could no longer tolerate the verbal abuse. I was never concerned because he was older, eighteen or nineteen. So I let him go. Usually north to Washington state, where he had a cabin. Or he went to stay with a friend of his mother's, JoAn Corrales, whom he had known since he was a child. And when older, he stayed with friends or went to Alaska to work on a salmon fishing boat. It was good for Christian to be away from the irrational behavior of a movie star father and live in households far away from Hollywood; households where there was a normalcy to everyday living. Fortunately, JoAn was a very kind, compassionate person who never asked for anything, although she was giving so much to Christian, not only in mothering, but also monetarily. She did this because she was a long-time friend of Anna Kashfi. And because she was a friend of Anna's, Marlon thought she had "a hidden agenda in extending friendship to Christian." I asked what he thought this hidden agenda was. He merely replied, "She's a friend of Anna's."

When I knew Christian was at JoAn's, I'd ask Marlon to send some money to her for Christian's upkeep as I knew the needs of a growing boy, but Marlon vehemently rejected my request and forbid me to send her anything. I didn't, as I thought Marlon might hear of it through Christian or her son, who was Christian's age, and think she had made a request.

I knew Christian didn't have any money, as Marlon never gave him an allowance because he "gave him a roof over his head, and food, and clothing, and transportation." If he wanted any pocket money, as I had suggested, Marlon again said, "Christian can go to work." I bought all his clothes and I gave him money for lunch, snacks, and cokes. He'd spend some of it on cigarettes in defiance of his father's "no smoking" edict.

When Christian was living at home, Marlon was almost always dieting, so we couldn't have the snack food boys his age yearned for after school. There were no cookies, Twinkies, pies, or cakes, and no cokes allowed in the house. Christian had a pal who lived two houses away and he'd run over after school. His friend's mother treated him to what he was missing at home.

One night, Christian asked if he could go to the movies with him. His mother was going to drive them to Westwood Village and pick them up after the movie. I gave him permission to go to the movie and said I would give him enough money to pay for both of them, popcorn, candy, and a drink. Christian added, "And a hot dog." I reminded him that he had been treated to cookies and milk and this was an opportunity to reciprocate.

I only had a hundred-dollar bill and a twenty. I wanted to give him 20 dollars for each. I went to see if Marlon had a twenty. He was reclining on the bed. I remarked I was going to check his wallet, which was on the bedside table; I needed twenty dollars to send Christian and his friend to the movies and I'd return it when I broke the hundred. He propped himself up with another pillow, said, "Doesn't he have his own money? Why are you paying for him?"

I explained why I wanted Christian to treat his friend. He asked, "Why are you giving them 20 dollars. That's too much." I replied I was giving Christian 40 dollars—20 for each. He exploded. He wanted me to give them five bucks!

To understand how hilarious this conversation was, you first must realize Marlon had not been to a movie house and paid for a movie ticket in 20 years or more. If Marlon wanted to see a particular movie, he'd call his agent, who would set up a private screening for Marlon and his guests at the studio, or

Marlon would go to a private screening at the home of his agent.

Now Marlon was telling me that when he was Christian's age, he paid 15 cents to see a movie, and as an adult he paid 35 cents. He was very aggravated, and I was beyond laughing. He didn't believe the cost of popcorn or candy in the movie theater, let alone the price of a ticket—about two dollars at that time. He was behaving as if I were a pickpocket. I finally convinced him by reminding him he was no longer being paid 150,000 dollars per movie, not one million per movie, but three million, plus a percentage. That's why I needed the extra 20 dollars to send his son to a movie.

And he watched as I lifted it out of his wallet.

Stranger still about this conversation, Christian wasn't a child who nickel-and-dimed you to the poor house. He seldom, if ever, asked for spending money other than what I gave him. He knew where I kept my petty cash and never went into it, unless I told him to take the money he needed. In spite of the fact that his father did not give him an allowance and he had no pocket money, I never had a penny missing while Christian and I lived at the house—neither did Marlon. Christian did not have light fingers.

That summer there had been another blowout with Marlon. During school vacation, Marlon sent Christian to Tetiaroa to work for the summer. Christian also took a few friends with him to work and earn some money. I only remember one friend lasting the summer. I was dismayed when I learned that Marlon made them pay for room and board.

Growing boys' food bills alone at a resort didn't leave the boys much earnings. I didn't think the boys should pay for their room and board. None of his other children or friends had ever paid for their food or dwelling when they visited the island. But he made Christian pay. Christian had to abide by a different standard. It wasn't fair. Marlon took a different view. When Christian went to the island, he worked and he paid. I fought hard to change Marlon's mind. I lost. Christian and the boys had to pay for their room and board.

What was ironic about this was that Christian consoled me because I didn't like what his father had done. I was very upset over my failure to convince Marlon to treat Christian and his friends as he did the other children and their friends—no charge for room and board. Though not as much as I, Christian, too, was upset at the obvious unfairness and didn't understand his father as Marlon didn't explain this decision.

Hurt, Christian questioned, "Why does he let the others get away with everything? Why does he treat me this way?"

I didn't have the answer.

One fall day the school principal called me and asked why Christian hadn't been to classes. My heart skipped a beat, and I then replied, "I have sent Christian off to school every morning." He informed me that Christian hadn't been to school in months. Months. I was terribly distressed. When confronted, Christian admitted that when he left each morning, he hadn't been going to school. He hated school and had dropped out.

Marlon took it in stride. He dismissed it with, "I was a high school dropout, too."

Now that Christian was no longer going to school, Marlon gave him an ultimatum—to get a job or go to work on the island. After the summer experience, Christian was not going to Tetiaroa.

I drove Christian to every gas station in Studio City in the Valley. No jobs, but loads of applications, which I helped him fill out at the kitchen table. Marlon had his nose out of joint because I was helping Christian—he thought Christian should look for a job himself and fill out the applications without my help. No one had helped him! Etc., etc., etc.

Christian made himself scarce and I was being asked every day if he was working. It was a rather tense period. Christian hiding out because he was afraid he'd be shipped out to the island, and Marlon putting on the pressure—he had to work. All I heard daily was Marlon saying to Christian that he was not going to keep him. And I was telling Christian not to worry; Marlon had to keep him until he was 21. Christian was in his mid-teens, but looked younger—and Marlon expected him to get a man's job. Christian would have to grow up fast. It was a bad time for me. To keep peace in the house, I was obliged to keep Christian hidden from his father. It pained me to tell him, "He's awake, keep out of sight." But Christian was grateful; he'd always thank me and tell me where he was going before he'd disappear.

Christian was very good about telling me when and where he was going. When he arrived at his destination, he'd telephone; if he left, he'd telephone and always let me know he was on his way home. Keeping me informed about where he was at all times was the only requirement I asked of him. His friends became aware of this and they would do the same. When they arrived at the house, they'd find me and tell me they were there, and when they were leaving, they'd tell me and call to tell me they had arrived home safely, as Christian did.

At this particular time, I'd ask him to stay the night at Mitch's, a friend. In the meantime, I'd try to find some type of work for him.

Marlon left town. But before he left, he gave explicit orders—Christian had to get a job or get out. I knew I had to do something to help Christian and placate his father. I contacted a contractor who had worked on the house addition and asked if he could use an apprentice—Christian needed a job. I'd pay his wages. It was during the rainy season and Malibu was flooded. Several houses were casualties of mud slides. He had contracted to clean up. Would Christian like a grunt job? He had no choice. I didn't pay his wages, he earned every dollar.

Christian spent weeks shoveling mud out of the homes of wealthy Malibu residents. He was up at seven each morning, had breakfast (cornflakes) and was off, yelling, "I'm leaving" at my door.

But all good things come to an end. Marlon returned and Christian was no longer working. It made no difference that Christian had worked while Marlon was away. Marlon said that since he wasn't working, he had to get out. I said he couldn't put him out—by court order he had to provide for him. "Do you want us to live elsewhere?"

"He's not staying here. Get him a ticket to Tetiaroa."

Once again, Christian was packed off to the island from where I received pitiful letters, begging me to rescue him. While I was working on his father, he took matters into his own hands. We were notified that he and a rowboat were missing from the island. He had left in the small boat heading for Tahiti. He wasn't a sailor. He was lost. Fortunately, he was picked up by a fishing boat and brought to Tahiti. Marlon was not happy with Christian, to put it mildly.

Christian was about to have his 16th birthday. I asked Marlon if he was going to allow him to come home.

"Absolutely not!"

I asked if he was going to Tahiti to celebrate it with him.

"Absolutely not!"

I then said I was going, as I felt 16 was a rite-of-passage year and one of us should be with him to celebrate it. I was then subjected to the "nobody celebrated my 16th birthday" lecture by Marlon. He did not want me to go to Tahiti.

Undeterred, I phoned my sister Marty and she agreed to accompany me to Tahiti for a week or ten days since her husband, Frank Pine, a B-25 pilot, was away working on a movie and she was free to accompany me.

I believe that was the happiest Christian had ever been to see me. Marty and I arranged a birthday celebration for him at Wong's Chinese Restaurant and even had a surprise date for him with the Wongs' daughter, whom he had shown an interest in. Christian had a wonderful time at his birthday dinner without his father.

I brought him from Marlon's house in Punaauia, where he had been staying, and put him up at the hotel with us in Papeete, where there was more activity. After being on the island where he was so unhappy, I wanted to let him run free and have some fun. Two nights later, in the middle of the night there was a knock at the door. Christian was ill with a raging fever. The doctor I summoned diagnosed the flu. Marty and I tended him for four days of our stay. After his recovery and a few days and nights on the town, I brought him home from Tahiti with us in spite of Marlon's dictum that he work on Tetiaroa.

* * * * *

To give me time for myself, I would spend weekends at the Beach, thereby giving Christian and Marlon alone time when I hoped they would bond. On Monday or Tuesday upon my return, I'd listen to Christian's complaints about his father's treatment, and he'd also swear never to go out to eat with Marlon again. Christian knew I always begged off going to dinner with Marlon. Because Marlon spent such little time with him, I felt Christian should dine with Marlon when asked, even though he complained to me.

One night, there was a gang at the house and Marlon suggested we all go to the Valley for dinner instead of ordering in. I wasn't going. Christian implored me to please come to protect him from his father. He was hungry, so I went along. Christian sat next to me, up close. Marlon realized why I was there and went after Christian big time. My glaring at Marlon across the table did nothing to stop him from holding Christian up to ridicule in front of his guests. Christian was so upset he could not eat.

Upon returning home, I told Christian I would never ask him to go out to dinner with his father again. I expressed my sorrow that I didn't take his complaints more seriously. I hadn't realized he was the recipient of such verbal abuse in public. For when Christian had complained, he had not been specific—it had just been that he hated having dinner with his father. From that evening on, if Christian had dinner with his father, it was his own choosing. I don't remember him choosing, just avoiding.

I, like Christian Brando, avoided dining in or out with Marlon.

After I had accompanied Marlon and friends to dine a few times, I begged off and wouldn't go to dinner with him. We would dine together when we traveled alone or when we shared a house, or shared a house with friends. When on location and he invited several people to stay, most times I found an excuse to move out. I could do without his behavior at the table.

Marlon, being who he was, naturally was the center of attention. Instead of knowing and accepting this, and graciously diverting attention from himself, Marlon had to make certain he was the center of attention. As his Aunt Bette said about him, he'd do cartwheels in the middle of a group of people for attention.

He had many ploys. As soon as all guests were assembled at the table, he'd start to perform. He'd take his fork or spoon and start flipping it into his water glass. Then he'd challenge everyone to do it. Then the one who succeeded would have to do it more times than he. This continued until he won. Bows and applause.

Another "fun thing" was to take his napkin and push a corner up his nose. Laughter. Of course, everyone was ordered to do the same as he wanted to see what we all looked like sitting with our dinner napkin dangling from our noses.

If we were in an Italian restaurant, he would take a strand of spaghetti, turn his head, sniff it up his nose and let it dangle while he ignored it and continued to eat. If the bread basket contained rolls, Marlon would immediately start a food fight, peppering his guests with all the rolls he could get his hands on.

Or, he would tell a joke inappropriate for when eating, or in mixed company, and no one would make eye contact while there was an embarrassed laugh. At times like that, if I made eye contact with Marlon, he'd call attention to it by saying, "Alice gave me 'the look'."

Then there were the times he held someone at the table up to ridicule. And if a girl had a zit or two on her cheek or chin, or near her nose, he'd call attention to it by directing everyone to her high cheek bones, her chin, or lovely nose. Of course, all everyone focused on were the zits. And the girl sat embarrassed while Marlon extolled the beauty of her face.

I found no humor in such conduct. Especially with business associates or newly-made acquaintances in mixed company at the dinner table at home or in a restaurant. I didn't participate in his nonsense at the table.

In all the years I knew him, he never grew up. He forever employed every trick to be certain he was the center of attention. And there wasn't a trick Marlon hadn't perfected to gain that attention.

* * * * *

Through the years Christian was coming and going. Subjected to his father's moods. It became a ritual. Hiding from his father. Then confronting him. Then leaving.

And so once again, Christian and Marlon were at loggerheads. This time we were in the Philippines where Marlon was acting in *Apocalypse Now*. I received a call from Barbara Luna, who was house sitting while we were away, saying Christian was at the house and she didn't know what to do. That was strange. I told her he lived there. Barbara then explained that Marlon said she was not to allow Christian on the premises. I asked to speak to Christian.

I discovered that while I was at the Beach closing my house and packing for a few months in the Philippines, Christian and Marlon had had a big blowout and he had run off. Now he was back. He had no money and nowhere to stay except at the house, since Marlon was away. It was storming and flooding in Beverly Hills. I talked to Barbara and told her to allow him to stay. Not to put him out in the rain. She was a lovely person and wished to allow Christian to stay, but she didn't want to offend

Marlon, her longtime friend. She said Marlon was adamant; Christian was not to be allowed in the house. She was conflicted, she wanted to hear from Marlon that Christian could stay. I said I'd talk to Marlon, and he or I would call back.

I approached Marlon about the situation. He was adamant—Christian could not stay in the house. I declared that in that case, since I was his guardian and I took my obligation as such seriously, I was leaving the Philippines and taking him home with me. But, if he allowed Christian to live at the house while we were away, I'd stay. He didn't want me to leave. And he didn't want Christian in the house. We were at an impasse.

I had to solve this so that both of them would win. Since Christian didn't want to return to the Northwest, there was only one solution. I'd send him back to the island, if that was agreeable with Marlon. Marlon didn't even want him on the island as he was going directly to Tetiaroa from Manila after he finished the picture. I prevailed only after I promised that Christian would be off the island before Marlon arrived. I felt that wasn't too much to promise as Christian didn't like the island and would be happy to leave.

I spent the rest of the evening arranging a flight out of Los Angeles for Christian and notifying the Tetiaroa office in Tahiti he was arriving. Though Christian didn't like living and working on the island, he realized that he had no money and nowhere to stay, so he gratefully accepted my solution to his problem. He realized it was of short duration—and, as I told him, he could work and earn some money. We'd deal with reconciling with Marlon upon my return.

After another big blowout, Christian was off again to Alaska, working on a salmon boat. Marlon again had told him to "Get the f--k out of *my* house." Christian was happy to oblige. We kept in touch by phone. Now Christian was about 20. Marlon wanted him on his own, taking responsibility for himself.

There were many, many father-and-son, violent, verbal clashes through the years. Of the many, these were only a few I became involved in, refereed, and negotiated solutions for.

It was at a time during these turbulent days and years Marlon confided that he and George Englund had had a big blowout the night before over parenting. According to Marlon, during the heated exchange George had told him in no uncertain terms that Marlon was a bad parent. He was very put out about it to put it mildly. And Marlon asserted, "I'm mad at George. I'll never speak to George again." "Never speak" lasted a few years.

Responsibility for a child from a broken home was not easy. I took Christian to a psychiatrist, going so far as to sit in on a few sessions to be certain he discussed his deteriorating relationship with his father. I sat for several hours while he saw the doctor alone. Marlon expressed his gratitude for what I was doing, but didn't change his attitude. Then, Christian said he liked the psychiatrist and was comfortable seeing him without me. I allowed him to go to the psychiatrist alone, but reminded him of his appointments, as I did with his father.

Then one day his psychiatrist phoned and inquired why Christian wasn't keeping his appointments. When challenged, Christian firmly declared he didn't need the psychiatrist; his father did. He wasn't going anymore.

You win some, you lose some. Still, I had to try.

But resentments kept building. Marlon was treating the other children differently. They were compliant. They weren't living in the same house with Marlon, putting up with his dark moods. They were "guests" in their father's house, intimidated by him, and overtly tried to please, whereas Christian confronted and stood up to Marlon—getting him in trouble.

Until Christian was 16 years old there was one Christian. Afterward, I observed behavior similar to his father. The acorn had not fallen far from the tree.

Christian was now exhibiting signs of volatile anger—these were expressed by slamming of doors, throwing whatever was within reach. This evolved into trashing his room the same way he had heard and witnessed. Now his demeanor had changed in regard to the children Marlon had fathered by different women. He began to express a hatred for them and his father when he, like Marlon, had anger explosions.

Resentments that had been submerged had built up during the years of being subjected to verbal abuse. I knew that since early childhood he had been confused by being told—without preparation—that the two-year-old visiting was another brother. He didn't comprehend how he could have a brother when his mother did not have any children but him. Where did this one and that one come from? He became wary of every new girl on the scene because he thought he'd have another brother. It must be remembered that this was a child who was cognizant that his parents had fought over him for years. He was the center of attention in their lives and the outside world. He was aware that when he went from school to school, he was known and treated differently. Now, instead of being an only child and getting all the attention, he had to share what little attention he had received from his father and others with several children he didn't relate to. And he sought identity elsewhere, where he was embraced as Marlon Brando's son.

He lived in his father's house, but was being ignored. His father was involved with women and didn't have time for or was unavailable to him when in need of parenting. He began to resent his father's girlfriends, but used them to his advantage. Then, as ever, he turned on them with verbal abuse and bad-mouthed them to others, until he needed them again. He, again like his father, courted favor with people when in need and after using them, they didn't exist. Until needed again.

His personality changed and now his confrontations with his father became more frequent and more hateful till they were both threatening to kill each other. I tried to reason with Christian, as I had with Marlon when he was threatening to kill his own father, but he was past understanding. He didn't accept the fact that he was never going to win an argument with Marlon. And through the years a hatred grew. This, with bonds of child to parent, developed into a love/hate relationship in both. There also developed a recognition by both that they were made of the same cloth. And each expressed this knowledge to me.

When Christian was a child, I protected and championed him when things got out of hand and I was on the premises. When he was older and I was his guardian, I continued to bring peaceful solutions to their angry outbursts. And when things became too much for Christian, he would lock himself in his room and lose himself in a marijuana haze, and beer cans would begin to turn up in his wastepaper basket. In a heart-to-heart I had with him about the direction his life was taking, he plaintively said, "Don't waste your time on me. I'm always going to drink beer and smoke marijuana until the day I die."

I took Christian to a psychiatrist and attended a few sessions with him, but he rejected the intervention with a flat statement, "He's crazy, not me!"

Marlon was not the only heavy in the drama unfolding. Christian developed a pattern of outrageous and troublesome behavior, especially on weekends. If he got into trouble, it greeted me when I returned from the Beach. Marlon just popped a Valium, locked himself in his room, and left me to deal with Christian and the situations.

So after a fight with Marlon and Christian was thrown out of the house or escaped from the threat of being killed, he would—because he had no funds—stay with his school friends, and later in life with friends he had made throughout his travels. And like his father, he would spin a yarn exonerating himself from any fault. I soon discovered that, along with bad-mouthing his father, at times he compounded it by including me to elicit sympathy from his latest benefactor. When I confronted him with this knowledge, he laughed it off with, "You know what I think about you."

After Christian left school at 16, the household became a battlefield and this continued throughout the years. Like Marlon had done in his youth, Christian was now living from girlfriend to girlfriend. And, like his father, the stories of his verbal and physical abuse were drifting back to me and Marlon. And Marlon was now seeing himself in Christian. The more trouble Christian got into, the more Marlon pushed him away and out as he related to himself what Christian was revealing in his behavior. "It's like looking in a mirror."

This conflict with Christian, along with all the monetary and familial problems, was chasing Marlon into avenues of escape. Christian, like Marlon, seemed to have no control over the addictions and demons that plagued him. And their entwined lives played out like a Shakespearean drama with me viewing from the wings as an audience of one.

When Christian became 21, he married Mary McKenna, a childhood friend. Unfortunately, it was of short duration and ended in divorce.

Christian now had to fend for himself. He could not return to his father's home; he could no longer consider it a port in a storm. He had to have permission to visit, as did the other children. Henceforth, Washington state was to become a refuge for Christian. Years earlier Marlon had bought a piece of property with a cabin for Christian, and he would live there when Marlon had "thrown him out." Now he decided that the northwest would be his home, far away from Hollywood and his father.

Through the years he had made friends there his own age and it was comforting to know Christian was near JoAn and her family, who also embraced him with their love and generosity.

Marlon tried not to be a movie-star father to the children, but there was no escaping it as they learned about their father's fame at their schools and from their mothers. Marlon Brando left Movie Star at the studio. But the children—Christian, Miko, Teihotu and Cheyenne, and their mothers, embraced it.

He was a movie star, they were the children of a movie star and were treated as such.

Marlon didn't allow the children to visit him while working. Miko was the exception when he came to Paris and asked to visit the *Last Tango in Paris* set as a birthday present. Also, Miko visited us for a week while we were staying at the Park Lane Hotel in London after filming on *Superman*. He was in his teens at the time, so he was exposed to conversations about the movie, since Marlon still had some work to do on the film.

Marlon, in Miko's presence, said he wanted to buy me a Rolls Royce for my role in his accepting *Superman,* and also for helping him through it. I thought that, more likely, he was trying to buy forgiveness for the very bad time he had given me in the country, where we had leased a house during the filming. I didn't want a Rolls Royce. A girlfriend, who was with Marlon, expressed surprise that he would give me a Rolls. I was repeating I didn't want one. Marlon was insisting I leave and buy one. Miko got into the act, urging me to take it. It became so ridiculous that to stop it, I said, "All right, Marlon, I'll buy a Rolls. Thank you very much."

Marlon didn't believe me. He turned to Miko and said, "I want you to go with her *now*. Make sure she buys the car." I was thinking, *Marlon drives my car more than his own vehicles, why does he want a Rolls?*

Miko was very excited for me. But he was due for a big letdown. We were informed at the Rolls Royce showroom where we looked at the cars that it would take two years to get one. I didn't order. I allowed Miko to tell Marlon about our experience. And I thanked Marlon again for the Rolls Royce.

Marlon had lucked out. I was going to stick it to him. Since he had been so insistent, I had decided I'd purchase the most expensive Rolls convertible made—loaded. I was going to make him pay for his behavior in the country.

I can also add the Rolls Royce to the Christmas gifts to Acapulco I didn't take.

* * * * *

Early in the year 2000, I received a very disturbing call from Marlon. After our greetings and inquiries into our health issues were put behind us, he proceeded to reveal that he was in dire financial trouble. His business manager had informed him he was greatly in debt and only had 12,000 dollars in liquid assets. His telephones, except for one line, had been cut off for lack of payment. He feared his utilities were next. And then bankruptcy. Would I please come up and straighten out his financial affairs for him as "it's driving me crazy?"

Wasn't this where I usually came in? Been there, done that. I knew Marlon was prone to lying and exaggeration to get what he wanted. And I hadn't been visiting as often as he expected. Also, I hadn't been staying with him when I did visit. I stayed with girlfriends or at a hotel, which bothered him. I determined to talk to his business manager to ascertain if the financial picture Marlon painted was that bleak before I committed myself to a few weeks with him that could turn into months.

I reminded myself, as Marlon had so many times, he was an actor. He was overwrought, but was it real? I decided I'd check it out first and make my recommendation as I knew that if it was as bad as he said, it was nothing I wanted to take on.

After talking to his business manager, I advised Marlon his business affairs were too complex with the different households and properties in different states and countries. And, since it was near tax time, I further mentioned how complicated his tax return was. Therefore, I suggested he needed a professional business manager. He exploded at the mention of a professional business manager, exclaiming they were why he was in this financial mess and had no money. I learned he had phoned JoAn Corrales in Kalama, Washington, where Christian was living, and asked who handled her business affairs—then made overtures to her advisers to take over the business management of his affairs, which they had refused.

Then JoAn agreed to take on the task of disentangling his financial affairs, not understanding what she was getting into.

She didn't know Marlon well enough to realize he never could cope with finances when she agreed to straighten out his financial mess. She also didn't understand that this commitment entailed the complexity of dealing financially with the different households and personalities besides Marlon. He, of course, jumped at the chance to dump everything into her lap so he wouldn't have to deal with any of it.

After JoAn Corrales had replaced Marlon's business manager, Marlon called and we discussed the state of his affairs. He was very upbeat, in contrast to the call he had made asking me to come up and stay with him for a few weeks to get his business affairs on track. In this call, he was enthusiastic about JoAn and Linda Pedula, an accountant, and the work they were doing to put his financial house in order—finding money and collecting monies owed from the government and other sources—and the new and different projects in work, which would bring him "millions." As usual he mentioned he'd be able to buy me another house to replace the one I had sold to help him out of a previous financial crisis.

Since this book is an answer as to why Marlon gave me a house in Newport Beach and a house in Bora Bora in the South Pacific, and why I sued Marlon's estate for monies owed, I'm including my remembrances of some of his calls in which he expressed his desire to do so.

It always bothered Marlon that he had been so broke that he had been obliged to ask me to help him out once again by selling my house and giving him the money.

In one call, after we exchanged our current personal well-being, and as always with Marlon, his current sexual exploits, he was very enthusiastic about a project with a Middle East country, stating they were going to end poverty in third-world countries, and at the same time "make millions." Again, he avowed how rich "we" were going to be and that I could have a house wherever I wanted to live.

During another telephone conversation, he spoke about his sexual activities at the age of 79, and I teased him about taking Viagra. Again money owed me was discussed. Our conversation was just months before he died, as Marlon was 80 on April 3rd,and he died two months later.

Marlon again called—this time to discuss ideas for a product to sell on QVC, home shopping. The few product ideas he came up with I thought involved too many other people and too much money, which he didn't have.

We were brainstorming to come up with an idea that would generate a great deal of money using Marlon's name. Two things I recall he was enthusiastic about were an earthquake-proof house and a way to air condition a house by drilling down 50 or 60 feet, etc., etc., etc. I don't remember the details because, as I listened to him, I realized this would require engineers and was not something that could get him out of the financial pit he was in—and certainly not something we could sell on QVC. So I steered him back by telling him I thought he should be personally involved—he would make more money that way—and suggested acting classes to be sold on QVC. He liked the idea and we discussed this at length, but we didn't make any decisions as to what he would do.

He remarked that he now had about 50,000 dollars he could invest. I advised him not to invest his own money, but to use "OPM." He asked what "OPM" was. "Other people's money," I said and proceeded to tell him about Aristotle Onassis who had revealed he had made his fortune with "OPM." We returned to a brief discussion of acting classes. Then he asked if I was okay financially and I assured him I was. He reiterated his previous comments to "hang in there" because "we" were going to make a fortune on acting classes. After I got off the phone, I wrote him in regard to my ideas for this project as he had liked my idea of acting classes and he wanted me to put my thoughts and ideas we had discussed down on paper and send it to him.

I didn't hear from him after I sent him the letter with my ideas for the acting classes, so I assumed he had dropped another project. But then he called and we again talked about QVC. And as if we had never discussed it, he told me he had an idea—he was going to give acting lessons. We were talking about how much money he could make, when abruptly he said he had to go because he had an appointment to have breasts made and he'd call back. I reacted with, "Breasts made!" He explained he was going to be dressed in woman's clothes so the actors would not be aware of Marlon Brando during the acting classes. He assured me he was serious about this project and again mentioned the money "we" were going to make. He ended the call by reiterating that he wanted me to have a roof over my head and financial security—completely ignoring my assurances I had both.

Lying For A Living, the acting classes, were discussed in subsequent calls. He enumerated the actors and actresses he had lined up, and he was pleased about that. And he seemed happy at the thought that he was doing something to make those millions and always related it to giving me anything I wanted. He never heard my entreaty not to think about it; he completely blocked it out.

Marlon phoned about another project—this one dealt with importing silks, etc., from China and selling them on QVC. Now he was going into the importing business with Anita Wylie. He wanted my input, so he asked me to call Anita and check out their plans—which I did.

I learned that Anita had already started to import silk goods from China. As I recall, she bankrolled the importing business to the tune of 20,000 dollars and Marlon, as his wont, was contributing his name, which he thought to be worth a great deal of money.

This conversation again was Marlon's road to millions. The deal with Anita, like many others, was abandoned, and subsequently she sent me some of the scarves and silk dresses she had imported.

It should be noted that Marlon was very serious about this project and had a meeting with a woman from QVC in regard to selling these China silk products. He even committed to personally appear on camera. Again, as with the acting lessons, he would dress as a woman with a gray wig and hawk his wares. This went nowhere as he never heard from QVC after their meeting.

Is it any wonder? It was all right to phone me with all his wild ideas, but it was another thing to have a meeting with Marlon where he'd have flights of fancy, if you didn't know him.

His obsession with making millions, buying me a house, giving me money, and taking care of me was beginning to worry me. Was he thinking of and regretting all the millions he had earned and spent with abandon? Millions were definitely on his mind, along with my well-being and his desire to buy a grand house for me. Were these calls a guilt trip? I tried to figure him out.

Sometime in late 2003 or early 2004, in a call from Marlon with the same discussion about the millions he could make, we explored what his name was worth. There had been an article in the paper regarding autographs and what stars' autographs were worth. Marlon's autograph on a Godfather photograph was listed as bringing in 2,000 dollars. This aroused a great deal of interest. He urged me to come up to the house for a few weeks—he wanted to give me his Godfather hat and his cape from Superman and asked if I knew where it was, as he hadn't seen it in a while. I told him where I knew it was, but he said it wasn't there. We explored the possibility that someone had taken it. I asked him not to start an interrogation of the employees. I would check, which I did, and discovered that it had been taken out of Marlon's closet, where it had hung for years, and transferred to the den closet. He also said we would go through all his possessions and I could have whatever I wanted in the house. But he especially wanted me to have the Godfather hat. We discussed his Godfather Oscar, which he had previously given me.

The thought went through my mind that he wanted all his drawers and closets cleaned out and didn't trust anyone else to go through them. But he continued with the giveaway by saying that he would sign as many photos as I wanted. That I could gather all the photos I had and all the photos I had filed through the years and he'd sign them all for me.

He also said that I should type a letter of authenticity that he would sign. I said my typing days were long over—I didn't have a typewriter, or a computer. He suggested that my niece, Mims, could type the letter of authentication and make copies for me. I phoned Mims and told her about the call from Marlon, and she typed and made copies of the letter as Marlon had suggested.

Marlon then discussed the possibility of making enough money from the sale of everything he gave me, and everything he signed, to take care of me. He felt very optimistic that it would happen.

I had been suffering from a very serious sinus infection, which required surgery, hospitalization, and recovery time, and put off driving up to Marlon's. And, as he was so full of life, and concern for me, I didn't think of Marlon dying. But did he?

After my operation I spoke to Marlon and his advice to me was, "Hang in there, kid, they're coming up with all these new drugs, and if we can hang on for another ten years, we'll live to be 150."

I remember replying, "Do you mean live, or exist?"

And we laughed at the vision of both of us at 150—hobbling around and drooling.

*****

When I decided, in 2002, to treat my niece's two elder children, Marisha, age 12, and Christopher age 14, to a Hollywood week of sightseeing: theater, Paramount studio lunch and tour, and a Universal City visit, I planned to stay poolside at the famous Hollywood Roosevelt Hotel. The hotel is located across the street from Grauman's Chinese Theatre on Hollywood Boulevard, where all the tourists mass to step in the footprints of the movie stars imprinted there. I mostly stayed with Marlon when visiting Beverly Hills, but I thought that this would be more convenient than staying in the hills with Marlon. Here we would be central and able to join the throngs walking the boulevard, looking for their favorite celebrity's star imbedded in the sidewalk.

When I called Marlon upon arriving at the Roosevelt, he became very upset because I had chosen to stay at the hotel instead of with him and insisted I move to his home immediately. My arguments for staying at the hotel prevailed. We made a date for lunch and he was appeased.

Marisha and Christopher knew who Marlon Brando was as they had heard that their mother, Mims, had spent one school vacation as Marlon's assistant during the filming of *The Missouri Breaks* on location in Montana. Mims went to Montana as an OC girl and came back a cowgirl. And they, like everyone who watches television movies, had seen *The Godfather*. Also, their Aunt Alice had worked for him.

But they were never privy to his eccentricities, for as when Marlon was working and left Marlon Brando, Movie Star, on the set, so too, when finished work, I left Marlon Brando on the hilltop on Mulholland Drive. Consequently, when we arrived for lunch at Marlon's even I wasn't prepared for his greeting.

In the background on the immense, green lawn three or four children were playing—laughing and chasing each other in a game of tag. And foremost at the top of the steps to the garden stood at regal attention this enormous giant of a grand figure, adorned in a dull gold brocade robe highly embossed with embroidery, his hands hidden in the wide sleeves covering his arms that were crossing his huge expanse. A six-inch-tall, gold-cloth, crown-like hat covered his head.

My God, I thought, *he's gone round the bend.* I wondered if he expected us to genuflect. But again, was he bestowing an honor upon me, trying to impress the children how highly he thought of me by the "out of a movie" scene in front of them—The Lord of the Manor greeting an honored guest?

I didn't know what Marisha or Christopher were thinking. I was afraid to look at the two behind me to read the expression on their faces.

I broke the spell he had created by greeting him loudly enough to be heard over the screaming children as we ascended the steps where he silently stood in all his splendor. I reached him and without a word, he embraced me in a rib-breaking hug. He clung to me so long I whispered, "Marlon, I think you'd better let me go, I want you to meet Mims's children."

He released me enough to greet them, and still with arm encircling me, we strolled toward the front door. Along the way we stopped several times as he pointed out a few things and introduced Marisha and Christopher to his children, who had grown in the years since I had last seen them. I took note of Marlon's shortness of breath as we ambled along and realized he was stopping to catch his breath, not just to call my attention to how high the oleanders had grown.

Upon entering the house, Marlon left and changed into a more comfortable yukata before joining us in the living room where he challenged Marisha and Christopher to a game of cards. He was unaware we had been playing cards together since they were very young children. After a time Christopher dropped out, then Marisha and Marlon went at it with great enthusiasm, playing a fast, noisy name called Slapjack. Marisha didn't know Marlon had to win, and she was beating him. Fortunately, lunch was announced or we'd be there all night as Marisha was just as determined to win as Marlon. He had met his match. She won.

During lunch, Marlon entertained us with his magic card tricks. Afterwards the huge-as-ponies dogs were brought on display—the massive St. Bernard and equally so Mastiff.

Angela, his assistant, entered at about that time and told Marlon he had a London call—an old girlfriend was on the line. Marlon turned to me with devilment in his eyes and urged, "You take it. You talk to her." When I refused his urgings, he told Angela to tell her he'd call back. I would have loved to hear the story he concocted about our visit, since he wanted her to know I was there with him. He hadn't forgotten that she had always been upset about our close relationship, which forever brought Marlon much delight. How interesting that, at this advanced age, he was still playing games where women were concerned.

Along with the shortness of breath I had noticed, I now realized Marlon looked aged and tired. So soon after the dogs were taken away, I eased us out, so he could return to his bed and rest.

I called the next day when I knew he'd be up and thanked him for his hospitality. But he was more interested in talking about what kept me so young. He marveled that I never change. I assured him I had. It was only his eyesight that had dimmed. That was when he confessed he had cataracts; that his sight was indeed dim and getting dimmer. Then he regaled me with all he could see. Especially since he had lost some weight. He was now able to see things he hadn't seen in years, except when he stepped out of the shower and caught a glimpse of himself in the mirror. Of course, being Brando, he was more graphic than I dare put into words.

*****

The last time I spoke to Marlon, he was very upbeat. I remember he started out by talking about one of the girls he had at his beck and call for years. He said in complete astonishment,

"Can you believe she really thought I loved her?" He wanted to know if he had ever told me he loved her.

We reminisced—about his many, many love affairs; about being "crazy"; about people we had met; the people we knew; about all we had been through together; about why he and I had never "made it" together. He wanted to know if it was because of all the girls that had been running through his bedroom during the early years—wanted to know if I ever cared for him romantically as he had about me. We talked about the good things and the bad—how I had helped him through so many of the bad, his illnesses, and how indebted and very, very grateful he was.

Then he switched from the nostalgia to a discussion of money—and, as always, the house: "Sweetheart, I'm going to buy you another house."

"Please stop worrying about a house for me. I'm happy living where I am. I don't need a house."

Ignoring my wishes, he reiterated, "I owe you, I want you to have a house." And then he qualified it by saying, "Or the money."

I laughed and lightly tossed off, "Okay, I'll take the money."

This caused him to remark that "we're" going to make so much money on QVC and on his other projects that we'd never have to worry about money again.

Before we terminated our call, he surprised me by a question, for he poignantly asked me, "Was I really as bad as people said I was?"

I almost said, "No, you were worse."

Instead I made light of the question, gently replied, with a little laugh, "No. You weren't."

He said he didn't think he was and was happy I didn't think he was as bad as was written about him.

That was to be our last chat. I was glad I held my tongue—and glad we had such a pleasant conversation. This was just weeks before he died on July 1, 2004.

I phoned Marlon the day before he died. I was unable to reach him.

It saddens me.

The Bells Toll

2004, June 29th, Tuesday—noonish—called Marlon—was told by the housekeeper, Angela, "He's sleeping."

When I asked, "How is he feeling?" she cheerfully replied, "He's wonderful!"

I left a message for him. I didn't receive a return call. Wasn't disturbed as at times Marlon took a day or two, or even a week or two, to return a call—especially if you were calling to ask him to recall a name from our past, as I was.

June 30th, Wednesday—I remember thinking, *Marlon is a night person, I'll call him tonight.* I called about 7:30 p.m. Received the answering machine and left the same message I had given the housekeeper. I wanted to confirm the name of a man from Cal Tech who was also an artist. I thought his name might be Jim Real—Marlon might know.

July 1st, Thursday—4:30 p.m. I received a call from JoAn. She said everyone was trying to locate Christian because Marlon was in intensive care and not expected to live. *How did this go from "HE'S WONDERFUL!"* my mind screamed.

7:00 p.m. Another call from JoAn. Marlon had died at 6:30 p.m.

I'm numb.

Did I hear correctly? No breaking news on television.

I phoned Jocelyn, Marlon's sister, to confirm. Got her answering service. This was not good.

Left message, "Is it true?" Asked her to call, "No matter how late you get in."

11:30 p.m. Jocelyn returned my call. "Yes, it's true. He died of cancer of the liver."

July 2nd, Friday morning—Still no "Brando dies" news on television. But the phones were still ringing—calls, calls, calls and rumors galore.

Noon—Called JoAn—asked her to phone Marlon's attorney, whom she knew quite well, and tell him to make a statement on behalf of the family to stop the wild rumors surrounding Marlon's death.

I felt I owed my friend that much.

Finally, mid-afternoon, the attorney released a statement. The world received the news, the eulogies begin, and friends and acquaintances, along with fellow actors, and fans worldwide, begin to mourn.

Marlon's wishes and instructions to me, if he died before I did, were very clear and precise.

"I want to be cremated. Jocelyn knows. Do not want anyone to see me dead. I want them to remember me as I was when they last saw me."

"I want some of my ashes to be buried here." (On the grounds of his home on Mulholland Drive in Beverly Hills where he lived for most of his adult life.)

"And some where me and Wally hiked. Florine will know. We took her hiking with us a few times."

"And some on Tetiaroa."

"And no services. And positively no memorial services." Marlon was emphatic about services and memorial services.

I have subsequently learned others had been told the same thing. After his death, I made his wishes known to his sister Jocelyn. She passed on his wishes to his immediate family since Jocelyn was informed by the hospital that she could not claim the body for cremation as Marlon had wished because she was not next of kin. The children were. Marlon was unaware of this. Marlon always spoke of Jocelyn as next of kin.

Were Marlon's wishes carried out?

There were a few open-coffin viewings at the mortuary for selected people. There was a 150-plus guest memorial. I received an invitation. In fact, I received three. From three different people; but did not attend in deference to Marlon's wishes. Neither did others for the same reason. Other very personal, long time acquaintances were not on the guest list and would have been if Marlon had wanted a memorial service and had made up the guest list before he died. They were rightfully pained by the snub.

One who invited me was a TV personality. She haughtily informed me the invitation to the memorial was for me alone; I could not bring anyone with me. I'd bet my life Marlon never told anyone he wanted an open-casket viewing and a Hollywood star-studded memorial. His sister would bear this out.

I learned that Marlon's ashes, along with Wally's, were tossed, on a windy day, in the desert of California. Where?

And rumor has it, some were taken to Tahiti to be scattered on his beloved atoll Tetiaroa.

Another rumor—which proved to be true—had some of his ashes sent through the mail in a baggy to Christian.

Had he made a life-held change? Were these his wishes that were carried out?

I don't know. Who cares? Does Marlon?

We can only wonder.

For now he's gone. Gone on the desert winds.

Yet, he lives on, in his many great, and not so great, films. And we'll now see him on our television screens in the spring, summer, autumn, and winter of his life. And we'll remember—remember our own seasons—remember watching in wonder Brando on the sound stages and distant locations, creating characters that will live on in these films. For we were there…oft-times helping to get him through the exhausting days. Days when his personal life was falling apart and chaos reigned.

This intensely private and personal life we were privileged to share. So many memories we've made together—memories that contain all the emotions known to man; the good, the bad, the ugly—the laughter, the pain. Memories to relive with mutual friends, who also shared his entire adult life—both film and personal. Memories to cherish and treasure, but yet some memories too personal to share.

His was a life squandered—a life unfinished. For even in death, he looms like a giant shadow over the lives he brought into this world, and also those he brought into his sphere.

He's gone.

Did he, will he, find his rest?

We can only listen to the desert winds that one day carried him soaring, then being spent, quietly and gently laid him to rest on the desert floor where he is destined to soar and fall again, and yet again, throughout eternity.

And so, for the last time, Mar:

Love and kisses,

Alice

*****

I end Part One with "love and kisses"—this is the way I usually ended notes to Marlon throughout our lifetime. It began when I started to work for Marlon. He left OOOOOO's and XXXXXX's signed Marlon on my tablet so that I'd see it first thing in the morning when I arrived at work. And through the years, I'd also receive messages from him signed the same.

As our relationship matured, so did I, and Marlon as well. And I felt safe in expressing, ever so lightly, feelings of caring without fear of being misunderstood. Thus, through the years we freely exchanged words of affection and I accepted his OOOOOO's and XXXXXX's without reservation—as he did mine.

A.M.

EPILOGUE

This is written to explain my lasting friendship with Brando, which was cemented in the first ten years of our relationship. At the beginning, Marlon and I were the only people in the house on a day-to-day basis, except for the different girls who passed through. Most of whom I never saw or met.

But as with any bachelor household, there had to be people to maintain the premises. And as much as Marlon was guarding his privacy, he had to admit certain people into his space. Therefore I hired, first, a crew to clean the house once a week. This didn't work out because of Marlon's sleeping habits. Then, he allowed me to hire a housekeeper. There were many. Since there was the constant money crunch, they lasted short periods. Also, there were those who didn't stay very long as they were intimidated by him and his moods and the lack of routine—his unorthodox sleeping habits.

It was years before there was a permanent housekeeper, and by this time, little children were on the scene. Marlon was forced to change his life style by the advent of children. And I had gotten him to clean up his act to a great extent in regards to drugs.

Also, I had hired a maintenance man who came by when I had a list of repairs, etc. I hired a gardener and a pool man. Marlon would complain about all the people around, but when I'd ask him if he wanted to mow the lawn, or get up on the roof to find and repair a leak in the skylight, or maintain the pool, he'd give me a dirty look and walk away.

There were times he complained he had no privacy; he was running into strangers. But he was the one making demands that I couldn't fulfill, and I had to hire experts.

At 36 years old, Marlon had no idea what it took to maintain a home, especially one with a business office, an acre of land, and a pool. He treated his home like a hotel. His previous secretaries did not have an office in his home. They came when summoned and departed. His girlfriends stayed—and went.

Now he had me on the premises, and I didn't always do his bidding. I drew lines. He buzzed me and asked me to bring him a coffee, which was simple. I knew how to boil water and spoon two teaspoons of powdered coffee into a cup and stir. But when he asked me to bring him some scrambled eggs and toast along with the coffee, I didn't hesitate to tell him I was not a short-order cook and, furthermore, I didn't know how to scramble eggs.

The day I told him that, he came running out of his room to the kitchen, called me from the office, got a small frying pan, put a chunk of butter in the pan, cracked two eggs into the butter, took a fork, broke the yolks, swished the mess around twice, stood back, turned to me as I watched, and snapped, "That's how you scramble eggs."

I started to snicker and said, "Let's see you make toast."

He was in no mood for humor. "Where's the toaster?" he demanded.

"You don't own one," I said, "But there's another frying pan, maybe you could put in a chunk of butter, put the bread in, and push it around."

"Buy a toaster," he snapped over his shoulder as he left the kitchen taking the frying pan and fork with him.

It didn't end there. The next day, he buzzed and again asked me to bring him scrambled eggs and toast with his coffee. I knew him well enough by this time to know he was testing me, so I was ready for him. I set up a tray with a linen cloth and had cut a pink camellia that I put on a folded linen napkin. I followed his routine and swished the eggs twice. But I added my own flourishes; I salted and peppered liberally and for an added touch a couple of dashes of Tabasco. Burned the toast in the toaster I had brought from home. But the coffee was made to his liking. I marched down the hall to his room and with a cheery "good morning" put the tray next to him on the bed. He looked at it and transferred it to his lap as he said, "Sit down. This looks wonderful!"

I sat on the edge of the king-sized bed furthest from him. He proceeded to eat the eggs with relish, never batting an eye, and, while picking up the burnt toast, exclaimed, "How did you know I liked my toast this way?"

By now I had to chuckle and commented, "I expected you to throw the plate of eggs across the room. I was ready to run."

He just smirked, gave me a piercing look, and, punching his words, said, "Do you think I'd give you the satisfaction?"

When later I heard his version of what I did, I discovered that I had put so much salt in the eggs that his lips puckered all day and so much Tabasco that when he went to the bathroom and had a BM—well, imagine the description of what puckered and his discomfort. He certainly had a way with words.

When I first began to work for Marlon, my job was to take care of all the everyday things that Marlon didn't want to be bothered with. I answered the phone, there was minimal correspondence, and I forwarded fan mail to Claire Priest Fan Mail Agency, which sent out photos and pertinent information regarding Marlon's career.

Marlon wasn't concerned with what he considered "piddling things." I soon discovered that almost everything was considered "piddling" and he didn't want to be bothered. His interest lay elsewhere—mainly the pursuit of ladies. So it quickly developed that he went his way and I went mine. I discovered that we both were well-suited to this arrangement. And our friendship flourished after a very, very bad start.

Since my office was in his home, I found myself slowly but surely involved in running his household. And before I knew what was happening, I was sucked into administrating not only his business affairs, but taking care of all his personal needs—buying his clothes, sundries, etc. Then I became involved in interior decorating with his Aunt Bette Lindemeyer, who was an interior decorator, and her assistant, Bill Huston. This led to making renovations and supervising building additions. When Marlon would despair of the noise and the mess, he'd leave town or the country until everything had been completed.

Needless to say, after years of my working alone, a secretary was hired to do secretarial work, such as it was, because my plate was too full. I accompanied Marlon on trips, both personal and business, and also when he traveled around the world as a UN ambassador for UNICEF. I worked with Marlon when he was filming, both at the studio and on location—local, around the United States, and foreign.

I also ran lines with him when he worked on a picture. At the time, it was just another duty and it wasn't until much later that I realized I had been not only cueing Marlon Brando, but at times acting with him, too.

Then there were the prolonged negotiations for the purchase of his atoll Tetiaroa. The atoll is 12 islands surrounding a lagoon. We joked that there were 13 islands at low tide. In some photos of the atoll you'll count 12 islands and in others 13 islands, which bears this out, though the 13th is merely a sand bar. In due time there was the building of an airstrip and bungalows, etc., tourism, and scientific experiments to be contended with.

Later Marlon purchased three bungalows on the island of Bora Bora. He kept one for himself, gave one to me, and one to Jay Kanter, his trusted agent. Jack Nicholson also purchased a bungalow next to mine over the water in the lagoon. I was in charge of overseeing the building and then furnishing the bungalows, which entailed many trips for months to Bora Bora. Marlon had turned Bora Bora over to me. This project was no small task.

Then there were the children and children visitations, and children's dental and medical needs, especially those from Tahiti. The household and life took on a new aspect with the advent of different mothers and children—and his ever-present girlfriends.

Throughout the years, there were also the people with medical problems that Marlon brought into his home while they were being treated. Of course, I was chauffeuring and caring for their needs. And the comfort of the many house guests.

Then came the addition of dogs. No lap dogs for Marlon—St. Bernard, a Mastiff, a German shepherd, and to top it off, a half wolf, half German shepherd. There also were, through the years, two cats, two lovebirds, a parrot, an ocelot, and a raccoon. And when Christian came to stay, his hamster and white mouse. Plus there were goldfish in the atrium pond and an aquarium. With all these animals, there were many hair-raising trips to the veterinarian in the San Fernando Valley. They also created many problems with the children and employees in the house.

I quit working for Marlon after *Quemada* (*Burn* in release in the United States) when we returned from filming the picture in Cartagena, Columbia. I moved back to Newport Beach for about two years.

Another big change in my personal and working relationship with Marlon occurred when, unbeknownst to me or anyone else, Marlon, who was petitioning the court for custody of his son, Christian, had submitted my name to the court as guardian for his child. I was accepted by the court. So Marlon and I came to an understanding. Now, along with the court and Marlon, I was legal guardian of his child. And by court order Marlon had to provide for me and Christian, which included living quarters for both. Marlon told me he had informed the court that I was living at his home from time to time. Now with guardianship I was compelled to.

So in a dozen or so years, I went from secretary, to personal assistant, to contractor, to guardian—and always friend. And I always shouldered more and more responsibility.

As the years went by and Marlon became involved in different social causes and different projects, along with developing Tetiaroa and writing, many secretaries were hired for the different projects. A secretary was also hired for the summer as both Marlon and I went to Tahiti, Tetiaroa, and Bora Bora in the South Pacific from June to September. So along with the influx of workers and secretaries, the children, their friends, and animals were also added to the invasion of Marlon's private domain.

There were times he found this all too overwhelming and he'd escape in a Valium haze, or lock himself in his room, or send everyone home until recalled, or leave for his island retreat—Tetiaroa.

Through the years Marlon and I had many conversations regarding his girlfriends, who didn't know and didn't understand our close relationship. Marlon enjoyed pitting one girl against another and didn't exempt me, regardless of our relationship. So when a girl brought up me, Marlon grasped on it with relish and would tell me what she had said about me and him, and about our relationship. I'd dismiss it as I knew what Marlon was up to. But this didn't deter Marlon. He would then make up lies and pass them on attributing them to me, thus trying to promote a "cat fight." They didn't know me so they were unaware that this was not my modus operandi. Rather than give him the satisfaction of a confrontation, I would stay at the Beach for a few days and by that time the girl would not be around and he would be plotting against someone else.

But in the eighties when he was pulling this, placating his current girlfriend, I told him I was sick and tired of his childish games and said I would just leave. By this time, I was only working three days a week. Christian was 21, married, and out of the house.

Marlon and I had a long talk about his situation and he agreed with me that I shouldn't have to deal with someone's emotional insecurities. Though if she thought about it, I should have been the least of her worries. It was all the other girls she didn't know about that were the problem. But they were invisible; I became the target of her emotional insecurity.

So Marlon pacified her by saying I was retiring, when in reality, he wanted me to set up an office in my home in Newport Beach. Therefore I went along with his retirement story and after summer vacation in the South Pacific, instead of returning to Beverly Hills, I went directly home and began to transform my sunroom into an office. I purchased an Apple computer, bought an answering machine, and set up shop. Marlon had asked me not to take any of my personal things from his home office, my bedroom when I stayed, as he wasn't ready to face my absence. So I left everything, knowing I could get anything at any time.

Setting up an office in my home was the worst thing I ever did. Even though I was "retired," Marlon and I let it be known to all that I would stay on as "consultant." Therefore I was available at all hours, day or night, to the secretaries and employees, business managers, lawyers, etc. And, of course, Brando.

He became impossible. He wanted to know where I was at all times. I would get message after message on the answering machine, day or night, berating me for not returning his calls if I was out. As if that wasn't bad enough, if I was not home and he called and didn't receive an immediate return call from me, he called my sisters, Boots and Marty. And if he couldn't reach them, he'd call my mother. I didn't call my sisters to tell them every time I left the house, so I'd get messages from them to call as soon as I returned, as Marlon was looking for me. After being together for 30 years in a close relationship, Marlon felt my absence at times unbearable, therefore the panic calls.

It didn't take me long to get rid of the answering machine. I don't have one to this day. I don't need to monitor calls like some people do. If I'm home, I'll answer the phone. And the computer ended up in a local school. Marlon was angry for a while to put it mildly, but he eventually got over it because there was nothing he could do.

It didn't take long before Marlon was trying to entice me back. Fortunately for me, I was having dental and physical checkups and was involved in community affairs, so I wasn't available to journey to Beverly Hills "for a few days." I knew that if I did, I'd be back on the three-days-a-week schedule.

He tried during Christmas week. Marlon called asking me to come up and help him get through the holidays. There were five employees at his beck and call and I felt he didn't need a sixth. Besides, I had a party to give and several I wanted to attend, plus our family traditional Christmas dinner and celebration.

While I was on the phone with him someone came in the room. Marlon stopped speaking and asked what the person wanted. I heard a woman's voice speaking. He listened and then exploded, "Don't bother me with that, get the f--k out of here before I break your f--king legs." I asked what that was about. He was still exasperated when he replied, "She told me the sink was blocked. No one can do anything. I have to do it."

I said, "Marlon you should not speak to her in that tone of voice, nor use that language." I had to hear how incompetent everyone was, etc., etc. I listened while he railed and then talked to him until he calmed down as I knew if I didn't, he'd do one of two things; pop a Valium or bring the girls in, and in the mood he was, give them all hell. It didn't sound as if it was going to be a very happy holiday season. But I advised him to be nice, tell them to call a plumber. Relax. It was Christmas.

After that call, I knew I could expect to receive others from him. It was only four months since I had left; it was too soon for me to return to spend time with him. He needed more time to accept that I was not coming back. He missed me, but I could do without all the chaos he created.

And I mentally thanked the girl for her insecurities that enabled me to enjoy the peaceful solitude and the freedom and time to pursue my own interests without squeezing everything in as I had done in the past.

It wasn't long before Marlon called and told me she was no longer around. She had caught him in bed with his housekeeper and that ended the relationship. It wasn't enough to make me return. I resisted his entreaties. I didn't need to contend with this new romantic entanglement.

Within the year Marlon was asking me to come up for a few days to meet the latest addition to his new family. And through the years this family grew to three children. Again Marlon was in court—with this extended family. And once again, he was confronted with lawyers' fees.

But by now he was not able to carry a film and command a large salary; he had no fallback. He was in failing health and hiding it from everyone, calling his friends on his good days and giving them glowing reports on his sex life; how well he looked for his age; how long we could live if we just hung in there because of the great advancement in medicine. He was looking forward to a ripe old age.

And his plans. Plans for making millions, plans for me, plans for overcoming poverty in the world.

All the dreams—yet to be fulfilled.

Marlon had always been reclusive, but it had been by choice. Now his body no longer responded as it had in his youth; his breath was shallow, his steps were slow. His bed was now his refuge instead of his playground. But his mind was unfettered and on a visit, he introduced me to a girl he had met on the Internet. He was still working the Brando charm. But he no longer awoke each day with a body he didn't know sleeping beside him. The sheets had turned from hot to cold. He was lonely. Still, sex addicted. Still dreaming about having a Chinese live-in.

His computer and the Internet had become his companions—these and movie rentals had become his entertainment. I could only embrace him and depart despite his urging me to, "Pay the driver and stay a few days."

The months passed.

I visited once more. He clung as he had many years ago when he was drowning in misery. I couldn't believe his condition, this old man, nor the condition of his house. I ached for him and pretended I didn't see the way he was living. I overlooked it, but I knew Marlon well enough to know he was looking at himself and the house through my eyes. After I departed, I was told that he had expressed himself as being ashamed, saying, "Of all the times for Alice to come up was now. I'm so ashamed."

His remark pained me.

There came a time when Marlon was overwhelmed by circumstances and he was asked, "Why don't you ask Alice to come up and help you?"

He vehemently said, "Absolutely not! Yes, I need her but, no!"

He became silent for a moment, then whispered sadly, "The man she knew doesn't live here anymore."

And he slowly rose from where he was sitting and shuffled down the hall toward the sanctuary of his bed.

After this, we only visited on the telephone—where he could still be Marlon Brando, the star who shone so bright and whose light had not dimmed.

PART TWO

BEVERLY HILLS, 1991-92

In 1991, Marlon phoned to inform me he was going to write his autobiography and asked if I would make myself available to him. Soon after he called again, this time asking me to come to his home as he needed to talk to me in person about his autobiography. This is when I discovered Marlon had an ingenious idea; he would ask ten or 15 of his intimates to write how they perceived him in not less than 25 pages—and he would write a critique of each submission. Each writer would receive 50,000 dollars if Marlon used their material. He later changed the amount to 25,000 dollars. My assignment: Contact all the people he selected and sell the idea to them. Then "keep on top of them," urging them to submit the material to Marlon as soon as possible.

This idea was immediately shot down by the publisher. They were not going to pay him millions unless he, not ten or 15 people, wrote the book.

But Marlon ignored them. He liked the idea and left for London, leaving me to carry on alone. I spent months encouraging the writers and urging them on while Marlon kept faxing, for he was anxious to obtain the material as soon as possible.

After all submissions were transmitted to Marlon in London, he didn't contact me or anyone else to let them know what he thought about the material. Now the tables had turned. Almost every day, one or all who had written were calling to find out if he was going to use their material and, if so, when they'd receive compensation. But, I discovered, Marlon never intended to use the material for his book—he thought this would be a good way to find out what everyone thought about him. Mission accomplished. He put us all to a test. We never knew whether or not we had passed. I think I flunked because I didn't hear directly from him for a few months. Of course, he was in Spain filming *Columbus* and was concentrating on that.

Then one day he called and said, "I'm not mad at you anymore."

"What were you mad about?" I asked.

"I don't knooow," he replied, drawing out "know."

"Well, Mar, next time let me knooow when you're mad at me so I can worry about what I did and why I'm not hearing from you. I thought after you returned from Spain, you were getting over jet lag and the women problems on location."

Actually, I'm certain that if he was mad at me, he really didn't remember why. But I remember. I had tweaked him a bit, pushed a few buttons, and since he was preparing to go to Spain, he didn't have time to think about verbally sparring with me. He, I'm certain, was concentrating on ways and means to postpone starting to work. Also, there were two serious problems with women in his life that were deeply disturbing him at that time, which he discussed with me by phone from London. Although I ventured solutions, he was apprehensive and he decided we'd talk upon his return; he couldn't consider solutions when he was also being plagued by problems caused by his accepting a role in *Columbus*. I had received calls and messages for him from Indian friends. When I had relayed the messages, it had disturbed him, but he needed the money; he couldn't join them and walk out in protest as they wanted. He asked me to explain his situation to them and smooth the waters for him, which I did.

The calls I received from Spain indicated he was giving everyone in his entourage a very, very bad time. I imagine my pushing buttons had added to his bad mood. This is what I overwrote about him and sent to London before he left for

Spain to film *Columbus*. The large caps were necessary because of his failed eyesight. Since I don't want to bore the reader with repetition, I have excluded some incidents I have written about in Part One from what I wrote and sent along to Marlon. For instance, I have eliminated Marlon's destructive behavior in New York City during the filming of *The Fugitive Kind*.

*****

MAR, YOU'RE PULLING MY LEG!

IF WE LIVE TO BE A HUNDRED, AND I HOPE WE DO, MAYBE I'LL KNOW MARLON BRANDO.

KNOW HIM? JUST WHEN I THINK I'VE GOT A HANDLE ON HIM, HE THROWS ME COMPLETELY. AN EXAMPLE: JUST RECENTLY, HE CALLED AND SAID, "ALICE, I'M GOING TO WRITE MY AUTOBIOGRAPHY."

HIS AUTOBIOGRAPHY! SEE WHAT I MEAN? I WOULD HAVE BET MY LIFE, WHICH I ASSURE YOU I VALUE HIGHLY, THESE WORDS WOULD NEVER, NEVER BE UTTERED BY MARLON BRANDO. IF I HAD MADE THE WAGER, I SUPPOSE I WOULDN'T BE ALIVE TO SEE THE BOOK'S PUBLICATION.

"I WANT YOU TO CONTRIBUTE YOUR PERCEPTIONS OF ME. YOU CAN WRITE ANYTHING. NO HOLDS BARRED," HE CONTINUED. MARLON, HE'S ALWAYS TESTING. WAS THIS ANOTHER TEST? OH, I HAD HEARD BOOK RUMORS. BUT THERE ARE ALWAYS RUMORS OUT THERE ABOUT MARLON. OBVIOUSLY, THIS WAS NO RUMOR, THIS WAS MARLON TALKING. THERE IS NO WAY I COULD TELL THE WORLD WHO MARLON BRANDO IS. I KNOW THAT AS SOON AS I PUT SOMETHING DOWN ON PAPER, HIS VERY ACTIONS WOULD CONTRADICT IT. FOR WHO HE WAS YESTERDAY, HE IS NOT TODAY.

AND YET THERE ARE CONSTANTS.

BUT AN AUTOBIOGRAPHY! WHY, MARLON, WHY? WHAT CRITERIA DO I USE TO ASSESS A LIFE?

THIRTY-FIVE YEARS OF SHARING A FULL LIFE IS NOT ONLY DIFFICULT, BUT IMPOSSIBLE, TO COMPRESS INTO "ABOUT 25 PAGES." BUT THIS IS MARLON'S AUTOBIOGRAPHY, NOT MINE. HE WANTED TO KNOW

HOW I VIEWED HIM WITH "NO HOLDS BARRED," SO I'LL STEP BACK IN TIME AND HAVE A LOOK AT THE MAN HE WAS AND THE MAN HE IS TODAY.

SOME REMEMBRANCES HAVE FADED, SOME HAVE LODGED IN MY MIND AND ARE AS CLEAR AS IF HAPPENING TODAY, AND SOME MEMORIES ARE JUST LIKE A KALEIDOSCOPE OF FLASHING IMAGES THAT SAY, "CATCH ME IF YOU CAN."

TOO SHORT A TIME IS ALLOTTED TO PURSUE THEM ALL—AND OF THOSE REMEMBRANCES THAT DO COME TO MIND IN WORD FORM ALONG WITH IMAGE, I CAN ONLY SAY THE CONVERSATION IS BEST OF MY RECOLLECTION.

MARLON AND I REMEMBER SOME EVENTS IN HIS LIFE DIFFERENTLY, AND WE SHOULD. I DIDN'T KNOW HIS THOUGHTS OR MOTIVATIONS FOR HIS ACTIONS AT ALL TIMES. I ONLY KNOW MY OWN PERCEPTIONS, SO, IN THIS SENSE, HIS TRUTHS SHOULD PREVAIL IF THERE ARE ANY CONTRADICTIONS IN OUR RECOLLECTIONS. THOUGH I ALWAYS KEEP IN MIND JACK BECK'S OBSERVATIONS IN REGARD TO MARLON...."HE HAS FAILURE TO RECALL CORRECTLY INCIDENTS WHICH ARE REVEALING ABOUT HIMSELF."

TO START WITH, MARLON BRANDO IS:

CHARISMATIC
HANDSOME
HUMOROUS
VITAL
EXUBERANT
SECRETIVE
CHALLENGING

WITH THE FIRST "HELLO," MARLON CHALLENGED ME BY ASKING HOW OLD I WAS. NOW, THAT WAS GETTING OFF ON THE WRONG FOOT WITH ME. NOT THAT I WAS AGE CONSCIOUS AT THE TIME, BUT TO THIS DAY, I'VE NEVER WANTED TO BE THOUGHT OF AS A NUMBER. YOU KNOW, SHE'S TEN, ISN'T SHE BIG FOR HER AGE; SHE'S 30, DOESN'T SHE DRESS YOUNG FOR HER AGE; OR SHE'S 40, DOESN'T SHE LOOK GOOD FOR HER AGE; AND SHE'S 50, YOU'D THINK SHE'D ACT HER AGE. YOU'RE NEVER THE RIGHT AGE.

I RECALL ANSWERING HIM, "OLD ENOUGH TO KNOW ENOUGH NOT TO TELL YOU."

I SOON DISCOVERED THAT MARLON RELISHED PUTTING PEOPLE OFF-BALANCE BY STATING SOMETHING IN SUCH A WAY THAT WHATEVER YOU ANSWERED DAMNED YOU. YOU KNOW, "WHEN DID YOU LAST BEAT YOUR WIFE?" QUESTIONS.

UNCONVENTIONAL
SELF-CONFIDENT

DELIBERATE
A FREE SPIRIT
TRUE TO HIMSELF
LACKS DISCIPLINE
MIDNIGHT FRIDGE RAIDER
STRAINED WILLPOWER

WHISTLE-BLOWER ALICE

IF YOU'RE NEVER THE RIGHT AGE, YOU'RE ALSO NEVER QUITE THE RIGHT WEIGHT TO SUIT EVERYONE, ESPECIALLY YOUR BEST FRIENDS. AND YOU CAN'T WRITE ABOUT MARLON WITHOUT WRITING ABOUT DIETS.

I DIDN'T HAVE DIET AWARENESS UNTIL I TEAMED UP WITH MARLON. YOU NAME THE DIET, MARLON HAS TRIED IT—AND EVENTUALLY, SO HAVE I. THROUGHOUT THE YEARS, I HAVE ACCUMULATED A THICK FILE FOLDER OF DIETS AND A BOOKSHELF FILLED WITH DIET AND HEALTH BOOKS.

MARLON'S FIRST DIET THAT I RECALL WAS CIGARETTES, BLACK COFFEE, STEAK, AND SALAD. IT WORKED. FOR HIM. IT'S DIFFICULT TO NUMBER HOW MANY TIMES THROUGH THE YEARS ALL THE FOOD THAT WAS CARTED OUT OF THE HOUSE BECAUSE HE WAS DIETING. THAT MEANT THAT THE STAFF HAD TO SQUIRREL FOOD IF WE WANTED TO NIBBLE. AT TIMES WE'D SUFFER PANGS OF HUNGER DURING THE DAY, ONLY TO BE TOLD THE NEXT DAY BY HIS CURRENT GIRLFRIEND WHERE SHE AND MARLON HAD DINED THE NIGHT BEFORE AND HOW HE HAD ORDERED

EVERYTHING BUT WHAT WAS ON HIS DIET PLAN. AND BETWEEN COURSES, HE'D SAY, "DON'T TELL ALICE." OR, HE'D DIET ALL WEEK AND BASKIN-ROBBINS DURING THE WEEKEND. I CAN'T IMAGINE MARLON'S WORLD WITHOUT ICE CREAM.

LIFE WASN'T A CONSTANT DIET. HIS USUAL ROUTINE WAS TO DIET BEFORE THE START OF A FILM. ONE FILM WHERE IT BACK-FIRED WAS *THE GODFATHER*. HE HAD DIETED SLIM AND THEN THEY PADDED HIM TO MATURITY. I GUESS YOU CAN'T WIN THEM ALL. ONE OF THE FUNNIEST EPISODES PERTAINING TO MARLON DIETING OCCURRED WHEN HE SIGNED FOR A FILM AT UNIVERSAL. JAY KANTER, NOW PRODUCER, SUGGESTED HE TRY A DOCTOR WHO HAD HELPED SOME STARS AT THE STUDIO SHED A FEW POUNDS BEFORE STARTING A FILM. THE DOCTOR HAD A GREAT SUCCESS RECORD ACCORDING TO JAY.

MARLON AGREED TO SEE THE DOCTOR, SO JAY MADE THE APPOINTMENT. AT THE APPOINTED TIME MARLON WENT TO THE DOCTOR'S OFFICE AND HAD THE REQUIRED PHYSICAL EXAMINATION, THEN CAME HOME WITH A DIET THAT HE TURNED OVER TO ME. HE WAS VERY PLEASED WITH THE DOCTOR AND THE DIET, WHICH CONSISTED MAINLY OF CHICKEN, FISH, VEGETABLES, FRUIT, COFFEE, OR TEA.

MY CONTRIBUTION TO HIS DIET EFFORTS WAS GROCERY SHOPPING FROM A LIST MADE FROM THE DIET MENUS. AFTER A FEW DAYS, I WONDERED ALOUD, "WHY AM I GOING TO THE STORE EVERY DAY, HAULING ALL THIS FOOD? I THOUGHT MARLON WAS DIETING."

"HE IS," WAS THE REPLY.

I RECHECKED THE DIET. THAT'S WHEN I NOTICED A LINE, "ALL YOU CAN EAT OF THE ABOVE" AT THE BOTTOM OF THE PAGE. AFTER CONSULTING WITH THE COOK, I DISCOVERED THAT MARLON TOOK THAT LINE LITERALLY. I CONFRONTED HIM AND HE BRUSHED ME OFF WITH, "I'M FOLLOWING THE DIET."

SO THAT DAY I WROTE DOWN ALL HE CONSUMED. I CALLED THE DOCTOR THE NEXT DAY AND TOLD HIM I THOUGHT IT A VERY STRANGE DIET FOR WEIGHT LOSS, THERE WAS MUCH TOO MUCH FOOD ALLOWED. I WAS OF THE OPINION THAT MARLON WOULD NEVER LOSE WEIGHT ON THE DIET HE HAD GIVEN HIM. THE DOCTOR INSISTED THAT HE WOULD LOSE WEIGHT AND ASSURED ME HE HAD NEVER HAD A FAILURE.

"YOU'RE GOING TO HAVE YOUR FIRST ONE," I PROPHESIED.

THEN I READ ALL THAT MARLON HAD EATEN THE DAY BEFORE—BREAKFAST AND LUNCH WEREN'T TOO BAD, BUT HALF A BROILER CHICKEN FOR DINNER, THEN THE OTHER HALF DURING THE NIGHT, PLUS A VARIETY OF VEGETABLES AND FRUIT REALLY GOT HIS ATTENTION. HE WAS AGHAST!

"WHERE DID HE GET THAT MENU?" HE CHOKED OUT.

"YOU GAVE IT TO HIM. BELOW THE DAILY MENUS THERE'S A LINE THAT SAYS, "YOU CAN HAVE ALL THAT YOU CAN EAT OF THE ABOVE." WHEREUPON HE SAID, "I'LL GIVE YOU MY RECEPTIONIST AND YOU GET HIM IN HERE AS SOON AS POSSIBLE." WHEN I TOLD MARLON THAT I HAD BLOWN THE WHISTLE ON HIM, HE WAS FURIOUS WITH MY TRAITOROUS ACT. HE LOVED THAT DIET. HE THOUGHT HE HAD DIED AND GONE TO

HEAVEN. HE WAS NEVER HUNGRY. THAT I COULD BELIEVE.

DID HE GO BACK TO THE DOCTOR? NO. BUT I DO THINK HE WAS JUST TRYING TO PROVE THE DOCTOR WRONG. THAT HE COULD HAVE A FAILURE. AND THE DOCTOR—HE NEVER CALLED ASKING WHERE MARLON WAS. I GUESS HE KNEW HE HAD MET HIS MATCH, AND HE WAS IN A NO-WIN SITUATION.

PASSIONATE
OUTLANDISH
CONTROLLING
KIND
SKEPTICAL
MISCHIEVOUS
ENTERTAINING
ABSENT-MINDED?

AUNTS DON'T GO TO MARLON'S PICNICS

MARLON, AS I SAID, USUALLY DIETED BEFORE FILMING, BUT BETWEEN PICTURES HE WOULD DINE OUT, HAVE LUNCHEON MEETINGS, OR DINNER GUESTS.

AND THEN THERE WERE HOLIDAYS.

IT WAS EARLY, THE DAY AFTER THANKSGIVING. BETTE LINDEMEYER, MARLON'S AUNT, CALLED AND ASKED ME TO PLEASE, PLEASE TAKE HER NAME OFF THE THANKSGIVING DAY GUEST LIST. THAT WAS MY FIRST CLUE THAT THANKSGIVING DINNER AT MARLON'S WAS A FIASCO AGAIN. THIS WAS THREE YEARS IN A ROW!

WHAT WAS THERE ABOUT THANKSGIVING? WHAT WAS THERE ABOUT MARLON AND DINNER PARTIES?

MARLON'S SISTER, JOCELYN, EACH YEAR MADE THE TURKEY DRESSING THEIR MOTHER HAD MADE FOR THEM WHEN THEY WERE GROWING UP. IT WAS A FAVORITE OF MARLON'S AND HE WOULD LOOK FORWARD TO IT EVERY YEAR. JOCELYN ARRIVED AT MARLON'S THANKSGIVING MORNING AND PUT THE TURKEY IN THE OVEN, THEN RETURNED TO HER HOME IN RUSTIC CANYON.

THIS PARTICULAR YEAR MARLON TOLD JOCELYN, "SLEEP IN, I'LL PUT THE TURKEY IN THE OVEN IN THE MORNING." BEFORE I LEFT FOR MY HOME IN NEWPORT BEACH, I TYPED OUT ALL THE INSTRUCTIONS AS PER JOCELYN'S REQUEST AND PUT THEM WHERE MARLON COULDN'T MISS THEM—ON THE FRIDGE.

AS BETTE TELLS IT, THEY ARRIVED, HAD DRINKS AND SOME LIVELY CONVERSATION, AND WHEN THEY QUERIED, "ISN'T IT TIME TO EAT?," THEY DISCOVERED TO THEIR DISMAY THAT THE THANKSGIVING TURKEY WAS STILL IN THE REFRIGERATOR.

"MARLON BOILED HOT DOGS," SHE FUMED. "NEVER AGAIN WILL I ACCEPT AN INVITATION FOR THANKSGIVING AT HIS HOUSE. I THOUGHT LAST YEAR WAS BAD ENOUGH, BUT THIS WAS TOO MUCH."

THE "LAST YEAR" SHE REFERRED TO, THE ST. BERNARD, TOTO, HAD STOLEN THE TURKEY FROM THE KITCHEN. WHEN I SAW THE DOG LOPE BY THE LIVING ROOM WINDOW WITH THE TURKEY, I SUMMONED MARLON. WE CORNERED TOTO OUTSIDE MARLON'S BATHROOM, WHERE MARLON WRESTED THE TURKEY OUT OF HIS JAWS. BUT TOTO GOT AWAY WITH THE

DRUMSTICK AND THIGH HE HAD CLENCHED BETWEEN HIS TEETH.

WE STOLE AROUND THE HOUSE INTO THE KITCHEN WHERE, AMID LAUGHTER, MARLON TRIED TO HIDE THE GAPING HOLE IN THE TURKEY WITH A BUNCH OF PARSLEY. IT DIDN'T WORK. IT STILL LOOKED LIKE A TURKEY WITH A MISSING LEG AND THIGH. THEN I TOOK OVER THE KITCHEN SINCE THE COOK WAS LYING DOWN IN MY OFFICE, STILL IN SHOCK, HAVING HAD A PANIC ATTACK OVER THE DISAPPEARANCE OF THE TURKEY.

WE DECIDED IT WAS BEST TO SLICE THE REMAINING TURKEY, AND I URGED MARLON BACK TO HIS GUESTS, TELLING HIM NOT TO SAY ANYTHING ABOUT THE DOG AND THE TURKEY. BUT HE THOUGHT OTHERWISE; IT WAS TOO GOOD NOT TO TELL. OF COURSE, BETTE WAS MORTIFIED BY THE DRAMA. SHE REFUSED TO SHARE THE TURKEY WITH THE DOG.

ENOUGH WAS ENOUGH FOR HER.

BETTE MEANT WHAT SHE SAID. SHE NEVER ACCEPTED AN INVITATION TO THANKSGIVING DINNER AGAIN.

HOW TO GIVE A PARTY—BRANDO STYLE

LEST YOU THINK THAT THERE WAS NO FOOD SERVED AT MARLON'S HOUSE, LET ME TELL YOU ABOUT THE DAY MARLON DECIDED HE WANTED TO HAVE A PARTY AND INVITE HIS FRIENDS: GEORGE, SAM, JAY, WALLY, PHILLIP. THERE WAS ONE REQUIREMENT ATTACHED TO THE INVITATION: EACH OF THEM HAD TO INVITE THREE GIRLS TO THE PARTY. THAT IS, ALL EXCEPT PHILLIP RHODES WHO WAS MARRIED TO MARIE.

"DO YOU WANT ME TO CALL EVERYONE?" I INQUIRED.

"NO, I'LL CALL THEM." HE REPLIED. "YOU TAKE CARE OF THE FOOD AND DRINKS AND EVERYTHING ELSE.

I GOT THE EASY PART.

AT THE APPOINTED TIME, TRADER VIC'S, WHO WAS CATERING THE PARTY, ARRIVED AND SET UP THE BUFFET TABLE AND BAR. THE FLORIST HAD DELIVERED THE FLOWERS. MARLON, AS USUAL, CHOSE "FALL IN LOVE" MUSIC AND WENT THROUGH THE ROOMS DIMMING LIGHTS. AFTER ALL WAS TO HIS SATISFACTION, MARLON HURRIED OFF TO SHOWER AND CHANGE.

SHORTLY, HE RETURNED AND MIXED US A DRINK BEFORE THE GUESTS ARRIVED. WE SAT ON SOFAS FACING EACH OTHER ACROSS THE COFFEE TABLE. AND WE SAT, AND SAT, AND SAT. FINALLY, AFTER MARLON HAD SAID FOR THE UMPTEENTH TIME, "WHERE'S EVERYBODY?" WE DECIDED EVERYONE WAS PLAYING A JOKE ON HIM. BUT WHEN HE INQUIRED, "WHAT DID THEY SAY WHEN YOU INVITED THEM?" I REALIZED WHAT HAD HAPPENED.

"I DIDN'T INVITE ANYONE."

"WHAT!" HE SHOUTED INCREDULOUSLY, "YOU DIDN'T INVITE ANYONE?"

"NO, YOU TOLD ME YOU WERE GOING TO CALL EVERYONE—LOADS OF GIRLS!"

WITH THAT WE BOTH RUSHED TO THE PHONES AND FRANTICALLY STARTED DIALING EVERYONE WE KNEW, ALL THE TIME THINKING OF THE MOUNTAINS OF POLYNESIAN FOOD IN THE WARMERS. WE WERE HUNGRY, BUT NOT THAT HUNGRY.

SUCH WAS NOT THE CASE IN LONDON, THOUGH, WHERE MARLON WAS FILMING *A COUNTESS FROM HONG KONG*. MARLON RECEIVED A CALL FROM PLAYWRIGHT TENNESSEE WILLIAMS, WHO WAS IN TOWN, SO MARLON INVITED HIM AND HIS COMPANION, BILL, ALONG WITH A FEW OTHER FRIENDS, TO DINNER. MARLON EVEN REMEMBERED TO TELL US GUESTS WERE COMING TO DINE.

AT THE APPOINTED TIME, THE GUESTS ARRIVED, HAD COCKTAILS, AND WENT IN TO DINNER. AND THAT'S WHEN THE COMEDY STARTED. (I had cocktails with everyone, but was skipping dinner.) THE COOK, GERTRUDE, PUT THE FIRST COURSE ON THE DUMBWAITER AND SENT IT UP TO THE DINING ROOM. THEN CALAMITY STRUCK. THE DUMBWAITER WITH THE FOOD GOT STUCK BETWEEN FLOORS. THE ALARMED COOK CALLED FOR HELP AND WE ALL GOT INTO THE ACT—STRUGGLING WITH THE DUMBWAITER. THE MAID, SECRETARY, CHAUFFEURS, I, AND MARIE RHODES WERE THE "ALL." AND THE MORE WE STRUGGLED, THE MORE PANICKED GERTRUDE BECAME.

EVERYONE GOT THE GIGGLES OVER THE SITUATION. NATURALLY, THE FLURRY IN THE KITCHEN ECHOED THROUGH THE SHAFT TO THE FLOOR ABOVE. AND MARLON WAS EXPRESSING HIS DISPLEASURE BY RAPIDLY PRESSING AND DEPRESSING THE FOOT BUZZER, ADDING TO THE NOISE AND CONFUSION IN THE BASEMENT KITCHEN. WE KNEW THIS WAS HIS WAY OF TELLING US HE WAS UPSET ABOUT THE NOISE EMANATING, THROUGH THE SHAFT, FROM THE KITCHEN, WHERE EVERYONE WAS DESPERATELY

TRYING TO UNFREEZE THE DUMBWAITER, HOPING TO RETRIEVE THE FOOD.

THINGS WENT FROM BAD TO WORSE BELOW AND ABOVE. MARLON COULDN'T TALK OR HEAR HIS GUESTS BECAUSE OF THE DISTRACTIONS—THE THUMPING AND LAUGHTER. THE ONLY THING THAT COULD BE DONE AT THAT POINT WAS TO FORGET THE FIRST COURSE. BUT THE SECOND COURSE WASN'T READY, AND THE SCURRYING AROUND IN THE KITCHEN WITH EVERYONE OFFERING TO HELP COULD NOW BE HEARD UPSTAIRS, TOO, AND WORD CAME DOWN THAT MARLON WAS FUMING—WITH EVERY NEW SOUND, HIS TEMPERATURE ROSE.

IT FELL UPON ME TO APPRISE MARLON OF THE SITUATION, WHICH HE SURELY HAD GUESSED. I REMEMBER GETTING A CHILLY RECEPTION. THEN I HURRIEDLY ARRANGED A RELAY FROM THE KITCHEN UP THE NARROW STAIRWAY TO ME OUTSIDE THE DINING ROOM, WHERE I PASSED IT ON TO THE MAID WHO WAS SERVING TABLE. BY NOW MARLON WAS FURTHER UPSET BECAUSE THE FOOD WAS LATE. HE HAD WANTED EVERYTHING TO BE PERFECT FOR HIS GUEST OF HONOR. BUT, AFTER DINNER WAS SERVED AND THE PLATES RETRIEVED BETWEEN COURSES, IT WAS DULY NOTED BY EVERYONE BELOW IN THE KITCHEN THAT MARLON NEED NOT HAVE BEEN CONCERNED AT ALL. TENNESSEE DIDN'T EAT A MORSEL. HE DIDN'T EVEN PUSH A PEA AROUND HIS PLATE. ALL HE DID WAS DRINK HIS DINNER. IN FACT, HE WAS SKUNKED WHEN HE LEFT THE TABLE.

UNPREDICTABLE
GETS EVEN (EVEN IF IT TAKES HIM FOREVER)
VULNERABLE
NOT CAUTIOUS IN VOICING OPINIONS ON WHAT HE FEELS STRONGLY ABOUT
DEMANDING
VOLATILE
DISTRUSTFUL

"MARLON DEAREST..."

MARLON, LIKE CRAWFORD, HATES WITH A PASSION THOSE WIRE HANGERS ONE GETS FROM THE CLEANERS. I THINK THE HANGERS KNOW THIS, TOO, BECAUSE ONCE IN A WHILE ONE SNEAKS INTO HIS CLOSET AND HIDES BETWEEN HIS SHIRTS. AND WHEN HE DISCOVERS IT, YOU CAN HEAR HIM ALL THROUGH THE HOUSE. HOLD YOUR HANDS OVER YOUR EARS, HE GOES BALLISTIC! HE MAKES IT SEEM AS IF WE INTENTIONALLY PUT A WIRE HANGER IN HIS CLOSET JUST TO TORMENT HIM. NOW, WOULD WE DO THAT TO YOU, MARLON? OF COURSE NOT!

DOESN'T ANYONE LIKE THOSE HANGERS?

LETTER EXCERPT: GEORGE ENGLUND TO MARLON: "I CALL IT LUCKY THAT YOU PUT PRIVATE AND PERSONAL ON THE ENVELOPE (FROM JAPAN) BECAUSE THERE IS ABSOLUTELY NO QUESTION THAT ALICE WOULD HAVE BLACKED OUT SEVERELY AS SOON AS SOME OF YOUR

FLAMBOYANT IMAGES PENETRATED HER TIGHTLY LACED CONSCIOUSNESS."

CHAMPION OF THE UNDERDOG
PLAYFUL
ENERGETIC
TENDER
ANIMAL LOVER

RESPONSIBILITY FOR MARLON INCLUDED HIS EXTENDED FAMILY AND ALL THINGS AROUND HIM, INCLUDING HIS PETS.

THERE ARE DOGS, AND THEN THERE ARE DOGS. LIKE ST. BERNARDS, HUGE, BUT PLAYFUL; MASTIFFS, SWEET AND GENTLE, BUT DROOLING; GERMAN SHEPHERDS, FRISKY AND DEVOTED, WHO FEEL THEY HAVE TO JUMP ON YOU AND KNOCK YOU OVER TO SHOW HOW MUCH THEY CARE; AND A WOLF DOG, WARY BUT SENSITIVE. NOT TO MENTION THE EXOTIC ANIMALS AND FARM ANIMALS. MARLON'S A TRUE LOVER OF ANIMALS—AND THEY HAVE A LIKE RESPONSE TO HIM.

THE LAMB:

ONE EASTER, MARLON THOUGHT THE CHILDREN SHOULD HAVE A LAMB. SO THE SAN FERNANDO RANCHES WERE SCOURED UNTIL A LAMB FOR SALE WAS LOCATED.

THE LAMB WAS DELIVERED TO THE HOUSE KICKING AND BLEATING ON GOOD FRIDAY EVENING. BUT WHERE

DO YOU KEEP A LAMB UNTIL THE CHILDREN ARRIVE NEXT MORNING? IN MY OFFICE BATHROOM, OF COURSE.

ON MONDAY MORNING WHEN I RETURNED TO WORK, I DISCOVERED THE LAMB AGAIN IN THE BATHROOM AND A NOTE ON MY DESK FROM MARLON: *FIND A HOME FOR THE LAMB*. QUESTIONING I LEARNED THAT THE CHILDREN HAD ALL BEEN FRIGHTENED AND SO HAD THE LAMB. WE SENT THE DARLING LITTLE THING BACK TO THE FARM.

THE RACCOON:

THIS WAS NOT RUSSELL, WHO MARLON HAD WHEN HE LIVED IN NEW YORK CITY. THIS WAS ANOTHER RACCOON. NO HOUSEHOLD PET WAS MORE DISRUPTIVE THAN THE RACCOON. HE WAS CRAZY ABOUT MY ANKLES. SEVERAL TIMES A DAY HE WOULD SNEAK IN UNDER MY DESK, NIP ONE OF MY ANKLES, AND RUN AWAY. I KNEW HE WAS LAUGHING AND SAYING, "GOTCHA AGAIN!" COMPLAINING TO MARLON DID NO GOOD. HE EXCUSED THE RACCOON AS, "HE'S ONLY BEING FRIENDLY." THIS KIND OF FRIEND I DIDN'T NEED. WHEN HE WAS OUT OF HIS CAGE, AS HE WAS WHENEVER MARLON WAS IN THE HOUSE, ALL YOU WOULD HEAR WAS INTERMITTENT SCREAMS. EVERYONE AVOIDED HIM, IF POSSIBLE. NO ONE WAS SAFE FROM A REAR ASSAULT.

THE HOUSEKEEPER AND HER HUSBAND THREATENED TO QUIT AFTER THE RACCOON ATTACKED HER AS SHE WAS BENDING OVER. WHEN I ANSWERED HER SCREAMS, SHE WAS ON ALL FOURS ON THE KITCHEN FLOOR, SCRAMBLING TO ESCAPE FROM THE RACCOON, WHO KEPT NIPPING AT HER FROM BEHIND. HE THOUGHT IT A

WONDERFUL GAME THEY WERE PLAYING AND DIDN'T TAKE TOO KINDLY TO MY ATTEMPTS AT SHOOING HIM AWAY FROM HER RUMP. SEEING I HAD NO SUCCESS, HER HUSBAND, WHO ALSO CAME RUNNING AT HER SCREAMS, JOINED IN, BUT BY THIS TIME THE RACCOON WAS HAVING ONE HECK OF A TIME AND WASN'T ABOUT TO GIVE UP THE FUN. HE HAD NEVER HAD SO MANY SCREAMING, CRAWLING, AND JUMPING AROUND. FINALLY, SOMEONE RAN FOR MARLON, WHO CAME AND RESCUED US FROM THE ATTACKING BEAST. THEN TO ADD TO OUR INJURIES, OUR HERO, MARLON, UTTERED NOT A WORD OF SYMPATHY. HE SIDED WITH THE SNEAKY RACCOON. AND WOULD YOU BELIEVE, HE BLAMED US FOR THE RACKET.

WOLFIE:

WOLFIE WAS ONE OF THE LOVES OF MARLON'S LIFE, AND MINE, TOO. HE WAS HALF WOLF AND HALF GERMAN SHEPHERD. PREDOMINANT IN HIS NATURE WAS THE WOLF HALF. MARLON PURCHASED HIM WHEN HE WAS AN ADORABLE PUP. FULL GROWN, HE WAS A BEAUTY.

UNBEKNOWNST TO ANYONE, WOLFIE HAD MADE A DEN UNDER A SHED HIDDEN AMONG THE BRUSH ON THE SIDE OF THE HILL OPPOSITE THE POOL AREA. ONE DAY WHEN MARLON NOTICED WOLFIE WAS MISSING, HE SEARCHED THE PROPERTY AND DISCOVERED THE DEN WITH NEWBORN PUPS.

AFTER A FEW HOURS, MARLON DECIDED TO MAKE A CHICKEN-WIRE YARD AROUND THE DOG HOUSE ON THE PATIO OUTSIDE THE KITCHEN FOR THE NEW FAMILY. WHEN HE HAD FINISHED, HE SAT WATCH ON

THE DEN, AND WHEN WOLFIE LEFT, MARLON CRAWLED INTO THE DEN ON HIS BELLY FOUR OR FIVE TIMES AND BROUGHT THE PUPS TO THE ENCLOSURE HE HAD BUILT. WE WENT INTO THE ENCLOSURE AND PLAYED WITH THE FROLICKING PUPS TO TAKE AWAY ANY FEAR OF US THAT THEY MIGHT HAVE AS WOLFIE WATCHED FROM A SHORT DISTANCE AWAY. NOW MARLON WAS IN THE UNENVIABLE POSITION OF HAVING TO ENTICE WOLFIE INTO THE ENCLOSURE. AFTER THIS WAS ACCOMPLISHED, ON MARLON'S ADVICE, WE WENT INTO THE HOUSE, THUS ALLOWING WOLFIE AND THE PUPS SOME TIME TO BECOME ACCUSTOMED TO THE NEW ENVIRONMENT.

A SHORT TIME LATER WE LOOKED OUT AND DISCOVERED THE ENCLOSURE WAS EMPTY. MARLON RECONNOITERED THE DEN SITE AND HEARD THE PUPS SQUEALING. AFTER ALL MARLON'S WORK AND BELLY CRAWLING, WOLFIE HAD TAKEN THE PUPS BACK TO THE SECURITY OF THE DEN. SO MUCH FOR MARLON'S ATTEMPTS AT TAMING THE WILD.

THE LOVE BIRDS:

MARLON AND I HAD A RUNNING FEUD OVER THE LOVE BIRDS. ADMITTEDLY, THEY WERE ABSOLUTELY BEAUTIFUL TO SEE. A FAN HAD SENT THEM TO MARLON IN A LARGE, LOVELY, WHITE CAGE WITH A LOVE NOTE. IN SPITE OF THE LOVELY CAGE, MARLON DECIDED THEY SHOULD BE ALLOWED TO FLY FREE...IN HIS ROOM. NEED I SAY MORE? THEY PARTICULARLY LOVED TO PERCH ON THE SILK LAMPSHADES. IN TWO DAYS OF FLYING FREE, THERE WERE LOVE DROPPINGS ALL OVER THE BOOKS ON THE BOOKSHELVES LINING THE WALLS.

ALL THE TABLES, CHAIRS, BED, ARTIFACTS, PICTURES BORE THEIR SIGNATURE. THEY DIDN'T MISS A THING. AND THE LAMPSHADES: ULTIMATELY, THEY HAD TO BE DISCARDED. SOON THE HOUSEKEEPER WAS HAVING FITS. I WAS HAVING FITS. MARLON WAS HAVING FITS— BUT WITH US.

THE LOVE BIRDS DIDN'T LAST TOO LONG. FINALLY, EVEN MARLON HAD HAD ENOUGH, BOTH WITH THE BIRDS AND US.

"FIND A HOME FOR THEM."

IT WASN'T EASY. IT TOOK A GREAT DEAL OF PERSUASION ON MY PART TO GET THE LOS ANGELES ZOO TO TAKE THEM.

SO MUCH FOR LOVE BIRDS. THEY PRODUCED ONLY STRAINED RELATIONSHIPS IN THE HOUSEHOLD— ANYTHING BUT LOVE.

THE OCELOT:

TIM THE OCELOT WAS ABSOLUTELY GORGEOUS. MARLON WAS HIS SOLE COMPANION AS NO ONE ELSE WOULD GO INTO MARLON'S ROOM, TIM'S TERRITORY, UNLESS MARLON WAS THERE. I ADMIRED HIM FROM A DISTANCE. BEAUTIFUL.

UNLIKE THE LOVE BIRDS, HE WAS AN EXTREMELY CLEAN ANIMAL. ONE DAY I WAS IN MARLON'S ROOM TALKING TO HIM WHEN I HEARD A SOUND FROM THE BATHROOM. WATER RUNNING?

"WHO'S IN YOUR BATHROOM?"

"THAT'S TIM, HE'S URINATING."

SMART ANIMAL, THERE WAS NO CLEANING UP AFTER HIM. OBSERVING THE OCELOT, IN THE PRESENCE OF MARLON, I WISHED I COULD TRUST WILD ANIMALS, BUT

WOLFIE WAS THE ONLY ONE I FELT COMFORTABLE WITH.

THE PARROT:

IF TIM THE OCELOT WAS CLEAN, NOT SO WITH THE PARROT WHOSE DOMAIN WAS THE ATRIUM. THE GARDENER COMPLAINED AND COMPLAINED, NOT TO MARLON, BUT TO ME. HE HAD THE UNENDING TASK OF CLEANING THE ATRIUM POOL AND HOUSE ENTRY AND WAS NOT VERY HAPPY ABOUT IT. I HAD TO PASS ON HIS COMPLAINTS TO MARLON, WHICH MADE IT SEEM AS IF THE COMPLAINTS WERE COMING FROM ME. THEREFORE, MARLON WAS NOT VERY HAPPY WITH ME.

PRETTY AS THE PARROT WAS, NOBODY, BUT NOBODY, WOULD HAVE ANYTHING TO DO WITH IT. THEN ONE DAY IT DISAPPEARED.

CATS:

MARLON INHERITED A CAT WHEN A GIRL HE HAD MET ON A MOVIE SET AND BEFRIENDED ENDED HER LIFE. WE FED IT EACH DAY AND TRIED TO MAKE FRIENDS, BUT MARLON WAS THE ONLY ONE THE CAT BEFRIENDED. THE CAT LIVED IN MARLON'S ROOM, ON HIS BED MOST OF THE TIME. SHE COMPLETELY IGNORED THE REST OF US AND THE REST OF THE HOUSE.

BUT THE GINGER CAT, SAM, WAS ANOTHER STORY. HE WAS A PEOPLE CAT. HE MADE FRIENDS WITH EVERYONE. HE WAS ALSO A PROWLER AND A BATTLER. HE SPENT AS MUCH TIME AT THE VETS, WOUNDED, AS HE DID AT HOME.

BEGUILING
DETERMINED
SINGLE-MINDED
CONDESCENDING
TOLERANT
HARD WORKER

MARLON HAS A PHENOMENAL MEMORY. THIS STATEMENT IS GOING TO SURPRISE MANY OF HIS BIOGRAPHERS WHO WROTE HE COULDN'T REMEMBER HIS LINES. BELIEVE ME, HE COULDN'T REMEMBER ONLY WHAT HE NEVER BOTHERED TO MEMORIZE. MOST OF THE TIME HE BRUSHED OFF THE DIALOGUE DIRECTOR, WHO WANTED TO EARN HIS SALARY, WITH, "THE LINES WILL ONLY BE CHANGED DURING THE REHEARSALS."

MARLON IS A QUICK STUDY. I KNOW BECAUSE WHEN I FIRST STARTED TO WORK FOR MARLON, SEVERAL MORNINGS WHILE HE WAS HAVING COFFEE, HE'D PICK UP HIS SCRIPT, ASK ME WHAT SCENE THEY WERE SHOOTING THAT DAY, AND HAVE ME RUN HIS LINES WITH HIM. NO MORE THAN THREE TIMES THROUGH THE SCENE AND HE'D HAVE HIS LINES DOWN PAT.

DURING THE FILMING OF *ONE-EYED JACKS,* MARLON AND WRITER GUY TROSPER KEPT PRODUCTION SECRETARY MARCELLA BRUCE AWFULLY BUSY TYPING SCRIPT CHANGES ON THE SET. SCENES WERE BEING REVISED EVERY DAY AND AT TIMES REWRITTEN BETWEEN SHOTS. BUT MARLON, THE ACTOR, DIDN'T GIVE THE DIRECTOR, BRANDO, ANY PROBLEM WITH DIALOGUE. FOR WHEN MARLON APPLIED HIMSELF, AS I

SAID, HE'S A FAST LEARNER. AH, BUT WHEN HE LEARNED ABOUT CUE CARDS AND EARPHONES, HE WAS IN ACTOR'S HEAVEN.

MARLON ALSO HAS A VERY RETENTIVE MEMORY. JUST TELL HIM SOMETHING ABOUT YOURSELF AND YEARS LATER, HE'LL DROP IT IN A CONVERSATION. SOME GIRLS HAVE CONFESSED TO ME THAT HE REMEMBERS THINGS SO FAR BACK THEY HAVE LONG FORGOTTEN THEM AND WISHED THAT HE HAD, TOO.

NAME A SONG. MARLON WILL KNOW THE WORDS AND MELODY.

MARLON WOULD SAY, "WHAT'S THE NAME OF THIS SONG?" THEN HE'D SING A LONG FORGOTTEN GOOD OLDIE OF WHICH THE NAME ESCAPES YOU. THEN ANOTHER, AND ANOTHER. NOTHING THE MATTER WITH HIS MEMORY.

WORK IS WHEN YOU'RE BORED TO DEATH BY WHAT YOU ARE DOING.
—karl lagerfeld

I DIDN'T THINK HARD WORK WAS MARLON'S QUEST IN LIFE, BUT HE WORKED HARDER ON HIS CRAFT THAN GIVEN CREDIT FOR BECAUSE HE MADE IT SEEM SO EASY. I MUST SAY THAT ONCE COMMITTED TO A PART, MARLON DID HIS HOMEWORK ON THE CHARACTER—DEVELOPING A CHARACTER FAR BEYOND WHAT THE

WRITER OR DIRECTOR ENVISIONED. A CASE IN POINT, *THE GODFATHER*, DON CORLEONE.

ANOTHER CASE IN POINT; *APOCALYPSE NOW*. I HAD LEFT MARLON ON HIS COTTAGE VERANDA OVERLOOKING THE LAKE, WRITING AND WORKING ON HIS SCENES IN *APOCALYPSE NOW* WITH A FULL HEAD OF HAIR. SOMETIME DURING THE NIGHT, MARLON SHAVED OFF HIS HAIR. THE FOLLOWING MORNING, I WAS TAKEN ABACK WHEN I SAW HIM. I DON'T KNOW HOW LONG MARLON HAD HAD THIS IN MIND FOR HIS CHARACTER, OR WHETHER IT WAS A SPUR-OF-THE-MOMENT DECISION, BUT IT CERTAINLY WAS A CORRECT ONE. AUTHOR JOSEPH CONRAD HAD DESCRIBED KURTZ, MARLON'S ROLE, AS BEING "AS BALD AS A BILLIARD BALL." MARLON ASKED ME NOT TO REVEAL WHAT HE HAD DONE AS IT HAD NOT BEEN PREVIOUSLY DISCUSSED WITH THE DIRECTOR, COPPOLA, AND HE WANTED TO SURPRISE HIM.

ALTRUISTIC
NOBODY'S FOOL
GETS EVEN—IF IT TAKES FOREVER
SECRETIVE
UNFORGIVING

NOW IT CAN BE TOLD

SO MANY UNTRUTHS HAVE BEEN WRITTEN ABOUT MARLON'S TIME AWAY FROM THE SCREEN PRIOR TO THE MAKING OF *THE GODFATHER*. IT HAS BEEN

REPORTED THAT NO ONE WANTED MARLON. WHY, I EVEN READ AN INTERVIEW IN WHICH MARLON HIMSELF SAID THAT HE DIDN'T WORK BECAUSE NO ONE WANTED HIM, THUS PERPETUATING THE MYTH. RUBBISH, MARLON, RUBBISH! THE TRUTH OF THE MATTER IS THAT I WAS INFORMED BY MARLON, AS WAS HIS LAWYER, NORMAN GAREY, NOT TO ACCEPT ANY SCREENPLAYS BECAUSE HE WAS NOT GOING TO WORK. HE WAS EXTREMELY BITTER ABOUT HIS CURRENT MARRIAGE AND HE EXPLAINED HE WAS GOING TO SUE FOR AN ANNULMENT.

WHAT HAD THAT GOT TO DO WITH WORK? CALIFORNIA HAD COMMUNITY PROPERTY LAWS. MARLON CONFIDED THAT HE DID NOT WANT TO HAVE ANY ADDITIONAL INCOME THAT COULD BE CONSIDERED COMMUNITY PROPERTY. HE WAS ADAMANT ABOUT NOT SHARING THE FRUITS OF HIS LABOR. HE PUT HIS CAREER ON THE LINE AND DECIDED NOT TO LABOR, NO MATTER HOW LONG IT TOOK TO GET HIS PERSONAL LIFE'S PROBLEMS RESOLVED.

HE THEN SWORE ME AND NORMAN TO SECRECY ABOUT HIS PLANS AS HE DIDN'T WANT ANYONE TO KNOW HIS REASON FOR NOT WORKING. THEREAFTER, ALL SCRIPTS SUBMITTED TO HIM WERE RETURNED UNREAD BY ME OR NORMAN, AND DOZENS CAME IN EACH MONTH DURING THAT PERIOD. SOME WERE DISCUSSED BY ME AND NORMAN AND WE CONCLUDED THAT HE SHOULD CONSIDER THEM. AT NORMAN'S INSISTENCE, I FOOLISHLY APPROACHED HIM ABOUT A SCRIPT WE HAD BOTH READ AND LIKED. WAS IT *BUTCH CASSIDY AND THE SUNDANCE KID*? I THINK IT WAS. I KNOW THAT WAS SUBMITTED. I SAY *FOOLISHLY*

BECAUSE I GOT MY EARS BURNED BY HIS REFUSAL. HE WAS FIRM IN HIS RESOLVE.

AS TIME WENT ON YOU'D THINK PRODUCERS AND WRITERS WOULD GET THE MESSAGE THAT HE WASN'T WORKING AND BECOME DISCOURAGED BY THE REJECTIONS. BUT IT DEVELOPED THAT EVERYONE HAD A SCREENPLAY THAT WOULD "BRING MARLON BACK TO THE SCREEN," SO WE WERE INUNDATED BY SCRIPTS ALL DURING HIS HIATUS. IN THE MEANTIME, THERE WAS MUCH PRESS AND SPECULATION ABOUT "BRANDO'S RETURN TO THE SCREEN."

I CAN'T RECALL A TIME HE WASN'T TURNING DOWN MORE PARTS THAN HE ACCEPTED, EVEN TO THIS DATE. FOR AS I WRITE THIS, THREE NEW SCRIPTS HAVE BEEN RECEIVED. WHERE DID MARLON EVER GET THE NOTION NOBODY WANTED HIM? AND THERE WAS PRESS COVERAGE AND SPECULATION ABOUT THIS, TOO. I CAN ONLY ASSUME THAT PRODUCERS AND WRITERS DIDN'T GET MARLON'S MESSAGE THAT HE WASN'T WORKING, ALTHOUGH NORMAN AND I DID. WE TOOK HIM AT HIS WORD AND WE DIDN'T BOTHER HIM WITH SCRIPT SUBMISSIONS. THEREFORE, HE DIDN'T KNOW HOW MANY, OR WHAT FILMS, HE TURNED DOWN.

OH, WE DID BOTHER HIM NOW AND THEN, BUT IN A JOCULAR MANNER. WE MIGHT ASK WHEN HE WAS GOING TO DECIDE TO WORK AGAIN. BUT WE KNEW THE DECISION WOULD BE HIS, NOT THAT OF THE PRESS, PRODUCERS, WRITERS, OR DIRECTORS. HIS DECISION ALONE.

AFTER HIS MARRIAGE WAS DISSOLVED AND A SETTLEMENT MADE, HE WAS NOT QUITE READY FOR

WORK. OTHER LEGAL MATTERS AND CONSIDERATIONS CAUSED DELAYS.

THE GODFATHER

NOBODY WANTED BRANDO FOR THE PART, EXCEPT THE AUTHOR, PUZO. AND HE STOOD ALONE, FIRMLY CONVINCED. THEN HE GAINED AN ALLY IN FRANCIS COPPOLA WHEN HE WAS CONTRACTED TO DIRECT. AND THE REST IS CINEMATIC HISTORY.

AFTER MARLON SIGNED ON FOR *THE GODFATHER*, HE SIGNED TO DO ANOTHER FEATURE, *THE NIGHTCOMERS*, WITH STEPHANIE BEACHAM—MICHAEL WINNER DIRECTING AND ELLIOTT KASTNER PRODUCING.

A VERY INTERESTING CONVERSATION TOOK PLACE IN THE DINING ROOM OF THE UNIVERSITY ARMS HOTEL IN CAMBRIDGE, ENGLAND, WHERE MARLON WAS FILMING *THE NIGHTCOMERS*. MARLON, HIS MAKEUP MAN PHILLIP RHODES, AND I WERE DISCUSSING *THE GODFATHER*. MARLON WONDERED WHETHER OR NOT IT WOULD BE A FINANCIAL SUCCESS. HE WASN'T VERY HIGH ON ITS BOX-OFFICE POTENTIAL. MARLON SAID HE THOUGHT IT WOULD ONLY MAKE ABOUT TEN MILLION DOLLARS. HE ASKED PHILLIP HOW MUCH HE THOUGHT IT WOULD MAKE. PHILLIP EITHER COULDN'T HAZARD A GUESS, OR REFUSED TO GUESS, BUT HE AGREED WITH MARLON MORE OR LESS. MARLON THEN ASKED ME HOW MUCH I THOUGHT IT WOULD MAKE, AND WITHOUT HESITATION I SAID, "50 MILLION." THEY BOTH HOOTED AND SAID I WAS HALLUCINATING. NEVER, NEVER, NEVER! I WOULDN'T CHANGE MY OPINION

EVEN THOUGH MARLON HAD A FEW UNKIND WORDS ABOUT IT, SO HE SAID, "I'LL BET YOU 50,000 DOLLARS IT WON'T MAKE 50 MILLION."

"I DON'T HAVE 50,000 DOLLARS TO BET."

"OKAY, I'LL BET 50,000 DOLLARS TO YOUR 10,000 DOLLARS."

I STILL REFUSED TO BET.

"IF YOU THINK IT'LL MAKE 50 MILLION, THEN YOU'D BET," HE GOADED.

"YOU WOULDN'T PAY OFF."

"YES, I WILL. PHILLIP IS A WITNESS."

"ALL RIGHT," I CAPITULATED. "WE HAVE A BET."

I COULD SEE MARLON MENTALLY COUNTING MY HARD EARNED MONEY.

LATER, I SAID TO PHILLIP, "WHAT DO YOU THINK?"

"I DON'T KNOW." HE SHOOK HIS HEAD. "50 MILLION IS A LOT OF MONEY."

THIS WAS 1972 AND 10,000 WAS A LOT OF MONEY, TOO!

NEEDLESS TO SAY, I WON THAT BET. BUT, OH, HOW WRONG MARLON AND I WERE IN THE AMOUNT OF MONEY *THE GODFATHER* WOULD MAKE AT THE BOX OFFICE! PUZO REVEALED THAT HE WAS, TOO.

HE'S THE COMFORT OF AN OLD TWEED JACKET IN THE DEPTH OF WINTER—OTHER TIMES THE IRRITATION OF A HAIR SHIRT ON A HOT SUMMER'S DAY.

—alice marchak

GREAT PERSONAL MAGNETISM
TORMENTER
PROVOCATIVE
FROSTY
DEMANDING
TEASE
ADVENTUROUS

MARLON WAS BORN ON APRIL 3RD AND I ON APRIL 13TH, IN THE SIGN OF THE RAM. WE'RE BOTH ARIES. IS IT ANY WONDER THERE WERE TIMES WHEN MARLON AND I LOCKED HORNS?

ONE OF THOSE TIMES WAS WHEN MARLON ASKED ME TO COME INTO HIS SITTING ROOM BECAUSE HE WANTED TO SHOW ME HIS NEW NIKON CAMERA AND LENSES. I HAVE TO SAY UP FRONT, CAMERAS DO NOT EXCITE ME. THEY NEVER DID. SO I WAS QUITE INDIFFERENT TO THE NIKON AND ALL THE ACCESSORIES MARLON WAS DISPLAYING.

BUT MARLON WAS SO EXCITED ABOUT IT, YOU'D THINK HE HAD DISCOVERED THE MISSING LINK. AND IT WASN'T LONG BEFORE THE REAL REASON HE WANTED TO INTEREST ME IN THE NIKON EMERGED.

"I WANT YOU TO GO DOWN TO THE CAMERA SHOP AND LEARN HOW TO USE THE CAMERA AND LENSES."

I STOOD AND LISTENED WHILE HE ENUMERATED ALL THE THINGS HE WANTED ME TO LEARN. WHEN HE WAS THROUGH, I SAID ONE WORD, "NO."

"NO?"

I COULD SEE HE DIDN'T BELIEVE HE HEARD ME CORRECTLY; I WANTED TO LAUGH.

"NO," HE REPEATED.

"IT'S YOUR HOBBY, YOUR CAMERA, YOU LEARN HOW TO USE IT."

"BUT I WANT YOU TO LEARN," HE WHEEDLED, TRYING TO CHANGE MY MIND, "THEN YOU CAN TEACH ME."

"I'M NOT INTERESTED IN PHOTOGRAPHY. I DON'T HAVE ANY DESIRE TO BE A PHOTOGRAPHER, OR A TEACHER OF PHOTOGRAPHY.

NOW HIS FRIENDLY MANNER CHANGED. "DO YOU MEAN TO STAND THERE AND TELL ME YOU'RE NOT GOING TO DO AS I ASK?" HE ENUNCIATED EVERY WORD.

I INSISTED. "IT'S YOUR HOBBY. YOU WANT TO BE A PHOTOGRAPHER. I HAVE NO INTEREST IN YOUR CAMERA." I PUNCHED EVERY WORD, TOO.

HE DIGESTED THIS, THEN VERY COLDLY SAID, "I DON'T WANT YOU TO EVER TOUCH THIS CAMERA."

"I WON'T," I REPLIED, "HAVE NO FEAR."

I KNEW BY HIS FROSTY DEMEANOR THAT I WAS IN DEEP FREEZE.

ALL I EVER SAW WERE SOME OUT-OF-FOCUS PICTURES AND PHOTOGRAPHS OF BODIES WITH NO HEADS. HEY, MAYBE THAT'S WHAT HE WAS PHOTOGRAPHING—BODIES. SO MUCH FOR THAT HOBBY.

MARLON PRESUMES THAT BECAUSE HE'S INTERESTED IN SOMETHING, EVERYONE SHOULD BE. NOT SO, MARLON, NOT SO.

THE NEXT THING MARLON TRIED OUT ON ME WAS THE RV. I DO NOT GET RAPTUROUS OVER A MOTOR HOME. A CADILLAC CONVERTIBLE, YES. MARLON DID NOT UNDERSTAND WHY I DIDN'T HAVE THE SAME FEELINGS FOR HIS RV. WHY I DIDN'T WANT TO DRIVE IT.

I WOULDN'T DRIVE HIS FOUR-WHEEL DRIVE, EITHER. HE TRIED EVERY PLOY TO BREAK ME DOWN, BUT I STOOD FIRM. I DON'T DRIVE AND MAINTAIN RV'S OR FOUR-WHEEL DRIVES. I'M NOT THE LEAST BIT INTERESTED IN THEM. IF THEY NEEDED GAS OR REPAIRS, SOMEONE ELSE HAD TO DO THE HONORS.

"THE OTHERS DRIVE THE RV, WHY CAN'T YOU?" HE'D QUERY.

"IF THEY WANT TO DRIVE THE RV, IT'S ALL RIGHT WITH ME," I'D REPLY.

AFTER AN EXCHANGE LIKE THIS, HE'D GO OFF EXASPERATED AT MY RECALCITRANCE AND HAVE A FEW HUNDRED HARSH AND UNKIND WORDS ABOUT ME TO ANYONE WHO'D LISTEN.

I THINK—NO, I KNOW—MARLON WANTED LADIES TO BE TOMBOYS. I DON'T FIT THAT IMAGE. HIS IDEA OF A WONDERFUL TIME WAS CRAWLING AROUND THROUGH BRAMBLES UP AND DOWN HILLS. HE'D COME BACK EXHILARATED. I'D LOOK AT HIS LADY FRIENDS, JILL FOR ONE, AND THEY'D BE DRAGGING, GROANING, "NEVER AGAIN, NEVER AGAIN."

HOW THRILLING CAN IT BE STUCK IN THE DESERT SAND SOMEWHERE IN THE INTENSE HEAT OF DEATH VALLEY? OR OUT IN THE BOONIES, BROKEN DOWN? MARLON LOVED THE EXPERIENCE. HIS GIRLFRIENDS WOULD ONLY INTONE, "NEVER AGAIN."

I ALSO REFUSED TO BE ENTICED INTO SPARRING WITH HIM. HE HAS THE GREATEST REFLEXES. HE'S FAST! WHEN I REFUSE, HE TEASES BY DANCING AROUND AND FLICKING ME WITH HIS FISTS, TRYING TO PROVOKE A RESPONSE. I JUST KEEP SIDESTEPPING AND DUCKING

AND DON'T LET HIM LURE ME INTO RESPONDING WITH A JAB OF MY OWN.

ONE DAY I DIDN'T MOVE QUICK ENOUGH AND HE CAUGHT ME WITH A SHARP ONE ON THE ARM. WHEN HE SAW THE BRUISE, HE WAS CHASTENED AND WAS CAREFUL IN USING ME AS A TEST OF HIS REFLEXES AGAIN.

OH, DOES HE LIKE TO TORMENT AND PROVOKE!

BUT, I MUST CONFESS THERE WAS ONE TIME, OR TWO, OR THREE, WHEN HE WORE ME DOWN. HE HAD BEEN PESTERING ME TO GO MOTORCYCLING WITH HIM. NOW, I KNOW GIRLS WHO WOULD JUMP AT THE CHANCE, BUT NOT ME, BRANDO OR NO BRANDO. THAT IS, UNTIL ONE DAY ON CATALINA, DURING THE FILMING OF *MORITURI*, HE CAUGHT ME IN A WEAK MOMENT. AFTER ABOUT 15 MINUTES OF NEGOTIATING, WE REACHED AN AGREEMENT: HE WOULDN'T TRY TO TURN MY HAIR GRAY. HE KEPT HIS WORD. HE WAS VERY RESPONSIBLE, BUT I WAS TOO APPREHENSIVE TO ENJOY THE OUTING.

YOU WIN SOME. YOU LOSE SOME. AND NEITHER OF US LIKES TO LOSE.

SPEAKING OF LOSING, MARLON AND I ARE VERY COMPETITIVE; HE WITH ME AND I WITH HIM. THAT DOES NOT MEAN HE'S COMPETITIVE WITH EVERYONE, OR IS HE? WE REALLY LIKE TO BEST EACH OTHER. (SPEAK FOR YOURSELF, ALICE.)

WHEN YOU'RE KNOCKING AT THE GATES OF HEAVEN, YOU'D BETTER STAY ON GOOD TERMS WITH THE DOORMAN.

—red foxx

COMPASSIONATE
MOODY
STRONG
DIFFICULTY IN ADMITTING HE'S WRONG
CONTEMPLATIVE
SPIRITUAL

MARLON WILL TELL YOU HE DOESN'T BELIEVE IN GOD. YET, WHEN HE'S VERY ILL OR ON THE BRINK OF DEATH, HE'LL MAKE ALL KINDS OF DEALS AND PROMISES WITH "GOD" AND ME, WHEN I'M AROUND.

IN 1975 WHEN MARLON RETURNED FROM GRESHAM, WISCONSIN, AND THE STORMING OF THE ABBEY, HE WAS A TRUE BELIEVER. AS HE TOLD ME, "BULLETS WERE WHIZZING PAST MY HEAD."

ON THAT TRIP HE MADE A FRIEND OF FATHER GROPPI, WHO WAS ALSO IN THE ABBEY WITH THE MENOMINEE INDIANS. DURING THE SHOOTOUT, FATHER GROPPI HAD GIVEN MARLON A MARYKNOLL BIBLE. WHEN MARLON RETURNED FROM GRESHAM, HE HAD ME ORDER A COUPLE OF HUNDRED BIBLES FROM MARYKNOLL, WHICH HE PASSED OUT TO EVERYONE WHO CAME BY THE HOUSE. I REMEMBER MARLON TELLING ME, "THE FLYING BULLETS ONLY MISSED ME BY THE GRACE OF GOD."

I ONLY KNOW, MAR, THAT'S WHEN YOUR HAIR REALLY STARTED TURNING GRAY!

AND IT SHOULD BE NOTED THAT'S WHEN I STARTED TURNING GRAY, TOO—ESPECIALLY WHEN I FOUND

MYSELF HANDING OUT BIBLES, AT MARLON'S REQUEST, LIKE SOME "RELIGIOUS" ON A STREET CORNER, TO EVERYONE WHO CAME TO THE HOUSE. OH, MAR, THE THINGS YOU'VE GOTTEN ME INTO.

THEN THERE WAS ST. JOHN'S HOSPITAL, INTENSIVE CARE. MARLON WAS THERE WITH WHAT WAS DIAGNOSED AS A HIDDEN ULCER. I HEARD HIM TALKING TO GOD. "I HOPE HE HEARD ME."

EVIDENTLY HE DID, MAR, YOU'RE HERE AND HE'S STILL LISTENING.

ANOTHER TIME, MARLON BECAME VERY ILL WHILE IN TAHITI. HE CALLED AND ASKED ME TO MEET HIM AT THE PLANE, SAYING HE WAS RETURNING BECAUSE HE WAS ILL. AS I WAS DRIVING HIM TO THE HOSPITAL, I HEARD HIM MAKING PLEADING NOISES THAT SOUNDED LIKE "GOD HELP ME, PLEASE GOD HELP ME."

SO MUCH FOR NOT BELIEVING IN GOD!

DEVOID OF VANITY
STRONG-WILLED
INDEPENDENT
PRANKSTER
GENEROUS
SYMPATHETIC

TENNIS SHOES ANYONE?

A 16-YEAR-OLD FRIEND OF ONE OF THE BOYS WHO BELIEVED IN THE AMERICAN DREAM OF ENTREPRENEURSHIP PURCHASED 250 PAIRS OF TENNIS

SNEAKERS. THE TENNIS CRAZE, WHICH HAD SWEPT OVER CALIFORNIA, HAD PEAKED AND WAS IN A DOWNWARD SPIRAL WHEN THE BOY GOT THIS GREAT BARGAIN IN TENNIS SNEAKERS. HE COULDN'T MOVE THEM AND NOW HE WAS STUCK. UNTIL MARLON HEARD HIS SAD STORY. YES, THAT'S RIGHT. MARLON BOUGHT THEM. AND, OF COURSE, HE NEGLECTED TO TELL ME, OR ANYONE ELSE. I DIDN'T LEARN ABOUT THIS ACQUISITION UNTIL THE BOY CALLED AND ASKED ME TO PICK UP THE TENNIS SHOES MARLON HAD BOUGHT. NATURALLY, I THOUGHT IT WAS ONE PAIR OR TWO. BUT 250! WHERE DID HE THINK I WAS GOING TO PUT THEM? HE DIDN'T CARE. THEY WERE MARLON'S NOW. THEY WERE NO LONGER HIS PROBLEM. BUT THEY DID BECOME MINE—AND THEY ENDED UP AT A BOY'S CLUB.

YOUNG AT HEART
NATURAL REBEL
CHARMING
ARTICULATE
CARES DEEPLY

AS AMBASSADOR OF GOODWILL FOR THE UNITED NATIONS (UNICEF), MARLON WORKED TIRELESSLY FOR YEARS AS A FUNDRAISER. HE ALSO SPENT MONTHS AT A TIME RECRUITING TALENT FOR THE YEARLY GALA FUNDRAISER, WHICH WAS HELD IN DIFFERENT CITIES EACH YEAR: NEW YORK, OSLO, PARIS, ETC. MARLON NOT ONLY SPENT MONTHS RECRUITING THE TALENT, BUT IF THERE WERE ANY LAST-MINUTE GLITCHES AND

THE "STAR OF THE GALA" FOR SOME REASON OR OTHER COULDN'T APPEAR, THEN IT WAS BONGO TIME WITH BRANDO.

HE WAS VERY GENEROUS WITH HIS TIME AND PURSE ON BEHALF OF THE WORLD'S POOR CHILDREN, REPRESENTED BY UNICEF, HAVING MADE FILMS ABOUT THE STARVATION OF CHILDREN IN INDIA AND ELSEWHERE, AS WELL AS TRAVELLING MANY THOUSANDS OF MILES FOR A FIRST-HAND LOOK AT SITUATIONS IN UNDER-DEVELOPED COUNTRIES, WHICH ENABLED HIM TO BE AN EFFECTIVE SPOKESPERSON FOR UNICEF.

OF HIS MANY TRIPS AROUND THE WORLD FOR UNICEF, I ONLY ACCOMPANIED HIM ON ONE. AS REPRESENTED, THIS WAS ALSO GOING TO BE A VACATION—A PLEASURE TRIP FOR ME AND MARLON. WHAT HE SAID WAS, "WE'LL WORK AND HAVE SOME FUN."

IT WAS A TRIP I REMEMBER WITH GREAT CLARITY. THE PRESS INTERVIEWS AT EVERY STOP: NEW YORK CITY, PARIS, ATHENS, BEIRUT, KARACHI, LAHORE, RAWALPINDI, NEW DELHI, BANGKOK, SYDNEY, FIJI, TAHITI. THEY REALLY WERE MOB INTERVIEWS. I DIDN'T REALIZE UNTIL THAT TRIP MARLON'S ENORMOUS POPULARITY AMONG ADULTS WORLDWIDE. I WAS AWARE OF THE ADORING YOUNG LADIES AT HIS GATE, BUT THIS WAS A REVELATION. DID I HAVE MY HEAD IN THE SAND! HE WAS MOBBED EVERYWHERE WE WENT, AND WHAT SURPRISED ME MOST, I THINK, WAS THAT MEMBERS OF THE PRESS WERE HIS BIGGEST FANS, NOT HOSTILE, BUT ADORING.

I ALSO LEARNED ON THAT TRIP HOW VERY GRACIOUS A RELAXED MARLON COULD BE TO EVERYONE WITHOUT EXCEPTION—THAT INCLUDED THE MEMBERS OF THE PRESS. BECAUSE IT WAS A TRIP ON BEHALF OF UNICEF, MARLON AGREED TO BE AVAILABLE FOR ALL PRESS CONFERENCES THEY HAD SET UP IN ADVANCE OF HIS ARRIVAL IN EACH COUNTRY. THESE WERE TO BE CONTROLLED, ORGANIZED AFFAIRS WHERE MARLON WOULD GET UNICEF'S MESSAGE OUT AND TRY TO RAISE THE CONSCIOUSNESS OF THE WORLD, WHICH HE DID VERY EFFECTIVELY AT EVERY NEWS CONFERENCE. BUT THAT WASN'T ENOUGH. THE PRESS WAS ON A FEEDING FRENZY. BRANDO WAS AVAILABLE. AND THEY ATE HIM UP.

NEW YORK CITY WAS A PIECE OF CAKE. PARIS WAS, WELL, SEMI-SANE. IF YOU COULD CALL SEMI-SANE THE HORDES OF PHOTOGRAPHERS AND JOURNALISTS ALL PUSHING AND SHOVING AND QUESTIONING AT THE SAME TIME, AND A FEMALE REPORTER IN MY SUITE AT THE RAPHAEL HOTEL IN MY BED. SHE THOUGHT SHE WAS IN MARLON'S SUITE AND IN MARLON'S BED. OR ANOTHER FEMALE REPORTER HIDING IN MARLON'S SUITE WHO REFUSED TO LEAVE WHEN HE RETURNED TO HIS ROOM AFTER THE PRESS CONFERENCE DOWNSTAIRS. AND NEITHER COULD I, AS MARLON DIDN'T WANT TO BE ALONE WITH HER FOR OBVIOUS REASONS. OR BEING CHASED THROUGH PARIS FOR TWO DAYS BY HER. SHE STAYED THE COURSE, SHE WAS THE LAST PERSON WE SAW AS WE BOARDED THE PLANE TO LEAVE THE CITY OF LIGHTS.

EVEN PARIS DIDN'T PREPARE US FOR ATHENS. ATHENS, WHERE MARLON WAS SMOTHERED BY THE

CROWDS SCREAMING, "BRANDO! BRANDO! MARLON! MARLON!" WHERE THE LIMOUSINE WAS ROCKED BY, NOT TEENAGE FANS, BUT INTERNATIONAL PRESS JOURNALISTS AND PHOTOGRAPHERS TRYING TO REACH HIM AND YELLING QUESTIONS AT THE SAME TIME, AMIDST A DIN THAT REACHED A HYSTERICAL PITCH. WHERE THE OFFICIAL WELCOMING CEREMONIES HAD TO BE CANCELLED BECAUSE THERE WAS NO MOB CONTROL. WHERE MARLON AND I COULDN'T GO THROUGH IMMIGRATION BECAUSE WE COULDN'T LEAVE THE LIMO THAT TOOK US FROM THE PLANE TO THE TERMINAL. WHERE HE COULDN'T LEAVE THE HOTEL WITHOUT HIDING ON THE FLOOR IN THE BACK OF THE CAR UNDER A BLANKET. I WOULD HAVE THROWN IN THE TOWEL THEN, BUT I WAS ONLY ACCOMPANYING HIM. HE SMILED THROUGH IT ALL, DIDN'T HAVE A RUDE GESTURE OR WORD FOR ANYONE. THE WORLD PRESS WERE MARLON'S NEWEST BEST FRIENDS. AT LEAST THAT WAS MY PERCEPTION.

BEIRUT, WHERE HE WAS AGAIN GREETED RAUCOUSLY, WHERE I WAS CAST ASIDE BY HIS RESCUERS FROM THE PRESS MOB AND ABANDONED AT THE AIRPORT WITH THE LUGGAGE UNTIL MARLON MISSED ME AND A HARRIED AND APOLOGETIC UNICEF REPRESENTATIVE SHOWED UP.

BEIRUT, WHERE MARLON WAS SMOTHERED WITH LOVE AND WHERE HE WAS FETED ROYALLY AND FELL MADLY IN LOVE WITH A PRINCESS FOR A FAST FEW HOURS, AND SHE WITH HIM. HE'LL PROBABLY DENY THIS, BUT I WAS THERE. I SAW IT ALL. I OVERHEARD THE "I LOVE YOU'S" FROM BOTH AND SAW THE PASSIONATE KISSES IN THE MERCEDES THAT TOOK US IN A HAIR-

RAISING MOTORCADE TO THE AIRPORT TO CATCH OUR PLANE. AND AT THE AIRPORT, THE KISSES OF FAREWELL FROM ALL THE LADIES WHO HAD FILED INTO OUR CAR AND THOSE WHO HAD ACCOMPANIED US IN THE MOTORCADE. MARLON WAS BATHED IN ADORATION AND HE GLOWED. HE GAVE AS MUCH LOVE AS HE RECEIVED THAT NIGHT.

AND IT CARRIED OVER TO OUR NEXT STOP, KARACHI. THERE WAS ANOTHER LOVE FEST. MARLON HAD IMBIBED A LITTLE TOO MUCH, IF YOU CAN CALL TWO OR THREE DRINKS DURING THE EVENING TOO MUCH—A LITTLE IS A LOT FOR MARLON—AT THE DINNER PARTY IN BEIRUT. THEN HE "FELL IN LOVE AGAIN" WITH THE HOSTESS ON THE PLANE EN ROUTE TO KARACHI. SHE LOOKED AT HIM ADORINGLY WHEN SHE PASSED BY. AND EVERY FEW MINUTES SHE STOPPED TO SEE IF SHE COULD BRING HIM SOMETHING TO DRINK. I WAS TRYING TO GET A FEW WINKS, BUT IN BETWEEN THE DRINKS SHE WAS BRINGING MARLON, HE KEPT NUDGING ME AND ASKING, "IS SHE AS PRETTY AS I THINK SHE IS?" AS HE SQUINTED AT HER WITH HIS NEAR-SIGHTED, BLUE EYES. I COULD TELL HE WAS FALLING IN LOVE AGAIN AND AS I SAID, HE DID. HE WANTED TO KNOW IF HE SHOULD GET HER TELEPHONE NUMBER. I FINALLY ASKED HER NOT TO BRING MARLON ANY MORE TO DRINK AS I WAS CERTAIN WE WERE GOING TO BE MET BY THE PRESS. HE TOLD HER NOT TO PAY ANY ATTENTION TO ME. SHE DID STOP THE STRAIGHT VODKA AND THEY DARKENED THE PLANE.

EVERYONE WAS TRYING TO GET SOME SHUTEYE, BUT MARLON KEPT TALKING LOUDLY TO ME. TRYING TO KEEP ME AWAKE WITH HIM IS WHAT HE WAS DOING.

SOMEONE COMPLAINED TO THE HOSTESS. SHE CAME BY AND POLITELY ASKED US TO KEEP QUIET AS OTHERS WERE TIRED AND TRYING TO SLEEP. SO WAS I, AND I WAS GLAD SHE CAME BY THAT TIME. BUT MARLON WAS NOT READY FOR SLEEP AND HE NUDGED AND WHISPERED, "LET'S TAKE THEM ON. YOU AND I CAN TAKE ON THIS WHOLE PLANE, CAN'T WE?" ALL WE NEEDED WAS A FIGHT. I FINALLY CONVINCED MARLON TO SHUSH AND SHUT HIS EYES.

WHEN WE ARRIVED IN KARACHI, I WAS EXHAUSTED. MARLON WAS EXHAUSTED, AND TO PUT IT PLAINLY, INTOXICATED. THE HOSTESS CAME BY AND REQUESTED US TO STAY IN OUR SEATS UNTIL THE OTHER PASSENGERS HAD DISEMBARKED AS THERE WERE PHOTOGRAPHERS AND JOURNALISTS ON THE TARMAC, AS WELL AS UNICEF REPRESENTATIVES.

WE STAYED ON THE PLANE, AND SINCE MARLON WAS IN NO CONDITION TO TALK TO THE PRESS, HE CONCOCTED A STORY FOR ME TO DELIVER. HE PUT ON HIS JACKET AND PUT UP THE COLLAR, THEN HE TIED AN ASCOT AROUND HIS NECK AND PUT ON DARK GLASSES TO HIDE THOSE BLOODSHOT BLUE EYES. I WAS TO TELL THE PRESS THAT MARLON WAS ILL. HE HAD A COLD AND COULDN'T TALK, BUT WITH REST AT THE HOTEL, MARLON WOULD BE ABLE TO MAKE THE SCHEDULED 2:30 P.M. PRESS CONFERENCE.

YOU CAN IMAGINE THE SITUATION WHEN MARLON DISEMBARKED. AT THE FOOT OF THE PLANE, REPORTERS AND PHOTOGRAPHERS HAD ASSEMBLED WITH STANDING MICROPHONES. WHEN WE CAME TO THE DOOR OF THE PLANE, THE YELLING STARTED AND WE NOT ONLY GOT A BLAST OF SOUND, BUT WERE ALSO

ASSAULTED BY A TREMENDOUS WALL OF HEAT. WE BOTH VISIBLY WILTED.

AS PER OUR ARRANGEMENT, I LINKED MARLON DOWN THE STAIRS TO WHERE A BATTERY OF MICROPHONES WERE WAITING. I APPROACHED THEM AND STARTED OUT BY THANKING THEM FOR COMING OUT SO EARLY TO GREET MARLON AND THEN TOLD THEM HE COULDN'T TALK AND ANSWER ANY QUESTIONS. THAT'S AS FAR AS I GOT BECAUSE UNBEKNOWNST TO ME, WHILE I WAS BEING THE GOOD SPOKESMAN, MARLON WAS BEHIND ME TEARING OFF HIS ASCOT AND JACKET AND PUTTING HIS ARM AROUND ONE OF THE JOURNALISTS PROCLAIMING LOUDLY, "DON'T PAY ANY ATTENTION TO HER, I DON'T HAVE A COLD. I'M DRUNK. LET'S GET OUT OF THIS BLASTED HEAT!" THEN GATHERING HIS LATEST BEST FRIENDS, HE WENT CHUMMILY ALONG TO THE TERMINAL, LEAVING ME STANDING THERE WITH EGG ON MY FACE.

A UNICEF REPRESENTATIVE AND I WENT THROUGH IMMIGRATION AND RETRIEVED OUR LUGGAGE. HE WAS WORRIED ABOUT MARLON, SO I SENT HIM OFF TO SEE IF HE WAS ALL RIGHT. WHERE WAS MARLON? AT THE BAR BUYING DRINKS FOR EVERYONE IN THE AIRPORT AT THAT EARLY HOUR.

AFTER I DID THE CUSTOMS BIT, MARLON AND HIS NEW PALS, THE PRESS, TUMBLED INTO CARS AND IT WAS OFF TO THE HOTEL, WHERE MARLON INVITED THEM TO HIS SUITE FOR BREAKFAST, DRINKS, AND MORE CONVERSATION. WHEN MARLON HAD HAD HIS INOCULATIONS, SOMEONE MUST HAVE USED A

PHONOGRAPH NEEDLE, BECAUSE HE JUST TALKED AND TALKED AND TALKED.

I DIDN'T JOIN THEM AT BREAKFAST. I WENT TO MARLON'S ROOM AND LAID OUT A CHANGE OF CLOTHES THAT HE WOULD WEAR AT THE PRESS CONFERENCE THAT AFTERNOON. THEN I WENT TO MY ROOM, DID THE SAME, AND WENT TO BED.

BUT I WAS UNABLE TO SLEEP. THE LAUGHING AND TALKING WAS TOO MUCH AND I BEGAN TO WORRY THAT THIS MIGHT TURN INTO ANOTHER "TRUMAN CAPOTE EPISODE." SO I HOPPED OUT OF BED, CAME OUT AND RAN EVERYONE OFF, MUCH TO MARLON'S CHAGRIN, BY SAYING THERE WOULD BE NO PRESS CONFERENCE IF THEY DIDN'T LEAVE AND ALLOW MARLON TO GET SOME MUCH NEEDED SLEEP. OVER MARLON'S PROTESTATIONS, THEY FINALLY DEPARTED.

THEN, I GAVE MARLON SOME VITAMIN B1 AND BUFFERIN TO WARD OFF A MAJOR HANGOVER. THAT IS, AFTER I HAD CONVINCED HIM I WASN'T TRYING TO POISON HIM AND POINTED HIM TOWARD HIS BEDROOM.

THE KARACHI PRESS CONFERENCE WAS A REPLAY OF PARIS AND ATHENS AND BEIRUT. MARLON HAD DECIDED BEFORE GOING DOWNSTAIRS THAT BECAUSE HE HAD ALREADY GIVEN THEM SO MUCH TIME AT THE AIRPORT AND IN HIS SUITE THAT MORNING, THE PRESS CONFERENCE WAS GOING TO BE SHORT. HE DIDN'T KNOW UN OFFICIALS HAD HAD TO CHANGE THE SITE BECAUSE THEY COULDN'T ACCOMMODATE ALL THE PHOTOGRAPHERS AND JOURNALISTS THAT HAD SHOWN UP. IT SEEMED THAT EVERYONE AT THE HOTEL WHO KNEW MARLON WAS THERE GOT PRESS PASSES—

OR THERE WERE A HUNDRED OR SO JOURNALISTS AND PHOTOGRAPHERS IN KARACHI THAT DAY. REGARDLESS, IT WAS ANOTHER MOB SCENE. BUT IF THE PRESS WAS OUT OF CONTROL, MARLON DEFINITELY WAS CONTROLLED. HE ARTICULATED THE POINTS HE WANTED TO MAKE ABOUT UNICEF AND VERY DEFTLY ANSWERED PERSONAL QUESTIONS. NEVER WAS HE SO CHARMING AND GRACIOUS AND ACCESSIBLE. AND THE PRESS, AS BEFORE, MADE THE MOST OF HIS ACCESSIBILITY.

NEXT, WE MADE AN UNSCHEDULED STOP AT LAHORE, WHERE MARLON WANTED TO VISIT WITH FRIENDS, AND THAT GAVE US BOTH TIME FOR REST AND RELAXATION. A COCKTAIL PARTY AT THE AMERICAN AMBASSADOR'S RESIDENCE WAS OUR ONLY OFFICIAL FUNCTION.

SO FAR, UNICEF OFFICIALS WERE VERY PLEASED BY THE GREAT AND SUCCESSFUL PRESS COVERAGE OF MARLON'S TRIP ON THEIR BEHALF. AND THEY SHOULD BE, BECAUSE MARLON WAS SURELY SPREADING AROUND ENOUGH GOODWILL THAT IF IT WERE MANURE ON GRASS, THE WORLD WOULD BE GREEN. AND HE WAS TIRELESSLY MEETING WITH UNICEF REPRESENTATIVES IN THE FIELD, GATHERING FACTS THAT GAVE HIM MORE INFORMATION TO DISPENSE.

LEAVING LAHORE, WE ARRIVED IN RAWALPINDI AFTER A TRIP BY CAR WHERE WE SAW THE UNBELIEVABLE MIGRATION OF HUMANS ALL ALONG THE ROAD. IT WAS AWESOME.

THAT MORNING WE HAD BEEN CHECKED INTO OUR ROOMS AT THE HOTEL BY LOCAL REPRESENTATIVES OF UNICEF WHO HAD MET MARLON'S ARRIVAL. THE HOTEL

HAD SEEMED RATHER QUIET AND SEDATE IN COMPARISON TO THE HECTIC SCENES WE HAD EXPERIENCED WHEN MARLON HAD CHECKED INTO PREVIOUS HOTELS.

UNBEKNOWNST TO US, A SOVIET MINISTER (KOSYGIN, IF MY MEMORY SERVES ME CORRECTLY) WAS HAVING A MEETING WITH PAKISTAN GOVERNMENT OFFICIALS ON THE DAY WE ARRIVED IN THE RAWALPINDI HOTEL. I LATER DISCOVERED THAT THE HOTEL HAD BEEN EVACUATED FOR THE MEETING. I IMAGINE SOMEONE HAD DECIDED TO ALLOW MARLON TO STAY SINCE WE HAD NOT BEEN NOTIFIED TO LEAVE.

MARLON WAS CATCHING UP ON SLEEP IN HIS ROOM WHILE I, IN THE MEANTIME, TOOK THIS FREE TIME TO WRITE SOME CARDS TO FRIENDS AND FAMILY. THEN I WENT TO THE LOBBY TO LEAVE THEM AT THE DESK FOR MAILING. EN ROUTE TO THE LOBBY, I NOTICED A SHINY BLACK LIMOUSINE DISPLAYING THE HAMMER AND CYCLE FLAGS PARKED NEAR THE ENTRANCE. THE SIGNIFICANCE DIDN'T REGISTER AT THE TIME, SO I WAS FLABBERGASTED WHEN ON MY ENTRANCE I WAS IMMEDIATELY SURROUNDED BY MACHINE-GUN-TOTING SOLDIERS. I COULDN'T UNDERSTAND WHAT THEY WERE SO EXCITED ABOUT, BUT I DID RECOGNIZE THE LANGUAGE THEY WERE MENACING ME WITH AS RUSSIAN. A TRANSLATOR MATERIALIZED AND SO DID AN UNIDENTIFIABLE HOTEL EMPLOYEE, WHO WAS SCREAMING, "WHAT ARE YOU DOING OUT OF YOUR ROOM? WHY AREN'T YOU IN YOUR ROOM? WHAT ARE YOU DOING HERE?"

HE WAS ASKED TO PRODUCE MY PASSPORT, WHICH HAD BEEN RELINQUISHED UPON REGISTRATION THAT

MORNING. THEY PERUSED IT, INTERROGATED ME UNTIL THEY WERE FULLY SATISFIED THAT I WASN'T AN AMERICAN SPY, THAT I TRULY WAS ONLY MARLON BRANDO'S SECRETARY. I WAS SUBSEQUENTLY ESCORTED BY AN ARMED GUARD TO MY ROOM, WHICH THEY PROCEEDED TO CHECK. THEY CLOSED MY BLINDS, WHICH I HAD OPENED, AND I WAS TOLD TO STAY IN MY ROOM, NOT TO USE THE TELEPHONE, NOT TO LOOK OUT THE WINDOWS. IF I CAME OUT, THEY WARNED, I'D BE SHOT ON SIGHT.

SO I HUDDLED ON MY BED IN THE DARKENED ROOM, RELIVING THE BIZARRE EPISODE WHICH HAD BEEN STRAIGHT OUT OF A B MOVIE, WONDERING WHAT I WAS DOING IN RAWALPINDI WHEN I COULD BE SAFE AT HOME IN THE GOOD OLD U.S. OF A.

AND MARLON SLEPT ON.

LATER THAT EVENING ROBERT PARRISH, THE DIRECTOR AND A FRIEND FROM EARLY PARAMOUNT DAYS, SURFACED OUT OF THE BLUE. HE HAD DISCOVERED THAT MARLON WAS IN TOWN AND ARRANGED TO PICK HIM UP, TAKE HIM TO DINNER, AND THEN, AS A REFRESHED MARLON PROCLAIMED, "ALICE, YOU CAN'T COME WITH US, WE'RE GOING OUT ON THE TOWN." WHATEVER "OUT ON THE TOWN" MEANT IN RAWALPINDI, PAKISTAN.

I DID GET THE IMPLICATION. BOB AND MARLON MUST HAVE HAD A WONDERFUL TIME "ON THE TOWN" BECAUSE WHEN BOB DELIVERED MARLON TO THE DOOR OF HIS SUITE LONG AFTER MIDNIGHT, BOTH OF THEM WERE BOUNCING OFF THE WALLS DRUNK.

I WAS AWAKENED BY THE AWFUL COMMOTION THEY MADE, BUT STAYED WHERE I WAS AS I HAD HAD MY

SHARE OF EXCITEMENT FOR THE DAY. BESIDES, I WANTED TO BE RESTED AS MARLON AND I WERE SLATED TO LEAVE AT DAYBREAK ON THE WEEKLY FLIGHT TO THE KHYBER PASS TO OBSERVE THE WAR. THAT'S RIGHT, OBSERVE THE WAR. I HADN'T BARGAINED FOR THIS, BUT MARLON WAS GUNG HO TO GET TO THE FRONT AFTER SOMEONE FROM UNICEF INFORMED HIM THERE WERE SOME INTERESTING PEOPLE UP THERE HE SHOULD TALK TO, SINCE HE WAS SO CLOSE.

I MUST CONFESS I WAS NOT AT ALL ANXIOUS TO GO. I'M NOT THE TYPE OF PERSON WHO FEELS THE NEED TO GO OVER NIAGARA FALLS IN A BARREL TO HAVE A FULFILLED LIFE. LIKEWISE, I DON'T BELIEVE IN CIVILIANS VISITING WAR ZONES, INCLUDING SENATORS AND CONGRESSMEN EXPOSING THEMSELVES TO ENEMY OR FRIENDLY FIRE. ESPECIALLY IF THE CIVILIAN IS ME. BUT MARLON HAD CONVINCED ME WE'D BE PERFECTLY SAFE. HE DOES HAVE WINNING WAYS—HIS WINNING ARGUMENT BEING, "WOULD THE UNITED NATIONS UNICEF OFFICIALS LET ANYTHING HAPPEN TO ME? NO WAY!" SO KHYBER PASS, HERE WE CAME.

AT DAWN I LET MYSELF INTO MARLON'S ROOM TO AWAKEN HIM FOR THE TRIP. HE WAS A SIGHT TO BEHOLD, SPRAWLED ACROSS THE BED. PULLING HIS LEG EVER SO GENTLY BECAUSE I DIDN'T WANT HIM TO JERK AND AWAKEN A PAIN IN HIS HEAD, I SANG, "GET UP, MARLON, WE'RE GOING TO THE KHYBER PASS TO SEE THE WAR." HE COULD ONLY GROAN, "GO AWAY."

"COME ON, MARLON, LET'S GO SEE THE WAR."

I ONLY URGED HIM BECAUSE I KNEW HE WAS GOING NOWHERE THAT DAY. FEELING SYMPATHETIC, I LEFT HIM FULLY CLOTHED, LYING AMONG THE RUMPLED COVERS IN THE DARKENED ROOM, AND SET ABOUT CONTACTING UNICEF OFFICIALS TO CANCEL OUR FLIGHT AND ABORT THE VISIT TO THE KHYBER PASS.

SINCE THERE WAS ONLY ONE PLANE A WEEK TO THE AREA, WE HAD TO FOREGO OUR VISIT TO THE WAR ZONE. THIS DIDN'T DISAPPOINT ME ONE BIT, BUT MARLON WAS SORRY NOT TO HAVE HAD THE OPPORTUNITY TO TALK TO SOME UNICEF MEN IN THE FIELD UP NORTH.

AFTER MARLON RECUPERATED FROM HIS NIGHT OF DEBAUCHERY WITH BOB PARRISH, WE RETURNED TO KARACHI, WHERE WE WOULD CATCH A PLANE AND CONTINUE ON OUR PREARRANGED UNICEF TRIP. THAT DAY, OR WAS IT THE NEXT, AS I PERUSED THE LOCAL NEWSPAPER, I CHANCED UPON A SMALL ITEM ON THE LOWER FRONT PAGE THAT CHILLED ME.

THE WEEKLY PLANE FROM RAWALPINDI TO THE KHYBER PASS HAD CRASHED IN THE MOUNTAINS. IT HAD COME DOWN IN TERRAIN THAT WAS INACCESSIBLE TO RESCUERS. NO ATTEMPT WOULD BE MADE TO REACH IT. THAT WAS ALL. IT WAS ALMOST LIKE A NEWS BULLETIN. ALMOST? IT WAS!

UPON READING IT, I IMMEDIATELY THOUGHT OF ROBERT PARRISH AND HOW PROVIDENTIALLY HE CAME TO RAWALPINDI AT THAT PARTICULAR TIME TO SCOUT FOR LOCATIONS, BUT IN REALITY HE SAVED ME AND MARLON FROM A MOUNTAINTOP GRAVE.

GRAPES, HOPS, AND SOUR MASH

I DON'T WANT TO LEAVE THE READER WITH A WRONG IMPRESSION OF BRANDO—ONE THAT IMPLIES THAT MARLON BRANDO IS A TWO-FISTED DRINKER.

CONTRARY TO WHAT I'VE WRITTEN ABOUT MARLON BEING INTOXICATED, MARLON IS NOT A DRINKER—HABITUAL OR OTHERWISE. IF THE TRUTH BE KNOWN, HE IS VERY SELDOM, IF EVER, IMBIBED. I'VE KNOWN MARLON FOR 35 YEARS AND NEVER, I REPEAT NEVER, HAVE I SEEN HIM COME HOME FROM THE STUDIO AND POUR HIMSELF A DRINK, OR HAVE A DRINK "WHEN THE SUN WENT DOWN," OR A COLD BEER ON A HOT DAY, OR WITH HIS BREAKFAST, LUNCH, OR DINNER. HE'S EXTREMELY STRONG-WILLED WHEN IT PERTAINS TO ALCOHOL.

THE EXCEPTIONS TO HIS ABSTINENCE ARE WHEN HE HAS DINNER GUESTS AND DRINKS ARE SERVED; WHEN HE HAS OR ATTENDS A PARTY; AND WHEN OUT TO DINNER, HE'LL ORDER A BOTTLE OF WINE FOR THE TABLE AND DRINK A GLASS OR TWO. SINCE HE'S NOT A SOCIAL LION, THERE ARE SEVERAL MONTHS OR EVEN YEARS BETWEEN DRINKS.

IN ALL THESE YEARS, ANYONE WHO HAS SEEN HIM INTOXICATED HAS SEEN A RARE SIGHT.

SO MUCH FOR THE CANARD OF BRANDO ALONE ON HIS HILLTOP, DRINKING HIMSELF TO OBLIVION. TAKE MY WORD FOR IT. THIS WILL NEVER HAPPEN.

SPEAKING OF DRINKING. I SAID I WASN'T GOING TO TALK ABOUT MARLON'S GIRLFRIENDS, BUT THERE'S ONE THAT DESERVES A FEW LINES FROM ME, IF NOT FROM MARLON. SHE WAS HAUGHTY, SHE WAS SNOTTY,

SHE WAS AMUSING IN HER HAUTEUR. SHE THOUGHT SHE HAD CLASS BECAUSE SHE TOLD YOU SHE HAD CLASS. SHE WAS A FUNNY DUCK.

BUT THAT'S NOT WHAT DESERVES THE FEW LINES. SHE WAS THE ONLY GIRLFRIEND MARLON HAD WHO "DRANK." SHE WAS WHAT CAN BEST BE DESCRIBED AS A CLOSET DRINKER. I ONLY SAW HER TAKE A DRINK ONCE, IN LONDON, BUT I KNOW I SAW HER INEBRIATED MORE THAN ONCE.

MARLON AND I HAVE A DISAGREEMENT ABOUT THIS. WE'VE BOTH KNOWN HER FOR YEARS. TRUE, HE'S SPENT MORE TIME WITH HER THAN I HAVE; THAT'S WHY I CAN'T BELIEVE HE WAS UNAWARE OF HER PROCLIVITY FOR BOOZE.

YOU DIDN'T NEED TO BE AN INDIAN TRACKER TO READ THE SIGNS. DID MARLON REALLY THINK THE HEADY PERFUME CONSTANTLY BEING SPRAYED HID THE ODOR EMANATING FROM HER PORES? AND WHAT ABOUT THE CLOVES SHE POPPED INTO HER MOUTH? TO HIDE THE BOOZY BREATH, MAYBE?

MARLON, I'M SURE, KNOWS THE DIFFERENCE BETWEEN UNDULATING AND STAGGERING, NO MATTER HOW CONTROLLED THE GAIT. OR DID HE REALLY THINK SHE WALKED LIKE THAT—LISTING WITHOUT A HINT OF BREEZE IN THE AIR?

AND, MAR, YOU DON'T THINK SHE WAS CROSS-EYED, DO YOU? BY NOON SHE HAD TROUBLE FOCUSING AND NEEDED "TO LIE DOWN FOR A LITTLE NAP," AS SHE WAS WONT TO SAY.

I DON'T KNOW IF MARLON EVER SAW HER DRUNK, OR EVEN TAKE A DRINK, BUT I PAID A BAR BILL, WITH HIS MONEY, IN TAHITI. I DON'T KNOW WHO DRANK THE

BOTTLE OF JACK DANIELS ROOM SERVICE DELIVERED TO HER. AND, OH YES, THE SECOND BOTTLE SHE ORDERED WHEN SHE WAS DEPARTING.

CHARISMATIC
FRANK
HONEST
IMPULSIVE
AMUSING
A FRIEND IN NEED

MARLON WAS GETTING FRUSTRATED ABOUT HIS HOUSE BEING BROKEN INTO ALMOST EVERY TIME HE WENT ON A TRIP. AND AT THIS PARTICULAR TIME IN HIS LIFE, HE WAS DOING A GREAT DEAL OF TRAVELLING. TRY AS WE MIGHT, WE COULDN'T KEEP HIS TRAVEL PLANS SECRET.

I FINALLY FIGURED IT OUT. ARMY ARCHARD'S COLUMN IN THE HOLLYWOOD REPORTER USUALLY HAD MARLON'S COMINGS AND GOINGS. AFTER A CALL TO ARMY, HE HONORED MARLON'S REQUEST THAT IF HE MENTIONED HIS TRAVEL PLANS, HE WOULD ALSO NAME THE PERSON, OR PERSONS, WHO WAS HOUSEGUESTING WHILE MARLON WAS AWAY. GOOD OL' ARMY.

SOON AFTER, MARLON AND I WENT ON A TRIP TO TAHITI. THIS WAS WHEN MARLON WAS NEGOTIATING FOR THE PURCHASE OF HIS SOUTH SEAS ISLAND, TETIAROA. JAY KANTER, HIS AGENT AT THE TIME, NEEDED A PLACE TO STAY FOR A FEW WEEKS, SO MARLON TOLD HIM THE HOUSE WAS HIS. AND ARMY

ARCHARD SPREAD THE WORD THROUGH HIS COLUMN THAT MARLON WAS GOING TO TAHITI AND JAY WAS STAYING AT HIS HOUSE.

A HAPPY JAY MOVED IN THE NIGHT WE DEPARTED. AND WHILE OUT TO DINNER WITH HIS THEN GIRLFRIEND AND NOW WIFE, KIT, YOU GUESSED IT, THE HOUSE WAS ROBBED—ALL OF JAY'S CLOTHES WERE STOLEN. BY SOMEONE WHO KNEW JAY, I IMAGINE. SOMEONE WHO NEEDED SUITS IN JAY'S SIZE.

P.S. JAY NEVER STAYED AT MARLON'S HOUSE AGAIN WHILE MARLON WAS AWAY. YOU DON'T HAVE TO WONDER WHY.

TAHITI

MARLON WAS LOOKING FOR A BOAT TO PURCHASE TO GO BACK AND FORTH TO TETIAROA, THE SOUTH PACIFIC ATOLL THAT HE HAD RECENTLY ACQUIRED. THIS WAS LONG BEFORE HE HAD AN AIRSTRIP BUILT. HE AND I PROWLED THE WATERFRONT OF PAPEETE, CHECKING ALL THE BOATS TO SEE IF ANY WERE FOR SALE.

STERLING HAYDEN WAS IN PORT WITH *THE WANDERER*. I HAD KNOWN HIM FROM PARAMOUNT STUDIO WHEN HE WAS UNDER CONTRACT THERE. SO I HAILED HIM, AND MARLON AND I WERE INVITED ABOARD. HE THOUGHT VERY HIGHLY OF *THE WANDERER* AND SEEMED VERY HAPPY TO GIVE US A TOUR. MARLON DISCOVERED THAT THE BOAT WAS FOR SALE. NO WONDER STERLING RHAPSODIZED OVER IT; HE HAD PROBABLY HEARD THAT MARLON WAS A

POTENTIAL BUYER. MARLON LOVED THE BOAT, AS I RECALL, BUT IT EVIDENTLY DIDN'T FIT HIS NEEDS BECAUSE HE DIDN'T BUY IT. I BELIEVE PETER FONDA LATER OWNED THE BOAT.

NOT THAT DAY, BUT EVENTUALLY, MARLON DID BUY A BOAT. AND THE MANNER IN WHICH HE PURCHASED IT MADE TONGUES WAG AMONG ALL THE NATIVES ON THE ISLANDS OF THE SOUTH PACIFIC.

I WASN'T WITH HIM ON THE TRIP TO TAHITI WHEN HE MADE THE PURCHASE. BUT THE WAY I HEARD IT, SOMEONE WHO KNEW HE WAS LOOKING FOR A BOAT TOLD HIM ABOUT ONE THAT HAD SUNK, BEEN RAISED, PAINTED, AND WAS FOR SALE AT A BARGAIN PRICE. MARLON, AS THE STORY GOES, SAID, "I'LL BUY IT."

HE'S THE ONLY MAN I'VE HEARD OF WHO EVER BOUGHT A BOAT SIGHT UNSEEN. TRUE STORY? ONLY MARLON KNOWS. BUT THE TAHITIANS LOVE TELLING IT ABOUT HIM.

MARLON RETURNED HOME FROM HIS TRIP TO TAHITI AND INFORMED US THAT HE HAD BEEN LUCKY: HE HAD FOUND A BOAT AND PURCHASED IT. NO OTHER INFORMATION WAS FORTHCOMING. NO PHOTOGRAPHS OF THE VESSEL. NO DESCRIPTION. JUST THAT HE WAS THE HAPPY OWNER OF A BOAT. OF COURSE, NO ONE KNEW THE "BOAT STORY," OR WE'D KNOW HE COULDN'T GIVE US A DESCRIPTION OF THE BOAT BECAUSE HE HADN'T SEEN IT HIMSELF. THAT IS, OF COURSE, IF THE "BOAT STORY" WAS TRUE.

SOME MONTHS AFTERWARD, MARLON AND I RETURNED TO TAHITI. HE HAD PAINTED THIS GLORIOUS

TRIP WE WERE GOING TO TAKE TO TETIAROA ON THE NEW BOAT.

AFTER OUR ARRIVAL, MARLON SPENT A WEEK IN PAPEETE BUYING NEEDED EQUIPMENT, FOOD SUPPLIES, ETC., FOR THE ISLAND. ALL THE SUPPLIES HE BOUGHT WERE TO BE SENT TO THE DOCK FOR OUR DEPARTURE AT WEEK'S END.

DEPARTURE DAY ARRIVED AND THERE I WAS IN MY WHITE TOPSIDERS, WHITE PANTS, NAVY- AND WHITE-STRIPED T-SHIRT, ALL SET FOR A CRUISE.

AT DAYBREAK, WE RACED INTO PAPEETE FROM MARLON'S HOME IN PUNAUUIA. WHEN MARLON PARKED THE CAR AT DOCKSIDE, I DID NOT SEE ANYTHING THAT LOOKED AS IF WE COULD "CRUISE" TO TETIAROA ON IT. MARLON HAD BOUNDED OUT OF THE CAR AS SOON AS HE HAD PARKED, SO I COULDN'T ASK HIM ABOUT THE BOAT.

MARLON WAS VERY HAPPILY GREETING EVERYONE ON THE DOCK, THEN STOOD CHATTING NEAR A SCRUFFY BOAT—A LARGER VERSION OF THE AFRICAN QUEEN—THAT WAS BEING LOADED WITH SUPPLIES. SHORTLY THEREAFTER, MARLON WAVED ME OVER AND HE INTRODUCED ME TO A FEW BAREFOOT TAHITIAN SAILORS. A MAN HAILED MARLON FROM THE BOAT. MARLON JUMPED ABOARD WITH ME FOLLOWING AND HE GREETED THE MAN, THEN TURNED AND INTRODUCED ME TO THE CAPTAIN OF THIS DERELICT.

ENGINES HAD BEEN STARTED AND WHEN I SAW THEM CASTING OFF, I SAID TO MARLON INCREDULOUSLY, "IS THIS IT?"

NONCHALANTLY HE SAID, "YES."

"I'M NOT GOING ON ANY SHARK-INFESTED OCEAN IN THIS," I CRIED AND JUMPED OFF ONTO THE DOCK.

MARLON YELLED, "COME ON, ALICE. IT'S OKAY."

"NO WAY, JOSE," I CALLED BACK.

NOW MARLON JUMPED ONTO THE DOCK. THERE ENSUED A CHASE AROUND THE WHARF THAT HAD THE TAHITIAN DOCK WORKERS BUG-EYED. THE TAHITIANS MUST HAVE THOUGHT WE WERE LOONY.

I DIDN'T GO. INSTEAD, I STOOD ON THE DOCK HUFFING AND PUFFING AND WAVED MARLON OFF. HE WAS YELLING BACK AT ME AS THEY PULLED OUT, "YOU'LL BE SORRY."

IT TURNED OUT TO BE ANOTHER OF MARLON'S ADVENTURES. OR SHOULD I SAY MISADVENTURES, FOR THEY NEVER DID MAKE IT TO TETIAROA. THE BOAT BROKE DOWN AT SEA. MARLON WAS PICKED UP BY A PASSING FISHING BOAT AND RETURNED TO PAPEETE. WHEN I ASKED, "WHAT HAPPENED?" HIS REPLY WAS A TERSE, "I DON'T WANT TO TALK ABOUT IT." SO WE DIDN'T.

I KNEW WHEN TO BACK OFF.

WHEN LAST I HEARD, THE BOAT HAD SUNK AGAIN OFF ONE OF THE ISLANDS IN THE SOUTH PACIFIC. MARLON STILL DOESN'T WANT TO TALK ABOUT IT.

ROMANTIC
DEPENDABLE
MANIPULATIVE
ANTI-SOCIAL
JUDGMENTAL
SENSUOUS
SENTIMENTAL
UNCONVENTIONAL

CRAZY LIKE A FOX

"I'M CRAZY," MARLON ANNOUNCED TO ME SHORTLY AFTER I STARTED TO WORK FOR HIM AT HIS HOME.

YES, I SILENTLY AGREED, *CRAZY LIKE A FOX*.

HE WAS SERIOUS, BUT HE NEVER CONVINCED ME HE WAS CRAZY. SURE HE DID CRAZY THINGS, BUT HE WASN'T CERTIFIABLE BY ANY WILD STRETCH OF THE IMAGINATION.

YET FOR YEARS HE WOULD EXCUSE HIS EXCESSIVE BEHAVIOR WITH "I'M CRAZY." I THINK SOMEONE, AND I ASSUME IT MUST HAVE BEEN A PSYCHIATRIST HE WAS SEEING, TOLD HIM HE WAS CRAZY, AND HE TOOK THAT AS GOSPEL INSTEAD OF GETTING ANOTHER OPINION. BUT IT SUITED HIS PURPOSE AS HIS REBELLIOUS, UNCONVENTIONAL BEHAVIOR WAS EXCUSED AND TOLERATED WITH THE PRONOUNCEMENT, "HE'S CRAZY." AND THOSE AROUND HIM VOICING THIS WERE ONLY AGREEING WITH HIM WHEN THEY SAID IT.

"CRAZY" ALSO CARRIED OVER TO HIS PERSONAL AND INTIMATE RELATIONSHIPS. HE TRULY BELIEVED ANYONE WHO BEFRIENDED HIM OR BECAME INVOLVED

WITH HIM EMOTIONALLY WAS CRAZY. HIS CREDO: ONLY A CRAZY PERSON WOULD GRAVITATE TOWARD ANOTHER CRAZY PERSON. CONSEQUENTLY, ALL MARLON'S WOMEN WERE IN THERAPY SOON AFTER BEGINNING A RELATIONSHIP WITH HIM. MOST OF THE TIME AT HIS INSISTENCE AND EXPENSE. OF COURSE, THEY WERE ALWAYS TRYING TO PLEASE HIM. IF MARLON SAID THEY NEEDED TO SEE A PSYCHIATRIST, THEY SAW A PSYCHIATRIST.

MARLON WOULD, FROM TIME TO TIME, URGE ME INTO ANALYSIS. I RESISTED, REASONING THAT IF HE WAS IN THERAPY BECAUSE HE THOUGHT HE WAS CRAZY, I WASN'T GOING TO ALLOW HIM TO PUSH ME INTO "CRAZY." EVEN WHEN HE INSISTED THAT I HAD TO BE CRAZY WORKING FOR HIM.

IN HINDSIGHT, MAYBE MARLON WAS RIGHT, AND THEN MAYBE HE WASN'T. MAYBE I WAS CRAZY TO WORK FOR HIM. WHO KNOWS "CRAZY?" ALL I KNOW IS, HE WASN'T CRAZY, BUT HIS ACCEPTANCE OF THIS ASSESSMENT SUITED HIS PURPOSE FOR A LONG, LONG TIME.

ALL MARLON KNOWS ABOUT WOMEN WOULD FIT IN A THIMBLE WITH ROOM LEFT OVER FOR SINATRA AND NELSON RIDDLE'S ORCHESTRA.

—alice marchak

LOVABLE
NONCONFORMIST
TORMENTED
GALLANT
BEWITCHING
SEDUCER
UNFAITHFUL

MUCH HAS BEEN WRITTEN ABOUT MARLON AND HIS WOMEN. I FEEL VERY UNCOMFORTABLE WRITING ABOUT "MARLON'S LOVE LIFE," EVEN WITH HIS URGING. HOW CAN I TELL THE WORLD HOW SAPPY HE IS WHEN HE THINKS HE'S IN LOVE, OR ACTUALLY IS IN LOVE? I JUST CAN'T, MAR, I JUST CAN'T.

CAN I TELL EVERYONE HOW MANY TIMES HE HAD ME AND BLANCHE, ANOTHER EMPLOYEE, CHANGING SOFT WHITE LIGHT BULBS TO SOFT PINK, REARRANGING FLOWERS, FLUFFING PILLOWS, DIMMING LIGHTS, ETC., ETC., ETC., WHILE HE PICKED OUT DREAMY MUSIC; VIVALDI, SINATRA, GLEASON.

BLANCHE AND I WONDERED LOUD ENOUGH FOR HIM TO HEAR US, "WHO'S COMING?" AND LAUGHED ALOUD AT HIM AS HE REARRANGED WHAT WE HAD REARRANGED AND CHECKED EVERYTHING AGAIN.

'WHAT IDIOT GIRL WOULD BE TAKEN IN BY ALL THIS NONSENSE?"

"I CAN'T THINK OF ANY."

OH, HOW WE LAUGHED. HOW HE GLARED. AND, OH, HOW WRONG WE WERE.

AND CAN I TELL HOW MUCH HE SUFFERED WHEN A ROMANCE WENT BUST? HOW HE WALLOWED IN MISERY TILL I ACCUSED HIM OF ENJOYING IT? NEVER, EVER HAVE I SEEN ANYONE SUFFER SO BEAUTIFULLY—NOT EVEN ME—AND GOD KNOW HE'S SEEN ME SUFFER THROUGH BROKEN ROMANCES.

AND THEN, AFTER ALL HIS AGONY, HIS ANGER AND DESIRE FOR REVENGE. REVENGE, AH, SWEET REVENGE! SOME OF HIS PLOTS FOR REVENGE WERE MASTERPIECES. BUT I HAVE TO LET HIM TELL ABOUT THE WOMEN WHO HAD "DONE HIM WRONG." I COULD NEVER MANAGE THAT BECAUSE I COULDN'T BEGIN TO DO IT JUSTICE.

I ONLY RECALL ONE GIRLFRIEND OF HIS THAT I CAN TRULY SAY I DIDN'T LIKE ONE BIT—AND TOLD MARLON SO. THEN, THERE WERE OTHERS I GENTLY NUDGED HIM TO MARRY—LOVELY, EXOTIC FRANCE NUYEN, AND DARLING JILL BANNER, WHO WAS ENGAGED TO MARLON FOR A TIME AND WHOM I THINK HE WOULD EVENTUALLY HAVE MARRIED IF SHE HAD LIVED. (MARLON RECONFIRMED THIS IN A CONVERSATION AS I WRITE; I WASN'T SURPRISED.)

ALL MARLON'S WOMEN KNEW MORE ABOUT MEN THAN MARLON DID ABOUT WOMEN. THEY LED HIM IN A MERRY CHASE. I THINK ONE OF THEM WOULD HAVE MADE HIM A GOOD LIFE'S COMPANION. BUT THEN, WHEN DID HE TAKE MY ADVICE?

THAT'S ALL I'M GOING TO DISCLOSE ABOUT THE WOMEN IN HIS LIFE. AFTER ALL, THIS IS HIS STORY, EXCEPT TO SAY THAT HE ALWAYS PICKED HIS OWN WOMEN. AND WITHOUT EXCEPTION THEY ALWAYS LACKED AT LEAST ONE OR TWO OF HIS REQUIREMENTS

FOR A PERFECT MATE—SUBCONSCIOUSLY LEAVING ROOM FOR REJECTION OF EACH.

IS HE STILL LOOKING? I CERTAINLY HOPE SO. WILL HE FIND WHAT HE'S SEARCHING FOR? NO. SHE DOESN'T EXIST.

MARLON HAS ALWAYS BEEN TRUE TO HIMSELF. WHAT DEMONS HE WRESTLED WITH ONLY HE CAN SAY. WHEN I FIRST STARTED TO WORK FOR HIM, I WAS UNDER THE IMPRESSION THAT HE REALLY DIDN'T WANT TO WORK. THAT WORK INTERFERED WITH HIS MISSION IN LIFE, WHICH AT THAT TIME WAS CHASING WOMEN—AND CATCHING THEM, I MIGHT ADD. THAT HE WANTED THE FREEDOM TO PURSUE. THIS WAS A TIME WHEN HE WAS EXERTING ALL HIS ENERGIES TOWARD AFFAIRES DE COEUR, RATHER THAN FILLING HIS POCKETS WITH GOLD.

MY IMPRESSION WASN'T TOO WRONG. HE EVEN CONFIDED ONE DAY THAT HE WOKE EVERY MORNING AND IMMEDIATELY BEGAN PLANNING WHAT GIRL OR GIRLS HE WAS GOING TO SEE THAT DAY.

LATER IN LIFE THAT CHANGED, BUT IT WAS MUCH LATER. MARLON NEVER HAD ONE GIRLFRIEND IN HIS LIFE. HE HAD ONE SPECIAL GIRLFRIEND WHO HE PROFESSED TO LOVE, AND TWO OR THREE STANDING IN THE WINGS.

ROMANTICALLY, MARLON WAS USUALLY WALKING A TIGHTROPE. I THINK HE LIKED LIVING ON THE EDGE. HE DIDN'T BLINK, EXCEPT ONCE THAT I KNOW OF. A GIRLFRIEND, WHO HAD COME TO TOWN FOR THE WEEKEND, WAS SITTING WITH HIM ON THE COUCH IN THE LIVING ROOM WHEN AN AIR WEST HOSTESS WALKED IN WITH HER OVERNIGHT BAG.

I THOUGHT I SAW AN AIR HOSTESS SASHAY BY MY OFFICE DOOR. I WALKED OUT TO THE KITCHEN TO ASK BLANCHE IF I HAD SEEN AN AIR HOSTESS OR IF I WAS HAVING EYE PROBLEMS. SHE SAID, "IF YOU ARE, BABE, THEN I AM, TOO." THEN WE DOUBLED OVER WITH LAUGHTER AT THE SCENE WE IMAGINED TRANSPIRING IN THE NEXT ROOM.

IT HAD HAPPENED SO UNEXPECTEDLY AND SO FAST THAT NEITHER OF US HAD HAD TIME TO WARN DEAR OL' MAR THAT "TROUBLE WAS ON THE WAY." IN NO TIME AT ALL, MARLON BUZZED AND ASKED ME TO COME TO HIS BEDROOM.

FIGHTING FOR COMPOSURE, I WALKED BY THE LIVING ROOM WITH THE TWO GIRLS SITTING OPPOSITE EACH OTHER ON THE WHITE COUCHES FLANKING THE FIREPLACE. I WAS HARDLY ABLE TO KEEP A STRAIGHT FACE, YET INWARDLY I SYMPATHIZED WITH THEIR PREDICAMENT.

WHEN I GOT TO MARLON'S ROOM, HE TUGGED ME INTO THE BATHROOM, WHERE HE WAS HIDING, AND HISSED, "YOU'VE GOT TO HELP ME!" AND THAT SET OFF SUCH A PAROXYSM OF LAUGHTER AT HIS BEING CAUGHT THAT WE COULDN'T TALK. WHEN I COULD SPEAK, I REFUSED.

"THIS IS ONE TIME YOU HAVE TO GET OUT OF IT YOURSELF." I LAUGHED AND STARTED TO LEAVE.

"YOU CAN'T LEAVE ME!" HE GRABBED ME AND TRIED TO HAUL ME BACK. WE STARTED TO WRESTLE, ME TRYING TO GET FREE OF HIS ARMS AND HE TRYING TO HOLD ME, LAUGHING ALL THE TIME.

"MARLON, IF ONE OF THE GIRLS COMES IN, WHAT WILL THIS LOOK LIKE, ME STRUGGLING IN YOUR ARMS?"

THIS REMARK RELEASED ME AND I LEFT HIM WITH A "GOOD LUCK" AND A GOOD LAUGH. I KNEW MARLON WELL ENOUGH TO KNOW THAT HE MIGHT FALL INTO THE FRYING PAN, BUT NEVER INTO THE FIRE BENEATH IT. HE'D COME OUT OF THIS UNSCATHED WITHOUT MY HELP—AND HE DID.

I MUST SAY, MARLON GAVE US A LOT OF GOOD LAUGHS. OUR HEARTS WERE YOUNG AND GAY THEN.

JILL, A GREAT LOVE OF MARLON'S, AND I WERE TELEPHONE BUDDIES. THERE WERE FEW PEOPLE SHE COULD TALK TO ABOUT MARLON, AND WHENEVER SHE FELT THE NEED TO EXPRESS SOMETHING ABOUT HIM THAT SHE WOULDN'T DISCLOSE TO ANYONE ELSE, SHE'D CALL. OTHER TIMES, SHE'D PHONE JUST TO HAVE A FEW LAUGHS—SOMETIMES AT MARLON'S EXPENSE. BUT ONE TIME SHE CALLED ME TERRIBLY UPSET ABOUT SOMETHING MARLON HAD DONE.

MARLON AND JILL HAD BEEN IN HAWAII EN ROUTE TO TAHITI AND TETIAROA WITH A COUPLE OF FRIENDS. MARLON PROVOKED AN ARGUMENT AND THEIR ENGAGEMENT WAS BROKEN. SHE DIDN'T GO TO TAHITI.

IT WAS ONE OF THE FEW TIMES SHE CALLED THAT WE DIDN'T LAUGH. NOW THAT SHE'S GONE I MISS THAT LAUGHTER.

WHO ARE YOU GOING TO BELIEVE? YOUR EYES OR ME?

AS FOR ME AND MARLON. IF YOU ASK, "ARE YOU IN LOVE WITH MARLON?" THE ANSWER IS, "NO."

BUT IF YOU ASK, "DO YOU LOVE MARLON?" THE ANSWER IS "YES"—AS IN TENDER FEELINGS.

I WILL HAVE TO CHANGE THAT ANSWER TO A QUALIFIED YES.

I SAY THIS BECAUSE THERE WERE DAYS WHEN I WOULD HAVE LIKED TO DROP-KICK HIM TO CATALINA. AND I'M CERTAIN THAT IF YOU ASK HIM, HE'D SAY THERE WERE DAYS OR MOMENTS WHEN HE'D LIKE TO DO THE SAME OR WORSE TO ME.

BUT SOME PEOPLE LIKE TO THINK OTHERWISE. THIS IS WHAT EVERYONE SAW ON THE SET AT UNIVERSAL STUDIO, WHERE MARLON WAS REHEARSING A SCENE WITH HIS CO-STAR, SHIRLEY JONES:

I WAS SITTING IN A DIRECTOR'S CHAIR WATCHING THE REHEARSALS—STAYING OUT OF THE LINE OF VISION OF THE ACTORS. NEVERTHELESS, MARLON SPIED ME AND SAUNTERED OVER, HUNKERED DOWN, AND LEANED TOWARD ME UNTIL OUR NOSES WERE KISSING. THEY HEARD HIM CHUCKLE AND SAW ME SMILE. THEY SAW US LOOKING DEEP INTO EACH OTHERS EYES AND WHISPERING, AND MARLON RISE AND RETURN TO REHEARSALS. LATER, A FRIEND WHO HAD OBSERVED THE BYPLAY, REMARKED TO MARIE RHODES, A FRIEND AND MARLON'S STAND-IN, "YOU CAN'T TELL ME THOSE TWO AREN'T LOVERS!"

SILLY GIRL! DON'T YOU BELIEVE YOUR EYES!

NOW IT CAN BE TOLD. HERE'S THE SCOOP:

MARLON SPIED ME SITTING IN THE DIRECTOR'S CHAIR AND SAUNTERED OVER, HUNKERED DOWN, AND LEANED TOWARD ME UNTIL OUR NOSES WERE TOUCHING, THEN WHISPERED, "CHECK MY BREATH." AND HE PARTED HIS LIPS AND EXHALED INTO MY FACE.

"IT'S SWEET," I SAID, "BUT IF YOU'D FEEL MORE COMFORTABLE IN THE SCENE, I HAVE BINACA IN MY BAG. WOULD YOU LIKE SOME?"

"SMILE," HE WHISPERED AND CHUCKLED, "DON'T BE SO SERIOUS." THEN HE CONTINUED, "NO, SHE'LL SMELL IT AND KNOW I WAS CONCERNED ABOUT MY BREATH."

"NOT TO WORRY. YOU'RE ALL RIGHT," I REPLIED.

SO ASSURED, HE ROSE FROM HIS HAUNCHES AND RETURNED CONFIDENTLY TO THE SCENE. MARIE AND I LAUGHED WHEN I EXPLAINED WHAT HAD TRANSPIRED.

SO MUCH FOR LOVERS! BUT THAT'S HOW RUMORS GET STARTED—PEOPLE BELIEVE THEIR EYES.

ANOTHER TIME, ANOTHER CROWDED SET. MARLON PULLED ME INTO HIS ARMS AND NUZZLED MY EAR AS HE LED ME THROUGH A COUPLE OF ASTAIRE AND ROGERS TWIRLS AND DIPS. THEN HE BOWED LOW, ROSE, AND BLEW ME A KISS FROM THE TIPS OF HIS FINGERS AS HE BACKED AWAY.

OH, MY! HOW ROMANTIC!

LET'S HAVE A RE-RUN OF THIS SCENE:

WHILE MARLON WAS SUPPOSEDLY NUZZLING MY EAR, HE WAS WHISPERING, "I WANT TO CHECK OUT THAT GIRL OVER THERE, THE ONE IN BLACK." SINCE HE WAS MYOPIC, HE SPUN ME CLOSER TO WHERE THIS BLACK SILK-STOCKINGED, LONG-LEGGED MOVIE EXTRA HE WAS INTERESTED IN WAS STANDING AND GAVE ME A FEW TWIRLS WHILE HE "CHECKED HER OUT."

SO MUCH FOR SUCH PUBLIC DISPLAYS OF AFFECTION. I COULD CITE OTHERS THAT OCCURRED DURING THE YEARS, BUT THESE WILL GIVE YOU AN IDEA OF HOW

THE WHISPERS I HAVE ENDURED ABOUT OUR SO-CALLED LOVE RELATIONSHIP GET STARTED.

MARLON HAD SO MANY LOVES DURING HIS LIFE, BUT, ALAS, I WASN'T ONE OF THEM. SORRY TO DISAPPOINT SOME PEOPLE.

LET'S HEAR IT FOR SENSUALITY!

I CONSIDER MARLON A VOLUPTUARY. BESIDES WOMEN, HE LIKES CASHMERE, SILK, AND THEN THERE WAS SATIN! SOMEHOW SATIN DIDN'T FIT THE IMAGE I HAD OF MARLON. NOT AT ALL. ONE DAY OUT OF NOWHERE CAME THE REQUEST.

"GET ME SOME SATIN SHEETS."

SINCE WHEN DID MARLON TAKE AN INTEREST IN SHEETS? HE NEVER CARED WHAT KIND OF SHEETS WERE ON THE BED—WHITE, BLUE, PRINT, ETC. CLEAN WAS ALL THAT INTERESTED HIM.

"SATIN SHEETS?" I QUESTIONED.

"YOU KNOW, SATIN SHEETS—BLACK, WHITE, PEACH."

"YOU WANT BLACK, WHITE, PEACH SATIN SHEETS."

"YEAH. A BUNCH."

I GUESS HE WANTED SATIN SHEETS. WILL WONDERS NEVER CEASE. NATURALLY, HE WANTED THEM YESTERDAY. NATURALLY, I COULDN'T FIND ANY LOCALLY. I FINALLY ORDERED SOME FROM A STORE ON THE EAST COAST. THEN I RECEIVED NOTICE OF DELAYED DELIVERY. THAT DIDN'T PREVENT MARLON FROM ASKING DAILY, "WHERE'S MY SHEETS?" TRYING MY PATIENCE.

FINALLY, A BUNCH ARRIVED AND A SET IMMEDIATELY ADORNED HIS BED.

NEXT MORNING WHEN I SAW HIM, I ASKED, "HOW'D YOU SLEEP?'

THERE WAS A GRUNT IN REPLY. HE WASN'T TALKING. DID I TELL YOU HE TAKES A WHILE TO FULLY WAKE UP? MOODY MORNING IS WHAT YOU COULD CALL IT.

THE FOLLOWING DAY I AGAIN INQUIRED, BUT THIS TIME MORE TO THE POINT, "WELL, MAR, HOW ARE THE SATIN SHEETS?" THIS TIME I GOT A "SWELL."

SO DAY AFTER DAY, ON WENT THE BLACK SATIN SHEETS, THE WHITE SATIN SHEETS, THE PEACH SATIN SHEETS. TILL ONE DAY THERE WAS AN EXPLOSION.

"TAKE THOSE SHEETS OFF MY BED!"

WHAT, MARLON, THOSE SATIN SHEETS YOU COULDN'T WAIT TO GET? THAT YOU ALMOST DROVE ME CRAZY ABOUT UNTIL THEY ARRIVED?

"NOW! I'M EXHAUSTED! I'VE BEEN SLIDING ALL OVER THE PLACE. I'M ON THE FLOOR A COUPLE TIMES A NIGHT. GET THEM OUT OF HERE!" HE MOANED.

END OF THE SAGA OF THE SATIN SHEETS, EXCEPT TO SAY WE HAD THE DEVIL OF A TIME TRYING TO GIVE THEM AWAY. IT SEEMS EVERYONE ELSE KNEW ABOUT SATIN SHEETS WHAT MARLON HAD TO EXPERIENCE THE HARD WAY.

ENDEARING
CANDID
WITTY
LONER
HOSPITABLE

DON'T FENCE ME IN

MARLON STARTS CLIMBING THE WALLS, FENCED IN, SMOTHERED, WHEN TOO MANY PEOPLE ARE IN THE HOUSE FOR ANY LENGTH OF TIME—HOUSEGUESTS WHO STAY ON AND ON AND ON. HOUSEGUESTS WHO START TO ABUSE HIS HOSPITALITY. HE'LL SEE HOW FAR PEOPLE WILL GO, AND THEN HE'LL CALL AN ABRUPT HALT.

ONE TIME HE LEFT FOR A WEEK IN THE DESERT TO GET AWAY FROM IT ALL. UPON DEPARTURE HE DIRECTED ME TO "GET RID OF EVERYBODY BY THE TIME I RETURN."

BUT, LIKE KAUFMAN'S CHARACTER IN *THE MAN WHO CAME TO DINNER,* A PARISIAN ARTIST, WHO WAS THE HOUSEGUEST OF ONE OF THE HOUSEGUESTS, WALKED THROUGH A PLATE GLASS WINDOW IN THE LIVING ROOM THE EVENING OF HIS FAREWELL PARTY. THE POOR GUY ENDED UP RECUPERATING FOR A MONTH ON A HOSPITAL BED IN THE GUESTROOM. FORTUNATELY FOR ME, MARLON'S WEEK AWAY TURNED INTO TWO, AND SINCE HE'S SUCH A COMPASSIONATE MAN, ON HIS RETURN HE COMMISERATED WITH THE UNFORTUNATE MAN.

THIS ISN'T TO SAY THAT MARLON DOESN'T LIKE HIS FRIENDS AROUND. HE DOES. OR, I SHOULD SAY *DID,* AS HE'S BECOME MUCH MORE OF A LONER AS HE HAS GROWN OLDER. IN SPITE OF THIS, HIS FRIENDS HAVE ALWAYS RECEIVED A WARM, OPEN-HEARTED WELCOME ON CROSSING HIS THRESHOLD. BUT HE'S A PERSON WHO NEEDS TIME ALONE, TO REFLECT, SORT OUT HIS

THOUGHTS, AND PLOT HIS PLOTS. TIME TO DECIDE WHAT HE'S GOING TO TOSS INTO THE BOILING CAULDRON HE KEEPS STIRRING. BUT HE DOES VALUE HIS QUIET TIMES.

I WAS AROUND A LONG TIME AND I UNDERSTOOD THIS ABOUT MARLON AND RESPECTED IT. WE BOTH HAD AN INSTINCT ABOUT EACH OTHERS' NEED TO BE ALONE AT TIMES. EVEN THOUGH I WAS WORKING FOR HIM AT HIS HOUSE, I GAVE HIM SPACE, AND HE, IN TURN, GAVE ME SPACE. MAYBE THAT'S ONE OF THE REASONS I WAS AROUND A LONG TIME. WHO KNOWS?

FRIENDS, ROMANS, COUNTRYMEN.
—shakespeare

A WALK IN THE WOODS WITH WALLY

AT THE MOMENT THE ONLY PERSON I CAN THINK OF THAT MARLON HAD WHAT COULD BE EXPRESSED AS NORMAL HUMAN RELATIONS WITH WAS WALLY COX. IT WASN'T A MARLON BRANDO MOVIE-STAR RELATIONSHIP. OTHER FRIENDS FROM HIS YOUTH DIDN'T HAVE THE SAME NON-STAR RELATIONSHIP. IT'S EPHEMERAL, BUT IT'S THERE.

AMONG OTHER THINGS, BOTH MARLON AND WALLY WERE ATTUNED TO NATURE. THEY WERE HIKING BUDDIES AND WOULD NEVER RETURN FROM THEIR WOODLAND FORAYS WITHOUT A BIRD'S FEATHER, A ROCK THAT HAD CAUGHT THEIR FANCY, WILD GRASSES, OR A GNARLED WALKING STICK. FOR YEARS, A

WALKING STICK MARLON BROUGHT BACK FROM AN OUTING WITH WALLY WAS KEPT JUST INSIDE THE DOOR OF HIS BEDROOM. I'VE NOTICED IT'S IN THE DEN NOW. THESE TREASURES, TO MY MIND, TOLD MORE ABOUT MARLON THAN ANYTHING ELSE. I ALWAYS CONSIDERED THESE A PART OF HIM AND WARNED ONE AND ALL NOT TO THROW THEM OUT. IN TIME, EVERYONE IN THE HOUSEHOLD GREW TO RESPECT THAT OLD STICK LEANING NEXT TO HIS DOORWAY. HIS ROOM DOESN'T LOOK THE SAME WITH IT NOW BANISHED TO ANOTHER PART OF THE HOUSE.

I REMEMBER WALLY WITH GREAT AFFECTION. HE WAS ALWAYS WELCOME AT MARLON'S HOME. HE'D STOP BY IN A NEIGHBORLY FASHION AS HE LIVED NEARBY. WALLY WAS THE ONLY PERSON WHO DID THAT—JUST DROPPED BY WITHOUT CALLING TO SEE HIS FRIEND WHEN THE SPIRIT MOVED HIM.

I REMEMBER ONE DAY HE DROPPED BY IN PARTICULAR. MARLON AND I WERE IN HIS SITTING ROOM. MARLON WAS TALKING WHEN WALLY CAME IN. THEY DIDN'T GREET EACH OTHER, WALLY MERELY JOINED US. WITHOUT ANY OUTWARD ACKNOWLEDGEMENT OF HIS PRESENCE, MARLON KEPT ON WITH HIS DISCOURSE. AFTER A FEW MINUTES OF SILENT ATTENTION, WALLY STOOD UP AND QUIETLY STATED, "THIS IS SOOO BORING." AND SLOWLY WALKED OUT. MARLON IGNORED HIS DEPARTURE AS HE HAD HIS ENTRANCE AND KEPT ON TALKING. BUT THIS FLAT STATEMENT, AND HIS DELIVERY, MADE ME CHUCKLE IN AMUSEMENT. WHEN I DID, MARLON JUST SHOOK HIS HEAD FROM SIDE TO SIDE AND SAID WITH AFFECTION, "THAT'S WALLY."

I DON'T KNOW ANYONE ELSE WHO WOULD HAVE DONE THAT, NO MATTER HOW BORING. AND, I DON'T KNOW ANYONE ELSE THAT MARLON WOULD HAVE ACCEPTED THAT PRONOUNCEMENT FROM WITHOUT CHALLENGING IT. BUT SUCH WAS THEIR FRIENDSHIP, THERE WAS NO CHALLENGE AND NO ARGUMENT ABOUT IT. MARLON ACCEPTED THE FACT THAT HE BORED WALLY—AT THAT MOMENT.

DEAR, DEAR WALLY. MARLON WAS SO ANGRY WITH HIM FOR DYING. AND I MISSED HIM TELLING ME HOW BEAUTIFUL HE THOUGHT I WAS EVERY TIME HE WALKED IN THE DOOR. HE CERTAINLY KNEW HOW TO MAKE MY DAY.

PERSONAL OBSERVATIONS AND THOUGHTS
—alice marchak

IT'S BEEN MY OBSERVATION THAT MARLON RELATED EASILY WITH CHILDREN, AND CHILDREN WITH HIM, NOT "MARLON BRANDO, MOVIE STAR." WHEN WITH YOUNGSTERS, HE KNEW THEIR INTERPLAY WAS HONEST. HE COULD ACCEPT THAT HONESTY WITHOUT RESERVATIONS. THIS, I SAW, HE COULD NOT DO WITH AN ADULT.

SO HIS RELATIONSHIPS WITH ADULTS WERE MORE OFTEN THAN NOT SUSPECT AND COLORED BY HIS PROFESSIONAL PERSONA—"STAR."

MARLON DIDN'T TRUST AMIABLE STRANGERS ENGAGING HIM IN AIMLESS CONVERSATION, HOWEVER WELL-INTENTIONED, OR FRIENDSHIPS PROFFERED WITH

ONLY SLIGHT ACQUAINTANCE. HOW WAS THIS? MARLON WAS CERTAINLY UNCOMMONLY HANDSOME OF FACE AND BODY. HE WAS CHARISMATIC, ARTICULATE. HE HAD GREAT PERSONAL MAGNETISM AND CHARM. WHY DID HE THINK HE DIDN'T ATTRACT ANYONE? THAT NO ONE WAS ATTRACTED TO HIM AS A MAN—A PERSON THEY WOULD LIKE TO KNOW AND, YES, LOVE. BUT HE THOUGHT PEOPLE ONLY SAW "MOVIE STAR."

SOMETIMES, I THOUGHT HE HAD AN INFERIORITY COMPLEX. THEN I'D TELL MYSELF, *BUT HE CAN'T FEEL THAT WAY.* I OFTEN FELT HE GREATLY REGRETTED NOT HAVING A HIGHER EDUCATION AND ENVIED PEOPLE WHO HAD A MYRIAD OF DEGREES. *BUT,* I'D TELL MYSELF, *HE'S A SAVVY MAN WHO HAS EARNED HIS DEGREES IN SELF-EDUCATION. HE DOESN'T HAVE TO TAKE A BACK SEAT TO ANYONE WHERE NATIVE INTELLIGENCE IS CONCERNED.*

MARLON DOESN'T TRUST ANYONE UNTIL THEY PROVE THEMSELVES, AND THEY GO THROUGH MANY TESTS TO EARN THAT TRUST. I, ON THE CONTRARY, TRUST EVERYONE AND THEN TAKE MY LUMPS.

THERE ARE TIMES, THOUGH, WHEN MARLON INVITES INTIMACY, EVEN ON SHORT OR NO ACQUAINTANCE. ON THE OTHER HAND, HE WILL FROST ANYONE WHO ENTERS HIS SPHERE UNINVITED. CONTRADICTORY IS HIS NAME.

MARLON ALSO HAD AN AFFINITY FOR ATTRACTING TROUBLED, PROBLEM-PRONE PEOPLE—PEOPLE WITH BROKEN WINGS. HE GRAVITATED TOWARDS MISFITS. THIS IS NOT NECESSARILY BAD. HE WAS A SYMPATHETIC

EAR FOR EVERYBODY'S TROUBLES, ESPECIALLY ANYONE WITH PROBLEMS OF THE HEART—MINE INCLUDED. HE WAS A PSYCHIATRIST TO HIS WORLD. AND, GOD KNOWS, MOST OF WHOM PEOPLED HIS WORLD WERE IN DIRE NEED OF ANALYSIS AND ADVICE.

BUT EVEN THAT IN TIME BECAME TOO MUCH FOR MARLON TO SHOULDER, FOR ONE DAY HE WEARILY ANNOUNCED TO ME, "THE CLINIC IS CLOSED." IS IT, MAR? I WONDER.

FRIENDLY
LOVING
CHARITABLE

YOU'VE HEARD TELL OF PEOPLE WHO'D "GIVE YOU THE SHIRT OFF THEIR BACK." WELL, MEET THE MAN WHO'D GIVE YOU THE COAT OFF HIS BACK.

MARLON COULDN'T CARE LESS ABOUT CLOTHES. HE'S GONE OUT OF THE HOUSE OR AWAY ON A TRIP AND RETURNED WITHOUT MOST OF HIS GARMENTS.

"DID YOU LEAVE YOUR SHEARLING COAT AT THE HOTEL?" OR "YOUR SWEATER...?" OR "YOUR CAMEL-HAIR COAT...?" OR "YOUR RAINCOAT...?" AFTER EVERY OUTING OR TRIP, I'D INQUIRE. I WOULDN'T GET A REPLY.

"TRY TO REMEMBER WHERE YOU LEFT IT SO I CAN SEND FOR IT," I'D PERSIST.

WHEN HE RETURNED FROM A TRIP, WE'D INVARIABLY HAVE THESE ONE-SIDED CONVERSATIONS ABOUT CLOTHES. HE'D TALK AROUND THE SUBJECT OF HIS CHARITY AS IF IT MADE HIM UNCOMFORTABLE. AND I

THINK IT DID. THEN HE'D MUMBLE SOMETHING LIKE, "THIS WOMAN WAS SITTING ON THE STEPS FREEZING WITH JUST A LITTLE SHAWL. AH, I, AH, PUT IT AROUND HER SHOULDERS. I WAS GOING TO THE HOTEL...."

YEAH, MAR, AND THE REST OF THE TRIP YOU FROZE YOUR BUTT OFF BECAUSE YOU DIDN'T BUY ANOTHER COAT FOR YOURSELF, AND NOW YOU'RE IN BED WITH "ALMOST PNEUMONIA."

OR, HE HAD MET A FRIEND WHO NEEDED A JACKET TO GO ON AN INTERVIEW AND MARLON'S WAS JUST SWELL. OR, SOMEONE FELL IN LOVE WITH HIS SWEATER. OR, HE JUST LEFT IT AND DIDN'T REMEMBER WHERE. "BUY ANOTHER, ALICE."

I REMEMBER THAT COLD WINTER WELL; THERE WERE TWO SHEARLING COATS THAT DIDN'T FIND THEIR WAY HOME, PLUS AN ASSORTMENT OF CASHMERE SWEATERS AND SCARVES.

IF ANYONE WISHED STRONGLY ENOUGH FOR SOMETHING AND MARLON CROSSED THEIR PATH, THEIR WISH WAS IMMEDIATELY FULFILLED.

HE'S A GIVER, A PROVIDER, NEVER A TAKER—IT SEEMS TO EMBARRASS HIM TO BE ON THE RECEIVING END OF A GIFT. I THINK HE FEELS HE SHOULD BE THE GIVER.

MARLON WILL NEVER BE "POOR." HE'LL NEVER BE "IN NEED." HE HAS IT WITHIN HIMSELF TO BE NEITHER. MARLON'S NOT INTERESTED IN ACCUMULATING "THINGS." OH, HE HAS WHAT I TEASINGLY CALL "HIS TOYS," BUT THEY ARE ALL UTILITARIAN.

HE HAS A WORKSHOP WHERE HE TINKERS AND A "BUNKER" THAT'S A MAN'S DREAM—A MINI HARDWARE STORE. ALL KINDS OF GADGETS THAT HAVE

SPECIFIC APPLICATIONS. A HAM RADIO, WALKIE-TALKIES, COMMUNICATION SYSTEMS, COMPUTERS, A FAX MACHINE, A XEROX MACHINE, TVS AND MUSIC SYSTEMS, A QUASAR, AND WHATEVER ELSE HE PLAYS AROUND WITH THAT HAS FLASHING LIGHTS AND BUZZING SOUNDS. AND "HOW TO" INSTRUCTION BOOKS TO USE ANY OR ALL. THE ONLY THING MISSING IS A ROBOT AND I KNOW I'LL DROP BY ONE DAY AND THAT, TOO, WILL BE THERE.

BUT NO KNICKKNACKS—TCHOTCHKES—FOR HIM.

THEN THERE ARE THE BOOKS, BOOKS, BOOKS: NON-FICTION, "HOW TO," AND CLASSICS. AND THE MAGAZINES. HE'S A SAVER OF "INTERESTING" ARTICLES OR THINGS THAT CAN BE RECYCLED. I'VE SAID OF MARLON THAT IF HE DIDN'T HAVE HOUSEHOLD HELP AND A SLEW OF SECRETARIES, HE'D BE LIKE THE COLLIER BROTHERS IN NEW YORK CITY WHO, IT WAS DISCOVERED AFTER THEIR DEATHS, NEVER THREW AWAY NEWSPAPERS, MAGAZINES, ETC., AND TUNNELED THEIR WAY THROUGH THEIR ROOMS OF PAPERS, MAGAZINES, BOOKS, AND JUNK.

MISCHIEVOUS
WICKED
WICKED
WICKED

MARLON GETS "MAD" AT PEOPLE AND THEN FORGETS WHAT HE'S MAD ABOUT. AT LEAST THAT'S WHAT HE'LL

SAY IF HE'S QUESTIONED. AND WHEN HE DECIDES HE'S NOT MAD ANYMORE, HE EXPECTS FORGIVENESS AND FORGETFULNESS. MAINLY BECAUSE HE'S FORGIVEN AND FORGOTTEN.

HE'LL USE THE MOST ELABORATE, FAR OUT RUSES TO MAKE UP. ONE NIGHT A FRIEND, ANITA, WHO MARLON HAD BEEN "MAD" AT, CALLED.

"ALICE ," SHE SAID, "WHAT ARE YOU DOING TO MARLON? WHAT'S GOING ON?"

"WHAT ARE YOU TALKING ABOUT? NOTHING'S GOING ON."

"MARLON CALLED," SHE CONTINUED, "AND TOLD ME 'ALICE IS TRYING TO POISON ME.'"

"OH, I CAN'T BELIEVE WE'RE HAVING THIS CONVERSATION. YOU DIDN'T BELIEVE HIM, DID YOU?"

"NO, I DIDN'T. BUT WHY WOULD HE GET SUCH A NOTION?"

SHOULD I TELL HER THAT WAS HIS WAY OF MAKING UP OR KEEP HER IN THE DARK?

"HE WASN'T FEELING WELL AND BEFORE I LEFT WORK TONIGHT, I GAVE HIM SOME BUFFERIN—I MADE SURE HE TOOK AND SWALLOWED THE PILLS WHILE I WAS THERE. IT CERTAINLY WASN'T POISON I MADE HIM SWALLOW."

AND SO THEY MADE UP. THEY WEREN'T "MAD" ANYMORE. BUT NOW HE HAD A "MAD" SECRETARY TO CONTEND WITH THE NEXT MORNING, FOR I CONFRONTED HIM IMMEDIATELY.

I WAS CONCERNED ABOUT THIS BECAUSE, AS I SAID TO HIM, GOD FORBID SOMETHING HE ATE POISONED HIM, OR SOMEONE "DID HIM IN," SHE WOULD CERTAINLY POINT THE FINGER AT ME.

HE SEEMED TICKLED AT MY DISTRESS AND POOH-POOHED ME SAYING, "NOBODY WOULD BELIEVE THAT, ALICE."

"THE POLICE WOULD," I COUNTERED, "AND I'D APPRECIATE IT IF YOU DIDN'T TELL SUCH STORIES."

HE LAUGHED AND DISMISSED MY CONCERN AS ANOTHER ONE OF MY FOIBLES THAT HE HAD TO PUT UP WITH. BUT I WAS SERIOUS, I DIDN'T LIKE BEING PORTRAYED AS ONE OF THE BORGIAS.

HE SAYS TERRIBLE THINGS ABOUT PEOPLE, AND IF YOU DIDN'T KNOW HIM, YOU'D BELIEVE HIM. HE'S THAT CONVINCING. AND, SOMETIMES, HE NEGLECTS TO TELL PEOPLE HE FABRICATED THE ENTIRE YARN.

THEY THEMSELVES ARE MAKERS OF THEMSELVES.
—james allen, *AS A MAN THINKETH*

AT THE BEGINNING I MENTIONED THAT MARLON IS CONTRADICTORY—AND YET THERE ARE CONSTANTS. I'LL ENUMERATE A FEW CONSTANTS WHICH WILL HELP OUTLINE A SKETCH I HOPE TO DRAW.

A DAY DOESN'T GO BY WITHOUT HEARING THE UTTERANCES FROM SOMEONE TO MARLON: "BUT YOU TOLD ME TO DO IT!"

"NOW, I'M TELLING YOU NOT TO DO IT!"

OR

"IF IT'S NOT RECORDED, I DIDN'T TELL YOU TO DO IT." (ARE YOU TRYING TO "GASLIGHT" US, MAR?)

THE TWO MOST OVERWORKED WORDS IN MARLON'S VOCABULARY: *ALWAYS*, AS IN, "YOU ALWAYS..."

NEVER, AS IN, "YOU NEVER..."

PEOPLE WHO KNOW MARLON WILL THINK I'VE SANITIZED THE OVERWORKED WORDS BY OMITTING THE F-WORD. TRUE. IT'S ANOTHER OVERWORKED WORD IN HIS VOCABULARY, BUT HE IS MOST CAREFUL ABOUT NOT USING IT IN FRONT OF, OR IN CONVERSATION WITH, LADIES. IF THE WORD SLIPS INTO THE CONVERSATION, HE IMMEDIATELY APOLOGIZES. (YOU GET POINTS FOR THIS, MARLON.)

HE WASTES OTHER PEOPLE'S TIME, YET HE'S VERY STINGY WITH HIS OWN TIME. (YOU GET MINUS FOR THIS.)

MARLON GIVES GENEROUSLY WITH MONEY AND MATERIAL THINGS. (YOU GET PLUS FOR GENEROSITY—HEAVEN SMILES ON YOU.)

HE'S A COLLECTOR OF INFORMATION. IF HE LIVES TO BE 150 YEARS OLD, HE'LL NEVER BE ABLE TO USE IT ALL. (THANK GOD FOR COMPUTERS OR, AS I SAID BEFORE, MARLON WOULD BE LIKE THE COLLIER BROTHERS.)

HE'S SHORT WITH PEOPLE; DOES NOT ALLOW PEOPLE TO EXPLAIN THEIR SIDE OR POSITION IN A CONTROVERSY. PREJUDGES. THE FIRST ONE TO HIM WITH A COMPLAINT OR A SOB STORY WINS.

(WHAT HAPPENED TO "INNOCENT UNTIL PROVEN GUILTY?")

FRANK AND HONEST, SOMETIMES TO THE POINT OF RUDENESS—DIRECT—NO SUBTLETY—CASE IN POINT—SOPHIA LOREN AND ANNA MAGNANI. (BOO! BOO! THROW HIM TO THE LIONS!)

HE'S A JOKESTER AND A PRANKSTER. A GOOD LAUGHER. CAN LAUGH AT HIMSELF. AT TIMES. (WHEN RATED, YOU GO OFF THE CHARTS.)

MARLON RECOGNIZES HIS OWN SHORTCOMINGS; HE CAN ENUMERATE THEM. HE MIGHT BE HESITANT IN BLOWING HIS OWN HORN. (DON'T BE SO HARD ON YOURSELF, MAR.)

IN CONVERSATIONS, HE USUALLY SETS THE AGENDA ABOUT WHAT YOU ARE TO DISCUSS. AND WITH WOMEN, IT'S USUALLY SOMETHING CONFESSIONAL. (IS THAT THE WAY TO WIN FRIENDS AND INFLUENCE PEOPLE?)

HE'S A SOLITARY MAN. RECLUSIVE. (HEY, THERE'S A BIG WORLD OUT THERE—THINGS TO DO, PLACES TO SEE.)

HE QUESTIONS HIS OWN DECISIONS. DOESN'T TRUST THEM. SO HE POLLS HIS FRIENDS BEFORE HE COMMITS HIMSELF, YET HE'S TRUE TO HIMSELF. (MAR, YOU'RE REALLY VERY PERCEPTIVE.)

MARLON BECOMES TOTALLY COMMITTED TO A CAUSE HE BELIEVES IN. HE DOESN'T ESPOUSE A CAUSE BECAUSE IT'S IN VOGUE, TRENDY, SO TO SPEAK. HE HAS AN INNATE AWARENESS OF SOCIAL INJUSTICE. (GO TO THE HEAD OF THE CLASS.)

HE'S SOMETIMES OUT OF STEP WITH THE REST OF THE WORLD. HE'S USUALLY ONE OR TWO STEPS IN FRONT. (HE DOES WALK TO HIS OWN DRUMMER.)

MARLON COULD NEVER BE CHARACTERIZED AS A SNOB. HE'S THE TYPE OF MAN WHO WOULDN'T MIND ENTERING YOUR HOUSE FOR THE FIRST TIME THROUGH THE KITCHEN DOOR OR THROUGH THE GARAGE FILLED WITH JUNK YOU CAN'T PART WITH. (WHAT MORE CAN I SAY?)

MARLON ACTS WITH INTENT AND PURPOSE. AT TIMES, THOUGH, WITHOUT THOROUGHLY THINKING THINGS THROUGH. (JOIN THE CLUB, MAR.)

HE'S A MASTER OF THE PUT-DOWN. BUT AT TIMES SO SUBTLE THAT PEOPLE AREN'T AWARE THEY'VE BEEN PUT DOWN. (PLEASE BE KIND, MAR, SOME HURTS WE CAN'T PUT A BAND-AID ON.)

HE'S A MUSIC LOVER. HE HAS RHYTHM IN HIS HEART AND IN HIS SOUL. (IN HIS BODY, TOO, HE'S A PEACHY DANCER.)

MARLON IS A PROVIDER. (NOT ONLY "LOAVES AND FISHES," BUT ALSO DIAMONDS AND PEARLS.)

"BRANDO THE GREAT"

MARLON AND HIS FRIEND DICK CAVETT HAVE A SHARED INTEREST—THE MAGIC CASTLE AND MAGIC SHOPS.

"PICK A CARD, ALICE."

I'M AWARE IT'S ANOTHER TRICK AND I INDULGE HIM, THEN TRY TO OUTWIT THE "WIZARD." BUT AFTER ALL THESE YEARS, MARLON'S STILL PULLING RABBITS OUT OF THE HAT, SO TO SPEAK, AMAZING ME WITH HIS SLEIGHT OF HAND AND FRUSTRATING ME AT THE SAME TIME BECAUSE I HAVE AGAIN FAILED TO "CATCH HIM AT IT."

NOW YOU SEE IT, NOW YOU DON'T. THE HAND IS QUICKER THAN THE EYE. HE'S MASTERED WHAT I KNOW ARE "TRICKS," BUT TO HIS GREAT CREDIT, HE WON'T REVEAL THE SECRET OF HIS MAGICAL POWERS. AT LEAST NOT TO ME.

IF FRUSTRATING ME WITH MAGIC ISN'T ENOUGH, HE WIPES ME OUT IN VERTICAL TIC-TAC-TOE, TOO.

CHALLENGING ME TO GAME AFTER GAME, ONLY TO HUMILIATE ME. OH, HE HAS ALLOWED ME TO WIN ONE OR TWO GAMES, BUT THAT'S HUMILIATING, TOO, BECAUSE I CATCH THE TWINKLE IN HIS EYES AND I KNOW THAT'S WHAT HE'S DOING—EVEN THOUGH HE SAYS WITH AN ANGELIC SMILE, "YOU'RE CATCHING ON." CATCHING ON, MY FOOT!

WHERE WERE YOU ON NOVEMBER 22ND, 1963?

MARLON AND I WERE IN TAHITI ON HOLIDAY WHEN NEWS OF KENNEDY'S ASSASSINATION FLASHED AROUND THE WORLD. CARLOS PALACIOS, THE CONSUL GENERAL OF CHILE IN TAHITI, HEARD THE NEWS ON HIS SHORTWAVE RADIO AND IMMEDIATELY DISPATCHED HIS WIFE, AGNES, TO TELL MARLON.

SHE ARRIVED AT MY FARE IN AN AGITATED STATE AND BLURTED OUT THE AWFUL NEWS TO ME.

"WHERE'S MARLON? CARLOS SENT ME TO TELL MARLON."

MARLON WAS IN THE LAGOON SNORKELING. WE RAN THE FEW YARDS TO THE BEACH FROM WHERE WE COULD SEE HIS SNORKEL MOVING BETWEEN THE CORAL HEADS.

WE SHOUTED HIS NAME, BUT HE WAS TOO FAR TO HEAR OUR CRIES, SO WE FLOATED AN OUTRIGGER CANOE THAT WAS BEACHED NEARBY AND PADDLED OUT. IT WAS THE FIRST TIME I HAD EVER PADDLED A CANOE AND WAS FEARFUL OF OVERTURNING AS WE ZIGZAGGED OUR WAY TO HIM.

MARLON SURFACED AT OUR APPROACH AND TURNED SILENT WHEN WE TOLD HIM, "KENNEDY HAD BEEN ASSASSINATED." WE LEFT HIM SITTING FORLORNLY ON A CORAL HEAD STARING OUT TO SEA, IMMERSED IN HIS OWN THOUGHTS OF A PRESIDENT HE HAD RECENTLY VISITED WITH IN CALIFORNIA.

MARLON THE ARCHITECT—OR MOVE OVER MRS. WINCHESTER, YOU'VE GOT COMPANY!

MARLON HAS A BIT, NO, MORE THAN A BIT, OF THE ECCENTRIC MRS. SARAH WINCHESTER IN HIM. SHE WAS THE NORTHERN CALIFORNIA WIDOW OF AN HEIR TO THE WINCHESTER RIFLE COMPANY. WHEN HER HUSBAND DIED SHE INHERITED MILLIONS. AS THE STORY GOES, SHE TURNED TO MEDIUMS AND FORTUNE TELLERS TO CONTACT HER LOVED ONES. ONE TOLD HER THAT AS LONG AS SHE KEPT BUILDING, SHE WOULDN'T DIE.

SO DAY AND NIGHT, CARPENTERS KEPT ADDING ROOMS, AND STAIRCASES, OR WHATEVER TOOK HER FANCY, TO THE VICTORIAN MANSION SOUTH OF SAN JOSE, WHICH UPON HER DEATH HAD 160 ROOMS.

WHEN I SAY MARLON HAS A BIT OF MRS. WINCHESTER IN HIM, I'M REFERRING TO HIS BUILDING PROCLIVITIES. HIS DRAFTING BOARD IS LOADED WITH SKETCHES, AND MODELS DOT HIS ROOMS AT ONE TIME OR ANOTHER. ARCHITECTS WITH PLANS DRAWN FROM HIS SKETCHES, ENGINEERS, AND CONTRACTORS ARE USUALLY IN CONSULTATIONS WHEN YOU VISIT.

BUILDING IS IN PROGRESS AT HIS ESTATE IN BEVERLY HILLS, AND ONGOING ON HIS ATOLL, TETIAROA. AND THEN THERE ARE PLANS GERMINATING TO BUILD IN NORTHERN CALIFORNIA. THE EXPERIMENTS AND INNOVATIONS ARE NEVER-ENDING.

IT ALL KEEPS HIM BUSY, BUSY, BUSY. SOME PEOPLE BUILD CASTLES IN THE AIR, MARLON DOES THEM ONE BETTER; HE NOT ONLY BUILDS THEM, HE CAN LIVE IN THEM.

MARLON DISMISSES SLINGS AND ARROWS WITH, "I DON'T CARE." BUT, I GUESS, I CARE ENOUGH FOR BOTH OF US.
—alice marchak

DEBUNKING THE BUNK

AS I'VE ATTESTED TO, MARLON TELLS TALL TALES. BUT IN HEART-TO-HEART, HE CAN BE SERIOUS.

DURING A SERIOUS CONVERSATION ONE DAY, HE TOLD ME HE HAD BEEN AT A PARTY, A MIXED BAG, AND, AS USUAL, HE SAT OFF BY HIMSELF. HE WAS JOINED BY A YOUNG MAN WHO APPRAISED HIM AND SAID, "DID ANYONE EVER TELL YOU THAT YOU LOOK LIKE BRANDO?"

NOW MARLON, PRANKSTER THAT HE IS, DECIDED TO HAVE FUN.

"OH, YEAH," HE SAID, "ALL THE TIME. WHY? DO YOU KNOW HIM?"

"MARLON'S A FRIEND OF MINE," THE STRANGER CONTINUED.

THIS REMARK GOT MARLON'S ATTENTION BECAUSE HE HAD NEVER SEEN THIS PERSON STANDING IN FRONT OF HIM BEFORE. AND THE MAN WAS TELLING HIM THEY WERE FRIENDS.

"YOU'RE FRIENDS, EH?" MARLON WAS GETTING READY FOR A ZINGER, BUT THIS "FRIEND" BEAT HIM TO IT.

"YES," HE SAID, "WE WERE LOVERS."

"WHAT DID YOU DO?" I ASKED, LAUGHING.

"I SAID TO MYSELF, 'MARLON, IT'S TIME TO SHUFFLE OFF TO BUFFALO.' SO I DID. I GOT OUT OF THERE FAST."

ANOTHER TIME WHEN RUMORS WERE CIRCULATING AND MARLON THOUGHT THEY'D REACH ME, HE VERY SUCCINCTLY SAID TO ME, "DON'T BELIEVE ANYTHING YOU HEAR ABOUT ME. NOT TRUE." HIS WORD IS ENOUGH FOR ME—THOUGH HE DID TELL ME WHAT HAPPENED TO CAUSE THE UNTRUE RUMOR TO START.

IT WAS REGARDING A PORNOGRAPHIC PHOTOGRAPH WHICH SOMEONE SOLD TO ANNA KASHFI FOR A REPORTED 1,000 DOLLARS. THE POOR WOMAN WAS THE VICTIM OF A HOAX. MARLON DENOUNCED THE ACCUSATION IN COURT AND THE PURPORTED PHOTOGRAPH WAS DISPATCHED BY COURT ORDER TO EASTMAN KODAK LABORATORIES AND THOROUGHLY EXAMINED. I HAD GATHERED PHOTOGRAPHS OF MARLON, FULL FACE AND PROFILE, BEFORE AND AFTER HIS BROKEN NOSE. THESE ALSO WERE SENT ALONG TO EASTMAN KODAK AS AIDS IN THEIR EVALUATION OF THE PHOTOGRAPH.

THE NOT SURPRISING RESULT: THE PHOTOGRAPH WAS VERY DEFINITELY NOT BRANDO. MARLON AND HIS

LAWYER, AS WELL AS ANNA KASHFI AND HER LAWYER, WERE NOTIFIED OF THIS FINDING. AND THAT EPISODE WAS CLOSED. OR SO MARLON THOUGHT.

EVEN THOUGH ANNA, BY THE EVIDENCE, WAS TAKEN IN BY SOME UNSCRUPULOUS CON MAN, EVERY FEW YEARS THE DOCTORED HOMOSEXUAL PHOTO TURNS UP. AFTER READING THIS, MAYBE FUTURE PURCHASERS OF THE PHOTO WILL WISE UP. THEY'RE BUYING A DEAD HORSE!

FORTUNATELY, I HAVE THE TYPE OF BRAIN THAT CAN RECORD A GREAT NUMBER OF UNRELATED THINGS WITHOUT COMMITTING THEM TO PAPER. ONE MINUTE IT WAS, "DON'T ANSWER THE PHONE."

THE PHONE RANG AND IT WAS, "ANSWER THE PHONE."

"DON'T MENTION MY NAME."

"CALL ME MARLON."

"TELL HER I'M OUT."

"IF SO-AND-SO CALLS, I'M IN."

RETAIN AND REJECT. REJECT AND RETAIN.

JUST A FEW MINUTES WITH HIM WHILE HELPING TO GET HIM ON HIS WAY FOR A LATE APPOINTMENT WAS MIND-BOGGLING AT FIRST.

IT WAS:

"CALL JAY. TELL HIM NO ON BEN HUR."

"CALL GEORGE. WHERE IS HE GOING TO BE TONIGHT? GET A NUMBER. I'LL CALL HIM."

"FRANCE IS COMING OVER LATER."

"CANCEL AARONSON. NO. DON'T CANCEL AARONSON."

"CALL JAY. I'LL DO BEN HUR."

"FIND OUT WHERE WALLY IS." (WALLY WHO?)

"WHERE'S MY KEYS?"

"DID YOU SEE MY SUNGLASSES?"

"I NEED A STREET MAP OF L.A.—OF CALIFORNIA."

"I WANT A BOOK—GEORGE WILL KNOW—ASK GEORGE."

"SEND FLOWERS TO STELLA." (STELLA WHO?)

"I HAVE TO TALK TO JAY ABOUT TIDD." (TIDD WHO?)

"I NEED A NEW ELECTRIC RAZOR."

"WHERE'S MY KEYS?"

"THERE'S A LIGHT BULB OUT IN THE BATHROOM."

"TELL THE GARDENER TO PLANT NIGHT BLOOMING JASMINE."

"WHERE'S MY WALLET? I CAN'T FIND MY WALLET."

"CALL DRUM CITY. FIND OUT WHEN MY DRUM WILL BE READY."

"GET ME SKETCHES IN SPAIN."

"I THINK MY CAR NEEDS GAS."

"I DON'T HAVE MY WALLET!"

"CALL WASSERMAN, TELL HIM I'M ON MY WAY."

NOTHING IN MY BACKGROUND PREPARED ME FOR THIS WHIRLWIND THAT ENTERED MY LIFE. THIS DEVILISH ROGUE WITH A ROVING EYE AND MIND. IF LIFE WAS A BANQUET, MARLON WAS FIRST AT THE TABLE, SO EAGER WAS HE TO SAVOR ALL THE DELIGHTS LIFE HAD TO OFFER. AND HE TOOK BIG BITES.

WHAT A DILEMMA I WAS FACED WITH. THOSE FIRST YEARS, I DIDN'T KNOW WHAT TO MAKE OF HIM. WHAT WAS FACT? WHAT WAS FICTION? WHAT WAS TRUTH? WHEN I THOUGHT HE WAS LYING, OR IF YOU WILL,

FABRICATING, OR STRETCHING IT, HE WAS TELLING THE TRUTH, AND VICE VERSA. WHAT WAS FANTASY? WHAT WAS REAL?

I DIDN'T KNOW.

BRANDO!

THIS WAS NO BROODING BRANDO WITH A TORN T-SHIRT, THIS WAS A FREE-SPIRITED, GALLOPING STUD. FANS WERE IDENTIFYING WITH WHAT AND WHO THEY SAW ON THE SCREEN. MARLON WAS STANLEY KOWALSKI TO THEM. MUCH LATER, HE WAS THE GODFATHER.

I HAD NO TIME TO ANALYZE THIS SCREEN PERSON—OR HIS PERFORMANCE. I HAD TOO MUCH TRYING TO UNDERSTAND THIS COMPLEX, MERCURIAL PERSON IN FRONT OF ME WHO ONE MOMENT TOLD ME HE WAS A VERY PRIVATE PERSON, AND THE NEXT WAS CONFIDING MOST INTIMATE THINGS. WHAT WAS HAPPENING HERE? HOW DID HE KNOW TO TRUST ME WITH SECRETS OF HIS HEART? THIS COULD BECOME A BURDEN IF I LET IT, BUT THIS "LONER," I THOUGHT, NEEDED A CONFIDANTE. LITTLE DID I KNOW HE HAD SEVERAL. BUT THINGS HE TOLD ME WOULD BE HINTED AT OR WHISPERED CONFIDENTIALLY IN MY EAR BY OTHERS, AND I WONDERED IF THIS WAS A TEST. BUT NO, IT WASN'T A TEST.

I SOON DISCOVERED THAT MARLON HAD A PENCHANT FOR CONFIDING. AND AS THE YEARS WENT BY, I KNEW THERE WERE DOORS SLAMMED SHUT, LEST HE BECAME TOO VULNERABLE TO ME. THE PAIN I COULDN'T LAUGH AT. OTHER THINGS I COULD. HE LET

ME LAUGH AT HIM AND WITH HIM. BUT OH, HOW DEEPLY HE FEELS, THIS MAN-CHILD.

I'VE GOT A SECRET! I'VE GOT A SECRET!

LET'S EXPLORE PRIVACY—HIS. HE'LL TELL YOU HE'S A VERY PRIVATE PERSON, WHICH MEANS HE'S ALSO SECRETIVE. BUT IS HE? HE'LL TELL ME A "DON'T TELL ANYONE" SECRET.

FOR EXAMPLE, ONE MORNING IN HIS DRESSING ROOM AT PARAMOUNT STUDIO, WHERE HE WAS DIRECTING AND STARRING IN *ONE-EYED JACKS*, HE TOLD ME IN THE STRICTEST CONFIDENCE THAT AFTER CHILD VISITATION THE EVENING BEFORE, HIS EX HAD COME AT HIM WITH A KITCHEN KNIFE. HE SPELLED IT OUT IN HARROWING DETAIL. I WAS NOT TO TELL ANYONE. O.K. IT WAS OUR SECRET. HE THEN LEFT FOR THE SOUND STAGE AND I FOLLOWED A SHORT TIME LATER, HUGGING THE SECRET TO MY BREAST. BUT BY THE TIME I REACHED THE SOUND STAGE, I WAS TOLD BY THREE PEOPLE I ENCOUNTERED ABOUT THE ATTACK. AND WHEN I ENTERED THE STAGE, I DISCOVERED THE ENTIRE SET WAS BUZZING ABOUT IT. WHAT KIND OF SECRET WAS THAT? WHAT ABOUT PRIVACY?

I REMEMBER HOPING HE DIDN'T THINK I HAD GIVEN HIS SECRET AWAY. I SOON LEARNED THAT MARLON TOLD SECRETS TO YOU, AND YOU, AND YOU. ASKING ALL OF US NOT TO TELL A SOUL. I'D HEAR THE MOST PERSONAL THINGS ABOUT HIM IN THE DAMNEDEST WAYS AND PLACES, AND THEY'D ALL ORIGINATE WITH HIM. HE STILL SAYS, "DON'T TELL ANYONE," AND THEN

IT'S ON THE EVENING NEWS. FROM THE BEGINNING OF OUR RELATIONSHIP, MY IDEA OF PRIVACY AND HIS WERE AT ODDS. NONETHELESS, HE IS A PRIVATE PERSON.

HOWEVER PERPLEXING, HE CERTAINLY KNOWS HOW TO KEEP ONE OFF-BALANCE. IN DUE TIME, I HAD TO STOP MYSELF FROM ABSORBING MARLON'S TRAITS. THERE ARE ENOUGH BRANDO CLONES OUT THERE. YOU HAVE TO BE STRONG. I DON'T MEAN TOUGH, BUT STRONG, TO WITHSTAND MARLON'S POWER TO BEND YOU TO HIS WILL. YOU COULD LOSE YOURSELF IF YOU WEREN'T VIGILANT. BUT I ONLY SOLD MY TIME IN THE MARKETPLACE. NOT MY BODY, NOT MY SOUL, AND NOT MY MIND. NEVERTHELESS, HE WAS A REFRESHING WIND BLOWING THROUGH MY LIFE.

FAME AND BRANDO—FROM MY VIEW

MARLON'S FAME WAS ALL-ENCOMPASSING. AS THE YEARS PASSED, MARLON COULD NOT ESCAPE IT BECAUSE AS EACH FILM HE MADE WAS RELEASED, FAME BECAME MORE ENVELOPING. AND THOUGH HIS PROFESSIONAL LIFE AND PERSONAL LIFE WERE LIVED ON THE FRONT PAGES OF THE WORLD'S NEWSPAPERS AND MAGAZINES, IT WAS HIS PROFESSIONAL LIFE THAT BECAME PERMANENTLY IMPRINTED ON FILM, ATTESTING TO HIS GENIUS AND MAKING HIM A LEGEND, WITH MORE POWER AND RECOGNITION—AND MORE FAME.

THERE CAN BE NO ESCAPE FOR MARLON FROM THE MAN WHO IS ADMITTEDLY THE GREATEST ACTOR, OR

ONE OF THE GREATEST ACTORS, OF OUR TIME, AND THE MYTH PROMULGATED BY HIS SILENCE IN THE FACE OF THE UNTRUTHS WRITTEN ABOUT HIM.

I DO BELIEVE THAT PART OF HIM WANTED THE RECOGNITION AND POWER THAT HIS INNATE TALENT BROUGHT HIM. ANOTHER PART HATED THE SELF THAT DELIGHTED IN THIS ACKNOWLEDGEMENT.

SO, DENYING AND HIDING THIS CONFLICT PREVENTED HIM THE FREEDOM TO ENJOY EITHER HIS PROFESSIONAL OR PERSONAL LIFE TO ITS FULLEST.

IN OTHER WORDS, THE PRICE OF HIS FAME WAS HIS FREEDOM, AND THAT'S A TRAGEDY. BUT HOW MUCH DID HE WILLINGLY CONTRIBUTE TO THAT PRICE? ONLY MARLON CAN SAY.

AND WHAT DO I NOW PERCEIVE? A MAN WHO LIVES ALONE ON A LOFTY PINNACLE OF FAME; WHO DESIRES NOTHING MORE THAN TO FIND A WAY DOWN BEFORE IT'S TOO LATE—WHILE THERE'S STILL TIME TO BE HIS TRUE SELF WALKING AMONG MEN.

IN SO FEW LINES I'VE TRIED TO GAZE THROUGH THE MIST OF TIME AND SKETCH A PORTRAIT OF A MAN I'VE KNOWN ALL OF MY ADULT LIFE AND HIS.

BUT AS I LOOK AT THE PORTRAIT I'VE DRAWN, I SEE NOT ONLY MARLON, BUT ALSO MYSELF...AND FRIENDS...AND ACQUAINTANCES.

*****

FAX NOT SENT

The reason not sent: Marlon, I learned, was en route to Spain for the filming of Columbus. I could no longer fax him. Further, I did not want to give him a dig in the ribs when he was starting a film—I knew the mood he'd be in since he always dreaded working and I didn't want to pile on.

JANUARY 17, 1992

TO: MARLON
FROM: ALICE

DEAR MAR:

I CAN ONLY ASSUME BY YOUR SILENCE THAT THE MATERIAL I SENT IS UNACCEPTABLE. SO BE IT.

I WROTE WHAT I UNDERSTOOD YOU WANTED, WHICH WERE SOME PROVOCATIVE OBSERVATIONS THAT WOULD STIMULATE, AND WHICH YOU COULD PLAY OFF—NOT YOUR REALITY, BUT, AS YOU STATED, OUR PERCEPTIONS.

OBVIOUSLY SOMEWHERE, SOMEHOW, I MISUNDERSTOOD WHAT YOUR INTENT WAS, OR IS. BUT, AS I SAID, I DID ONLY WHAT I HAD UNDERSTOOD YOU WANTED.

I DON'T FEEL THAT IGNORING THE OBVIOUS BY A WALL OF SILENCE IS VERY PRODUCTIVE AS FAR AS YOUR BOOK IS CONCERNED. IF YOU RECALL, I WAS VERY RELUCTANT TO GO "PUBLIC" IN REGARD TO YOUR PRIVATE LIFE, AND STILL FEEL THE SAME. THIRTY-FIVE YEARS OF PROGRAMMING IS NOT EASILY EXORCISED. I SHOULD HAVE FOLLOWED MY INSTINCTS IN THIS

REGARD, BUT THAT'S HINDSIGHT. AS JEFF BROWN SAID THE OTHER EVENING, "I'D LIKE TO HEAR SOMETHING. I PUT WEEKS INTO THAT." I FEEL THE SAME.

I BELIEVE IF MY SUBMISSION WERE ACCEPTABLE, I WOULD HAVE HAD SOME RESPONSE. EVEN IF IT'S AN OUT-AND-OUT REJECTION.

AS I STATED IN MY COVER LETTER, I WROTE ENOUGH SO YOU COULD DELETE A WORD, PHRASE, OR SEQUENCE—AND NOW I ADD ALL. AT THIS POINT, I FEEL THE LATTER WOULD BE PREFERABLE AS IT WON'T GET ANY MORE ACCEPTABLE IN PRINT AND I DON'T WANT ANYTHING I'VE WRITTEN TO BE IN PRINT UNDER A CLOUD.

YOU CAN RETURN IT TO ME WITH A REJECTION SLIP AND I'LL FEED IT INTO THE SHREDDER, PAGE BY PAGE. UNLESS, OF COURSE, YOU WISH TO USE THE MATERIAL FOR WORD COUNT, THEN TRASH IT.

OLE! OLE!

ALICE

AUTHOR'S NOTE

In 1992 Marlon called again and asked me to "come on up and stay a month with me." He needed help with his autobiography. He said that George Englund was negotiating a deal and would co-write, and he needed my input. We three would work together. He didn't have any money—family problems had depleted his cash—and his emotional health was at an all-time low. His daughter's drug and mental problems, acerbated by the tragic death of the boy she loved, the father of her child, tormented him. His fallback when there was a lack of money had always been, "I have to make another movie."

Only this time, he was grossly overweight, he had aged, he was pushing 70—he lacked the fire of youth. He couldn't wrap his mind around the thought of emoting while the camera rolled. But his mind was very active, imagining the millions dangling before him, and he grasped at the idea of a book like a thirsting man lost in the desert, stumbling upon an oasis with a life-saving well.

I did not become actively involved in any of the negotiations with the publishers, nor did Marlon, he left everything to George. He kept me informed of George's progress till at last a deal was firmed, then I agreed to "come on up for a month or so" to help him get organized. Marlon was thankful he didn't have to "go to work." Whereas acting is the lifeblood to some, and a joy, to Marlon it was a descent into the fires of hell.

As Marlon did when committed to a movie, so now he began to thwart George's progress with the book. He began to plot—plot ways whereby he could write the book at his leisure, balking at deadlines. Where he had been dragging and was so low, he now had perked up. George was nailing down the book deal. Now that it was time for Marlon to begin producing, he began sabotaging. I wondered if George realized what he had let himself in for—if he had forgotten the lessons learned from working with Marlon at Paramount when setting up his production company, Pennebaker, or later directing Marlon in *The Ugly American*, and their many abandoned projects for Tetiaroa. I had a premonition life would repeat itself.

As I listened to an animated Marlon plotting and planning, I felt sorry for George when he discovered that Marlon came up with the ingenious idea to have 15 or 20 people write their perceptions and he would then critique what they had written. The reason I felt for George was that he'd have to sell the idea to the publishers.

Marlon, in the meantime, was pressed for money. He thought when he, or when George in this case, received word that a publisher was interested, he'd be handed millions and they'd work out literary details later. He'd write at his convenience. He did not know anything about writing a book and less about the publishing business. When no money was immediately forthcoming, he was back to square one.

His emotional problems again came to the fore. He had to go to Paris as his daughter's psychiatrists needed Marlon's presence at treatment sessions, as well as her mother's and family, if she were to get well.

But first, Marlon was required in London for consultations and finalization of legal matters regarding his appearance in *Columbus*—he had to once more emote for a living. Life was crowding him, for he also was expecting to become a father again in California.

He was very grateful that I was shouldering the burden of refurbishing his house and taking that pressure off him. We fell into a familiar pattern; I was once again sharing his home and shouldering his problems.

Columbus was to be filmed in Spain. Soon after I arrived at his home, Marlon was off to Europe to face his familial problems there, leaving George to face and sort out his literary problems, and me to urge his choices into writing their perceptions of him, along with fixing his house, which was a disaster when I arrived.

The publishers, of course, rejected Marlon's idea—he'd have to write the book himself. Now I became a conduit as Marlon didn't wish to speak directly to anyone concerning the format of the book.

Marlon was a law unto himself. He didn't think rules and regulations, social mores, or now literary methods of procedure, applied to him. He was Marlon Brando. I was fearful that if he received a book advance it would have to be returned.

Nevertheless, George and I continued on. When all submissions had been received and I had sent them to Marlon, it was as if Marlon had fallen off the face of the earth. No one could reach him. I heard from the publishers, but I could only fax messages to Marlon. I didn't hear from George. It was as if the autobiography, which by now had taken up eight months of my time, no longer existed. Marlon and George had words about the book. And when we finally spoke, Marlon did not want to talk about it.

"Later," he said. But later never came.

Marlon called when his son was born; a book was never mentioned. Calls and faxes went back and forth—no mention of the book. Marlon went to Spain to film *Columbus*. No calls referencing the book. He was working on the film. I didn't press. When Marlon wanted to talk, he'd talk.

Marlon finished *Columbus*. I was notified of his date of arrival from Europe. As usual, he asked that everyone be told that he wanted to be alone—they would be notified when to return to work.

I had finished all the repairs—a new kitchen floor had been installed, breakfast room furniture cleaned, laundry room cleaned and painted, bookshelves in den repaired and books dusted and put in order, pantry shelves cleaned and repaired, Marlon's suite cleaned—papers filed, torn wallpaper repaired in TV-computer room, walls of windows washed, Marlon's workshop and "bunker" cleaned, and all tools organized. A new hand-tied bamboo trellis covered the terrace surrounding the house and vines planted that would eventually cover it, outdoor wicker furniture painted, and cushions cleaned. Marlon's truck and automobile serviced, washed, and gassed. Orchids and freesias filled the rooms, and fresh fruit overflowed a large bowl on the kitchen counter.

As a rule I stocked the refrigerator before leaving the house when Marlon returned from a trip. But this time I received word from one of his assistants she would be coming by the house with food prepared by a friend of hers. I was given to understand that Marlon was on a new eating regimen and had hired her to prepare his food. Therefore, I didn't purchase food, except for a large bowl of assorted fruit. She arrived before my departure and put several small plastic cartons of food in the refrigerator. I didn't know what was in the cartons and wasn't curious enough to check them.

Next to arrive was a secretary who had accompanied Marlon to Spain and returned directly. She said she had some purchases requested by Marlon she was going to take back to his bedroom. It should be noted that secretaries were not allowed in the house without permission from Marlon. He had erected an office building that had a kitchen and bathroom and they all operated from there. I was the only one who came in and out of his home at will. Also, I never stayed in the guest house when I visited. I stayed in the house with him, in my old quarters.

Marlon did not want me staying alone in the house during the night with only two large dogs and had suggested I hire security. Since the house was so run down and needed a great deal of work, I had told Marlon I'd like to hire Carlos, who had worked on Tetiaroa and was now back in town to do the maintenance I required. I had asked that he be allowed to sleep in the den, instead of hiring a stranger to stay with me. Now, Carlos came to pick up his stuff and left.

Marlon and his assistant, who was returning from London with him, were due home at 8:30 p.m. I only had to be certain no one was in the house and put on lights throughout the house before I departed. Night was already upon us.

I started in the kitchen and worked my way through the house down to Marlon's suite, flipping on lights. I walked into his room and turned on the lamp on the left side of his king-sized bed. The light, though dim, flooded his bed and scared the wits out of me. Lying on the right side of the bed was a naked girl. My eyes popped out of my head. It was a life–size, big-busted, naked, inflated girl.

Now I had seen everything. Or had I?

Marlon's secretary came out of his dressing room/bathroom, saw me, and became very agitated. She had explicit instructions from Marlon, "Don't let Alice see it."

She explained that Marlon had called and asked her to go to a sex shop and buy it, among other sex items, inflate it, and put it on his bed. Can you believe she did it? I couldn't.

Well, I knew he was a sex addict, so I don't know why I was so surprised.

I don't know what else she bought. I didn't ask. Wasn't interested. I couldn't get out of there fast enough after I gave her my word I wouldn't tell Marlon I had seen his toy.

Everyone was now out of the house and I could leave. I said my goodbyes to the Mastiff and St. Bernard dogs and took off for the Beach.

It wasn't too long before his assistant called to say she and Marlon had arrived home. She further stated that he was very upset because, "There's nothing to eat in the house." I explained there was food in the refrigerator. Another of his assistants had brought it.

"There's only a few small cartons," she replied.

"That's what she brought according to her arrangement with Marlon," I informed her.

"There's only two bananas," was the next complaint.

"There's a big bowl of fruit," I stated. "I had bought a couple of apples, oranges, peaches, and a large bunch of grapes along with bananas."

"There's only two bananas," she repeated.

"Someone may have eaten a banana. I wasn't watching the fruit to see if anyone had taken any. With all the other fruit, two should be enough."

"Marlon likes bananas, you should have bought more," she continued, repeating, "and he's upset because there's nothing in the house to eat."

I had the feeling Marlon was at her elbow.

Nothing was said about the cleanliness of the house, the new floor, or other repairs. I got off the phone after this ridiculous exchange about bananas and food Marlon had one of his assistants supply. I waited for her to call me and complain about the "naked lady" on Marlon's bed. I waited...and waited...and waited.

After *Columbus*, I never heard from either George or Marlon in regard to the book, even though I spoke to Marlon. When *Songs My Mother Taught Me* was published, Marlon called and, as I've written, laughed about all the money he received for the book.

*****

The saga of Brando does not begin nor end with me. Too many peopled his life and have their own story to tell. And I have shown but the tip of the iceberg through what I have elected to reveal. I have written about a very short period of time considering the many hours in the days and years I've known and spent with Marlon.

Every day brought new drama from the fertile mind of the man known as Marlon Brando. The waking hours spent on his bed looking at the ceiling was not spent in idle dreaming. Yes, there were some dreams, but in the early days, as throughout his life, there was more planning and plotting than dreaming.

I have only told fragments of my story to explain why I sued Marlon's estate, and in doing so I deliberately did not bring forth in depth other relationships that came and went in both our lives. As I said, people in Marlon's life have their own story to tell. Carlo Fiore, Anna Kashfi, George Englund, Tarita Teriipia, Bernard Judge have already done so in print, while others have appeared in documentaries, telling of a Brando they worked with, for, or met. Perhaps others will come forward with their own personal story. I hope so.

I've opened the door—how many will follow? I don't know. What I do know is there will be many questions screaming for answers. And I will answer them—in some form or another.